The School Reading Program

The School Reading Program

A Handbook for Teachers, Supervisors, and Specialists

Richard J. Smith *University of Wisconsin, Madison*
Wayne Otto *University of Wisconsin, Madison*
Lee Hansen *Ann Arbor Public Schools*

Houghton Mifflin Company Boston
Dallas Geneva, Illinois Hopewell, New Jersey Palo Alto London

Library of Congress Catalog Card Number: 77-77993

ISBN: 0-395-25452-3

Contents

Preface

The School Reading Program is addressed to reading specialists, classroom teachers, and administrators concerned with reading curriculum development. The reason for addressing the book to professionals in all three roles is that the greatest potential for curriculum improvement lies in the combined efforts of all three. The narrower the working distance between instructional leaders and teachers, the greater the opportunities for improving the quality of instruction that students receive. Therefore, this book is intended to be a resource for educators working together to improve the quality of reading instruction in both elementary and secondary schools.

The professional experiences of the three authors allow them to speak from firsthand experiences as public school teachers, reading specialists, school administrators, researchers, and university professors of reading methods courses. In the book each of the three discusses the aspects of reading program development about which he is most knowledgeable and with which he has worked. The suggestions for reading program improvement offered in each chapter are, therefore, drawn from the author's work experiences as well as from studies and the writing of others in the area of reading curriculum and instruction.

The book has been compiled to serve as a basic text in courses designed for the study of reading curriculum development, such as "The Supervision of Reading Programs," "Guiding the School Reading Program," "Administrators and Reading," and "Improving Reading Instruction." Professors and students in advanced courses in reading methodology may also find the book useful as a basic or supplementary text, especially in courses that raise curriculum issues or focus upon programmatic aspects of reading instruction.

Administering the School Reading Program (Wayne Otto and Richard Smith, Houghton Mifflin, 1970) was the starting point for this new text. Because of the extensive changes and additions that were made, however, *The School Reading Program* is more than a revision. The authors and publishers sampled opinion widely about what was needed in a textbook that gave direction in the development of school reading programs, and their findings pointed toward a substantially expanded version of *Administering the School Reading Program.* Accordingly, an additional author was added to the writing team, and the present book was written to reflect the expressed needs of the professionals whose opinions were surveyed.

The authors and the publisher are grateful for the assistance of those who made professional reviews of the manuscript. These reviewers, to whom we give thanks, are H. Donald Jacobs, Arizona State University; Karl D. Hesse, University of Oregon; and P. David Pearson, University of Minnesota.

The School Reading Program

Chapter 1 An orientation to the reading program

This handbook is for teachers, supervisors, and specialists who are responsible for school reading programs. As a resource for people with diverse roles and specific responsibilities, the contents must address diverse aspects of both the reading program and the reading process. The overall purpose is to provide direction for collaborative efforts to improve the teaching of reading through program improvement.

But diversity can obscure.

Chapter 1, then, provides the reader with a broad view of the book and the reading program, which are dealt with in separate sections. Both sections include the authors' beliefs and inclinations regarding the development of reading programs, and taken together they should orient the readers to the organization and content of the book.

About the book

The most important factor in reading program development is the teacher. Therefore, this book is designed to help teachers do the best possible job of teaching students to read. But teachers do not work alone. To do their jobs well they need training, instructional materials, supervision, and all the other components that make good reading programs. With this in mind we have addressed a broader audience than teachers themselves: supervisors, reading specialists, administrators, and other educators, as well as teachers, who contribute to students' development in reading.

Many topics included in this book are usually not discussed in length in reading methods textbooks. For example, we give considerable attention to the in-service education of teachers, the evaluation of school reading programs, the role of reading specialists, the development of programs for students with reading problems, and other topics that are important to program development but are not necessarily germane to discussions of teaching methods. Nevertheless, program-related topics cannot be discussed without regard for instructional methodology. In addition, a discussion of instructional materials cannot ignore how the materials are used; one on evaluating reading programs cannot ignore pupil evaluation; one on programs for correcting reading problems cannot stop short of teaching methodology. Consequently, some redundancies may appear in this book. We decided that showing the interrelatedness of program components was more important than eliminating redundancy. The coherence of the individual chapters should benefit from that decision.

TWO REALITIES

One of the first realities that a student of reading program development must accept is that no two school settings are alike. Each classroom, school building, and school district involve unique personalities, personality combinations, political power bases, financial resources, community standards, and other factors that interact in the development of reading programs. Because of the uniqueness of school settings within which reading programs function, no book about reading program development can speak directly to all of the immediate concerns of a particular teacher, supervisor, or specialist. Yet philosophies, theories, research findings, model programs, opinions, and observations can cut across idiosyncratic interests and needs by offering counsel and guidelines that can be adapted to fit given conditions. Therefore, readers of this book will find clear-cut answers to some of their personal questions, guidelines for arriving at answers to other questions, and at least some direction for seeking out answers to most of their questions about reading program development. This book, then, is a handbook of facts and ideas that must be combined, adapted, and tried out to meet unique needs at particular times. In short, the book is offered as a resource for building dynamic reading programs, not as a blueprint for a preconceived program.

Another reality is that reading programs for the elementary and the secondary school share many needs, resources, and responsibilities, but each has some that are unique. Because this is a handbook for both levels, we discuss aspects of program development that are shared by both without reference to level. We also identify and discuss separately those aspects of program development that seem to be different for elementary and secondary schools. We have, however, chosen to stress the similarities more than the differences because teachers, supervisors, and specialists at all academic levels are working with the same process and are trying to attain the same goal of having every student realize his or her full reading potential. But equally important is the fact that teachers, supervisors, and specialists who participate in reading program development must frequently work at both academic levels. In fact, as such concepts as *individualized instruction, continuous progress,* and *mainstreaming* gain impetus, the line that separates the elementary from the secondary school is diminished, especially insofar as the reading curriculum is concerned. Although teachers, supervisors, and specialists may continue to focus their work at one academic level, their need for knowledge of all levels becomes increasingly important.

FROM THEORY TO PRACTICE

Like teaching, program development requires the application of philosophy and theory to practice. Program developers who know only philosophy and theory are not fully prepared for their jobs. On the other hand, a study of case histories, descriptions of programs, and procedures for building certain kinds of programs is not sufficient preparation for facing the uncertainty of future needs and becoming involved in the decision-making process. Therefore, we have attempted to include philosophy, theory, opinion, research findings, and practical concerns in our discussions because decision making and program development require a sensible melding of all these ingredients. The readers' task is to put them together to meet personal challenges.

One way for teachers, supervisors, and specialists to prepare for working with actual problems that test their beliefs, theoretical background, and practical knowledge is to practice with some tough ones. The final chapter in this book presents eleven multifaceted problems that should present a real challenge. We offer solutions for each problem in eleven coordinated responses. Readers can test their problem-solving abilities and then compare their solutions with the authors'.

The problems can be used most effectively if they are saved until all the chapters have been studied. Although each problem is keyed to specific chapters, the complexity of the problems makes responding to them easier and more productive if the entire book has been studied first. In courses on reading program development, the problems can be used effectively as a final activity. Students in the course form study groups, and each group is assigned one or more problems. The group prepares a response to its assigned problem or problems and makes a presentation to the entire class. After each presentation, the entire class—including the presenters—reads the response in this book and compares the solutions. Alternatively students can prepare responses individually and then compare them to those of the authors. However they are used, the problems should help students bring their philosophies, theoretical knowledge, and experiential backgrounds together in the search for solutions to practical problems related to reading program development.

About the program

In the second edition of *Corrective and Remedial Teaching* (1973), Otto, McMenemy, and Smith drew a distinction between *developmental program* and *developmental teaching*:

> The term *developmental program* generally has a broad meaning, whereas the meaning of *developmental teaching* usually is somewhat more restricted. Typically, the goal of the developmental program is achievement in the basic school subjects that approaches the limit of each pupil's capacity. Thus, the developmental program subsumes the entire curriculum at all grade levels as well as specialized instructional programs designed for pupils with particular needs. Developmental teaching, on the other hand, usually is designed for the normal child who moves through the school experience without special problems. The result is that when we speak of a school's overall developmental program we typically are speaking not only of regular classroom instruction (developmental teaching) but of special instruction—corrective, remedial, adapted, accelerated—as well. (p. 33)

We have preserved this distinction and the broad definition of the developmental program in this book.

COMPONENTS OF THE READING PROGRAM

The overall developmental reading program as we conceive it is schematically represented in figure 1.1. The essential point is that

5

Figure 1.1 **A schematic of the reading program**

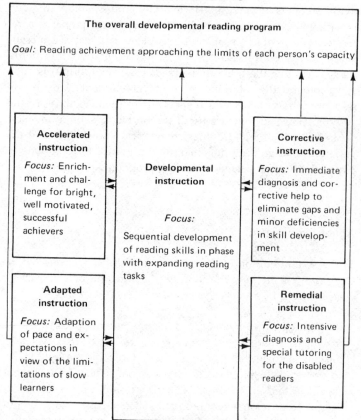

Source: Adapted from Wayne Otto and Richard J. Smith, *Administering the School Reading Program* (Boston: Houghton Mifflin, 1970), p. 28. © 1970 by Wayne Otto and Richard J. Smith.

there should be a single, overall reading program. The several specialized instructional programs are interrelated and contributing but subsidiary parts. We shall define and describe model subsidiary instructional programs, but we encourage teachers, supervisors, and specialists to make their own adaptations.

The overall developmental reading program

The ultimate goal of the reading program is reading achievement that approaches the limits of each person's capacity. The focus is upon the individual, not upon groups or grade-level performance, because mean scores of groups can be misleading and grade-level performance may be beneath the aspirations and capabilities of some individuals and beyond the grasp of others. All instructional efforts are clearly subsumed by the goal of near-capacity achievement for each individual, whether the efforts are essentially classroom developmental or clinic remedial. The overall program must provide a master plan that includes the articulation of objectives and a coordination of instructional efforts. The specifics of the master plan—objectives, administrative arrangements, specialized personnel—are discussed in detail in the chapters that follow. They must, of course, be arranged in ways that are appropriate and practicable in given situations.

There *must* be a master plan. Without it special programs, provisions for specialized personnel, and within-classroom developmental teaching programs are likely to be disorganized. Remedial teaching, for example, is isolated drill unless it is coordinated with the learner's experiences in the classroom. Similarly, second-grade reading is only an arbitrary collection of skills unless it is coordinated with first-grade and third-grade reading. Reading coordinators are likely to do little more than fight brushfires unless they have some overall guidelines. With a well-conceived overall plan, the whole can be more than the sum of its parts.

Keeping in mind the need for coordination, we can examine some specific instructional plans within the total program. Subprograms and classification schemes do not necessarily add up to a total program, but a consideration of several aspects can help to clarify the scope of an adequate program.

Developmental instruction

The focus of developmental instruction is upon the sequential development of reading skills in phase with expanding reading tasks. Schiffman (1966) has stated it well:

> The developmental program involves systematic instruction at all school levels and in all content areas for those who are developing language abilities commensurate with their general capacity levels. This developmental program is the responsibility of every teacher, affects all the pupils, is provided for in the regular curriculum, and is a continuous, ongoing process. A balanced program includes instruction in the basal, curricular and recreational reading areas. (p. 241)

Put another way, *developmental instruction* is the regular classroom teaching program that is pitched to and adequate for

7

the normal child who moves through the skill development sequence without complications. This is not to say that any slapdash approach will do. On the contrary, because developmental instruction carries the main thrust of the overall program, it should receive major attention in planning and substantial support in execution. There is still no definitive research to show that a particular administrative setup (for example, graded or ungraded, interclass or intraclass grouping) or a particular instructional approach (basal, multibasal, experience, self-selection) is best. Probably there never will be. The most satisfactory approach is to offer the best possible developmental instruction with existing resources and personnel. This approach can be successful if the emphasis is placed upon the individuals in the program.

Corrective, accelerated, adapted, and remedial instruction—to respond to special problems and/or needs—must, of course, be carefully coordinated with the ongoing developmental program.

Corrective instruction

The purpose of corrective instruction is to provide immediate diagnosis and corrective teaching to eliminate gaps and minor deficiencies in skill development. Offered by the classroom teacher within the framework of regular developmental instruction, it is actually an integral part of the general program. It is differentiated from developmental instruction here mainly to underscore the need for constant assessment of skill development and prompt provision of additional instruction when needed. Many skill development problems can be corrected with relative ease if they are detected and corrected before they lead to more generalized breakdowns in the skill development process and, in turn, to the failure-frustration-failure effect that saps motivation and destroys positive self-evaluation.

Efficient corrective instruction can be provided only if there is a continual, systematic assessment of individual skill development. Once-a-year achievement testing is far from adequate for spotting problems in skill development. What is needed is a scheme for constant and specific skill assessment. If teachers are given assistance in becoming aware of the scope and sequence of skills involved in the reading process and provided with concrete bases for making judgments about their pupils' skill development status, they will be able to make the assessments. (The matter of skill-based teaching is discussed in detail in chapter 3.)

Corrective instruction, which is provided within the framework of regular developmental instruction, is used when the need is detected and for the individuals who need it. Thus, a child who is having difficulty with, say, three-consonant blends might be taken aside for special help; or ten pupils who are having trouble in following the sequence in narrative materials might be taught as a group; or an entire class might be given a series of lessons designed to increase reading speed. Typically, the instruction will be designed to reteach or reinforce skills or subskills previously introduced in developmental instruction. There is a double payoff for well-conceived, systematic corrective instruction: pupils who need additional help get it, but (equally important) those who do not need it *do not* get it. Too often we continue to bludgeon pupils with boring activities for which they have no need.

Accelerated instruction

The last point on corrective instruction is extremely relevant to accelerated instruction where the focus is upon providing enrichment and challenge for bright, well-motivated, successful achievers. Every experienced teacher knows pupils who have been bored, or worse, because they are tied to a group or a grade level. Concern for the individual must make us sensitive to the needs for accelerated as well as corrective instruction; it is as nonsensical to repeat what has been mastered as it is not to repeat what has been missed.

Accelerated instruction should proceed from a systematic assessment of individual skill development. Once a child has a solid skill development base, the pace of instruction can be quickened, the scope broadened, or both, without concern that essentials are being missed or passed over too lightly.

Adapted instruction

In the typical school setting the children who seem to fare the worst in spite of their teachers' endless concern belong to a group that we shall call *slow learners*, children whose IQs fall roughly in the 80 to 90 range. These children do not achieve at grade level in reading or any other school subject. Consequently they become a source of great concern to every school person who stubbornly clings to grade-level performance as the minimum acceptable level for each individual. Virtually everyone on a school staff knows and accepts the bell-shaped curve of normally distributed intelligence, which shows that about one-fourth of the children in school have IQs below 90. The same people know that grade-level performance is an artifact and that equal numbers of children perform above and below it. Thus some children cannot achieve at grade level because of their limited intellectual ability.

Yet so-called remedial reading classes are cluttered with slow learners, ostensibly with the expectation that they will catch up; teachers ceaselessly attempt to "motivate" their slow learners to do better; and slow learners continue to be assigned tasks they cannot handle. Apparently many of us are able to accept limited capacity as an abstract cconcept but not as a fact.

Children with limited ability are likely to benefit much more from adapted instruction, where the pace and long-term expectations are modified in view of their limitations, than from remedial or corrective instruction, where the expectation is that the deficit can be overcome. This is not to suggest that anyone should be arbitrarily branded as a slow learner and abandoned. On the contrary, the slow-learner category should be applied only after careful assessment. Once the fact of limited capacity is established, the adaption of subsequent instruction is a demonstration of concern for the individual.

Adapted instruction is probably best provided within the regular classroom or, where classrooms are not the basic instructional units, in a generally heterogeneous context. Thus slow learners are not segregated into homogeneous groups. The materials and procedures used in adapted instruction are less important than the pacing of instruction. The main problem of slow learners is that they are unable to proceed in skill development as rapidly as children who have average or better intelligence; consequently, they quickly drop behind, and their whole skill development sequence gets out of phase. Only when the pace of instruction is realistically adapted are the majority of slow learners able to make the most of their limited abilities. Careful, systematic assessment of skill development provides the key to realistic pacing in adapting instruction just as it provides the key to focused corrective instruction.

Remedial instruction

This is the place for intensive diagnosis and special tutoring for the disabled reader. Remedial instruction differs from corrective instruction in degree and from adapted instruction in expectations. Remedial instruction is reserved for pupils with disabilities so severe that they need more intensive help than can be provided through corrective instruction, but in either case the expectation is that achievement deficits will be eliminated or reduced as a result of the teaching. In adapted instruction, there is no expectation of achievement at grade level or better; the instruction is geared to the limited abilities of the individual.

Some modification of the administrative setup is necessary to provide teacher time, adequate materials, and an optimum setting for the provision of the intensive diagnosis and tutoring required by a remedial situation. Assuming that remedial work is reserved for pupils with problems too severe to be handled through developmental or corrective instruction in the classroom, it is necessary to establish a situation in which the required special help can be provided. The arrangements can range from specially staffed clinics (either centrally located, with children transported to the facility, or mobile, with the unit transported to the children) to individual remedial teachers (itinerant remedial teachers responsible to more than one school, remedial teachers assigned full time to a single school, or regular teachers with some specialized training given released time from the classroom to offer remedial instruction). There are advantages and disadvantages for each setup. The decision as to which is best can be made only in terms of local needs and resources. (Guidelines for making the decision are given in later chapters.)

For a more detailed discussion of the corrective and remedial aspects of the total reading program, see the second edition of *Corrective and Remedial Teaching*, second edition (Otto, Mc-Menemy & Smith, 1973, chaps. 3–9).

Some final words

We have discussed several aspects of a well-rounded reading program to underscore the need for different types of instruction; but, as we have said, classification schemes do not make a program. A coherent reading program is the result of a careful coordination of well-conceived parts.

We have two final points. First, a reading program cannot be copied from a book or purchased, neatly packaged. It must be developed by the entire staff within a local context. Second, a good reading program need not be more costly than a poor one. Some of the most expensive programs are the poorest. Flashy hardware, shelves of materials, and specialized personnel often offer a false sense of security. While monetary support is important, dollars alone cannot purchase a good reading program.

THE READER IN THE PROGRAM

Given a sensitivity to individual needs and aspirations and a reading program with sufficient breadth and flexibility to provide the framework for individual development in reading, the

11

remaining need is to consider the placement of the student in the program.

Who and why

Each student should be placed in a reading program on the basis of the best available estimates of his or her *general ability* and his or her *achievement in reading*. The *who* and *why* of program placement, then, are determined on the basis of comparisons of learning capacity and actual achievement.

First consider general ability or learning capacity. Although you must recognize the limitations of intelligence tests and IQ scores, an example based on IQ scores demonstrates some of the factors to consider.

Given the formula CA (chronological age) × IQ (intelligence quotient) = MA (mental age), a ten-year-old with an IQ of 90 has a mental age of nine, and a ten-year-old with an IQ of 120 has a mental age of twelve. Both children would be in fifth grade if they had started school at the age of six and had continued without retention. Thus, the child with the 90 IQ has the mental age, or capacity, of a fourth-grader; the child with the 120 IQ has the capacity of a seventh-grader. On a straight MA = Capacity basis, the learning capacities of the two children differ substantially despite their placement in the same grade. Obviously, concern for each individual would dictate that the two children be exposed to sharply differentiated instruction within the same grade level. (One would be a candidate for adapted instruction and the other a candidate for accelerated instruction.)

Unfortunately—or perhaps fortunately—straight MA = Capacity conversions are not to be taken without at least two grains of salt. First, the ten-year-olds have both lived for the same length of time and, let us assume, have been exposed to similar experiences. Assuming perfect IQ assessment (which, admittedly, is assuming a great deal), the 90 IQ child might do better than the average nine-year-old on the basis of his more than a tenth of a lifetime's additional experiences, and the 120 IQ child might be at a disadvantage in competing with twelve-year-olds because of his substantial dearth of experiences by comparison. Second, IQ scores from any source are not absolute numbers, but IQ scores from group tests need corroboration from other sources.

An estimate of a child's learning capacity can be made if his or her IQ is known. If this estimate is combined with other facts and common sense, it can be the basis for the student's tentative placement in the developmental program, but the placement must be modified in view of *actual achievement* in reading. Some children's reading achievement is below their learning capacity level. Grade level is not a realistic achievement criterion because some children are capable of doing much better and others are not capable of grade-level performance.

The main point is that the bright child who is achieving only at grade level may need corrective help, and the slow learner who is achieving below grade level may need adapted rather than remedial teaching. Of course, reading test scores, like IQ test scores, must also be taken with a grain of salt. Both capacity and actual achievement contribute to the *why* that helps to determine *who* should receive particular instructional consideration in the total developmental program.

What and where

If reasonably accurate, reliable estimates of general ability and specific reading achievement are available, it is possible to specify the aspect of the total developmental program that is likely to provide the most appropriate instructional focus for each child. In figure 1.2 the appropriate focus for three levels of capacity and three levels of reading achievement is given. The schema is not adjusted for anticipated group size. The expectation is that in a normal situation the majority of pupils—with capacity in the average range and achievement in the grade level (grade level plus or minus three to nine months, depending on the grade) range—would fall in the developmental category. With the understanding that each category is only roughly delimited in the schema, we can suggest some guidelines for assigning pupils.

Figure 1.2 **Placement of a student in the reading program, based on general capacity and actual achievement**

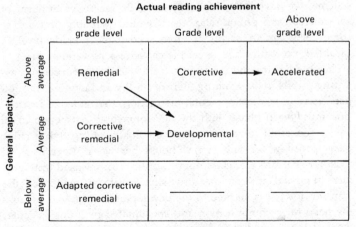

Source: Adapted from Wayne Otto and Richard J. Smith, *Administering the School Reading Program* (Boston: Houghton Mifflin, 1970), p. 36. © 1970 Wayne Otto and Richard J. Smith.

Children with capacity and reading performance in the average range can be taught adequately in the regular developmental program. The average range of reading performance covers roughly a six-month band (grade level plus or minus three months) by the end of first grade to an eighteen-month band by seventh-grade level and above. Teachers must, of course, remain vigilant to detect changes in performance that signal a need for corrective or accelerated instruction.

Slow learners, children whose IQs range from 90 to 80 and below, should be given adapted instruction where the pace and expectations are realistically modified to be in line with their capacity. There is also a possibility that slow learners will perform below their capacity level. When the gap is substantial, they should not be excluded from remedial instruction.

Remedial instruction should be reserved for children who are performing substantially below their capacity levels and appear to require intensive, individual diagnosis and tutoring beyond what can be provided in the developmental or corrective context. We prefer to call these children *disabled* rather than *retarded* readers, because the latter may carry a connotation of mental retardation, which is not intended. In general, children in the middle elementary grades who are reading two or more years below their capacity levels (the gap must be decreased or increased for lower or higher grades) should be considered candidates for remedial reading. (In practice, grade level may be the criterion. In this case, bright children who read at grade level but substantially below their capacity level pose a problem because they clearly need some additional help but are precluded from remedial reading. They should not be ignored. In the figure 1.2 schema, we have indicated corrective help for them. In terms of self-concept and public relations, it would probably be troublesome to designate bright children who read at grade level as disabled, no matter how great the capacity-achievement gap.)

If remedial instruction is to serve its ultimate purpose of assisting pupils in overcoming their disability and moving into full participation in developmental instruction, the remedial instruction must be in phase with the developmental instruction in all areas. Too often remedial instruction is something that a child participates in for only a few hours per week. Regardless of whether specialists or classroom teachers with released time provide remedial instruction, provision must be made for the transfer of what is learned to the developmental context. Because the need for communication and coordinated planning is acute, we feel that remedial teaching is, in general, better offered in each child's home school building than in a centrally located clinic.

Corrective instruction is provided to overcome moderate skill deficiencies and to fill in gaps in skill development. A general rule of thumb is that corrective teaching should be considered for children in the middle elementary grades whose achievement is one to two years below capacity. The gap must be increased or decreased at other grade levels. Corrective teaching is provided for individuals and groups within the general context of developmental instruction. The same is true for accelerated instruction, which is offered to pupils who need additional challenge.

When

There is only one point to be made here: when the individual is given prime consideration, there can be no generalizations about when certain things should happen. For some children the age of six is much too early to begin developmental instruction and for others it is much too late, for they may have learned to read at home or they may have grown weary of waiting. To treat a child who has reached an arbitrary school entrance age as an individual is to accept and to teach that child as he or she is.

Remedial instruction cannot be deferred until fourth grade, as it is in some schools. It must be given when the need is recognized before the negative overlay of failure has become thick and tough.

Adapted instruction must begin the moment the child starts to lag. No child should be subjected to the frustration and anxiety inherent in instruction that always moves too fast. And no child should be subjected to the boredom inherent in instruction that always moves too slowly and stops short of any challenge.

To put the focus on the individual reader in the reading program is to remove all that is arbitrary from the program. Our intent in discussing aspects of the program has been to ensure the awareness of the need for each type of instruction, not to impose more tracks and categories. If the aspects of the program we have described appear to impose arbitrary barriers, then they, too, must be eliminated.

Bibliography

Otto, Wayne, Richard McMenemy, and Richard J. Smith. *Corrective and Remedial Teaching*, 2nd ed. Boston: Houghton Mifflin, 1973.

Schiffman, G. "Program Administration within a School System." In John Money (ed.). *The Disabled Reader*. Baltimore: Johns Hopkins Press, 1966, chap. 15.

Chapter 2 The reading process

An elementary teacher works every day in the classroom helping young children learn to read—assigning a workbook lesson, helping a student to sound out a word, asking a question that will clarify meaning. The teacher moves with the confidence of a professional with many years of experience and many student successes.

Such a teacher seems to know what he or she is doing. Through many years of experience, he or she has developed a theory of the reading process and of human acquisition of that process. The teacher may not be able to articulate that theory very well if someone were to ask, "Can you describe what happens when a person reads?" or "How can someone best be taught to read?" But the basic premises of a theory are present, guiding each instructional decision that teacher makes.

Theory has been defined as "a system of assumptions, accepted principles, and rules of procedure devised to analyze, predict, or otherwise explain the nature or behavior of a specified set of phenomena" (*The American Heritage Dictionary of the English Language*, p. 1335). That is precisely what that elementary teacher uses—a set of assumptions, principles, and procedures—to make instructional decisions while teaching reading.

The teacher acquired these theories from training and study with specialists in the field of reading, from experience as a reading teacher, and from a belief that may never be explained. The theory probably did not come from a single source. It is a long and slow accumulation of bits of knowledge and belief about the reading process.

Thus the issue is not whether a teacher should take the time to formulate a theory of the reading process. That has already occurred. The issue, rather, is whether the teacher needs to treat his or her own theories as tentative and thus subject to ongoing scrutiny, and be aware of and participate in the continuing scholarly dialogue about the process.

This chapter explores that act of theorizing about the reading process. The chapter does not survey or categorize the current theory building and research in reading. That has already been well done by others. (See Singer and Ruddell, 1970, or Davis, 1971.) Nor do we propose to defend a particular theory or set of theories.

Our intent, rather, is to convince the reader that theories of the reading process are important to teachers and that participating in the ongoing scholarship is essential if the practice of teaching reading is to reflect the best knowledge available.

The importance of theory

In the hectic day-to-day business of managing a classroom, it is easy for the teacher to justify a decision not to worry about the sifting sands of scholarship in reading. Certainly lack of time and energy, little perceived relevance to the teacher's immediate situation, and an often meager background for understanding the theoretical complexities are reasonable excuses. However, we can present five compelling reasons why teachers should make the study of the scholarship of reading and reading instruction part of their ongoing professional responsibility.

First, modern reading scholarship enjoys an intellectual rigor that it has never before had. Reading, in short, is no longer a kitchen science; it is no longer the victim of helter-skelter, one-shot research and theorizing. That tradition has been replaced by careful, systematic, theory-based research. As Kling (1971) notes, "Perhaps the most striking generalization that emerges from the literature is that research in reading has been shifting rapidly during the last five years from an atheoretical to a theoretical base with concomitant interest in developing models of reading and more nearly adequate definitions of it" (p. 2–2). Moreover, there is probably less consensus than at any other time in recent history as to how the reading act occurs and how it is learned.

The implications of this shift are clear for the practitioner. We are rapidly developing a far better perception of the reading process and how it can best be taught, and these improved perceptions are making our vision far more complex. If teachers are to formulate classroom practices that reflect the best knowledge that we have about how reading occurs and is taught, then they must understand the emerging theories and must participate actively in the dialogue and debate that occurs as different theories collide.

A teacher's careful understanding of theory is also required by the need for order and system in pedagogy. Although teaching is an art and learning only a partially understood mystery, theory provides the important patterns for an artist's decisions. Williams (1974) says it well:

> Teachers are practitioners, and any good practitioner seeks to develop solid foundation in theory. A theory will not, of course, provide simple, straightforward answers to a teacher's questions about how to handle a particular child in a particular instructional situation or in a particular management crisis. But the knowledgeable teacher can draw upon what theory and research tell him, and he can use his general understanding to help provide a basis for developing and evaluating instructional programs in general and for making rapid and effective decisions as to how to handle specific, individual problems as they arise. (p. 533)

Without theory, practitioners would be reduced to confusion each time they faced a new instructional decision. A mastery of the best that theory has to offer will help ensure that the best pedagogical decisions are made.

The need for order in the reading curriculum is a third reason for practitioners to have a sound understanding of reading theories. Children become fluent and powerful readers only after an extended period of learning and development. The chances that students will develop in an optimal fashion are greater if their development has been guided by a consistent theory of the reading process. Thus, it is important that practitioners understand and can communicate to one another the theory that is guiding their instructional decisions in reading. Teachers in a school who dialogue with one another on alternative theories of the reading process will, as a group, arrive at a consistent and sound position.

Teachers who lack a thorough understanding of the alternative theories of the reading process are virtually at the mercy of the publishers when they select reading materials. Although publishers base their materials on a prevalent reading theory, teachers will have difficulty assessing the appropriateness of the materials and their supporting theoretical foundation unless they have an insight into theoretical alternatives.

The pedagogical demands being made of reading teachers by the public are far more rigorous than ever before. This is yet a fourth reason for a teacher to have a sound understanding of the impact of theory on reading instruction. Most school communities are no longer satisfied if only 50 to 70 percent of the students can read well. The public believes that if better instruction is provided, all children will learn how to read.

Although this is a somewhat unrealistic expectation, it is equally true that reading scholars are beginning to help children who find it difficult to learn to read. Their findings suggest that it is no longer necessary to ignore the reading skill needs of children with limited intellectual capacity, children with different cultural or linguistic backgrounds, or children with reading-related learning disabilities. If teachers are to work successfully with these children, they must be on the forefront of research and theory building.

A final reason why teachers must take an interest in reading process theories is perhaps somewhat less practical than the previous ones; it is, however, no less important. Teachers are closer to children and to the reading process than anyone else who is concerned with reading. As day-to-day practitioners, they are in an excellent position to participate in the act of theory building. Theory building in this area is likely to occur more quickly if a partnership between scholars and teachers is forged that allows both groups to participate in the process of learning more about the reading act. Teachers will not become part of this partnership until they have a better understanding of and appreciation for the many different reading theories.

Scholarship and the reading process

The process of reading and learning to read is the object of an intense scholarship search. All of the current theories of the reading process are nothing more than approximations to a mysterious act that we do not understand. No reading theory as yet is adequate to explain all of the mysteries of reading. All theories that purport to describe the reading process "leak" when they are tested against the realities of that process.

Attempts by scholars to build theories of the reading process are somewhat like the six blind men:

> It was six men of Hindustan,
> to learning much inclined,
> who went to see the elephant,
> (though all of them were blind);
> that each by observation
> might satisfy his mind.

19

We all know what happened: the first man thought the elephant a wall, the second a spear, the third a snake, the fourth a tree, the fifth a fan, and the last a rope. The poet concludes:

And so these men of Hindustan
disputed loud and long,
each of his own opinion
exceeding stiff and strong,
though each was partly in the right,
and all were in the wrong!

John Godfred Saxe

A practitioner studying the theoretical foundations of reading immediately faces what appears to be a jungle of research studies, theoretical treatises, and informal speculations. When these messages are looked at in isolation or compared with one or two others, they often do not seem to fit together into a reasonable pattern. There are, however, some concepts that will help the practitioner sort out the attempts at theory building in reading. We will review several of those concepts and then will share a proposed paradigm for viewing theory building of the reading process. The purpose of the paradigm is to help the practitioner who wishes to delve into this theory.

Reading theories can be described in a variety of ways. First, scholars speak of macrotheories and microtheories. A microtheory of the reading act attempts to describe one small part or segment of it. An attempt to describe the perception process that goes on as children attend to visual letter cues is an example of microtheorizing. A macrotheory attempts to describe the entire reading act.

Scholars also distinguish between developmental theories and descriptive theories. A descriptive theory is an attempt to describe the actions of a mature reader as he or she reads a message. A developmental theory is more likely to frame the explanation of the reading act in terms of how the process is learned.

Finally, scholars contrast molecular and holistic approaches to theory building. A molecular theory attempts to break the reading act into a sequence of more explicit behaviors (skills) that go together in a relatively linear fashion. In a molecular approach to theory building, it is assumed that if six or eight different kinds of skills have been identified, these skills go together in some systematic, building-block fashion to create the reading act. The holistic theorist may break the reading act into a series of component parts but suspects that the parts fit together in a complex, interrelating fashion that can never be fully understood because of the dynamic quality of reading. Moreover, this theorist views attempts to break the reading act into a series of aspects or parts as an artificial attempt to describe something that cannot in reality be broken apart.

It is reasonable for a practitioner aspiring to study the theoretical foundations of the reading process to ask exactly how many blind men are studying the elephant. Kling (1971) suggests there are five separate research and theory traditions. Several of these traditions can be further subdivided, particularly where the tradition has existed for some time. Table 2.1 provides a graphic picture of the five traditions and their subordinate areas. The table briefly describes each tradition and cites two or three references that either give an overview of the tradition or highlight a significant work from that tradition.

The five traditions are psychology, psycholinguistics, information processing, sociolinguistics, and the biobehavioral sciences. Psychology has a longer tradition of scholarship in the area of reading than any of the other four. Thus, more work has been done on studying reading from a psychological perspective. Kling further divides the psychological tradition into five subtraditions: the perceptual-conceptual tradition, the behavioristic tradition, the nativistic tradition, the cognitive tradition, and the psychometric tradition.

Most educators are familiar with the behavioristic traditions of Pavlov (classical conditioning) and Skinner (operant conditioning). Considerable work has been done to explain language acquisition and the reading process from the behavioristic perspective, but most attempts present considerable conceptual problems for modern theorists, primarily because the simplistic elegance of the stimulus-response approach does not adequately explain the complexities of the reading process. Staats and Staats (1962) is characteristic of a behavioristic description of the reading process.

The perceptual/conceptual tradition draws heavily on the visual perception theories from psychology to explain the initial acts of decoding. Such theories are less useful in explaining higher-order reading processes of comprehension. Gibson's (1970) work is exemplary in this tradition.

The cognitive tradition is typified by the work of such theorists as Piaget (1970) and Brunner, Goodnow, and Austin (1966). Theoretical work within this tradition relates the reading process to the cognitive development of the child.

Nativistic theories emerge from the premise that language is biologically based and is the manifestation of human species–specific cognitive roots. Nativistic psychologists tend to look for

Table 2.1 **Theories of the reading process**

Tradition	Description	Examples
1. Psychology		
a. Behavioristic	a. Based on Pavlovian classical conditioning or Skinnerian operant conditioning	a. Staats and Staats (1962), Carroll (1964)
b. Perceptive	b. Extension of perception theories of Broadbent (1958) and others	b. Gibson (1970)
c. Cognitive	c. Explanation of language acquisition as stages of cognitive development; based on traditions of Piaget (1970) and Brunner (1966)	c. Williams (1971), Elkind (1970)
d. Nativistic	d. Based on theories of language acquisition as a biological predisposition of humans	d. Lenneberg (1967)
e. Psychometric	e. Use of measurement theory to infer factors of reading	e. Davis (1971) Bormuth (1971)
2. Psycholinguistics		
a. Grapho-phonology	a. Sound/symbol relationships and their acquisition	a. McNeill (1970), Fant (1967)
b. Syntax	b. The grammatical structure of language and its acquisition	b. Chomsky (1965)
c. Semantics	c. The study of meanings that are attached to words and other symbols	c. Deese (1969), Ruddell (1970), Goodman (1968)
3. Information processing	Use of computer information-processing concepts to describe the reading process	Venezky and Calfee (1970), Kelly (1967)
4. Sociolinguistics	Individual and group differences that affect language acquisition	Bernstein (1971)
5. Biobehavioral sciences	Attempts to describe language behavior physiologically and chemically	Pribram (1969), Geyer (1971)

Source: Based on data from Davis, Frederick B. (Ed.), *The Literature of Research and Reading with Emphasis on Models,* Graduate School of Education, Rutgers University, New Brunswick, N.J., 1971, 640 pp. (Distributed by IRIS Corp., P.O. Box 372, East Brunswick, N.J. 08816)

language behavior universals across cultures. McNeill's (1970) work is characteristic of the nativistic tradition.

The psychometric tradition from psychology has attempted to use the discipline of measurement and testing to tease from human reading behavior the specific skills that make up the reading act. For example, a psychometrist will propose seven or eight discrete reading skills, develop test items for each of those skills, collect the items into a single test instrument, administer that instrument to a group of readers, and attempt through different statistical procedures to find distinct skill factors that are present in the readers' responses to test items. Davis (1971) and Bormuth (1971) are perhaps the best-known spokespersons from the psychometric tradition.

The major contributions of psycholinguistics to the theories of the reading process have occurred during the last twenty-five years. This research tradition has identified three kinds of information: phonology, syntax, and semantics. Phonology probes the linkages between the graphic systems of written language and the phonological systems of oral language. Syntax explores the grammatical structures of the language. Semantics investigates various strategies that the mature reader uses to obtain meaning. Spokespeople for this tradition include Chomsky and Halle (1968), Osgood (1966), and Ruddell (1970).

Information processing is a much more recent science, and its contributions to reading theory are as yet modest in number though important in concept. This tradition relies heavily on concepts from cybernetics, systems analysis, and general communication theory. Athey (1971), Hansen (1971), and Venezky and Calfee (1970) speak for this rapidly emerging tradition.

Sociolinguistics is a tradition of investigation that has provided insights on important individual differences among children. As Kling (1971) notes, "These include differences in dialect, differences among ethnic groups and information processing skills, differences in cognitive style, and differences arising from affective factors" (pp. 2–3). Sociolinguistics, an infant science, is just beginning to make significant contributions to a better understanding of the reading process.

Not to be overlooked is the work of the biobehavioral scientists. Their study of the neurological and physiological bases of psychological behavior, though seemingly some steps removed from the reading process itself, may eventually make a significant contribution to a better understanding of that process. At the very least, the biobehavioral line of investigation ought to be helpful in either corroborating or refuting scholars who have taken an extreme behavioristic or nativistic stance toward the

23

process of reading. Geyer (1971), Pribraum (1969), and Lorenz (1969) typify the biobehavioral tradition.

Three theories

Earlier we suggested that a practitioner must be concerned with attempts to describe the reading process. In this section, we would like to support that thesis by example. Our intent is to explore briefly three theories that bear on a description of the reading process. Each theory comes from a separate research tradition; each takes a somewhat different point of view. Following each description, we will suggest the implications of the theory for practice. (In choosing these three we in no way suggest that we favor them over others. We have selected these because they reflect the current divergent thinking in the field of reading.)

CAREFULLY CONDITIONED RESPONSES

The theory

Carroll (1970) describes the mature reading process as a complex and carefully integrated hierarchy of conditioned responses to an equally well-organized system of stimuli. According to Carroll, as we read, our eyes make a discrete series of fixations across the line of print. Each fixation, though extremely brief, is long enough for the eye to pick up and transmit to the brain various stimuli that are present in the span of that particular fixation. We may also receive, though less clearly, stimuli from neighboring fixations in the line of print.

These fixations, or the stimuli, are the words and other symbols present in the immediate vicinity. According to Carroll, we attend to the whole word as a distinct "gestalt-like" stimulus, which evokes a learned response. We do not sound the word out subvocally; we receive it as a total image.

If you are a skilled reader, you do not have to stop to figure out the pronunciation of a familiar word from its spelling; you are hardly conscious of the spelling at all. Still less do you attend to the particular phonetic values of the letters; in reading the word "women" it would scarcely occur to you to note that the "o" in the first syllable stands for a sound that rhymes with /i/ in "whim." The printed word "women" is a gestalt-like total stimulus that immediately calls to mind the spoken word that corresponds to it—or if not the spoken word itself, some underlying response which is also made when the word is spoken. (p. 293)

Carroll notes that the process of word recognition is not well understood; it is one of the unknowns in the whole problem of pattern perception about which psychologists know little. He does suggest, however, that "because the recognizability of a word is apparently correlated rather highly with its frequency of use, word perception seems to be a skill that depends upon large amounts of practice and exposure" (p. 294).

Carroll suggests that the mature reader recognizes words he or she has not seen in print before by attending to known stimuli within the new word; the reader thus picks out letters and patterns of letters that provide reasonable cues about the pronunciation of the word and thus some clue to its identity.

Finally, Carroll notes, the reader combines the words into larger stimulus units that evoke more complex responses:

The "essential" skill in reading is getting meaning from a printed or written message. In many ways, this is similar to getting meaning from a "spoken" message, but there are differences, because the cues are different. Spoken messages contain cues that are not evident in printed messages, and conversely. In either case, understanding language is itself a tremendous feat, when one thinks about it. When you get the meaning of a verbal message, you have not only recognized the words themselves; you have interpreted the words in their particular grammatical functions, and you have somehow apprehended the general grammatical patterning of each sentence. You have unconsciously recognized what words or phrases modify those subjects or predicates, and so on. In addition, you have given a "semantic" interpretation of the sentence, assigning meanings to the key words in the sentence. For example, in reading the sentence "He understood that he was coming tonight" you would know to whom each "he" refers, and you would interpret the word "understood" as meaning "had been caused to believe" rather than "comprehended". Somehow you put all these things together in order to understand the "plain sense" of what the message says. (p. 296)

The process of reading, according to Carroll, is not learned as a total unitary response. It is not learned all at once, and it is not

25

learned as a "slow motion imitation of the mature reading process. It has numerous components, and each component has to
be learned and practiced" (p. 297).

It is not clear in what order these components are learned or if
the order is the same for all children. Carroll says that there are
eight components, and they all must be acquired before reading
maturity is achieved. These eight components are:

1. The child must know the language that he is going to learn
   to read.
2. The child must learn to dissect spoken words into component sounds.
3. The child must learn to recognize and discriminate the letters of the alphabet in their various forms (capitals, lower
   case letters, printed, and cursive).
4. The child must learn the left-to-right principle by which
   words are spelled and put in order in continuous text.
5. The child must learn that there are patterns of highly probable correspondence between letters and sounds, and he
   must learn those patterns of correspondence that will help
   him recognize words that he already knows in his spoken
   language or that will help him determine the pronunciation
   of unfamiliar words.
6. The child must learn to recognize printed words from whatever cues he can use—their total configuration, the letters
   composing them, the sounds represented by those letters,
   and/or the meanings suggested by the context.
7. The child must learn that printed words are signals for
   spoken words and that they have meanings analogous to
   those of spoken words. While decoding a printed message
   into its spoken equivalent, the child must be able to appre-
   hend the meaning of the corresponding spoken message.
8. The child must learn to reason and think about what he
   reads, within the limits of his talent and experience.

The mature reader has practiced these eight skills so well that
they blend together into one unified performance.

The implications

The view of the reading process and its acquisition that Carroll
presents is not unpopular. Though some experts might quarrel
with him on particulars, there are many others who view reading
as an elaborate list of discrete skills, each of which must be practiced and learned separately. Many teachers share a similar perception of reading and build their programs accordingly.

If you as a teacher share a theory of the reading process similar to Carroll's, your reading program in all likelihood will have the following general characteristics:

1. Considerable emphasis will be placed throughout the instructional program on the development of a large and well-practiced repertoire of sight words.
2. Attention will be devoted to recognizing letters of the alphabet when their size and shape varies.
3. Letter-sound identification will be taught, but largely as a tool for recognizing words not seen before in print. Thus, phonics will not be taught as thoroughly as it might in other theories.
4. Reading is the task of unlocking written words into their spoken equivalents and then extracting meaning, a two-stage process.
5. Each component skill must be learned separately.
6. Each skill must be practiced consistently and continually, to be mastered.
7. The process of uniting the components into a total skill will occur naturally as individual components are mastered with increasing sophistication.

A PSYCHOLINGUISTIC GUESSING GAME

The theory

Carroll suggested that reading is a fairly precise, if complex, process. Goodman (1967) disagrees: ". . . the common sense notion I seek here to refute is this: 'Reading is a precise process. It involves exact, detailed, sequential perception and identification of letters, words, spelling patterns, and large language units' " (p. 259). He suggests that reading instead is a psycholinguistic guessing game in which the reader makes partial use of available language cues to make tentative decisions about meaning and then to confirm, reject, or refine these decisions as reading proceeds and additional cues are picked up: "Efficient reading does not result from precise perception and identification of all elements, but from skill in selecting the fewest, most productive cues necessary to produce guesses which are right for the first time. The ability to anticipate that which has not been seen, of course, is vital in reading, just as the ability to anticipate what has not yet been heard is vital in listening" (p. 260).

As research evidence for his position, Goodman provides analyses of the oral reading efforts of young readers. A young reader who is given fairly difficult passages to read will make a series of errors while reading the sentences orally. These errors, which Goodman calls "miscues," lead to a better understanding of the nature of the psycholinguistic guessing game. Goodman views these miscues not as careless mistakes but as traces of the tentative processing of minimal cues. Thus, reading is an interactive process between the reader and the printed page. It is not the plodding act of processing one fixation after the next, as it appears at the end of the reader's nose:

> No, the "end-of-the-nose" view of reading will not work. The reader is not confined to information he receives from a half inch of print in clear focus. Studies, in fact, indicate that children with severe visual handicaps are able to learn to read as well as normal children. Readers utilize not one, but three kinds of information simultaneously. Certainly, without graphic input, there would be no reading. But, the reader uses syntactic and semantic information as well. He predicts and anticipates on the basis of this information, sampling from the print just enough to confirm his guess of what's coming, to cue more semantic and syntactic information. Redundancy and sequential constraints in language, which the reader reacts to, make this prediction possible. Even the blurred and shadowy images he picks up in the peripheral area of his visual field may help to trigger or confirm guesses. (p. 266)

To summarize his model of the reading process, Goodman suggests the following eleven steps:

1. The reader scans along a line of print from left to right and down the page, line by line.
2. He fixes at a point to permit eye focus. Some print will be central and in focus, some will be peripheral; perhaps his perceptual field is a flattened circle.
3. Now begins the selection process. He picks up graphic cues, guided by constraints set up through prior choices, his language knowledge, his cognitive styles, and strategies he has learned.
4. He forms a perceptual image using these cues and his anticipated cues. This image then is partly what he sees and partly what he expected to see.
5. Now he searches his memory for related syntactic, semantic, and phonological cues. This may lead to selection of more graphic cues and to reforming the perceptual image.
6. At this point, he makes a guess or tentative choice consistent with graphic cues. Semantic analysis leads to partial

decoding as far as possible. This meaning is stored in short-term memory as he proceeds.

7. If no guess is possible, he checks the recalled perceptual input and tries again. If a guess is still not possible, he takes another look at the text to gather more graphic cues.

8. If he can make a decodable choice, he tests it for semantic and grammatical acceptability in the content developed by prior choices and decoding.

9. If the tentative choice is not acceptable semantically or syntactically, then he regresses, scanning from right to left along the line and up the page to locate a point of semantic or syntactic inconsistency. When such a point is found, he starts over at that point. If no inconsistency can be identified, he reads on seeking some cue which will make it possible to reconcile the anomalous situation.

10. If the choice is acceptable, decoding is extended, meaning is assimilated with prior meaning, and prior meaning is accommodated, if necessary. Expectations are formed about input and meaning that lies ahead.

11. Then the cycle continues. (pp. 269–270)

The implications

Goodman's theory of the reading process is significantly different from Carroll's. For Goodman, reading is a meaning-seeking rather than a meaning-extracting process. The classroom implications are clear for the teacher who accepts this alternative tradition:

1. Learning to read begins with the process of comprehension, that is, seeking meaning from the written-symbol system.

2. Students must be introduced gradually but simultaneously to phonic, grammatical, and semantic cues.

3. Context is critical to meaning, and no words should be introduced except in the context of a larger message.

4. Stress should be placed on the concept represented by a word in the context of other words. Dictionary definitions of isolated words are meaningless for reading.

5. Students' miscues can be used to suggest the kind of instruction that will be most helpful.

THE LARGEST MANAGEABLE UNIT

The theory

The third model of the reading process represents an entirely different tradition from the first two. The work of Venezky and Cal-

fee (1970) reflects an information-processing tradition, complete
with its complex concepts and computer terminology. Information-processing models might seem unnecessarily complex to
many practitioners. However, the growing library of research
about the reading process increasingly suggests that the mature
reading process is complex.

Venezky and Calfee suggest that a competent reader is anyone
whose w/o ratio and achievement score on a general reading test
approach that of the general adult population. (The w/o ratio is
the ratio of comprehension of written materials to the ratio of
comprehension of oral materials.)

The input-output model describes the competent reader. The
input is the message printed in the English language; the output
is something called "understanding."

Three concepts are key to Venezky and Calfee's description of
the reading process: *high-speed visual scanning, dual processing,*
and a search for the *largest manageable unit (LMU).* Figure 2.1 provides a schematic of their model.

The scanning process is directed by the reader's background
knowledge and by his or her immediate knowledge of the message in question. General background knowledge includes the
general nature and structure of written materials, concepts, and
properties that the reader uses to define reality (either real or
imagined), language habits, and common grammatical patterns.
Immediate knowledge is message specific. General background
knowledge is stored in what Venezky and Calfee call the Integrated Knowledge Store (IKS), and specific information (from
the message being read) is stored in the Temporary Knowledge
Store (TKS). The IKS and TKS are roughly analogous to long-term
and short-term memory.

Three additional storage units aid the scanning process.
There are the Associative Word Store (AWS) and the Low
Frequency Store (LFS). Word identifications are made by
parallel-search of the Associative Word Store (AWS), or if not
found there, by search of a larger, less-well organized store
(the Low Frequency Store—LFS). The AWS contains the most
frequently encountered items, organized for retrieval on the
basis of initial letters, final letters, and word length. Using
some minimal amount of information (first letters, plus length,
plus expectancies derived from previously scanned material),
a match in the associate store is attempted; if made, the remainder of the word is compared to the stored item; a mis-
match at this point will cause further searching in the table.
(Many items in this table, like *the* and *of,* function as single perceptual units.) An item not matched in the associative store will

Figure 2.1 **A schematic of a reading model**

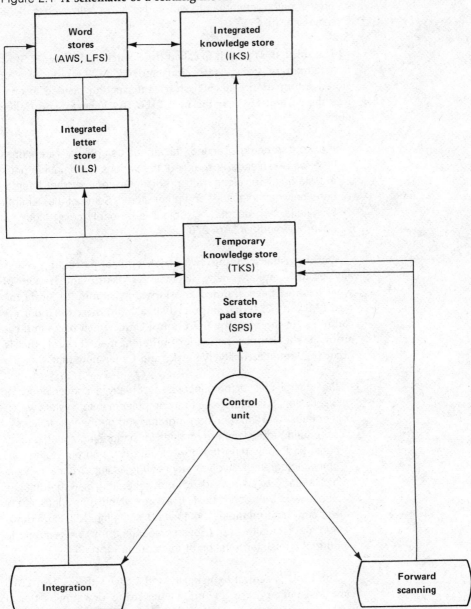

Source: From Richard L. Venezky and Robert L. Calfee, "The Reading Competency Model," in Harry Singer and Robert B. Ruddell (eds)., *Theoretical Models and Processes of Reading* (Newark, Del.: International Reading Association, 1970). Reprinted with permission of the authors and the International Reading Association.

be compared to items in the Low Frequency Store; failure to find a match immediately will cause subvocalization and re-scanning. (p. 275)

The third storage unit is called the Scratch Pad Store (SPS). It is a temporary storage unit characterized by a rapid decay of stored information. The SPS stores information needed to analyze the current LMU or the next LMU. As Venezky and Calfee note:

> If a word is being scanned, its various components are stored here; as a sentence is scanned, the various grammatical units are stored here, along with predictions derived from interactions between this store and other stores. Some of these might be: "finite verb needed," "subject is probably next," "look for adverbial modifier." (p. 278)

During visual scanning, two major forms of processing generally occur simultaneously: "syntactic-semantic integration of what has just been scanned and forward scanning to locate the next LMU" (p. 274). In computer-like fashion, these functions are controlled in the brain by the Control Unit, which paces and co-ordinates the complex network of different mental events that is occurring simultaneously. Venezky and Calfee note that

> the control unit, or homunculus, is chiefly a convenience for discussion. It is analogous to a computer monitor system which mediates between running programs and peripheral devices—scheduling jobs, locating routines for performing specific functions, and controlling the flow of data into and out of the machine. Integration involves connecting isolated units to what has already been picked up and generating new predictions about what will occur next. If a form which is in focus is not smoothly interpretable, the forward scanning will slow down and may actually stop. (Reverse scanning may be required to correct a misinterpretation or misreading.) (pp. 274–275)

The LMU is central to Venezky and Calfee's theory. An LMU can consist of a phrase, a word, a letter string, or a single letter. It is the largest meaningful unit that can be perceived rapidly at any instant during the scanning process. The size of that unit will depend on the reader's skills and the complexity of the message. As we noted earlier, the purpose of forward scanning is to locate the next LMU. Forward scanning makes a tentative identification of the LMU; syntactic-semantic integration seeks to confirm the earlier tentative identification by relating it to both

General Knowledge (IKS) in the reader's background and Imme-
diate Knowledge (TKS) obtained by previous syntactic-semantic integration. If the initial tentative identification of the LMU is not confirmed by integration efforts, rescanning must take place.

> Scanning, therefore, is central to the reading process, and involves a balance between two processes: integration and forward scanning, the former being strongly dependent upon the latter. If the material requires excessive attention during integration, either because of perceptual or conceptual difficulty, forward scanning is restrained. The balance between integration and scanning, however, may also be controlled by the intent of the reader: reading "light" novels or other materials requires primary attention to forward scanning with little integration. Digestion of dense writings, on the other hand, requires extensive integration with limited forward scanning. Poorer readers may not be able to shift the balance between these two processes for different materials and goals. (p. 276)

Forward scanning and integration lead to comprehension as information from temporary storage locations is moved into permanent storage locations. Furthermore, forward scanning, integration, and comprehension occur in a highly interdependent fashion and very quickly in the competent reader.

The model Venezky and Calfee propose, though complex, is obviously a general one, which requires considerable further development and testing. It is, however, an example of theoretical work in information processing that is being applied to reading.

The implications

The Venezky and Calfee model of the reading process suggests several specific implications for the reading teacher.

First, since oral language is the underlying system from which reading is an extension, attention must be devoted initially to each child's oral language development, both listening and speaking.

Second, the need to build up the storage centers which the brain's processing network accesses suggests a building-block approach to reading with considerable initial attention to sound-symbol patterns. This suggests early work with each student on phonological generalizations. Venezky and Calfee deem a sight vocabulary to be less valuable than the acquisition of sound-symbol generalizations.

Third, Venezky and Calfee suggest the following sequence of skills. Note the early emphasis on word-attack skills.

Preliminary Skills
a. Left-to-right, top-to-bottom orientation for printing.
b. Awareness that writing can be translated into speech.
c. Discrimination of letters and words.

Aural-Oral Skills
a. Manipulation of separate sounds in words, either in reception or production.
b. Blending of sounds into familiar words.
c. Connecting words into familiar words.

Letter-Sound Skills
a. Linking letters to sounds.
b. Discriminating cues which indicate which of several sounds is to be attached to a letter.

Processing Skills
a. Balancing of forward scanning and integration.
b. Using stored information to aid in forward scanning.
c. Searching for units larger than letters or single words.

From theory to practice

Theories of the reading process tend to be complex and burdened by jargon. It is easy for the reader to get so bogged down with individual theories that he or she ignores the overall message in this chapter. Perhaps it will be useful to review its contents.

We have suggested that theories of the reading process are not only what scholars study; such theories are also the stuff of which practice is made. A reading teacher has a notion of the reading process; though perhaps fragmentary and unarticulated, it is still present when that teacher makes decisions about an individual student or the total reading program. The strength of the decision will rest on the soundness of the assumptions that teacher makes about the reading process. The soundness of those assumptions is ultimately tested by whether the student learns to read well.

We are not suggesting that theories generated in a scholar's study or laboratory are inherently superior to what a teacher believes. No theory of the reading process is above suspicion. All need to be held tentatively and tested continually. What is needed is improved communication between scholars and practitioners so that each can learn from the other.

Some teachers will say, "Enough of theory; give me something practical." Let's for a moment pose some very practical questions that a reading teacher must confront if he or she is to develop a reading instruction program. As you address each question, consider the role that theory must play in deciding the issue.

1. Do we begin reading readiness programs by having children learn the names of letters or the characteristic sounds of letters?
2. Do we begin reading instruction with the child's own language (vocabulary and syntactical structures) or with a controlled vocabulary and syntax from standard written English?
3. Do we develop a strong and sizable sight vocabulary for each child?
4. Do we begin reading instruction with the sound/symbol unit, the word, or the sentence as the basic unit of communication?
5. Do we teach sound/symbol generalizations or the pronunciation of each word encountered?
6. Do we defer comprehension instruction until decoding skills have been mastered?
7. Do we use an augmented alphabet (for example, i.t.a.) to simplify learning the English sound/symbol system?
8. Should we teach a sequence of separate and discrete reading skills or naturally introduce skills as they fit the reading task?
9. Should we attempt to teach comprehension skills beyond literal comprehension?
10. Can comprehension be taught as a set of hierarchically ordered skills?

Many more questions could be asked. These are practical questions, for a reading program cannot be effectively designed and implemented until the teacher comes to grips with most of them. None of the questions can be answered unequivocably; each must be answered tentatively in the light of theory. Thus, a theory of the reading process is not a luxury; it is a necessity.

Summary

We have attempted in this chapter to make a case for theories of the reading process and reading instruction. We rejected the common notion that theories and theorizing are foreign to teachers. Rather we suggest that every reading teacher uses a theoretical base. We have also suggested at least five reasons why teachers should take an interest in the scholarship that produces new reading theory.

Research and scholarship in reading have been quite productive during the past two decades, and many new lines of investigation have been opened. Without a conceptual map, the practitioner can easily get lost. In this chapter, we have provided such a map for examining reading theory.

Finally, we have explored three very divergent theories of reading. We selected these not because we necessarily favor them but because they illustrate vividly the contrasts that are currently evident in the field. By reviewing what each theory infers about reading instruction, we suggest how one's approach to reading instruction will be guided by what one believes about the reading act.

Bibliography

The American Heritage Dictionary of the English Language. New York: Houghton Mifflin Company, 1969.

Athey, Irene J. "Language Models and Reading." In F. B. Davis (ed.), *The Literature of Research in Reading with Emphasis on Models.* New Brunswick, N.J.: Rutgers University Graduate School of Education, 1971, pp. 6-3-6-99.

Bernstein, B. "A Sociolinguistic Approach to Socialization: With Some References to Educability." In J. J. Gumperz and D. Hymes (eds.), *Directions in Sociolinguistics.* New York: Holt, Rinehart, and Winston, 1973.

Bormuth, John R. *On the Theory of Achievement Test Items.* Chicago: University of Chicago Press, 1970.

Bruner, J. S., J. J. Goodnow, and M. Austin. *Studies in Cognitive Growth.* New York: Wiley, 1966.

Carroll, John. "The Nature of the Reading Process." In Harry Singer and Robert B. Ruddell (eds.), *Theoretical Models and Processes of Reading.* Newark, Del.: International Reading Association, 1970, pp. 292–303.

Chomsky, Noam. *Aspects of a Theory of Syntax.* Cambridge, Mass.: MIT Press, 1965.

———, and M. Halle. *The Sound Pattern of English.* New York: Harper and Row, 1968.

Davis, Frederick B. (ed.). *The Literature of Research in Reading with Emphasis on Models.* New Brunswick, N.J.: Rutgers University Graduate School of Education, 1971.

Deese, J. *Psycholinguistics.* Boston: Allyn and Bacon, 1970.

Elkind, D. "Reading, Logic, and Perception: An Approach to Reading Instruction." In D. Elkind (ed.), *Children and Adolescents: Interpretative Essays on Jean Piaget.* New York: Oxford University Press, 1970, pp. 136–150.

Fant, G. "Auditory Patterns of Speech." In W. Wather-Dunn (ed.), *Models for Perception of Speech and Visual Form.* Cambridge, Mass.: MIT Press, 1967.

Gibson, E. J. "The Ontogeny of Reading." *The American Psychologist* 25 (1970): 136–143.

Geyer, J. J. "Comprehensive and Partial Models, Related to the Reading Process." In F. B. Davis (ed.), *The Literature of Re-*

search in Reading with Emphasis on Models. New Brunswick, N.J.: Rutgers University Graduate School of Education, 1971, pp. 5-1–5-51.

Goodman, Kenneth. "Reading: A Psycholinguistic Guessing Game." *Journal of the Reading Specialist* 6 (May 1967): 126–135.

———. *The Psycholinguistic Nature of the Reading Process.* Detroit: Wayne State University Press, 1968.

Hansen, Duncan N. "Information-processing Models for Reading-Skill Acquisition." In F. B. Davis (ed.), *The Literature of Research in Reading with Emphasis on Models.* New Brunswick, N. J.: Rutgers University Graduate School of Education, pp. 7-45–7-71.

Kelley, K. L. *Early Syntactic Acquisition.* Santa Monica: Rand Corporation, 1967.

Kling, Martin. "Quest for Synthesis." In F. B. Davis (ed.), *The Literature of Research in Reading with Emphasis on Models.* New Brunswick, N.J.: Rutgers University Graduate School of Education, 1971, pp. 2-1–2-18.

Lenneberg, E. H. *Biological Foundations of Language.* New York: Wiley, 1967.

Lorenz, Konrad. "Innate Bases of Learning." In K. H. Pribram (ed.), *On the Biology of Learning.* New York: Harcourt, Brace, and World, 1969, pp. 13–93.

McNeill, D. "The Development of Language." In P. H. Mussen (ed.), *Carmichael's Manual of Child Psychology,* 3d ed. New York: Wiley, 1970, 1: 1061–1161.

Osgood, C. E. "Interpersonal Verbs and Interpersonal Behavior." *Technical Report No. 64.* Urbana: University of Illinois, Group Effectiveness Research Laboratory, 1968.

Piaget, Jean. "Piaget's Theory." In P. H. Mussen (ed.), *Carmichael's Manual of Child Psychology,* 3d ed. New York: Wiley, 1970, 1: 703–732.

Pribram, K. H. (ed.). *On the Biology of Learning.* New York: Harcourt, Brace, and World, 1969.

Ruddell, R. B. "Psycholinguistic Implications for a Systems-of-Communication Model." In H. Singer and R. B. Ruddell (eds.), *Theoretical Models and Processes of Reading.* Newark, Del.: International Reading Association, 1970, pp. 239–258.

Singer, H., and R. B. Ruddell (eds.), *Theoretical Models and Processes of Reading.* Newark, Del.: International Reading Association, 1970.

Staats, A. W., and C. K. Staats. "A Comparison of the Development of Speech and Reading Behavior with Implications for Research." *Child Development* 33 (1962): 831–846.

Venezky, Richard L., and Robert L. Calfee. "The Reading Competency Model." In Harry Singer and Robert B. Ruddell (eds.), *Theoretical Models and Processes of Reading.* Newark, Del.: International Reading Association, 1970, pp. 273–291.

Williams, Joanna. "New Theories of Reading: What Do They Tell Us." *Teachers College Record* 75, no. 4 (May 1974): 553–561.

Chapter 3 Basic skills in perspective

When approaches to the teaching of reading are discussed and procedures for improving school reading programs are considered, one issue that inevitably comes up is the role and prominence that should be given to the basic reading skills. The issue is not easily resolved because it turns out to involve much more than a straightforward decision to accept or to reject the teaching of skills. Relatively few would advocate the elimination of skills. Instead, the issue is beclouded by problems of which skills are important, how much prominence skills should have in the total program, whether skills should be pinned down with instructional objectives, what the nature of instructional objectives is, whether a skill management system should be adopted, whether teaching skills will result in a neglect of important knowledge, whether the "affective domain" will be neglected. These are legitimate problems, which need solutions. Unfortunately more time and effort are being spent raising and discussing the questions than in attempting to deal with them.

The ultimate problem for people who use skills to teach learners to read seems to have two parts: Is a skill development approach to teaching reading defensible? Is it sensible? The question is the ultimate one currently because there will be no definitive answers to the ancillary questions about teaching skills for the next two or three decades. The jury is out—or, more properly, still awaiting presentation of the evidence. But in the meantime school is in session and the people who teach school need to make decisions about teaching skills.

In this chapter we shall deal with both the defense and the sense of teaching skills. Our position is that skills ought to be given prominence, particularly in the early stages of teaching reading. We believe that much of the concern about teaching skills is misdirected. The problem seems to be that some critics and some practitioners have been bedazzled by the trappings that are sometimes—and as often as not, inappropriately—

associated with teaching skills. We shall attempt to view the teaching of skills in perspective.

Otto took up the gauntlet in an answer to a poem by Elaine M. Roberts, in which she expressed her concern about skills:

There are lists after lists
Of skill after skill
To confuse any mind
Or make it most ill.
They have to be useful—
How could they be wrong?
For I read them all day
And half the night long.
If a kid ever masters
These skills I have read
He'll be either a robot,
Or else he'll be dead.

Roberts, 1974

The appeal for perspective came in this reply:

Poems are made
By fools like us;
But Elaine M. Roberts
Has made such a fuss
About teaching kids skills
To help them read
That I find myself moved
By a powerful need
   To say something to her and to all of her ilk
   that may or may not be poetic. She says that
Lists of skills
Have inflicted ills
On her mind and confused her.
And her kids, the poor dears,
Have fulfilled all her fears
Which, it's plain, hasn't amused her.
   So I'd like to offer a bit of advice.
If you can't see the forest because of the trees,
That problem's solved with the greatest of ease:
   Step back; get it all in perspective.
   Likewise . . .
If your pupils can't read in spite of their skills,
There's just one thing needed to cure all the ills,
   And that, dear Elaine, ISN'T invective.
   It's perspective.

Otto, 1975

39

We deal more definitively with skills in perspective in the pages that follow. First, we offer a rationale for teaching skills. Then we deal with some of the more persistent concerns that are being expressed about teaching them. Finally, we offer some guidelines for a workable approach to teaching reading skills in perspective.

Why skills?

Subskills can be identified and taught with positive effects on reading performance. Yet children comprehend long before they are taught a single comprehension skill, and teachers can help them to understand a passage without teaching them any specific skill. In fact, children often learn to decode words without any teaching at all. So on the basis of common-sense observations, one can wind up advocating either a *holistic* or a *subskills* approach to teaching reading.

The debate between supporters of these approaches is likely to continue for decades. In fact, it may never end because the terms for picking a winner are not very clear. Empirically, we are likely to find that for some purposes teaching skills produces the most reliable results, and for others a holistic approach best suits the needs of teachers and learners. Philosophically, we will continue to find justification for doing what best suits our inclinations. The controversy is a positive force in reading education, because controversy keeps us on our toes. Meanwhile, we aim to strike a working balance. The question before us is, Why teach skills?

We offer a pragmatic answer: because we need skills to focus instruction . . . or to individualize instruction . . . or to differentiate instruction . . . or simply to plan instruction —whatever term one prefers to describe a process whereby teachers

- Decide what is teachable and ought to be taught
- Find out what individuals already know
- Teach individuals—probably along with other individuals who have similar needs—what they do not know

We are not suggesting that all of schooling or everything that goes on in schools can or should be dealt with in such a prescriptive way, but we are convinced that basic reading instruction is enhanced when there is focus.

Anyone who rejects the notion of focused instruction probably will reject skills; conversely, the expectation would be that anyone who rejects skills will likely reject focused instruction. Not so. Many authors who write reading methods texts say little or nothing specific about skills, yet they rhapsodize about individualization and urge their readers to take a diagnostic approach to teaching. Such urging is like telling people to shoot at a target without saying what or where the target is—or whether the shooting should be done with a shotgun or a rifle. The identification of specific skills brings precision to diagnosis and focus to instruction. Attention to specific skills is the price we pay for focused instruction.

The question of whether the price is right comes closer to the concerns of teachers than any debate about holistic and subskills conceptions of the reading process. Some teachers who value skills and recognize the potential benefits from teaching them hold back because they claim to be wary of teaching skills in isolation. If the price of efficient, focused teaching were indeed skills in isolation, then the price would be too high, it is utter nonsense to teach skills for their own sake. Other teachers who value skills cheerfully do the extra planning and record keeping— which are the true price of a skill-centered approach to teaching reading—because they are convinced that the price is right. They don't worry about skills in isolation because they don't teach them that way. Skills are necessary because teachers need them to sharpen the focus of their teaching. But they must be sensibly chosen and they must be kept in perspective.

SOME PERSPECTIVE

Otto (1975) has made some comments about reading skills that are directed specifically to comprehension skills and also underscore the need to view them in perspective.

> Even a cursory search of the literature will yield dozens of lists of comprehension skills. Every basal reader and every curriculum guide will yield still another. But examine most of them closely and you have reason to hold skill lists in low esteem. The skills listed tend to be so general or so specific that they can serve no function in teaching or learning. More often than not the essential *literal* aspects of comprehension are neglected in favor of the more esoteric interpretive and creative aspects, and there seems to be no concern whatever for whether the skills are in fact teachable. If I thought that was the best we could do, I would want to cast the first stone to put skill lists and skill listers out of their misery.

I believe that we can do better. We can extrapolate from the literature and from the experiences of successful teachers to identify skills that can and should be taught; then we can follow up with research to examine the outcomes of such efforts.

Once we concern ourselves with sensibly chosen skills—skills that are both important and teachable—I think there will be less tendency to view them or to teach them in isolation. I see skills and the teaching of skills as the *substance* and the *means* for sharpening the process of developing reading comprehension. Skills must be identified, taught, and applied in context. In perspective skills can be the vehicle for moving children to independence in their reading comprehension. Without the explicit focus of skills, I'm afraid we abandon too many learners while they are still dependent on the crutches of "classroom questions," "directed reading activities" and other alternatives to explicit skill development. The alternatives, too, need perspective.

The essential point is simple: Skills make sense if they are viewed with common sense.

MORE PERSPECTIVE

So far we have been concerned mostly with the pragmatic aspects of teaching reading by stressing the basic skills. There is also substantial theoretical support for a skills—or, more properly, a skills-in-perspective—position. Samuels (1974) examined the theoretical support in a carefully conceived paper, which includes an examination of the controversy over holistic and part methods of instruction, a comparison of speech and reading acquisition, an analysis of current knowledge of skill hierarchies in reading, and some implications for reading instruction. His inferences on reading instruction bear repeating here because they speak directly to the question at hand.

A major point made by critics of the subskill approach is that fractionating the reading process interferes with the essential characteristic of reading, which is comprehension. This point is well taken. Many teachers who use the subskill approach have lost sight of the fact that the subskill approach is simply a means to an end. What has happened in many classrooms is that goal displacement has occurred and the means have become ends in themselves. In using the subskill approach care must be taken to prevent the subskills from becoming the focal point of instruction. Once again, perhaps, this point should be made, that it is important for the child to get ample practice reading meaningful and interesting material in context.

While agreeing with the critics of the subskill approach that too much emphasis can be placed on these subordinate skills, the critics probably are in error in failing to recognize the importance of subskills in the developmental sequence of skill attainment. Just because fluent readers are able to derive meaning from the printed page is no reason to believe that beginning readers can do the same or that we can transfer the sophisticated strategies of the fluent reader to the beginning reader. While it is true that sophisticated strategies can be taught to the less sophisticated, these transfers of skills have been accomplished by doing a task analysis of the sophisticated strategies and teaching these subskills to the beginner.

As the advocates of the holistic approach point out, the essential element of reading—deriving meaning—is destroyed by taking a whole and breaking it down. However, current research suggests that before one deals with wholes, smaller aspects have to be mastered first. For example, before one can visually process letter clusters as a unit, individual letters have to be unitized. The controversy between letter-by-letter and whole word processing in word recognition seems somewhat resolved now that we have evidence to indicate that familiar words can be processed by fluent readers as a unit while unfamiliar words tend to get processed letter-by-letter.

Many critics of the subskill approach suggest that meaningful reading material should be given to a child and subskills should be taught when the student asks for help or shows evidence of needing particular skills. This approach has shortcomings when one realizes the logistical and managerial problems facing the teacher with a large group.

With regard to this last point, it is important to consider that many students do not know what kind of help to request and many teachers are not sufficiently trained to diagnose and pinpoint the cause of the student's difficulty. Even when the teacher is able to diagnose the cause of the problem with accuracy, the managerial problems of giving individual help as needed loom so large as to make the system difficult to operate, if not unworkable. It would seem more manageable to assume on a priori grounds that there are certain subskills beginning readers require. These skills would be taught routinely to students. For those students who fail to master these skills, additional time could be allocated and different methods could be tried.

Earlier in this paper the point was made that the adverse relationship between holistic and subskill approaches may not exist. Both approaches recognize there are subskills. Subskill approaches start with smaller units and move to larger and more complex units. On the other hand, the holistic approach begins with the larger unit and moves to smaller units. One of the important factors differentiating the two approaches is that of sequencing. In considering this factor, we must think about which tasks and which unit size one would use to start instruction and how one would program the sequence of skills to be taught as the student progresses in skill.

Another similarity between the two approaches is that both recognize the importance of diagnosis of difficulty in reading and the need to remedy the problem. The subskill approach, however, attempts to reduce the number of students who will experience difficulty with reading by teaching the prerequisite skills before a problem appears. The subskill approach, therefore, would appear to be more efficient in terms of teacher time.[1]

We need skills. Teachers need them to systematize instruction and to teach efficiently. Readers need them to approach the complex task of reading efficiently and effectively.

Concerns in perspective

Perhaps, as Samuels suggested, nobody seriously denies that there are subskills in reading or even that teachers ought to teach them. Yet criticisms directed toward trappings that often accompany an inclination to teach skills—accountability, behavioral objectives, skill management systems, criterion-referenced assessment, and concepts of mastery—tend to be seen as criticisms of the basic notion of teaching skills. Properly directed, many of them would be perfectly valid. But misdirected and/or misinterpreted as they are, valid criticisms of the trappings tend to erode confidence in the skills themselves.

SOME SPECIFIC CONCERNS

Lest we reject skills for the wrong reasons, we need to examine some of the criticisms that seem to be aimed more at the trappings than at the skills.

[1]By permission of the author.

A "reading-as-skills" perspective

Klein (1975) has said that "classroom management procedures
evoke a 'reading-as-skill' perspective." From that perspective, he
says, "Reading ability is associated with the development of
skills related to identified components of the reading act which
are isolated and used for instructional grouping. Learning to read
is equated then with a mastery of those skills identified which
typically call for performing decoding tasks and answering comprehension questions based upon thinking-oriented concepts,
e.g. comparing-contrasting, cause-effect, inference, etc." (p. 253).
The tone of Klein's presentation suggests that skills are too superficial to bother with, and he is no more positive about
classroom management procedures: "At a time when most of us
are not sure about the nature and/or purpose of much of education, when many are searching for the structures and processes of
knowledge which constitute learning domains, classroom management advocates, as a whole, tend not to be concerned with
such questions. Objectives are terminal, learning is task-
oriented, and by the nature of its own design, reading via
classroom management is an end-state product, the route to
which is specifically delineated" (p. 354). He finally concludes
that the whole skills–classroom management enterprise is im-
moral.

Teachers are almost certain to get jumpy about skills when
they are criticized in *Elementary English*. But they should not mistake an eloquently stated point of view for a recitation of facts. In
our experience we have observed that the people who are inclined to devise and use classroom management procedures are
no more likely to be ignorant and arbitrary than the people who
criticize them. Presentations like Klein's, which hold up the most
heavy-handed and poorly conceived excesses imaginable in implementing classroom management procedures as if they were
representatives of the entire movement, create a good deal of
sound and fury but fail to deal with real issues.

The concept of mastery

Johnson and Pearson are among the critics who are concerned
about the notion of mastery in relation to skill development.
They have cited Bloom (1968) and Terwilliger (1972) to support
their argument that mastery is an elusive and unattainable goal
of skill development. Both Bloom and Terwillinger, however, are
discussing matters that are far removed from anything that
teachers mean when they talk about skills. Bloom is concerned
with mastery of an entire subject area:

45

Most students (perhaps over 90 percent) can master what
we have to teach them, and it is the task of instruction to find
the means which will enable our students to master the subject
under consideration. Our basic task is to determine what we
mean by mastery of the subject and to search for the methods
and materials which will enable the largest proportion of our
students to attain such mastery.

And Terwilliger deals with problems associated with the concept
of mastery at that same level of application.

The point we wish to make is that much of the concern about
mastery is not directed at skills at all, but at concerns that currently remain at a highly theoretical level. Nevertheless, because
serious attempts to teach skills usually involve some sort of judgment about adequacy of performance, or criterion, or mastery of
specific skills, the theoretical concerns tend to be generalized to
what ought to be very mundane decision making. Nevertheless,
the teaching of skills has been questioned, and effective programs for teaching skills have been abandoned because of concern for such inappropriate arguments.

Legitimate questions can, of course, be raised about mastery
at the specific skill level. The most critical one, as Johnson and
Pearson (1975) point out, is "What does it mean to master a
skill?" Here such matters as test validity and common sense come
into play. A valid mastery test must represent the skill as it is to
be applied. (Validity is discussed in more detail later.) And any
application of the notion of mastery must involve at least a minimum of common sense. Without common sense one might tend
to be dazzled by statements like Johnson and Pearson's (1975):

> If you show us a child who has mastered the level X main
> idea test, we can demonstrate his or her lack of mastery simply
> by increasing the conceptual difficulty of the words or contex-
> tual relationships. Comprehension is, by its nature, an ongo-
> ing, never-ending process. It can have no precise starting or
> stopping point.

Of course, no sensibly arranged list of skills would relegate
"main idea" to a single level. But more basic than that, no sensible practitioner would ever assume infinite knowledge of "main
idea" because a learner passed a test at a given level and with
given materials.

Perhaps the most straightforward way to deal with the mastery problem as it relates to teaching reading skills would be to

drop the word *mastery*. Although a properly conceived skill can indeed be mastered in a given context, we would not want to see skills thrown out because of disagreement about what it means to master them. There is no need to bog down in theoretical concerns when all that is needed is a way to demonstrate progress in skill development. (A pragmatic way to handle skill mastery is presented in the final section of this chapter.)

Psycholinguistic naiveté

In some circles any attempt to identify and teach skills is considered evidence of psycholinguistic naiveté. Johnson and Pearson (1975) have articulated the position as well as anyone: "Psycholinguists and others have argued that the division of the reading process into component skills is unrealistic because the reader uses all the information available in the text. Printed materials contain a great deal of redundancy: morphemic, syntactic and graphic" (p. 758). They point out instances where focus on a specific skill could disrupt a more global response to multiple language cues, and they conclude that the fragmentation inherent in skill-centered teaching denies the nature of language.

Once again, the need for viewing skills in perspective is quite apparent. There is no denying that where there is focus on specifics there is not simultaneous concern for more global aspects that may be present. Yet to say that focusing on skills denies the nature of the language is like saying that focusing on a tree or a butterfly or a mountain denies the nature of the landscape. The whole may be greater than the simple sum of its parts, but the fact is that it is parts that combine to make up the whole. Is one naive to examine the parts in order to get a better view of the whole?

The charge of psycholinguistic naiveté can be countered with a charge of pedagogical naiveté. Johnson and Pearson (1975) cite the following transgression by skills advocates: "If you consider a sentence like 'the girls were walking with their friends,' there are three indicators of plurality which children might use to understand the passage. Yet, in *some* skills monitoring systems, a certain stress would be placed on testing and teaching the final *s* plural marker" (p. 759). What could be more naive than to suggest that everything *can*, or *should*, be taught at the same time, and begrudge the teaching of the final *s* as a plural marker simply because there are more complex ways to figure out plurality?

But charges and countercharges aside, the basic point is quite simple. One does not deny the complexity of language or of

47

linguistic processes by focusing on the component bits. The denial would come if one were to insist that the component bits be kept in isolation. We have yet to find anyone who does.

Engineering syndrome

Johnson and Pearson (1975), Klein (1975), Brown (1973), Apple (1972), and Simons (1973, 1974) have written articles in which they deal explicitly—and generally with an overt negative bias—with the trappings associated with the teaching of skills: accountability, behavioral objectives, skill management systems, systems management procedures, performance-based competency. In each case they examine one or more of the trappings, but they never (with the exception of Johnson and Pearson) deal with skills and/or skill development. Taken together, the authors are expressing their legitimate concern about an engineering syndrome or mechanistic orientation in education.

This is not the place to try to deal infinitively—or even superficially—with the issues these authors address. But the fact is these issues far transcend the issue of whether or not to teach basic reading skills. To those who value the teaching of reading skills, the danger is that the specific issue will be lost to the larger ones. We should not, for example, abandon the teaching of reading skills because we reject the notion of accountability. We should not reject skills because we question whether all of education can be described by behavioral objectives. Yet we do see the water muddied by such important and related but not requisite concerns.

Validity of instruments

We have already acknowledged the need for valid assessment instruments. If skills are worth teaching, they are worth assessing. There can be no quarrel with the demand for well-conceived, efficient, reliable, and valid assessment instruments.

The problem is that some critics point out flaws associated with the instruments of some skill development systems as if they were the flaws of all such instruments. Those same critics also tend to dwell on the limitations of instruments designed to assess skill development as if they were unique to such instruments. Sloppy tests are sloppy tests, no matter what they are designed to measure.

The main validity concern is that proficiency with specific skills will in fact be reflected in an ability to cope with running text. Ultimately the teaching of any set of specific skills must stand or fall in view of that outcome. If we start with instruments that have demonstrated reliability and face validity, we can be satisfied if we get overall performance that meets our goals.

Hierarchies, interests, expense

The matter of hierarchical arrangement of skills can be troublesome. Some critics say that until a hierarchy has been worked out empirically, any list is not likely to be very useful in teaching; others feel that logical hierarchies are adequate. Practitioners know that skills will be taught in some kind of sequence simply because they can't all be taught at the same time. Realists acknowledge that currently there are no empirically validated hierarchies and that the research problems are so complex that there will not be any for some time. Meanwhile, it seems sensible to be satisfied with sequences that are worked out with regard to logical order, available research, and the practical demands of the classroom.

We agree with the critic who says that too much attention to specific skills can dull a learner's interest in reading. Lack of interest would surely be the outcome of mindless skill teaching. But fortunately, skill development does not just happen. Skills are taught by teachers who can make judgments about how much is too much.

And to the critic who says that skill development programs are expensive, we cannot say anything at all. There are too many variables, and expense is always a relative matter.

THE IMPLICATIONS

We have observed that the basic reading skills ought to be taught explicitly and systematically and that skill acquisition is important in learning to read. We must defend our position because when the trappings of teaching skills are attacked, the skills are likely to go out with the trappings. Our concern is not that teachers will deny the need to teach skills but that they will abandon their efforts to teach them explicitly and systematically. And our experience suggests that when skills are not taught explicitly, they may not be taught at all. Although some children have learned to read spontaneously, without any formal skill development, others have failed to read because they were not bright enough, or motivated enough, or mature enough, or lucky enough to put it together for themselves. If we expect to teach reading, we need to teach the skills.

49

Criticisms directed at the trappings that may be associated
with teaching skills need to be dealt with directly, not by soft-
pedaling the teaching of skills. The excesses of certain accountability procedures, the unthinking application of behavioral
objectives, the proliferation of lists of skills, the inclination to
isolate skills from their context, the mechanistic overtones of skill
management systems, the false security of mastery—all of these
concerns and others are real, and they deserve thoughtful attention. Ultimately the success of any skill development program
will depend on how well these concerns are handled.

We must recognize the general concerns about teaching skills.
But in the meantime, school is in session and most of us want to
teach skills in a way that is sensible and coherent for both
teachers and learners.

Teaching basic reading skills

Otto has worked for more than a decade to develop and try out a
system designed to help teachers teach the basic reading skills.
(General outcomes of those efforts [Otto, Chester, McNeil, and
Meyers, 1974; Otto and Chester, 1976] and the principal product
of those efforts [Otto and Askov, 1974] are described elsewhere.
Readers who are interested in the specifics should peruse the references cited for we do not propose to present them here. Instead, we will draw upon the experience we gained in developing a specific system as we discuss a general approach to
teaching the basic reading skills.) One approach can proceed as
shown in figure 3.1.

IDENTIFY ESSENTIAL SKILLS

Given that skills will be taught, some decision must be made
about *what* skills. The first step, the identification of specific
skills, must be taken decisively. We have seen so-called skill development programs launched with a commitment to no particular skills, just to the notion of teaching skills. The specifics are left
up to individual teachers or, most often, to the available materials. In such instances nobody knows what to do because there
are no goals. A workable approach to skill development must
begin with the identification of specific skills that are judged to
be essential to successful reading performance.

Figure 3.1 A schematic for basic reading skills

Identify essential skills

↓

State objectives

↓

Examine and monitor individual's performance

↓

Identify appropriate teaching/learning activities and materials

↓

Evaluate results

Benefits

The benefits of identifying essential skills are discussed throughout this chapter; briefly, skills provide the basis for focused instruction and for systematic learning.

Concerns

Anyone who attempts to specify essential reading skills is confronted with two main questions. Although we readily acknowledge that there is no definitive, research-based answer to either
of them, we feel we can answer them with enough confidence to
permit us to proceed.

First, what are the essential reading skills? Nobody knows for
sure. There are many lists of skills, and many successful teachers
of reading seem to know intuitively what they are. Still, the ultimate list of essential skills remains to be discovered. The question is confounded in part by the fact that children appear to
need certain skills while they are learning to read that become
unimportant once they have become mature readers. Mature
readers can respond to minimal cues that would be inadequate for
beginning or less sophisticated readers. Thus, analyses of the
skills of mature readers may be inadequate for identifying the
skills essential for teaching reading. The question is further confounded by the disagreement among authorities as to how reading ought to be defined. Some definitions are very broad; others
are limited. We do not propose to suggest the ultimate definition, but the fact is that until there is one accepted definition of
"reading," there can be no single list of essential skills.

The second question concerns the sequence of skills. The
painstaking and expensive research that would arrange essential

skills in a hierarchy has not been done and is not likely to be
done in the foreseeable future. The work is too expensive in
terms of time and resources available, and, more important, it is
too dependent on the particular definition of reading that a researcher might have. Nevertheless, skills must be taught in some
sequence because, in some instances, there is a logical progres-
sion from one to another and, if nothing else, all of the skills
cannot be taught at the same time. Pragmatically, then, once
skills have been judged essential, they should be arranged in a
sequence that makes sense to the people who will be teaching
them. The sequence can be modified on the basis of experience
and research findings.

STATE OBJECTIVES

Curriculum libraries are filled with dusty lists of skills. The dust
is undisturbed because few people have found these lists—no
matter how painstakingly they may have been worked out—to be
very useful. Small wonder, because the usual skill list goes something like this:

> The child
> > Has phonic analysis skills
> > > Beginning consonant blends

This statement indicates that a knowledge of beginning consonant blends is judged to be essential, but it offers nothing specific regarding what the skill amounts to in performance terms,
what might constitute adequate performance, or how one should
try to teach it.

If a skill is worth listing, it is worth specifying in a way that
permits teachers to teach it. For the beginning consonant blends
skill, a statement like this would be useful:

> Given real or nonsense words beginning with the consonant
> blends *st, sk, sm, sp, sw, sn,* and *sc,* the child (1) identifies the two
> letters that stand for the initial blend in words pronounced by
> the teacher; or (2) identifies words that begin with the same
> blend as a stimulus word pronounced by the teacher, and (3) pro-
> nounces words that begin with the blends listed above.

This expanded statement offers a description of what the skill
amounts to in terms of expected performance, a basis for judging
adequate performance, and at least an inkling of what might be

done to teach the skill. In effect the statement sets an objective for a specific skill.

Objectives—particularly behavioral objectives—are hailed by some as the salvation of teaching and damned by others as the hemlock that makes it too bitter to bear. The truth is that when objectives are sensibly used, they can make a positive contribution, particularly in a basic skill area like reading. A little bit of common sense can go a long way in thinking about and dealing with objectives.

Benefits

Niles (1972) has presented one of the most sensible analyses of the potential impact of objectives in teaching reading that is available. She acknowledges their dangers but also points out four potential advantages. First, the most obvious benefit is that "no one can tell whether he has arrived anywhere unless he has a clearly marked goal that he will recognize when he gets there. Behavioral goals are very clearly marked" (p. 106). Second, because objectives are written in terms of what a student is expected to be or do, a curriculum built in terms of objectives has the potential to be student centered rather than subject centered. Third, because objectives can define goals clearly, there is potential for more truly diagnostic teaching on a day-to-day basis. Fourth, with clearly defined goals, teachers can pay attention to the performance of individual students in ways that have been elusive in the past.

Concerns

Sensibly used objectives offer some very real benefits, but they also pose some concerns. The list that follows identifies our most persistent concerns about objectives and indicates how we are attempting to deal with them.

Limitations of objectives A school completely dominated by objectives, particularly behavioral objectives, would be a dreadful place. There would be no spontaneity, no seizing of teachable moments, few smiles, and few tears. There would be order and precision, but there would be little appreciation and only the most careful aspiration. There might even be skills galore without any inclination to apply them.

The limitations of an objective-based world are obvious, but they need not apply to an objective-based approach to reading instruction. It is one thing to pin down essential skills in reading

53

with stated objectives and quite another to say that every move a
teacher makes ought to be objective directed.

Prescriptive and descriptive objectives For some skills, objectives
can be prescriptive: that is, the objective can state the expected
outcome and the criteria for satisfactory performance. The objective for beginning consonant blends that was given earlier is a
good example of a prescriptive objective. With a minor addition,
it could also meet the criteria for a behavioral objective as described by Mager (1962), Bloom, Hastings and Madaus (1971),
and others. All that is lacking from the objective as it is given is
an explicit statement of the *expected competence* or *mastery* level.
The competence level was left unstated for reasons to be discussed later, but an "eight out of ten tries" criterion could be easily inserted. The point is that with some skills, the expected outcomes are quite clear and they can be prescribed in advance.

With other skills, however, the outcomes cannot—or should
not—be stated in such a definitive way—for example, an interpretive reading skill like predicting outcomes. If we really
want a child to predict an outcome, we must be prepared to listen not only to the prediction but also to the reasons for which it
was made. There can be no prescriptive objective because there
is no "right" answer or predictable outcome. Many critics of objectives appear to base their case almost entirely on this point.
They reject objectives completely because the classic behavioral
or prescriptive objective is inadequate to deal with certain goals
(or skills, or outcomes, whatever happens to be the topic of discussion).

Eisner (1967) talked about *open* and *closed* objectives when he
confronted the problem:

> To state an objective in terms clear enough to know what it
> [the terminal behavior] will look like requires that behavior be
> characterized in advance. This is possible when one is working
> with closed concepts or closed objectives. When one is deal-
> ing with open objectives, the particular behavior cannot be
> defined by a preconceived standard; a judgment must be
> made after the fact. When educational ends are directed to-
> ward open objectives, the form and content of the pupil's be-
> havior are identified and assessed after the educational activity
> concludes. (p. 279)

We prefer the terms *prescriptive* and *descriptive* for objectives that
are *closed* or *open*. But the point is precisely the same: In some instances it is quite appropriate to prescribe expectations in advance, and in others it is realistic simply to make a statement that
describes relevant activities.

We are inclined to use prescriptive objectives for the skills in such areas as word attack, study skills, and literal comprehension and to use descriptive objectives in the self-directed, interpretive, and creative reading areas. The differentiation of objectives enables teachers to deal with important reading skills for which they have not yet devised—and perhaps never should—means to anticipate and prescribe outcomes.

Scope of objectives in reading In the present framework, the scope of objectives would be the same as the scope of essential skills identified. Of course, scope will depend on the definition of reading chosen. A narrow definition would be limited to word attack and, probably, literal comprehension skills. We have chosen a somewhat broader definition that includes word attack, study skills, comprehension, self-directed reading, interpretive reading, and creative reading skills. The scope of any skill development program ought to reflect the definition of reading that is acceptable to the people who teach the program. Unfortunately, too many programs are adopted first so the definition of reading implicit in the program is forced on the users.

Levels of objectives Objectives are commonly stated at three levels. First, at the most abstract level, objectives are broad, general statements that specify goals for an entire school, guide program development, and/or identify courses and areas to be covered. Second, at a more concrete level, objectives are stated in terms that make them appropriate for analyzing general goals into more specific instructional goals. Third, at the most specific level, objectives are so explicit that they prescribe a particular route to attain the goals at the second level, and they provide the detailed analysis that is required by a programmed approach to instruction. At the first level there are few objectives that guide entire programs. At the third level, there may be almost infinitely many objectives that prescribe every step in a learning sequence. We believe that the mid-level of specificity is the appropriate one for the instructional objectives that guide skill development in reading.

Mid-level objectives serve to establish attainable, observable goals without being too general for day-to-day application or so specific as to dictate instruction. They set milestones or checkpoints and also permit teachers considerable flexibility in the route they choose to follow. Teachers can then take an objective-based approach to reading instruction without losing sight of the student. The objectives we offer as examples in the Appendix are all written at the mid-level of specificity.

55

Criterion for mastery A classic behavioral objective includes an explicit statement of the *expected competence* or *mastery* level. Purists on objectives would argue that an objective is worthless if it describes behavior but fails to set a criterion for judging mastery of the behavior described. Others would insist that adequate performance of a particular objective might vary from one person to another or even from one situation to another. We must admit to having been on both sides of the argument at one time or another. And, in view of everything we've learned, common sense tells us to stay on both sides at the same time.

An explicit criterion for mastery of objectives for word attack skills and study skills is probably both realistic and desirable. In our work with criterion-references measures, we set the criterion at 80 percent of the items correct on the criterion-referenced paper-and-pencil test for each skill. The reason for this criterion, rather than 90 or 100 percent, is that we acknowledge that no test is perfect. A person might answer two out of ten items incorrectly because those items are difficult to understand, misleading, or out of line with previous experience. Some users of criterion-referenced measures feel that 90 percent is a more appropriate criterion, and they seem to be able to apply it with no difficulty. The point is that with definitive objectives like those in the word attack skills and study skills areas, an explicit and demanding criterion seems realistic in view of assessment practices and desirable in terms of the level of performance required in order to handle basic tasks. Recall the beginning consonant blends objective. The behaviors called for can be assessed straightforwardly, and, more important, they are absolutely essential to successful word attack. So it is with virtually all of the objectives for word attack skills. The objectives for the study skills are similar in that they, too, call for definitive, task-specific behaviors.

On the other hand, we have begun to see a need for a more flexible criterion in judging the adequacy of performance related to the objectives for comprehension skills. Although a child who misses even a few beginning consonant blends would probably be quite unsuccessful in reading, the child who succeeds in identifying the main idea of passages 60 percent of the time—and thereby fails 40 percent of the time—demonstrates substantial, though certainly improvable, reading ability. In the first instance, anything less than virtually perfect performance amounts to failure; in the other, any success at all demonstrates an ability to tackle and cope with the task. To set an 80 percent criterion for the comprehension task would be, if not unrealistic, counterproductive in terms of diagnostic utility. Any other criterion level would be as arbitrary as 80 percent, of course, so we are not inclined at this time to set any criterion for the comprehension objectives. Thus, the objectives serve their prime purpose of prescribing expected behaviors, but they do not establish a level of adequate performance. Teachers can set that level for individuals in view of prior performance, prior instruction, the context in which the comprehension skill is to be applied, and the instructional options that are available.

To sum up, objectives really aren't the fearsome monsters some critics have made them. Like any other tool, they can be used sensibly or insensibly.

EXAMINE AND MONITOR INDIVIDUAL'S PERFORMANCE

The identification of skills and the statement of objectives make efficient diagnosis and continuous monitoring workable in the teaching of reading. Objectives provide a basis for criterion-referenced assessment (see chapter 7), which is designed to examine performance in terms of expected behaviors.

Benefits

Niles (1972) has summed up the major benefit. "Individualization in the past, what there has been of it, has tended to focus mostly on the element of time—all children doing the same work but at different rates . . . objectives have the potential to create a situation not only in which some students don't do the work at all—if they have already reached the objective—but in which other students may have several options of ways to reach the objective" (p. 107). The acquisition of reading skills tends to be highly idiosyncratic, particularly among children who have the least difficulty learning to read, so the need for individualization is very important. Children who learn skills quickly and, in many instances, independently can focus only on the few skills that give them some difficulty if there is systematic and continuous diagnosis. Others can be given all the help they need before their failure in reading becomes the main cause of their general academic failure.

Concerns

At least three very practical concerns must be addressed if the assessment and monitoring of skill development are to be efficient and productive.

57

First, the matter of choosing or devising assessment instruments and/or procedures must be considered. Objectives provide a basis for criterion-referenced assessment, but they do not provide the actual instruments or procedures. It is not enough simply to say—as we have seen in too many instances—that each teacher is free to look informally for the behaviors called for by each objective. There is a certain superficial appeal in being free to do one's own assessing, but the process soon collapses. Without provision for some reasonably rigorous assessment procedures, objectives tend to be little more than a security blanket: they provide comfort but no clout.

We have found that a combination of criterion-referenced paper-and-pencil tests and more informal performance tests meets most assessment needs. The paper-and-pencil tests offer efficiency in terms of administration and scoring, and the performance tests offer the flexibility and credibility required for daily operations. *Focused Reading Instruction* (Otto, Chester, McNeil, and Meyers, 1974) describes the ways in which we have attempted to deal with these concerns.

IDENTIFY TEACHING/LEARNING ACTIVITIES AND MATERIALS

Appropriate instruction involves more than focusing on strengths and weaknesses in skill development. It also requires providing differentiated instruction for students with different learning preferences and styles. Even with a common objective, different children will continue to have different instructional needs as they pursue the objective. Once specific skills and objectives have been established, materials and procedures can be organized for efficient retrieval.

Benefits

Many more materials and procedures for teaching reading exist today than any teacher could use, or even examine sensibly, in a lifetime. By organizing them around their own skills/objectives, teachers gain access to the materials and procedures they need for a specific purpose and at a given time. Teachers who are aware of and have access to a wide range of teaching options can be true eclectics in their teaching. An eclectic does not follow any one system or approach but knows many options and chooses the one that is best for a given student at a given time in a given situation.

Let the critics rave about the dangers of dehumanization and mechanization in systematic skill development. Look at the positive side and see an orderly presentation of endless options for meeting the needs of individuals. We know many teachers who feel that their escape from the lock step of basal readers came when they could become the eclectic teachers of skills that they had always wanted to be.

Concerns

One concern is that adequate resources be allocated for doing the job of organizing existing materials and activities around the skills/objectives of the program. A search of existing materials takes more time than teachers are able to squeeze out of their already crowded schedules, so time must be released and assigned to the task. Some system for keeping records of the materials and activities once identified must be devised, and responsibility for seeing to it must be assigned. And, of course, when available materials are inadequate for certain skills, additional materials must be acquired or devised.

The second concern cannot be dealt with as easily as the first. We have encountered little difficulty in identifying adequate materials and activities for teaching most of the essential skills except in the area of comprehension. More often than not, the materials offered in this area are either tied very explicitly to a particular notion about what comprehension is or not really addressed to any particular skill at all. The outcome is that very few materials can be identified that have both an explicit skill focus and reasonable compatibility with an eclectic approach to teaching skills.

Our inclination, then, is to devise our own materials rather than to abandon teaching the skills. We have begun a project in which we are attempting to develop means for focusing on skills and skill development activities during the reading process. In other words, skill-related activities are interjected in content materials so the reader is exposed to both skill development activities and content in a single operation. Teachers can and often do the same kind of thing when they discuss a reading assignment with their pupils. We are trying to systematize the process.

EVALUATE THE RESULTS

Otto, Chester, McNeil, and Meyers (1974) have summarized the benefits and our concerns:

59

Two levels of evaluation are essential when specific skills are the focus of instruction. First, there must be assurance that the skill-related objectives are being reached. Second, there must be assurance that the attainment of specific objectives is accompanied by functional reading ability, and ability to cope with the reading tasks encountered both in and out of school. The payoff for focused reading instruction comes at this second level.

We focus on essential skills and specific objectives in order to systematize teaching and encourage efficient learning. But the mastery of specific objectives is meaningless unless it is accompanied by an ability to get them all together and to read connected text. Many opportunities to apply the skills must be provided, and assurance that functional reading ability is increasing must be sought. Any evidence of a breakdown at either level is a signal to go back and reevaluate the entire process.

A breakdown in specific skill development may indicate too rapid pacing, inappropriate teaching, overwhelming personal difficulties, or other problems that can be identified through re-examination. A breakdown in functional reading ability may indicate inadequate skill mastery, inability to apply known skills, or inappropriate choice of reading materials at a given stage of skill development. Such problems, too, can be identified through re-examination. The main advantage of a skill-centered approach to reading instruction is that it establishes a basis for tracing back to see what went wrong if the desired end results are not forthcoming. We can do a better job of teaching if we first decide exactly what we want children to learn. (p. 41)

Sources of skills and objectives

Many lists of "essential" reading skills are available in the literature, and all of them share the limitations discussed earlier in this chapter. Lists of objectives are becoming readily available too. Some publishers offer complete objective-based programs, some offer objectives and criterion-referenced tests only; the options are varied. The best procedure is to examine those that seem to meet local needs and to pick the one that meets them best. Better yet, put together a local adaptation of one or more for a program that is tailored to fit precisely.

We will not attempt to list available options here. New programs are being added constantly, so any list would become outmoded too soon to be very useful. Furthermore, the composition and ordering of skill lists are changing rapidly as new research becomes available. In a period of rapid change, it is best to keep up with the current literature and current publishers' catalogs rather than to rely on a standard. An example of a list of skills and objectives, however, is given in the appendix to this book. We have worked with it extensively, but we do not offer it as anything more than an example. Readers may find it useful for purposes of comparison, as a starter or as a basis for general discussion. The list is limited to dealing with the skills and objectives for a developmental reading program at the elementary school level.

Our inclination is to stress basic skill development at the elementary school level and the application and extension of the basic skills at upper school levels. Consequently we do not offer a list of higher level or content area skills for postelementary school levels. Of course, the skills and objectives in the appendix could be modified to be appropriate for postelementary school programs designed for learners who failed to develop the basic reading skills in the normal setting.

Summary

Skills need to be given prominence in teaching reading, particularly at the early stages of reading instruction. Whether one favors a skill-based curriculum in reading or a somewhat softer line in treating reading skill development, a focus on the important skills is a pragmatic matter. The identification of important skills is essential for efficient diagnosis, systematic organization of instructional materials and procedures, and effective assessment of the outcomes of reading instruction. Our discussion provides perspective for viewing skills and skill instruction.

Benefits and concerns associated with the development and implementation of a skill-based approach to teaching reading are considered. Many apparent critics of teaching basic reading skills are, in fact, criticizing the trappings—such as instructional management systems, behavioral objectives, criterion-referenced tests, and accountability schemes—that are frequently part of skill-based programs. We maintain that the trappings often are ill conceived and/or badly used and so should not adversely affect

attitudes toward teaching skills. Pragmatic ways for dealing with
the problems encountered in teaching skills are suggested.

Bibliography

Apple, M. W. "The Adequacy of Systems Management Procedures in Education." *Journal of Educational Research* 66 (1972):
10–18.

Bloom, Benjamin S. "Learning for Mastery." *Evaluation Comment*
1 (1968).

Bloom, Benjamin S., J. T. Hastings, and G. F. Madaus. *Handbook
in Formative and Summative Evaluation of Student Learning.*
New York: McGraw-Hill, 1971.

Brown, A. " 'What Could be Bad?' Some Reflections on the Accountability Movement." *English Journal* 62 (1973): 461–463.

Eisner, E. W. "Educational Objectives—Help or Hindrance?"
School Review 75 (1967): 250–282.

Johnson, Dale, and P. D. Pearson. "Skills Management
Systems: A Critique." *The Reading Teacher* 28 (1975): 757–764.

Klein, M. L. "The Reading Program and Classroom Management:
Panacea or Perversion?" *Elementary English* 52 (1975): 351–355.

Mager, Robert F. *Preparing Instructional Objectives.* Palo Alto:
Fearon, 1962.

Niles, O. S. "Behavioral Objectives and the Teaching of Reading." *Journal of Reading* 16 (1972): 104–110.

Otto, Wayne. "A Poem." *The Reading Teacher* 28 (1975): 403.

———. "Design for Developing Comprehension Skills." Invited
paper for the research seminar, Development of Reading Comprehension, Sponsored by the International Reading Association, Newark, Delaware, July 1975.

Otto, Wayne, and E. Askov. *The Wisconsin Design for Reading Skill
Development: Rationale and Guidelines,* 3d ed. Minneapolis: National Computer Systems, 1974.

Otto, Wayne, and Robert Chester. *Objective-Based Reading.* Reading, Mass.: Addison-Wesley, 1976.

Otto, Wayne, Robert Chester, John McNeil, and Shirley Myers.
Focused Reading Instruction. Reading, Mass.: Addison-Wesley,
1974.

Roberts, E. M. "A Poem." *The Reading Teacher* 28 (1974): 75.

Samuels, S. J. "Hierarchical Subskills in the Reading Acquisition
Process." Address to the Hyman Blumberg Symposium on
Research in Early Childhood Education, Johns Hopkins Uni-
versity, November 1974.

Simons, H. D. "Behavioral Objectives: A False Hope for Education." *Elementary School Journal* 73 (1973): 173–181.

———. "Behavioral Objectives and Reading Instruction." In Malcolm P. Douglas, ed., *38th Yearbook of the Claremont Reading Conference*. Claremont, Calif.: Claremont Graduate School.

Terwilliger, J. S. "Some Problems Associated with the Concept of Mastery." Mimeo. University of Minnesota, 1972.

Chapter 4 Teaching students to value reading

The first prerequisite for valuing reading is to have the skills necessary to decode the printed language. However, there are students at all academic levels, as well as adults, who have good basic reading skills and who let these skills deteriorate for lack of practice. For good or bad, the television industry has done a much better job of promoting viewership than teachers have done promoting readership. Too many students are not learning to value reading as a product of their learning how to read.

The fact that numberless people have learned how to read and yet do so reluctantly or very little cannot be attributed entirely to weaknesses in instructional reading programs. Certainly other factors contribute to this problem. Society offers numerous other activities that vie for people's time and permit them to be pleasantly and even productively occupied. Because people have increasing numbers of resources other than print for information and recreation, teachers must become more aware of the necessity to help students realize what reading can do for them that other resources cannot.

Educators should think seriously about the changing role of reading in our society and make wholehearted attempts to structure reading programs that teach students the benefits of reading, as well as reading skills. Reading is no less important to the well-being of individuals and society now than it was before television and the expansion of other leisure-time resources. Reading is still a phenomenon that fosters personal and societal growth in a way and at a level that other phenomena cannot duplicate.

Our thesis in this chapter is that instructional reading programs must be evaluated on how well they impress upon students what reading can do for them that other communications media and recreational activities cannot. Where programs don't perform this function, changes should be made. Our purpose in this chapter is to identify aspects of reading programs that should be evaluated in terms of how well they are being used to teach students to value reading. We have identified five aspects that seem to have great potential for showing students the value of reading. For all five, we shall discuss possible problems and offer some suggestions for curriculum improvement.

Fostering higher-level reading behavior

THE PROBLEM

At all academic levels, developing higher-level reading behaviors is important and is often neglected. Too many students with the ability to read thoughtfully and with sensitivity do not. They have not been taught how to involve themselves with an author's thoughts and feelings beyond simple understanding. They are pragmatic readers only; they read to answer simple comprehension (often objective-type) questions on developmental reading exercises, to get a general notion of a content area reading assignment, or to answer questions on a reading achievement test.

After a number of years of only pragmatic reading, they come to believe that good reading is no more than a matter of getting the right answers to postreading questions that do not require higher-level reading. Eventually many of these students become so mechanical and superficial in their reading that they cannot communicate with an author. In effect, they become dependent upon someone else's questions to tell them what is worthwhile recalling about a reading selection; and relatively few, if any, of the questions tap the best intellectual and emotional responses they are capable of giving. They do not learn to think or feel about a reading selection, and they do not learn to discuss a selection without a structure provided by instructional materials and/or teachers' questions. Consequently, the act of reading is not included in the process and need of language usage that Langer (1966) described:

> The process of transforming all direct experience into that supreme mode of symbolic expression, language, has so completely taken possession of the human mind that it is not only a special talent but a dominant, organic need. All our sense impressions leave their traces in our memory not only as signs disposing our practical reactions in the future but also as symbols, images representing our "ideas" of things; and the tendency to manipulate ideas, to combine and abstract, mix and

65

extend them by playing with symbols, is man's outstanding characteristic. (p. 65)

Certainly the kind or level of cognitive and affective behaviors readers engage in during and after reading a selection depends upon their total personal growth and upon the selection itself, as well as upon the questions or tasks they are given. What a reader takes away from a selection depends greatly on what he or she brings to it and also on what is in the selection. It would be incorrect to teach reading as if every student were going to be capable and/or motivated to read everything with both cognitive and affective barrels blazing. Some students are less capable of higher-level cognitive and affective behavior than others, and some who are capable of higher-level reading behaviors are interested in using reading only occasionally and only to get the facts or whatever else can be obtained from lower-level reading behaviors. Reading at the lower cognitive and affective levels is a legitimate and worthwhile use of reading skills. To fault reading programs that don't result in all students' using higher-level reading behaviors with everything they read is not justified. However, there is a justification for faulting reading programs that do not try to teach students to engage in higher-level reading behaviors when they want to or when they should read for purposes that require higher-level cognitive and affective behaviors with material that is suitable for the utilization of those behaviors.

Otto, McMenemy, and Smith (1973) have conceptualized the reading process as a hierarchy of three complex behaviors: translation-comprehension, organization-internalization, and utilization. The second stage, organization-internalization, is a combination of both cognitive and affective behaviors that require more of the reader than simply knowing the words in a selection and understanding the basic message they encode. Readers who organize and internalize a selection apply, analyze, evaluate, and synthesize the content of a message and react to it with appropriate affective responses. In other words, higher-level reading behaviors go beyond basic understanding and simple acceptance or rejection of an idea. They involve the cognitive behaviors above the level of comprehension in the hierarchy of cognitive behaviors delineated by Bloom et al. (1965) and above the level of receiving in the hierarchy of affective behaviors delineated by Krathwohl et al. (1964). The following model illustrates Otto, McMenemy, and Smith's conceptualization of reading as a three-stage process and the hierarchy of cognitive-affective behaviors they would place within the organization-internalization stage.

Stage 1:   *Translation* (word recognition)-*Comprehension* (simple understanding of the message)

Stage 2:   *Organization-Internalization*
evaluating   characterizing
synthesizing   valuing
analyzing   responding
applying

Stage 3:   Utilization (for information or recreation)

Because no one knows exactly how the thinking process and the emotions function during the reading process, any breakdown such as the one presented above, especially for stage 2, must be based more upon conjecture than scientific evidence. Nonetheless, the experience of many good readers shows that some reading selections can be thought about at different levels or in different ways and that different kinds of affect can be aroused and entertained or rejected by the reader. Students who have not been given the kind of reading instruction that makes them aware of the range of behaviors that may be called into play as part of the act of reading and have also not been given reading experiences that foster using the range have been denied an important part of their reading education.

Our work with students and teachers at all academic levels has convinced us that teaching higher-level reading behaviors is a curriculum area that needs attention. Other educators have also spoken to this need. Osenburg (1962) examined the assumption that students who are identified by objective tests as superior readers also possess the other mental powers for comprehending and explaining what they have read. His subjects, high school seniors enrolled in the accelerated English programs of four high schools, had scored on nationally used standardized objective reading tests at or above the eighty-fifth percentile. These students were asked to identify the subject of a poem and explain their answers. Since the subject was not named in the poem, the students had to keep all the facts presented in mind and select a subject to which *all* the author's descriptions (not just some) would apply. Osenburg describes the responses of the 46 percent of the students who identified the subjects incorrectly: "Most incorrect answers resulted from careless reading or from an inability to draw logical inferences or from both. Some students jumped to their conclusions apparently after having read only a part of the poem, either skimming over the remainder or ignoring it entirely." From this study and a related one, which measured the difference between the ability to recognize a correct

67

answer and to recall it, Osenburg concluded that "superior" readers are superior only in their ability to recognize a correct answer on an objective test; they have not necessarily developed higher-level reading skills.

Hafter and Douglas (1958) studied college students who were failing because of reading disability. They concluded that the chief difficulty is not in the basic skills of word recognition and comprehension but in the thinking skills involved in most reading activities. They estimate that two-thirds of the students entering college have this difficulty. Adler (1940) writes of his experiences with the immature reading of college juniors and seniors and their consequent inability to obtain full value from reading a literary selection. Clearly no school can conclude that it is developing high-powered readers because its students score high on objective reading tests or go to college. Adler described the situation: "The defect which the [reading] tests discover is in the easier type of reading—reading for information. For the most part, the tests do not even measure the ability to read for understanding. If they did, the results would cause a riot" (p. 69). Our experience is that Adler's assessment is still valid today in spite of the changes in reading program development since 1940.

What is it that these students with a potential to develop high-level reading skills do not do? The answer is that for whatever reasons, they take away from a selection only a little of what they bring to it in terms of intellectual power and emotional sensitivity. They do not use the appropriate range of their cognitive and affective capabilities in reading materials. They should be comprehending the stated and the implied meanings of authors; they should be recognizing and appreciating the nuances of language and subtleties of meaning; they should be anticipating as they read and reflecting upon what they have read; they should be applying, analyzing, and evaluating the author's ideas and creating new ones synthesizing their immediate reading and their previous knowledge and experience; they should feel satisfaction, frustration, delight, uneasiness, or other personal reactions; they could and should be changed by certain reading experiences. Jennings (1965) says, "The one aspect of mature reading that appears most obvious and immediate is the difference we feel within ourselves as a consequence of this reading. This may be as trivial as a matter of having read one more book or as great as a turn-about in political belief or religious conviction" (p. 142). However, too many students rarely, if ever, read as their total personal maturity permits. Consequently, they do not perceive reading as a valuable experience. They do not realize the power of reading to stimulate enriching and satisfying cognitive and affective behaviors. The result is an apathetic or even negative attitude toward reading.

SUGGESTIONS FOR CURRICULUM IMPROVEMENT

The key to developing higher-level reading behaviors lies within carefully constructed reading-related activities. For students to experience and gain satisfaction from using the full range of their cognitive and affective powers, they must respond to questions and tasks that direct their thoughts and feelings above the levels of simple understanding of the author's message and acceptance or rejection of it.

The questions and tasks students are asked to respond to relative to reading selections should be broad enough to give them thinking room. They should allow for a variety of possible responses or points of view rather than a response that can be quickly evaluated as correct or incorrect. Asking students to speculate about the personal characteristics of an author, to add a character or lines of dialogue to a narrative, to project two characters ten years into the future, or to evaluate the decision made by a character or a point of view expressed by the author are examples of questions (broadly defined) that give students thinking room and develop reading power.

Converting short stories to radio dramas, tape-recording plays, dramatizing situations described in print, choral reading of poems, discussions, debates, and instructional conversations are all examples of activities for students to plan and do in connection with the reading of printed materials. High-level affective behaviors are also fostered through participation in these nonthreatening yet relatively sophisticated cognitive tasks.

A teacher who wants to foster positive attitudes toward reading and a perception of reading as a valuable activity because of the personal enrichment it can bring will try to construct questions and activities that involve students in writing, speaking, listening, illustrating, dramatizing, problem solving, and thinking creatively about reading materials that are suitable for promoting those kinds of higher-level cognitive behaviors and the concomitant affective behaviors they elicit. Other reading-related activities that raise the level of students' cognitive and affective responses to reading selections include illustrating book jackets; creating television commercials for books; debating a proposition implicit in an essay, a textbook, or a poem; writing classified newspaper advertisements for certain literary characters who might want to buy a car, rent a room, or buy a house; create tape-recorded radio plays or commentaries that might be coordinated with colored slides, sound effects, commercials, and background music. Smith and Barrett (1974) devote most of two chapters to descriptions of reading-related activities that have been used successfully to help students in the middle grades have higher-level thinking and aesthetic experiences with printed material. Most of their activities can also be used at lower and higher academic levels.

One final point seems important: Reading curriculums that include the utilization of higher-level reading behaviors to teach students to value reading must look at outcomes that go beyond scores on reading achievement tests. Of course, students should score well on reading achievement tests, but they should also be able to:

○ Debate propositions formulated from reading selections
○ Rewrite short stories as plays and produce them
○ Dramatize situations in historical accounts
○ Converse with others about their reading experiences
○ Discuss the merits of ideas advanced by authors
○ Engage in other activities of the kind we value for citizens in our society

Fostering higher-level reading behaviors to help students value reading is not an educational frill. It must be given major attention so the school reading program will produce students who read, as well as students who know how to read.

Selecting good reading materials

THE PROBLEM

When students have developed some independent reading ability and the thrill of being able to "say the words" diminishes, the quality of the material available for them to read is vitally important to their learning to value reading. Interesting characters, vivid descriptions, and unified and coherent paragraphs permit students to empathize, visualize, and think through ideas. Some developmental materials have elaborate word attack cues, comprehension questions, work sheets, and other instructional aids but are poorly written or not relevant to the students' experiences and interests. Attractive packaging and gimmickry sometimes hide dull, meaningless material but the real power of attraction between a reader and a reading selection resides in the selection itself.

SUGGESTIONS FOR CURRICULUM IMPROVEMENT

Although there are classics in children's and adolescent literature, no one can predict what material a particular student will value at a given time. Therefore a variety of materials (magazines, newspapers, biographies, novels, fiction, nonfiction) need to be readily available to students at all times during their schooling. These materials must range in difficulty and interest levels to accommodate the various reading abilities within groups of students. School districts that put most of the financial resources available for reading curriculum development into materials for developing reading skills at the expense of well-stocked and current central and classroom libraries are making a mistake.

All schools, elementary and secondary, should have committees that keep student reading materials current, varied, interesting, at various levels of reading difficulty, and of high quality. "Quality" needs a word of explanation. We mean materials that present characters, situations, points of view, morals, and other aspects of narrative and expository writing clearly, in good writing style, and with justice to all socioeconomic, religious, and ethnic groups. Quality thus encompasses both content and the author's craft.

Decisions about the quality of printed material are highly individual. Nonetheless, a careful scrutiny of materials by the teachers and students who will read them and respond to them will reveal those that have potential for generating intellectual and emotional responses. Guidelines for selecting materials for students are available from various sources known to all qualified librarians. However, those that are prepared by members of some organization should be supplanted by common sense judgments by those who will be using the materials. Material that would be rejected in one school district at some given time may be acceptable and indeed needed at another time or by another district.

The members of materials selection committees should include students, teachers, school administrators, parents, qualified librarians, and reading specialists. Their combined judgments should identify which materials will be helpful to students' growth in reading, their total personal growth, the educational objectives of the school, and, ultimately, social progress. A broad base of school and community support for the materials students

71

select or are assigned to read is also needed. Without question, committees of the kind we are describing do not readily and perhaps never arrive at consensus. But compromise is part of life in a democratic society, and providing thought-provoking, emotion-arousing, well-written reading selections for students is worth the effort.

We want to add a cautionary note to people purchasing materials that depict members of minority groups or materials that have minority group members as central characters. Until the later 1960s or early 1970s, materials about and for members of minority cultures were in short supply. The relatively recent concern with and pressures to develop materials about and for minority cultures have promoted their writing and production. Some of the new materials appear to have been produced more for the purpose of taking advantage of a ready market than for the purpose of providing well-written, fair, carefully researched depictions of minority cultures that appeal to majority as well as minority groups. Therefore, these kinds of materials need special consideration by selection committees, which should include or at least consult with members of various minority groups with expertise in the areas of children's and adolescent literature.

Providing school time for reading

THE PROBLEM

One characteristic of American society is the attempt to fill every waking moment with purposeful activity. Boredom is becoming a precious, or at least a scarce, commodity. Affluence and/or easy credit has permitted at least one generation of Americans to neglect the free public library in favor of TV viewing, Little League baseball, snowmobiling, camping, cycling, water skiing, and so forth. The need to open a book to kill a little time no longer exists. Most reading is now done for very pragmatic reasons, even by good readers. Consequently time spent out of school is being decreasingly used to discover the joy of reading. In fact, many students perceive out-of-school reading as an intrusion on the other diversions available to them.

The same flurry of activity and organization of time observable in American society as a whole is also characteristic of the school curriculum, both elementary and secondary. The expansion of knowledge in all curriculum areas had made the process of preparing young people for citizenry and either college or a job in twelve years plus kindergarten a difficult task indeed. When various special interest groups flex their political muscles the school adds another special class to the curriculum and devises another scheduling plan to accommodate what are referred to as "additional educational opportunities" within a curriculum that's already brimful of opportunities and increasingly organized like an industrial plant assembly line.

The perception that "just sitting around reading" is wasteful of precious school time and tax dollars is another dimension of the problem. Reading for information and pleasure should be considered a legitimate and desirable aspect of the school curriculum; however, not all parents are as concerned about having their children practice their reading skills and acquire positive attitudes toward reading as they are about having their children learn basic reading skills. Indeed, parents may seriously question or even object to using tax monies to give students reading time.

SUGGESTIONS FOR CURRICULUM IMPROVEMENT

Good readers who value reading are usually able to recall a period of time in their lives when they read voraciously. Just as playing the piano or playing tennis well requires hours of practice to acquire the skills and subsequent appreciation for the performance of the activity, reading also demands hours spent practicing the requisite skills and learning to value reading. Unfortunately, both out-of-school time and school time for many students is too filled with other activities to make room for reading. Since teachers and administrators can do more to control school time than they can to control out-of-school time, school time should be reallocated. If students at all academic levels are to read more, the school will have to provide time for that reading. (This recommendation does not preclude educating parents to the need for limiting out-of-school distractions and for providing students with materials, time, a physical environment, and encouragement for reading at home. However, the key seems to lie in curriculum revisions that result in reading's becoming an important part of every school day.)

The best way for the school to provide reading time for students lies within the USSR (Uninterrupted Sustained Silent Reading) model provided by Hunt (1967). Hunt advocates setting aside a certain part of the school day for silent reading as a regular part of the curriculum. During this time, all students, and in some schools teachers, administrators, secretaries, maintenance workers, and community members who participate in the program read self-selected materials—newspapers, magazines,

73

comic books, novels, biographies, catalogs, repair manuals, and so forth. The only material that is not read during this time is assigned material, material that people feel obliged to read, or material that violates community standards.

The purpose is to build silent reading activity into the curriculum at all academic levels as an important educational offering. Silent reading of interesting material becomes a legitimate expenditure of school time for students, administrators, teachers, and others who can and should be good models for students learning to value reading. Unless school time is provided for silent reading, the students who need it most will be least likely to have that need met.

Providing students with good models

THE PROBLEM

Students need models to emulate in regard to reading behaviors. If they see people reading only when they are required to read or hear people talking about reading only in terms of finding answers to questions, they may never learn that print can be used for other than pragmatic purposes.

Many students do not have good reading models in their families. In many families, television is the medium used most for information and recreation. The intellectual and emotional responses that are shared most within these family groups are those stimulated by each family's favorite programs. Consequently, if these students are going to have good reading models, the school will have to provide them.

The reading habits of teachers have been studied enough to validate the suspicion that students are being taught reading by adults who do not themselves turn often to reading for personal fulfillment and enrichment. It is deplorable that many American teachers, especially elementary schoolteachers, are not reading enthusiasts. From the results of a study that investigated the reading habits of college students, most of whom were planning to be elementary school teachers, Odland and Ilstrup (1963) drew the following implications:

Among a group of individuals who will be elementary classroom teachers there were many who seemed to possess an interest in reading and who had developed a power of selection which would guide their reading toward worthwhile literature. It cannot be ignored, however, that there were many individuals who read very little in books or in magazines. There is also cause for concern when one observes the popular choices of the students in books and magazines. In fact, there would seem to be a basis for asking if the adults who accept the responsibility of teaching young children the values of reading really consider reading a valuable medium of communication. (p. 86)

We have talked with many classroom teachers at academic levels from kindergarten to grade 12 about their personal reading habits. The majority report that they do not read as much as they would like to or feel they should because of a lack of time. To expect them to read less on the job than when they were students seems plausible because of the many demands placed on teachers in and out of school. Duffey (1973) studied the reading habits of a select group of two hundred elementary teachers in 1972 and compared his findings with those of a similar study he had conducted in 1966. Twenty percent reported reading no professional journal regularly at all in 1972, 11 percent did not remember having read a book within the year before the survey, and 50 percent had no book in mind that they intended to read. Duffey concluded, "Differences observed between the two groups of teachers are considerably less extensive than the similarities; the compelling similarity is the amount of non-reading reported by so many teachers in both groups, 1966 and 1972."

Studies of the reading habits of secondary teachers find the same results. Hipple and Giblin (1970), who investigated the reading habits of 386 English teachers in Florida, concluded that "the practicing secondary teacher in Florida is not likely to be engaged in much professional reading related to either education in general or to teaching English in particular." Although the subjects in their study might have done considerably more non-professional than professional reading, they probably did not, especially in light of the studies by Jones (1950), Abraham (1952), and Hawkins (1967). All three investigated the reading habits of college students, many of whom were preparing to be teachers. The results of their studies revealed the same general trends. For the most parts, the respondents confined their reading to daily newspapers, periodicals such as *Life* and *Reader's Digest,* and popular fiction. The two most common reasons for not doing more recreational reading were jobs and course assignments. A more recent study of teachers' reading habits was done by Bingham (1975), who used a questionnaire to investigate the reading habits of all 1,164 members of the Wisconsin State Reading Association. In the 580 questionnaires returned, Bingham found a great similarity between the responses of her subjects and the responses of those in the studies done previously.

75

Bingham noted, "Throughout this questionnaire in response to various items, the respondents expressed regret and frustration that their reading, both professional and recreational, was severely limited by lack of time. Job responsibilities, family demands and course work obligations were all cited as reasons for this lack of time. Apparently church and civic activities also interfered with reading. An occasional comment was that hobbies such as gardening and sports activities took precedence over reading."

Jacobs (1956) has noted the relevance of the reading habits of teachers to developing good reading habits in students: "The teacher who would promote reading interests on the part of children, then is clearly one who knows that communication not only is essential to human behavior but is also a truly individual achievement. Such a teacher has felt the impact of reading in his own living: the pursuit of stimulating ideas; the impact of lasting impressions of beauty gained from authors' creative uses of written language; the challenge to stretch new meanings and insights; the testing of old ways of behaving; the delights in coming again to familiar writings, the sharp pang of awe in the presence of greatness; the tingling anticipation of new worlds. Such a teacher would want to share this splendid bequest with children" (p. 23). Johnson (1956) opines, "a fondness for reading is something that a child acquires in much the same way as he catches a cold—by being effectively exposed to someone who already has it" (p. 123).

SUGGESTIONS FOR CURRICULUM IMPROVEMENT

Providing good models of reading habits for students to emulate is similar to providing more time for their reading. Accomplishing change is easier to do by modifying school conditions than by changing family life-styles. Students need to be exposed in the school context to people who read in their presence and who express implicitly and explicitly the sense of satisfaction they derive from reading. Obviously, the greatest need is good examples by teachers and administrators. Getting other people in the community to utilize the resources of the school for information getting and recreational reading also merits consideration.

The matter of teachers' reading habits is important. Women and men who spend their working lives educating young people should themselves value and use reading as a regular part of their daily lives. Teachers should be buyers of one of the most important products they want to sell to their students: reading.

The fact that some teachers apparently are not avid or even regular readers might be traced to two possible causes: some people who become teachers are essentially more nonintellectually inclined than they are intellectually inclined, and teacher-training programs tend to retard or have a negative effect on the development of reading skills and/or habits. If the latter is the case, then the same conditions and resultant deleterious effect on reading growth is probably true of professions other than education also. In other words, higher education may have the same built-in problems relative to fostering positive reading attitudes and skills that elementary and secondary education have. The problems may be simply assignment overload, too difficult materials to read comfortably, and no special time set aside for recreational reading. If the problem lies with the attraction of nonintellectuals to the teaching profession, then the solution lies in better recruitment and hiring procedures. Probably both conditions are factors that contribute to the problem.

From the time they enter teacher-training programs, students should be encouraged in all of their education courses to maintain a varied reading program. They should be told explicitly that recreational, as well as assigned, reading is an important part of their development as teachers. Candidates who cannot develop an interest in reading should be counselled out of teaching-training programs at both elementary and secondary levels. This may sound like a harsh measure to take, but we endorse it.

Reading skills improvement classes should be available to prospective teachers who need vocabulary, comprehension, and rate training. Reading achievement tests could be given to teachers in training and referrals to reading improvement programs made for those who are poor in reading achievement, regardless of their high school grades.

Teachers of education courses must become good models themselves by sharing their reading interests and materials with their students and by preparing students for assigned materials that are likely to cause vocabulary, comprehension, or rate problems. College students need help in reading difficult materials with economy of time and good understanding, just as elementary and secondary school students do.

Interviewers who talk to prospective teachers should consider the candidates' reading habits and abilities, in addition to factors more typically related to employment. They need to avoid hiring teachers who are reluctant readers and to impress those they do hire with the importance of continuing to read both for their professional and personal growth and to provide students with good models. Art teachers, music teachers, science teachers, coaches—

all teachers—will be a positive force in teaching students to value reading if they themselves value reading and let their values be known.

In schools where USSR is part of the curriculum, teachers should not correct papers when their students are reading. They should read too. They need to let students see them reading and to talk with students about the reading they and their students are doing in and out of school.

Idealistic as it may seem, we believe that administrators should provide reading time for all teachers, in the same way that they provide time for correcting papers and planning lessons. And boards of education should provide administrators time for reading so that they are not out of step with the students and teachers. The specific arrangements for creating these conditions will need to be worked out individually for each school district, but they are worthwhile campaigning and working for.

Finally, schools should encourage community members to do some of their reading in the school library where students can see them and perhaps even discuss their reading interests. It would not be inappropriate to invite community members to join class discussions, book clubs, and other activities and organizations that are direct outgrowths of reading. In fact, some sincere values for reading as a force for various kinds of personal enrichment could be pleasantly shared in these school-community encounters.

Teaching reading-thinking strategies

THE PROBLEM

One reason that many students do not learn to value reading is that they have not learned reading-thinking strategies that help them to extract ideas from print with an economy of effort and with an appreciation for both the quality of the ideas and the craft of the author. They begin reading a selection with no particular purpose. They never pause to reflect upon what they are reading and to put the author's ideas into their own personal language. They are largely unaware of the precise vocabulary, careful organization, and perhaps beautiful figures of speech or creative analogies employed by skillful authors. When they finish the selection, their eyes have been more active with the material than their minds. Consequently, they do not give reading the value it deserves.

For some students the lack of value they attach to reading because they do not employ good reading-thinking strategies may be attributed to their lack of motivation to apply their intellectual "muscle" to their reading. For other students, the problem may be that they were never taught how to read with their intellectual muscles flexed.

SUGGESTIONS FOR CURRICULUM IMPROVEMENT

More emphasis should be given to teaching reading-thinking strategies to students at all academic levels. The teaching should begin as soon as students have learned to decode the first stories in their initial instruction and continue throughout their schooling in both special reading classes and in all content areas that utilize reading materials.

Teaching the sender-message-receiver paradigm

One approach for helping students to value reading is to keep them aware of the concept of reading as a communication process. Students who perceive print as an encoded message that originated in the knowledge and perceptions of another person and that can be decoded and responded to with their own personal knowledge and perceptions will learn to appreciate the highly personal element in all reading. The sense of responding to another person is much different from responding to a piece of paper with printed letters on it.

Getting students to think about the sender-message-receiver paradigm can be accomplished by periodically asking about the author's motivation for writing his or her message, the form of the written discourse the author chose and the likely reason for choosing that form, and their personal reactions to the ideas and/or feelings expressed in the message. The following four questions apply to most reading selections and can be asked to keep students aware of the personal element in all written discourse:

1. Why do you think the author wrote what he (she) did?
2. Who was the author's intended audience?
3. Did the form of the message (poetry, essay, narrative, emphasis on facts, emphasis on interpretation of events) fit the purpose of the author and the audience for whom it was intended?
4. As the author's audience, what did the message do for you

79

(made you angry or happy, gave you information, confused you)?

These questions might be modified for different selections and for different age groups, but they are core ones for highlighting the sender-message-receiver paradigm.

Focusing attention on the author's craft

No one can tell someone else what to appreciate. One person's Mozart is another person's Beatles. However, it is possible to alert students to aspects of the author's craft that may appeal to them.

Teachers learn what their students value. Calling students' attention to a well-developed argument, a good analogy, an image-provoking figure of speech, a clever and persuasive appeal, a carefully chosen word, a thorough description, or some other device of a good writer might foster a sense of value for a reading selection that would not occur if their attention were not called to it. Students have a way of overlooking writing that deserves careful examination. Teachers should examine the reading material they assign for samples of the author's craft they think might be appreciated and consequently valued by their students at a particular time in the growth of their value systems. Eventually teachers can ask their students to share examples of good writing they find in their nonassigned reading. To use just one example, the headlines for major articles on newspaper sports pages are often colorful, descriptive, and appealing to student readers. Of course, some class time must be devoted to the sharing of the examples of author's craft the students find; but the contribution to the development of students' attitudes toward reading and their overall valuing of reading may be ample payment for the time invested.

Teaching reading for a purpose

The efficient reader reads for specific purposes. He or she may set these purposes, or they may be set by someone else. The object is for the reader to become increasingly self-reliant in determining reading purpose.

Reading for purpose can be as simple as scanning a chapter to find a name or a date or as sophisticated as becoming thoroughly familiar with a character to portray him in a play. Mature readers recognize the wide range of possible reasons for reading, select one or more reasons prior to each reading act, and proceed with their purpose in mind. Their reasons may vary from the need to escape from a busy day to the desire to master the concept behind a mathematical formula. In any case, they know what they want to get from the reading.

Because they have an objective, mature readers emerge from their reading experience with a distinct and valuable communication. These results are quite different from those reached by nondirected readers, who often emerge with only some general notions of the content they have passed through. Mature readers have what they want; immature readers often don't know what they have when they finish reading, and if they do know, they frequently don't know what to do with it.

Good readers are always ready to change their original purpose or add purposes as they read. They may start a chapter in a history book to learn the effects of a particular legislative decision on the economy of a state. Shortly they may decide to find out the political motivations of the legislators who made the decision. Their objective changes, but they are always in purposeful pursuit. The beginning reader may read to discover what Father has in the box and then to discover what the family will do with Father's surprise. The reader is not just reading; he or she is reading to find things out. The mature reader who meets two different characters in a novel may wonder how they will solve the conflict that is certain to arise in an anticipated meeting. He or she may search for clues to a character's feelings or words that describe a scientist's frustration. The immature reader does not read with this kind of inquiring mind.

One of the writers is reminded of the many times he taught Jack London's *Call of the Wild* to average-ability tenth-grade English classes. For each assignment of one or more chapters, the classic admonition was given: "Read it carefully so that we can discuss it tomorrow." Sometimes a little motivation was added: "This is an exciting chapter. You'll enjoy it." The discussion the following day was almost always extremely one-sided. It proceeded something like this:

"Well, do you agree with me that this is an exciting chapter?" Some affirmative nods, some shoulder shrugging, some heads turning toward the window. "Obviously some of you enjoyed it. Can you tell us what you liked about this particular chapter?" "Anyone?" Pause. "Sally?"

"It was exciting and interesting."

"Jack?"

"I agree. It was interesting and good adventure. And exciting."

"Did anyone notice the way the author used words that gave

the reader a vivid picture of the action taking place and almost made him feel as if he were there?" Evidently no one did. "Open your books to the first page in the chapter. Listen to this sentence and notice the descriptiveness of the verbs as well as the adjectives. 'He was *crying* with *sheer* rage and eagerness as he *circled* back and forth for a chance to *spring* in.' Close your eyes for a moment. Try to picture that. Imagine yourself sneaking up to take movies of that moment before open conflict." Heads turning back from the windows. Some straightening up in the seats. Some looks of concentration. Some looks of satisfaction in discovery. "Let's consider another aspect of this chapter. What did London seem to be saying in this chapter about the relationship between the civilized and the primitive?" Attentive silence. "Are you sure we read the same chapter?" Some smiles, some more shrugs. "All right, listen, and I'll tell you what this chapter is all about." Through his years of teaching tenth-grade English, the teacher became the best teller of *Call of the Wild* in the school and perhaps in the entire state. The pessimists in the class must have felt very stupid and convinced that they would never learn to read properly, and the optimists must have felt very fortunate to have such a smart teacher. And one day it occurred to the teacher that if the students were told to watch for some of these things as they read, they could discover *Call of the Wild* for themselves and thereby value it more.

Students at all academic levels need to know that a reading selection is written for a purpose. An author decides what responses he wants from a reader. He or she writes to inform, to give pleasure through carefully selected words, to persuade, etc.

Teachers need to acquaint students with materials written for different purposes and to show how personal purposes may be realized from given selections. Students might be asked to discuss the purposes of the authors of selections supplied by the teacher. Or they might be encouraged to ask questions about selections before they read them. Another good teaching procedure is to have students list purposes for which they might read and then match their lists with selections that are likely to satisfy those purposes.

Probably the best way to teach students to read for purpose is by assigning, prior to reading, questions or other tasks that can be satisfied through the selection. Skillful questioning is a means of stimulating different kinds of thinking while reading. Writing tasks, specified prior to reading but to be completed after it, are effective in giving students experiences in reading for purpose. The key word is *preparation*. The reader who is prepared to gain certain ideas or feelings from a selection is more likely to have a personally productive reading experience than one who is not reading for clearly defined purposes.

Teachers at all academic levels and in all content areas should teach reading for purpose. The elementary teacher should begin a child's development in this regard in keeping with the child's total personal development and with suitable reading materials. As the child grows and her or his reading materials become more sophisticated, his or her purposes for reading and ability to achieve those purposes should grow accordingly. Each content area and each sequential stage of the curriculum present different opportunities for expanding a student's ability to read for purpose.

Teaching students to reflect upon and organize ideas

Most writing is a highly organized process. Authors usually structure their ideas according to an organizational pattern: a most-important-to-least important organization, a least-important-to-most important organization, a building-to-a-climax organization, a cause-effect organization, and so forth. Some writers use a pattern that has one main or topic idea in each paragraph; others choose to let more than one paragraph support or build to a summary idea. Transmitting ideas efficiently via print requires the reader to tap into the organizational plan of the author and to pause occasionally to reflect upon and to organize the ideas in his or her own mind.

Reading comprehension and retention of what is read are both enhanced by reflective, organized reading in which ideas are connected and weighted in the mind of the reader. Comprehension is more than coming to grips with ideas in isolation; it is a careful relating and sorting of ideas into an existing cognitive structure. Ausubel (1964) comments pertinently:

> Since potentially meaningful material is always learned in relation to an existing background of relevant concepts, principles, and information, which provide a framework for its reception and make possible the emergence of new meanings, it is evident that the stability, clarity, and organizational properties of this background crucially affect both the accuracy and the clarity of these emerging new meanings and their immediate and long-term retrievability. If, on the other hand, cognitive structure is unstable, ambiguous, disorganized, or chaotically organized, it tends to inhibit meaningful learning and retention. Hence, it is largely by strengthening relevant aspects of cognitive structure that new learning and retention can be facilitated. (p. 234)

83

Good readers pause in their reading periodically to relate new ideas to old and to sort both into a stable coherent cognitive structure.

Thorndike (1917), after studying mistakes students made in reading paragraphs, concluded the following:

> Understanding a paragraph is like solving a problem in mathematics. It consists in selecting the right elements of the situation and putting them together in the right relations, and also with the right amount of weight or influence or force for each. The mind is assailed as it were by every word in the paragraph. It must select, repress, soften, emphasize, correlate and organize, all under the influence of the right mental set or purpose or demand.

These reactions or responses to a selection result in good comprehension and retention and consequently valuable reading experiences.

Teaching students to pause at important spots in a reading selection to reflect upon and to organize their thinking requires teachers to be thoroughly familiar with the materials they assign. They must understand the structure of the material and why it is structured as it is. Without this knowledge, it is impossible for them to help students with the reflecting and organizing process.

Students at all academic levels need specific instruction in organizing their reading. Just as setting a purpose for reading becomes a more sophisticated process as more sophisticated materials are introduced into the curriculum, so does the process of reading organization. Therefore, students begin to develop the ability to organize their reading in the primary grades and continue to do so through their entire school careers. Poor readers often apply to complex materials reading-thinking strategies that are suitable only for simple materials.

To teach reflective and organized reading, teachers need to make students aware that writing is organized, different materials are organized differently, and the reader must pause occasionally to decide which ideas are important and which are not and to relate and sort them accordingly.

Sometimes overhead projections can be helpful in teaching students how to organize their reading. Transparencies showing clear-cut organizational patterns may be projected for student viewing and discussions. Excerpts from different kinds of materials (a story with a surprise ending, a social studies article, a science text) can illustrate how a reader needs to direct his or her thinking to get the most from each selection.

The best procedure for helping students attain good comprehension and retention by organizing and reflecting upon their
reading is to give them specific directions on where to pause in
their reading and what to think about during that pause. The
first responsibility of the teacher is to make a careful survey of assigned selections to identify logical breaking points for students
to pause in their intake of ideas. The second responsibility is to
construct one or more thinking questions for students to respond
to (in writing, orally, or with inner speech) when they come to
those places. For example, teachers might say, "Put a little check
mark after the third paragraph on page 132 to remind you to
pause in your reading at that point. On the handout that I prepared to help you think through this chapter, you will find a
question to think about after the third paragraph on page 132.
Put another check mark after . . ." The question might be something like, "In your own words, what were the three major reasons why Congress did not want to declare war?" Or, " 'What do
you think Henry Aaron did after he hit the home run that tied
Babe Ruth's record?' (a) retired from baseball; (b) tried to beat the
record; (c) became a team manager; or (d) enrolled in college to
study for a new career?" The questions can take many forms and
can be at almost any level of difficulty. The idea is simply to keep
students thinking in a logical fashion about what they are
reading.

Teaching rate flexibility

A frequent complaint of people who avoid reading is that they
read so slowly. In effect, they are saying that they would value
reading more if they could read faster. Improving reading rate is
truly an important factor in helping many reluctant readers value
reading more. Fast readers do not necessarily comprehend better
than slow readers, nor do slow readers necessarily comprehend
better than fast readers. There are both fast and slow readers who
have good comprehension. Therefore, the problem is not only
one of improving comprehension. Efficiency and the degree of
pleasure desired from reading are also involved in the matter of
varying reading rate and style.

Reading rate is a misleading term; *rate of comprehension* is more
descriptive. Since comprehension is the objective of the reading
process, moving the eyes rapidly across lines of type is not in itself reading. Consequently, a reading rate score is meaningless
without an accompanying comprehension score. Furthermore,
reading rate and comprehension scores mean little unless one
knows the kind of material from which the scores were obtained
and why the reader was reading it.

85

Efficient readers let their rate be governed by the material they are reading and their purpose for reading it. They have many different reading needs and can move from one speed to another to enhance their comprehension and pleasure. They may change their rate from selection to selection or within a selection. For example, they know that the best way to read a novel is to begin on the first page and proceed to the last. They also know that a chapter in a textbook may be read best by surveying the entire chapter quickly and noting what seem to be key sentences before they begin a page-by-page reading. Within a selection, mature readers may move quickly through several paragraphs and then read a particular sentence slowly and carefully. They may halt their reading completely at times to savor the visual imagery produced by a vivid description or to ponder an intriguing idea. They employ more subvocalization with a poem and may even read it aloud. A mathematics problem may also require considerable vocalization to be understood. The context surrounding an unfamiliar word may need to be searched to find the meaning of the word, or an account of a sequential scientific process may need to be retraced to ensure comprehension and retention. Efficient readers shift rate gears as they move through written communication.

The ability to vary reading rate is often lacking in beginning readers. It needs to be developed carefully from the time the child starts to master the most basic reading skills, and development needs to be continued as the child progresses to more and more sophisticated materials. In the initial stages of reading instruction children are too concerned with decoding and meaning-getting processes to be trained in reading flexibility. Therefore, it is wise to postpone such training until they have indicated their relative mastery of basic decoding and comprehension skills. However, once these skills are finally in hand, they are ready to be taught how to vary their rate and style. Some children learn to be flexible readers without specific teaching, but many require the help of a teacher.

Teachers must first of all teach students that the world is full of many different kinds of reading materials, which generate different ideas and feelings. It is important to ask different kinds of questions about varying materials and assign different kinds of tasks for different reading experiences. Students at all academic levels should have opportunities to discuss why they select certain materials to read, what different materials offer, and what specific reading selections have done for them. Discussing how they read particular selections also illuminates the concept of flexibility. Specific directions for reading a certain selection are often helpful. For example, students may be told to scan the entire selection before reading, to pause and reflect at designated words or passages, and to read other designated passages rapidly. In this way they get the feel of reading flexibility.

It is better not to emphasize reading rate with students who do not have good word recognition skills. However, students who have good word recognition skills can rather easily be taught to read faster with no loss of comprehension. Timed exercises with reading selections at a difficulty level appropriate for the student's vocabulary and comprehension achievement will increase the rate. Three kinds of mechanical devices purport to be helpful: tachistoscopic devices, film projection devices, and pacer or accelerator devices. There are numerous claims of success from teachers who have used these devices to increase students' reading rate, but many educators seriously question their value. The problem of transfer from the machine to the book cannot be denied, and the criticism that good readers don't read in the mechanical fashion prescribed by the particular setting of the machine seems valid. Since regressions are frequently the cause of slow reading, placing an index card over each line of print as it is read may serve to break the habit of regressing and thereby improve reading rate. Two things should be kept in mind: Exercises to increase rate should always include comprehension checks, and students must be taught the desirability of slow reading for some materials and/or some purposes.

Teachers may use a number of measures to discover whether students are varying their rate and style of reading appropriately. Checking the time students take to read different kinds of reading materials is one evaluation technique. Asking them to retrace their progress through a selection or through two different selections telling how they varied their reading attack within or between the selections sometimes demonstrates development in reading flexibility. Asking them to locate the answer to a particular question within a specified period of time is revealing, and so is giving them a limited amount of time to read and summarize a selection. Obviously, the selections used for these evaluations need to be carefully chosen and the tasks assigned keyed to the content and difficulty of the material.

DEVELOPING VOCABULARY

Students with meager vocabularies often fail to read selections with complete comprehension and often fail to appreciate some

87

of the fine shades of meaning and precision of expression embedded in certain words. Vocabulary development is without question an important factor in teaching students to value reading.

One way to enlarge vocabulary is through wide reading. Students who read much may use reading experiences to enlarge their vocabularies. However, since wide reading does not guarantee vocabulary development, the reader must consciously attempt to improve his or her vocabulary. In this regard, the student with a meager vocabulary may be characterized not by a failure to read but by a failure to take advantage of the opportunities for vocabulary development that reading offers.

The kind of vocabulary development we mean is not only the addition of previously unencountered words to a student's reading vocabulary but the utilization of words from this vocabulary in his or her speaking, writing, and listening vocabularies. It is also the kind of development that causes the student to respond differently to shades of meaning in the same word used in different contexts and in words that are nearly, but not quite, synonymous.

Speculating about the number of words and word meanings in the English language, Laird (1957), says,

> Three quarters of a million? That would seem conservative, and we still have to define "a word." Some of these so-called "words," forms which have come to us with some continuity, have many uses. If one thinks of these words as the carriers of units of meaning, then many of the words single in form become multiple in use and meaning. Many words have dozens of meanings. . . . A rough check of random sections in various dictionaries suggests that we may safely say there are more than twice as many named meanings in English as there are recognized words. How many named meanings does a writer of English have before him, then, when he tries to compose a sentence? Two million? Certainly there are many times what any human being could ever learn, or learn to use. And yet we are constantly obtaining new words. (p. 53)

Since English writers have myriads of words and meanings at their disposal, readers of English must be skillful interpreters of words. They must know that a word has meaning in a particular context, and they must respond to words not as fixed but as changing entities. Mature readers recognize this phenomenon and learn new meanings for words as they encounter them.

Efficient readers have a variety of means at their disposal for learning new words. They do not rely on one method alone for analyzing words. They know that the words surrounding an unknown word may define the latter for them and thus search the context for clues to its meaning. They also know that analyzing the structure of a word may disclose its meaning. Good readers use roots, prefixes, and suffixes to aid them. They may use phonic skills to move a word from their sight word vocabulary to their listening vocabulary, which may contain the troublesome word. If all these strategies fail, good readers have well-developed dictionary skills to rely on and a positive attitude toward using the dictionary.

A necessary characteristic for those who use reading experiences to enlarge their vocabulary is a curiosity about words. They want to know where words come from, what they mean, how they change their meanings, how people react to them, and so forth. They wonder why an author used a particular word, and they appreciate the choice of a well-chosen word. They incorporate in their reading a search for new words and the answers to the many questions prompted by their interest in words.

Teachers at all academic levels are in an excellent position to help students use their reading experiences to enlarge their vocabularies. Besides teaching them various word analysis skills, they can teach them about the nature, history, and power of words and give them reading materials that stimulate interest in and respect for words. Poetry, carefully selected to match the interests, maturity, and reading ability of students, is often used successfully. Discussions of words used in advertising communications awaken students to the persuasive power of words. Alerting students to key, descriptive, or unusual words in a selection they are about to read is another good procedure. There are informative, humorous, and profound writings about words that may give students new insights and increased sensitivity to words. Hayakawa (1949) writes about "snarl-words" and "purr-words," and Carl Sandburg (1922) cautions readers to beware of using "proud" words.

Children in the primary grades can supply words to describe pictures and take part in other pleasant and meaningful activities that lead to vocabulary growth. There is no scarcity of methods to enlarge vocabulary through reading with students of all ages. The need is to take the time to construct lessons and motivate students to understand the concept of vocabulary development through reading, make vocabulary development part of their reading experiences, and use newly acquired words in effective speaking and writing activities. Students must have opportunities to use their increasing vocabularies in speech and writing;

they will forget the words they learned if they do not practice them. When students do use newly learned words, the teacher must acknowledge this manifested growth and provide suitable rewards.

Teachers should discuss new words that students learn while they read or familiar words found used in an unusual way or in an especially effective way. If students know that this activity is a regular part of the curriculum, they will learn to be prepared. This is a good evaluation activity for all content area classes in the secondary school, especially where supplementary reading is liberally assigned or strongly encouraged. Asking students to define or substitute words used in their writing is a way to determine whether they understand the words they are using. Careful listening to student reports and discussions and careful reading of student writing will also permit an evaluation of the transfer of words met in reading to speech and writing. Some teachers require students to keep notebooks or periodically submit short reports of their observations of words while reading. If called for sparingly and in a spirit of genuine sharing, these can be effective evaluative exercises, as well as good instructional procedures.

Summary

We have identified five aspects of school reading programs that need evaluation if students are to be taught to value reading. We have discussed the importance of fostering higher-level reading behaviors, the need to select good materials, the need to provide school time for reading, the importance of providing students with good models, especially teacher models, and the effect that teaching specific reading-thinking strategies can have on the efficiency with which students get meaning from print and thereby learn to value reading.

For each of the aspects, we offered specific suggestions for reading curriculum development at both the teaching and the administrative level. Reading specialists who are responsible for providing in-service education for teachers should find our suggestions helpful to them in their work with classroom teachers, special reading teachers, and school administrators.

The first step on the road to valuing reading is the development of basic reading skills. However, basic reading skill development and learning to value reading should be seen as more interdependent than independent within the context of the total

school program. How closely they work together should be apparent from our discussion of teaching reading-thinking strategies, which are skills efficient readers use to make their reading
more productive, more enjoyable and therefore more valuable to
them.

Learning to value reading and actually using it frequently are
also highly interdependent. The more time students spend reading, the better readers they will become and the more they will
learn to value reading.

The social context for reading has changed and will continue
to do so. But reading remains one of the most powerful forces for
personal and societal development available to most people. It is
one of the most valuable resources in our culture and should be
taught as such.

Bibliography

Abraham, William. "The Reading Choices of College Students." *Journal of Educational Research* 45 (1952): 459–463.

Adler, Mortimer J. *How to Read a Book.* New York: Simon and Schuster, 1940.

Ausubel, David P. "Some Psychological Aspects of the Structure of Knowledge." In Stanley Elan (ed.), *Education and the Structure of Knowledge.* Chicago: Rand McNally, 1964.

Bingham, Adelaide. "The Reading Habits and Preferences of Some Members of the Wisconsin State Reading Association." Master's thesis, University of Wisconsin, 1975.

Bloom, Benjamin S., et al. *Taxonomy of Educational Objectives: Handbook I: Cognitive Domain.* New York: McKay, 1956.

Duffey, Robert V. "Teacher as Reader." *The Reading Teacher* 27 (November 1973): 132–133.

Hafter, Irma T., and Frances M. Douglas. "Inadequate College Readers." *Journal of Developmental Reading* 1 (1958): 42–53.

Hawkins, M. L. "Are Future Teachers Readers?" *The Reading Teacher* 21 (1967): 138–140.

Hayakawa, S. *Language in Thought and Action.* New York: Harcourt, Brace & World, 1949.

Hipple, T. W. and T. R. Giblin. "The Professional Reading of English Teachers in Florida." *Research and the Teaching of English* 5 (1971): 153–164.

Hunt, Lyman C. "Evaluation through Teacher-Pupil Conferences." In *The Evaluation of Children's Reading Achievement,* edited by Thomas C. Barrett. Newark, Del.: International Reading Association, 1967, pp. 111–126.

Jacobs, Leland. "Goals in Promoting Permanent Reading Interest." In *Developing Permanent Reading Interests,* edited by Helen M. Robinson. Chicago: University of Chicago Press, 1956.

Jennings, Frank. *This is Reading.* New York: Bureau of Publications, Teachers College, Columbia University, 1965.

Johnson, Wendell D. *Your Most Enchanted Listener.* New York: Harper and Row, 1956.

Jones, Harold D. "The Extracurricular Reading Interests of Students in a State College." *School and Society* 72 (1950): 40–43.

Krathwohl, David R., et al. *Taxonomy of Educational Objectives: Handbook II: Affective Domain.* New York: McKay, 1964.

Laird, Charlton. *The Miracle of Language.* New York: Fawcett World Library, 1957.

Langer, Susanne. "The Prince of Creation." *The Borzoi College Reader.* New York: Knopf, 1966.

Odland, Norine, and Therese Ilstrup. "Will Reading Teachers Read?" *The Reading Teacher* 17 (November 1963): 83–87.

Osenburg, T. C. "Conceiving Objective Reading Tests: A Minority Opinion." *Journal of Developmental Reading* 5 (1962): 275–279.

Otto, Wayne, Richard A. McMenemy, and Richard J. Smith. *Corrective and Remedial Teaching*, 2d ed. Boston: Houghton Mifflin, 1973.

Sandburg, Carl. "Primer Lesson." In *Slabs of the Sunburnt West.* New York: Harcourt, Brace & World, 1922.

Smith, Richard J., and Thomas Barrett. *Teaching Reading in the Middle Grades.* Reading, Mass.: Addison-Wesley, 1974.

Thorndike, Edward L. "Reading as Reasoning: A Study of Mistakes in Paragraph Reading." *Journal of Educational Psychology* 8 (1917): 323–332.

Chapter 5 Tools of the reading curriculum: Materials and equipment

Selecting materials, one of the many interrelated instructional decisions that reading teachers must make, is as important a decision as any other instructional decision discussed elsewhere in this book.

Although the selection of reading materials will not in and of itself result in satisfactory reading achievement, we believe that selection is an important component of reading instruction. Thus, we shall examine the role of reading materials in the instructional process, the types of materials and equipment available, the process of evaluating and selecting these tools, the readability of materials, and the human relations content of reading material.

The role of materials

The major criterion a school district often uses to decide if curriculum revision is necessary in reading is the condition of the materials being used. If a commercial reading program has been used for several years, if several new teachers have been hired, or if a publishing company has announced a new basal series or remedial program, the district leaders will often decide that it is time to revise the reading program. Officials may not care that the present materials are working well; the issue is that the district is not up to date.

Materials should support reading instruction, not control it. As Hubbard (1976) notes:

Textbooks can become ends in themselves, purchased from a persuasive book salesman, seized at a book fair because of the colorful pictures or the self-correcting workbook pages, embraced because "we have always used that book," or assigned so "the kids have something to do." But the textbook must not be an end in itself, a necessary evil or a crutch. It must be selected to help support well defined purposes of the curriculum. (p. 1)

When teachers, administrators, and reading specialists start to guide the selection of materials or equipment, they must already have some instructional decisions well in hand. Specifically, they must have a clearly written statement of philosophy about the reading act and the act of reading instruction, a statement of curriculum that includes broad goals and more specific anticipated outcomes, a plan for evaluating students and program, and a skill sequence and some attention to reading attitudes and values. They must also consider the organizational structure and the abilities and professional attitudes of those who will also be using the materials. Finally, and most important, they should have an exceedingly clear perception of the students' needs, abilities, likes and dislikes. Only as these pieces of the reading instruction system fall into place can the role of materials be anticipated. As figure 5.1 notes, planning for reading instruction is a series of concentric circles. It begins with the students and their

Figure 5.1 **Student-centered planning for reading instruction**

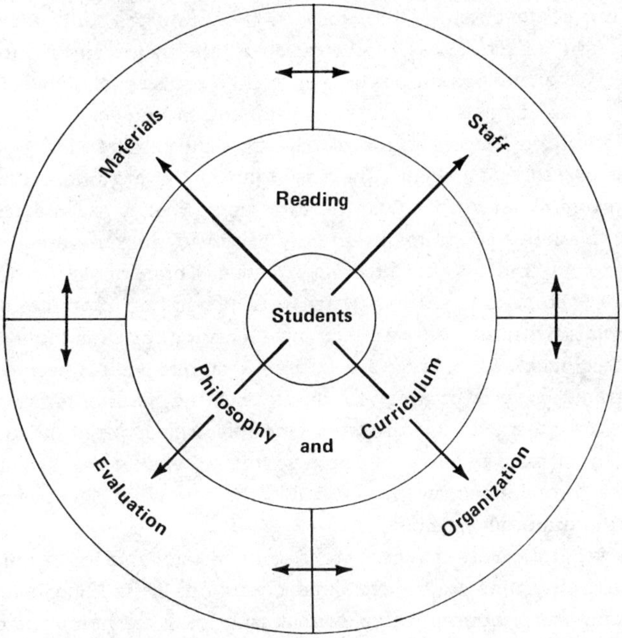

needs, evolves through the broad philosophic dimensions of curriculum and reading, and finally arrives at considerations of materials, evaluation, staffing, and organization. In short, actual selection occurs later in the planning process, not early.

The wide range of materials available for reading instruction has its genesis in the many divergent theories of how to teach reading. These theories are applied to reading programs. And then the debate rages: Reading program A is better than program B, but both are superseded by C. The research conducted during the 1960s by the U.S. Office of Education has laid some of these arguments to rest. As Early (1976) notes:

> These studies reflected the decade's overriding concern with method, pitting one approach against another. Altogether, five different basal series, three phonics programs, two linguistic programs, and two i/t/a programs were tried out in classrooms across the country. The results were evaluated with the same tests. Among classes using the same methods, sharper differences showed up on end-of-the-year testing than appeared between classes using the different methods under comparison. This surprising result led many to infer that teachers, not methods, were responsible for the differences. (p. 299)

Apparently different theories of reading instruction and the materials that support them do not make the most difference in reading achievement. Other factors, including the skill, experience, and effectiveness of the teacher, are major contributors. Thus it is erroneous for a school system to expect that a change in reading programs will result in improved reading scores.

Debunking the mystique of reading materials had led to two other excesses, however. The first follows the argument that if the program does not make the difference, then it should be all right to change programs frequently or to use one program at one grade level and another at the next level. This practice in some school systems has led to a patchwork of reading programs and materials without continuity or articulation. Reading materials are best used when they are part of a stable, well-thought-out program. The best strategy to use in teaching reading effectively is to design a reading program carefully, select program materials to support it, and develop a system to evaluate it. If evaluations are satisfactory, you should continue with the program and the materials selected.

A second excess is switching a student back and forth among reading programs within the same classroom. If the theories buttressing the programs differ dramatically or if the nomenclature used is different, this changing can do more harm than good. Again, a stable program taught conscientiously and carefully will be far more effective than the short trial of a variety of materials that often do not bear any logical relationship to one another.

Finally, we must confront the issue of who selects the instructional materials. We believe that foundation materials to support the reading program can best be selected by the individual school. Philosophy and curriculum can be developed at the district level, but materials must be selected by the teachers, who are closest to their students. District-wide adoptions, particularly in larger school districts, are probably cost efficient; but they are often tyrannical and ineffective. A program unsuited to the needs of the students in a particular school or incompatible with the personality and attitudes of the school's teachers will not succeed. Every teacher who is going to use a new reading program must have a role in the decision. That cannot be done when ten to fifteen teachers on a committee are making selections for several hundred other teachers.

Types of reading materials and equipment

The role that materials and equipment play in reading instruction is made no easier by the wide range of them available. There are reading materials and equipment available to support every conceivable reading theory or approach: readiness material, basic instructional material, programmed material, remedial material, reinforcement material, vocabulary machines, vocabulary-controlled magazines, and on and on. Without a road map, a practitioner can easily be fooled by the terrain. Let's try to sort some things out.

BASAL READING PROGRAMS

Beginning with the legendary McGuffey readers, basal readers have provided the foundation for the initial acquisition of reading skills. Smith and Johnson (1976) note that "there is a nine-to-one chance that you were taught to read by means of a basal reader. It has been estimated that currently, more than four out of five children are instructed through this approach" (p. 94). These programs are characterized by a controlled vocabulary of high-frequency words, a scope and sequence of word identification skills and comprehension skills (see, for example, figure 5.2),

Figure 5.2 Scope and sequence

	Kindergarten—Levels 1, 2		Readiness—Level 3
	LEVEL 1/Read-It-Yourself Books A&B	LEVEL 2/Read-It-Yourself Books A&B	LEVEL 3/Read-It-Yourself Books A&B
VISUAL SKILLS (Continued)	•Matching and recognizing letters and numerals ‡	•Matching words ✓	•Recognizing word forms that are the same and different ✓
CONCEPT DEVELOPMENT	•Ordering a sequence *	✓	✓
	*Associating numerals with number of objects *	✓	✓
		*Identifying number/numeral correspondence *	*Recognizing numerals ✓
			*Recognizing numerals *
	*Counting objects *	✓	✓
	*Recognizing textures, temperatures and relative size *	✓	✓
		•Relating picture of concept to its opposite *	✓
		•Describing cause and effect *	✓
		*Distinguishing between fantasy and reality *	✓
			*Understanding locational concepts *
		*Understanding time concepts *	✓
CRITICAL THINKING	•Making inferences and predicting outcomes *	✓	✓
	•Classifying *	✓	✓
		•Naming two classifications for an object *	✓
	*Solving problems *	‡	*Drawing conclusions ✓
COMPREHENSION	•Following directions *	✓	•Following four-part directions ✓
	•Naming object by hearing description ‡	•Completing an oral statement with spoken word that fits context *	•✓

✓ Review and maintenance or further development   ✓ Review and maintenance with further testing
• Review and maintenance with further development

Source: Reproduced from *Scope and Sequence, Levels 1–36, Series r, The New Macmillan Reading Program*, 1975. Reprinted by permission of the Macmillan Publishing Co., Inc.

98

and graded reading material that attempts to match the interests of students from kindergarten through grade 8. Smith and Johnson (1976) suggest that basal reading programs

> are comprehensive and are designed to comprise the total program (though many authors and publishers urge the use of supplements as well) to help children progress from the status of nonreaders, through the stages of reading acquisition, into refined, fully developed mature readers. With such a goal, most basal programs contain a variety of printed material designed to span the elementary school experience from kindergarten to grade six or eight. Basal programs typically include a number (eight to fifteen or more) of basic textbooks, an equal number of accompanying workbooks, comprehensive teacher's manuals, supplementary books, magazines and wall charts, a variety of audio-visual aids, and a full assortment of pre- and posttests intended for diagnosis of reading needs and assessment of mastery of skills and materials. (p. 95)

In recent years, severe criticism has been leveled at basal reading series; nevertheless, they remain the singular most popular approach to teaching reading in American elementary schools. Heilman (1972) lists several criticisms of the basal program:

1. Materials are dull and repetitive.
2. Language is often artificial and culturally removed from the student's language.
3. Story material is often without literary merit.
4. Insufficient emphasis is often placed on teaching sound-symbol relationships.
5. Reading materials often discriminate against women, minorities, and non-middle-class persons.
6. Round-robin reading is encouraged by the organization of the materials.
7. A static, three-group approach to reading instruction is encouraged, with little shifting of students from group to group as necessary.
8. Little provision is made for individualized, continous-progress instruction.
9. Little incentive is provided the teacher to get interested or enterprising students out of the basal program and into more challenging material.

These criticisms were probably justified a decade ago. Since 1970, however, considerable progress has been made to improve these programs, both through the help of federal research and development efforts and through the renewed efforts of textbook publishing companies.

Recent developmental reading programs reveal so many changes that it is almost a misnomer to refer to them as basal programs. Rather, it is more appropriate to think of them as instructional systems. They are characterized by:

1. Better incorporation of contemporary linguistic and psycholinguistic theory into the initial stages of reading instruction.
2. Greater consideration of the literary and informational merits of the reading material used for reading instruction.
3. Greater sensitivity to sociocultural stereotyping of women, minorities, and lower socioeconomic class persons.
4. A more psychologically sound scope and sequence of word recognition and comprehension skills.
5. Greater attention to critical and creative reading activities.
6. A larger variety of program components, including readiness kits, developmental readers, corroborating workbooks, skill-builder kits, flashcards, magazines, records, and tapes.
7. A systematic integration of all program components through a teacher-management system that encourages an individualization of instruction.
8. A sophisticated testing system, including placement tests, skill mastery tests, and informal achievement tests.
9. Teachers' manuals that are rich in suggestions and strategies for improved classroom instruction in reading.

Clearly basal programs are much better than those available even five years ago. Unfortunately, they still cannot solve every elementary school's reading instruction problems; they still can be improved upon.

LINGUISTIC READERS

The contributions of modern linguistic and psycholinguistic theory to reading instruction are considerable. Since Bloomfield's (1933) work in the 1930s, a considerable body of scholarship about language and language acquisition has grown. During the late 1960s and early 1970s, these contributions led to the introduction of instructional materials based on linguistic theories of language acquisition. Often, however, these linguistic-oriented reading instruction materials are confused with phonics materials.

There are some rather important differences between phonics
and linguistic-oriented reading material. *Phonic programs* teach
students directly the sound/symbol relationships between speaking and reading and teach them to blend these simple
sound/symbol patterns together to form words and other larger
units of meaning. A *linguistic approach* attends to families of
words that have similar linguistic patterns but are distin-
guishable by minimal cue differences: *fat, cat, rat, sat.* Through
this inductive practice with minimal cue differences nested in
larger word units, the student begins to acquire word-decoding
power. This learning occurs without actually practicing the
sound/symbol pattern in isolation.

The linguistic and phonics approaches lend themselves to a
variety of instructional strategies: early linguistic materials made
liberal use of nonsense words (figure 5.3.); some authors use a
programmed learning approach (figure 5.4). Workbooks filled
with drill and practice exercises are also numerous.

Figure 5.3 **The use of nonsense words in a linguistic program**

az	av	az	ac	az
	az	af	az	as

daz	daz	das	daz	daf
	dav	daz	dal	daz

gaz	daz	gaz	gat	gaz
	gaz	gan	gaz	gad

haz	gaz	hap	haz	haz
	haz	haz	hag	han

laz	haz	laz	haz	laz
	laz	gaz	laz	lan

Source: Reproduced from Leonard Bloomfield and Clarence L. Barnhart,
Let's Read (1963), Fig. 3 © 1963 by Clarence L. Barnhart.

Figure 5.4 **A programmed linguistic approach**

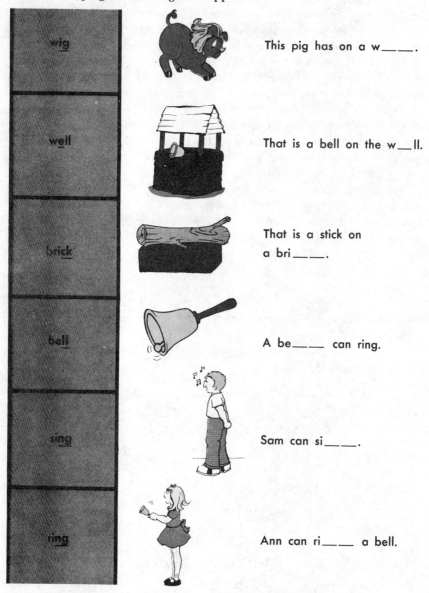

This pig has on a w____.

That is a bell on the w__ll.

That is a stick on a bri____.

A be____ can ring.

Sam can si____.

Ann can ri____ a bell.

Source: Reproduced from C. D. Buchanan, *Programmed Reading Book 4*, rev. ed. (New York: Webster Division, McGraw-Hill [a Sullivan Associates Program], 1968), p. 15 © 1968 Behavioral Research Laboratories.

Though popular and controversial during the early 1970s, linguistic and phonics materials have been somewhat eclipsed by the inclusion of linguistic and/or phonics instruction in modern basal programs. This early enthusiasm has also been tempered by the instructionally ineffective and somewhat stereotypic approaches used early in the movement.

Though not linguistic or phonic in origin, *augmented alphabet approaches* attempt to make the acquisition of sound/symbol relationships easier by using an alphabet where every symbol can be linked with its own unique sound. Conversely, the English alphabet of twenty-six letters is spread over forty-five phonemes, where a phoneme is a distinctive speech sound. Augmented alphabet approaches are designed for beginning reading only and require an eventual transition to normal English orthography. One of the more popular augmented alphabets, i/t/a, is shown in figure 5.5.

There are materials available that teach beginning reading using such an augmented alphabet. The approach has persisted for about ten years in the United States, but it is still not very widely regarded. Though rigorously researched and critiqued on all sides, the augmented alphabet approach has been slow to catch on as much because of the cost of retraining teachers and the large investment in materials as by the research or theoretical criticism.

SUPPLEMENTARY MATERIALS

In addition to the materials that form the foundation of a kindergarten through grade 8 reading program, there are many kinds of *supplementary materials* designed to meet special purposes: kits, workbooks, books designed as remedial reading material, and so forth. These materials are usually designed for older

Figure 5.5 **The i/t/a alphabet and representative words**

Source: Reproduced from H. J. Tanyzer, "What You Should Know About the Initial Teaching Alphabet," *Hofstra Review*. Copyright 1966 *Hofstra Review*, Winter, 1966, Hempstead, N.Y.

students who appear to be lagging behind their peers in the development of reading skills and power.

Remedial reading materials normally stress the same skills as developmental programs do. Their reading selections and format, however, are designed to appeal to older students. Teachers must select remedial reading materials carefully because some of those on the market are poorly conceived and inferior.

ADAPTED READING MATERIALS

Within other curriculum areas—such as language arts, science, and social studies—*adapted materials* have been developed to provide help for poor readers. Included are high-interest/easy-vocabulary books, magazines, and newspapers, adapted classics, and even adapted textbooks. These materials can be useful in motivating older students to read; however, they must be chosen carefully and used judiciously to prevent the further deterioration of a student's reading self-concept and the ostracizing of that student by more able peers. When a few students in the class use adapted reading materials and the rest work with more challenging materials, the self-concept of the poorer reader can be damaged if the teacher does not plan carefully.

PAPERBACKS

Paperback books often form part of the developmental reading program in the middle grades and in high school. In some school systems, they are treated as consumable materials. A fresh supply is provided to classrooms for classroom libraries each year. Students are encouraged to pick out their favorites, swap with one another, and tell others which books they find particularly interesting. Paperback programs cannot substitute for a sound skill-oriented developmental reading program, even at the middle grades, but they can motivate students at the secondary level to practice their reading skills and acquire the reading habit.

READING MACHINES

A final kind of supplement for the reading program has received its impetus from the pervasive technological revolution. *Reading machines* are mechanical devices designed to increase reading

speed, eye span, and word recognition. Many schools have purchased them, particularly to use in remedial reading instruction
for older students. Unfortunately technology is not going to salvage the poor reader. Such machines, in fact, may be harmful if
they consume time that might be spent more profitably in carefully tailored instruction by a sympathetic and skillful teacher.

SKILL DEVELOPMENT SYSTEMS

A *skill development system* is a carefully sequenced and hierarchical series of behavioral objectives strands that break the acts of
decoding, comprehension, and study down into more manageable instructional sequences. Such systems are the products of
the germinal work on individualized, continuous progress instruction by Gagne (1965), Bloom, Hastings, and Madaus (1971),
and Popham (1971). They usually include a series of pre- and
posttests, prescriptive assignments, and management forms and
records so that the progress of each student can be charted.
Chapter 3 includes a comprehensive description of these systems.

Selecting reading materials

Selecting materials for a reading program often is not a very systematic process. Busy teachers do not have the time to think systematically about the criteria or strategies for selecting materials.
More often than not, materials are purchased as the result of a
persuasive textbook salesperson, the recommendation of another
teacher, a colorful brochure, or a cursory examination of the material.

If reading materials are to be carefully and judiciously selected, some attention must be given to the screening and selection process. First, a school or school system should have a carefully enumerated selection policy and process in which the
following issues must be considered:

1. What roles will various professional staff, parents, and students play in the selection process?
2. Who will make the ultimate decision?
3. What is the relationship of materials selection to the other
   decisions required for program change—for example, philosophy development, curriculum development, testing and

105

evaluation development, professional staff training, cost effectiveness of the program?

4. How long will materials be retained once they are selected?
5. What shall reading materials be evaluated for (that is, what are the criteria against which materials will be examined)?
6. What is the selection process and time frame?
7. How will the materials that are to be examined be identified and secured?

Let's reflect in more detail on some of the issues of reading materials selection.

A PRODUCT SEARCH

It is not possible for a teacher or a group of teachers to be aware of all possible materials that might meet their needs. Typically teachers will build a list from materials they have been exposed to. Sometimes they will work with a reading specialist, although he or she may not be aware of everything that is available either. Furthermore, the teachers or specialist may forget about materials currently in production and not yet distributed.

A product search is a far more professional way to approach the process of determining what is available and what will be identified for review. The search should begin with a set of specifications for the kind of material being sought. Using the specifications, a teacher or materials committee can use any or all of the following strategies to uncover the widest possible range of appropriate materials.

1. Share your specifications list with your librarian and ask him or her to nominate any materials that meet the specifications.
2. Send letters with the enclosed specifications sheet to all the major materials companies and ask them to nominate any materials they market that fit.
3. Refer to materials reviews in recent reading and language arts professional journals and check the review against your specifications sheet.
4. Study instructional materials catalogs with your specifications close by to determine if any materials listed fit your needs.
5. Send your tentative list or identified materials and your specifications sheet to an instructional materials reference librarian (most schools of education have such a center) for review and additions.

6. Send your tentative list of identified materials and your specification sheet to an independent reading specialist for review and additions.

Obviously it is not necessary to use all of these strategies each time you wish to select a piece of material. However, the more far-reaching the decision (such as the purchase of a developmental reading program in the middle grades for an entire school or school system), the more carefully the product search should be conducted.

SCREENING AVAILABLE MATERIALS

The list of reading materials that meet the initial specifications may be quite lengthy; thus it will not be possible to do an in-depth evaluation of each piece of material on the list. An initial screening, required to eliminate from consideration materials that need not be studied in depth, might be conducted at an instructional materials preview library (most universities and larger school systems have such libraries) using three or four key criteria. These criteria will depend on the situation but might include compatibility with the school's reading philosophy, compatibility with the school's curriculum, and cost.

If, for example, your philosophy for initial reading skill acquisition is based on a total language approach, you may decide to eliminate immediately any programs that begin reading instruction with a heavy emphasis on sound/letter relationships. If your curriculum purports to individualize reading instruction in junior high school, you will probably wish to eliminate any material that does not include that kind of instruction. Finally, if your budget will not allow materials costing more than five dollars per child, it is probably futile to examine materials costing ten dollars per child.

EVALUATING READING MATERIALS

If reading materials are to be evaluated in a manner that is fair and objective, considerable time and attention must be devoted to the process to compare the characteristics and qualities of the competing materials. We will list eight areas of concern; of course, there may be others too.

Reading philosophy

As we suggested in chapter 2, all strategies and practices in reading instruction are based on some theory, and there are many competing theories. Moreover, each of us has our own theory (philosophical belief system) about how reading is best learned. So too does each piece or set of reading instruction materials.

It is critical to articulate these theories before you search for reading materials. Then, as you work, you can test your philosophy against that implied or stated for the materials you are evaluating. A final word of caution is in order: Do not look only at the author's statement of reading philosophy in the preface or teacher's manual. Examine the materials carefully to be sure they remain consistent with your stated philosophy throughout.

Reading curriculum

Reading is a complex, multifaceted skill. Educators differ in their opinions of the importance of various facets. For some, reading instruction is confined to initial decoding skills and simple comprehension skills. Others include critical thinking through reading, creative reading, recreational reading, and research or study skills as integral components of reading instruction. Each component can also be further broken down into sets of concrete skills that help to define comprehension or critical reading or study skills. These decisions ultimately make up the reading curriculum, that is, the plan for what instruction in reading is to occur. It is vital that teachers define their curriculum before they begin a search for materials. Then they can test their ideas against the curriculum proposed through the classroom materials. Without a reasonable match, the materials will not help students reach the goals set for the reading program.

Readability of materials

Every written message, including materials for reading instruction, is prepared for a specific audience. We assume that an attempt has been made to match the difficulty of that message (its vocabulary, sentence structure, and logic development) with the perceived skills of the intended audience. If, for example, a supplementary reader has been designed for the sixth grade, it should be readable by the average sixth grader. Some educators will even assume that most sixth graders can read the material. These conclusions may be incorrect, however. No teacher or administrator should assume that materials they are evaluating are readable by the students for whom they are intended. Always check the readability of the material by using a readability formula or by informally using a sampling of the materials with a wide range of students in a classroom setting.

Concept load

Although related to readability, the concept load of a written message is a distinctly different issue. All writers make certain assumptions about previous knowledge (basic facts and concepts) that the reader will possess in order to read the message successfully.

Concepts embedded in a message and not adequately explained are particularly suspect in preventing comprehension. These broad or abstract images for complex ideas or sets of related experiences are an effective shorthand for human communication. However, when misused, they are a common source of miscommunication.

A common misuse of concepts is to load them into a message without adequate explanatory material. If the reader's images for the concepts being used do not adequately match those of the writer, the reader may not be able to read the material at all or may misunderstand what he or she does read. This can happen in materials designed for reading instruction as easily as it can in materials designed for any other curriculum area.

Cultural and ethnic balance

The treatment of women and racial and ethnic minorities in instructional materials has come under critical scrutiny. Often these materials support stereotypic beliefs regarding the human characteristics or cultural roles of women, blacks, Chicanos, native Americans, and others. These images are unjust to persons who identify with these groups and unfair to all students who will unwittingly be exposed to them. An evaluation of materials for reading instruction must therefore include a careful examination of the cultural and ethnic balance of the material. Educators conducting such an evaluation may want to employ a multi-ethnic specialist to help, because many people, whatever their background, may miss subtle examples of stereotyping or cultural prejudice that their culture has made them insensitive to.

Organization and format

Most teachers and administrators devote considerable attention to examining the organization and format. They look at the breakdown into units or chapters, the use of pictures, captions, highlighting, and subtitles, the presence of color, the use of different shapes and sizes of types, the functional use of white space, and the availability of teacher's manuals and other supplementing material.

They sometimes devote less attention to the use and appropriateness of introductory or summary questions, the effectiveness of paragraphing, the appropriate use of detail, chronological sequence, or logical development (for example, concrete to abstract), or the instructional exercises or activities included in the material.

Durability

Instructional materials are packaged in a variety of ways. Covers can be hard or soft, bindings sewn or stapled, paper of varying weight and quality. Certainly the durability must meet the expectations set for the instructional material.

Cost

Cost is often one of the most important variables in a study of competing materials, yet it often receives little systematic attention. Attention should not only be given to the direct cost of the materials but also to the cost of supplementary materials (multimedia materials, games, kits, and other printed materials) necessary for the success of the program. Hidden costs—such as the replacement cost for consumable components or the costs of inservice training for teachers who will use the material—must also be considered.

A scale may help teachers judge each piece of material against each criterion characteristic. It could run from *weak* to *strong,* or perhaps from *omitted* to *consistent.*

Figure 5.6, developed by elementary teachers and principals in one school system, provides an example of one such materials evaluation plan.[1] Its purpose was to help teachers select developmental reading materials to support a kindergarten through grade 8 reading curriculum. These teachers were particularly interested in skill acquisition, management, and balance and content. The forms provide a brief description of the material, as well as a graph for summarizing numerically the results obtained on subsequent pages.

---

[1] These materials are displayed by the courtesy of the Madison, Wisconsin, Public Schools.

Figure 5.6 **A materials evaluation plan prepared by the East Area Reading Leadership Team, Madison, Wisconsin, Public Schools (1976)**

East Area—Analysis of reading material

Direction Sheet

This instrument is to be used to analyze reading materials. It is divided into three major categories: SKILLS, MANAGEMENT and BALANCE. [See the next six pages.] The scale will point out strengths and weaknesses of any given set of reading materials. A summary of your analysis is located in graph form on page 112. . . . There is also a place on this page to specify all the components of a set of reading materials. If the set has several levels, you will need to use one copy of the scale for each level.

INSTRUCTIONS FOR USE OF THE RATING SCALE

Reading materials are to be rated on a scale from 0 to 5.

	seldom	occasionally	consistently	
(0	1	3	5	)

A box is also included for marking items that do not apply.

- If the item is represented but poor in quality, mark a low number on the rating scale.
- If the item is not represented and you feel it should be, mark a 0.
- If you do not expect the item to be in the materials, check the "Does not apply" box.
- The comment space is there for you to use if you wish to make notes.

INSTRUCTIONS FOR USE OF THE SUMMARY GRAPH

You will need to find the average of each sub-category by adding the score of each item and dividing by the number of items scored *only*. This average is then recorded on the summary graph, as the sample indicates. Items that "do not apply" are not averaged in.

INSTRUCTIONS FOR USE OF THE COMPOSITE GRAPH

Transfer information from the summary graph to the composite of reading materials. This composite will show a total reading program for a grade level. To see a total school program you will need to look at K–5th grade composites. List materials as the composite sample indicates. Instead of listing each book, average the summary graphs for a grade level of books within a series.

Source: East Area Reading Leadership Team, Madison, Wisconsin, Public Schools.

Figure 5.6 **A materials evaluation plan** (cont.)

EAST AREA – ANALYSIS OF READING MATERIAL

Publisher	Copyright
Title	Level

Description:

Materials Include:

- [ ] Activity Cards
- [ ] Dittos
- [ ] Games
- [ ] Manipulatives
- [ ] Paperbacks
- [ ] Progress Charts
- [ ] Story Cards
- [ ] Study Cards
- [ ] Tapes
- [ ] Teachers Guide
- [ ] Tests
- [ ] Textbooks
- [ ] Visual Aids
- [ ] Word Cards
- [ ] Workbooks

Others (specify) ....

SUMMARY GRAPH

RATING SCALE
(Average Scores)

5.0—
4.5—
4.0—
3.5—
3.0—
2.5—
2.0—
1.5—
1.0—
.5—
0—

Word Attack
Vocabulary
Comprehension
Study Skills
Teacher Edition
Pupil Text-Content
Pupil Material-Text Format
Workbook-Content
Workbook-Format
Tests-Content
Tests-Format
Supplementary
Lang. Arts
Self and Others

SKILLS

MANAGEMENT

BALANCE

Figure 5.6 **A materials evaluation plan** (cont.)

EAST AREA-ANALYSIS OF READING MATERIAL
Rating Scale

Instructions for rating:

☐   0 — 1   3 — 5
Does not apply Omitted Seldom Occasionally Consistently

INSTRUCTIONS: Circle ONLY ONE rating for each category.

SKILLS		
1.0 Word Attack	Rating	Comments
1.1 Does the program put emphasis on the following learning strategies?	☐ Does not apply	
1.11 Sight	☐ 0 1 2 3 4 5	
1.12 Phonetic	☐ 0 1 2 3 4 5	
1.13 Structural Analysis	☐ 0 1 2 3 4 5	Avg.
1.14 Contextual	☐ 0 1 2 3 4 5	
1.14 Picture	☐ 0 1 2 3 4 5	
2.0 Vocabulary	☐ Does not apply	
2.1 Is the rate of introduction appropriate for students to learn?	☐ 0 1 2 3 4 5	
2.2 Does the material provide opportunities for student to apply knowledge of new words in other modes of communication?	☐ 0 1 2 3 4 5	
2.3 Does the material encourage the development of student independence in determining word meaning?		
figurative-literal	☐ 0 1 2 3 4 5	
context clues	☐ 0 1 2 3 4 5	
dictionary	☐ 0 1 2 3 4 5	Avg.
history	☐ 0 1 2 3 4 5	
prefixes—suffixes	☐ 0 1 2 3 4 5	
3.0 Comprehension	☐ Does not apply	
3.1 How well do the questions/activities help students with literal comprehension?	☐ 0 1 2 3 4 5	
3.2 How well do the questions/activities help the students with inferential comprehension?	☐ 0 1 2 3 4 5	
3.3 How well do the questions/activities help the students with critical evaluation?	☐ 0 1 2 3 4 5	
3.4 How well do the questions/activities stimulate creative thinking?	☐ 0 1 2 3 4 5	Avg.
4.0 Study Skills - Do the materials help the student develop these skills?	☐ Does not apply	
4.1 Following oral directions	☐ 0 1 2 3 4 5	
4.2 Following written directions	☐ 0 1 2 3 4 5	
4.3 Use of:		
Dictionary	☐ 0 1 2 3 4 5	
Encyclopedia	☐ 0 1 2 3 4 5	
Maps, tables, graphs	☐ 0 1 2 3 4 5	
Card catalog	☐ 0 1 2 3 4 5	
Other IMC resources	☐ 0 1 2 3 4 5	
4.4 Use of:		
Table of contents	☐ 0 1 2 3 4 5	
Index	☐ 0 1 2 3 4 5	
Glossary	☐ 0 1 2 3 4 5	
Headings	☐ 0 1 2 3 4 5	
4.5 Use of:		
Skimming and scanning	☐ 0 1 2 3 4 5	
S.Q. 3R Survey, Question, Read, Recite, Review)	☐ 0 1 2 3 4 5	
Outlining	☐ 0 1 2 3 4 5	
Footnotes	☐ 0 1 2 3 4 5	Avg.
A Bibliography	☐ 0 1 2 3 4 5	

Figure 5.6 **A materials evaluation plan** (cont.)

Rating Scale

Instructions for rating:

☐   0 – 1   3   –   5
Does not apply   Omitted   Seldom   Occasionally   Consistently

INSTRUCTIONS: Circle ONLY ONE
rating for each category.

MANAGEMENT		
1.0 Teacher Edition - Content	Rating	Comments
1.1 Do the lesson plans in teacher edition include the following: 1.11 Background information	☐ Does not apply	
1.12 Objectives of story	☐ 0 1 2 3 4 5	
1.13 List of needed supplementary materials	☐ 0 1 2 3 4 5	
1.14 Synopsis	☐ 0 1 2 3 4 5	
1.15 Bibliography	☐ 0 1 2 3 4 5	
1.16 Directions for new vocabulary	☐ 0 1 2 3 4 5	
1.17 Suggestions for related activities	☐ 0 1 2 3 4 5	
Teacher Edition - Format		
1.2 The proximity of teachers guide to story is: (check one) ☐ separate ☐ same page ☐ end of story		
1.3 Is the plan concise?	☐ 0 1 2 3 4 5	
1.4 Rate the physical construction Durability Binding Size Illustrations Type	☐ 0 1 2 3 4 5 Avg.	
2.0 Pupil Materials - Text - Content	☐ Does not apply	
2.1 Do the activities reinforce the lesson?	☐ 0 1 2 3 4 5	
2.2 Do the activities involve other communication modes? 2.21 Listening	☐ 0 1 2 3 4 5	
2.22 Viewing	☐ 0 1 2 3 4 5	
2.23 Writing	☐ 0 1 2 3 4 5	
2.24 Speaking (drama, puppetry, etc.)	☐ 0 1 2 3 4 5	
2.25 Designing (films, illustrating, posters, etc.)	☐ 0 1 2 3 4 5	
2.3 Do the activities encourage creative construction?	☐ 0 1 2 3 4 5	
2.4 Are the stories of high interest?	☐ 0 1 2 3 4 5	
2.5 Does it provide the student with a wide range of reading experiences?	☐ 0 1 2 3 4 5	
2.6 Do the stories have good literary quality? Distinctive literary style Sound characterization Dialogue that flows naturally	☐ 0 1 2 3 4 5 Avg.	
3.0 Pupil Materials - Text Format	☐ Does not apply	
3.1 Are illustrations appropriate? 3.11 Are they graphically clear?	☐ 0 1 2 3 4 5	
3.12 Are they within the experiential level of the children?	☐ 0 1 2 3 4 5	
3.2 Is the print appropriate for the student? 3.21 Size - layout - color	☐ 0 1 2 3 4 5	
3.22 Word spacing	☐ 0 1 2 3 4 5	
3.3 Are there annotations to aid students?	☐ 0 1 2 3 4 5	
3.4 Rate the physical construction Durability Binding Size Illustrations Type	☐ 0 1 2 3 4 5	

Figure 5.6 **A materials evaluation plan** (cont.)

MANAGEMENT		
	Rating	**Comments**
3.5 Is the sentence length appropriate	☐ 0 1 2 3 4 5	
3.6 Do the stories vary in length?	☐ 0 1 2 3 4 5	
3.7 Is there a glossary?	☐ 0 1 2 3 4 5	
3.8 Is there a pronunciation key?	☐ 0 1 2 3 4 5	Avg.
3.9 Is there a table of contents?	☐ 0 1 2 3 4 5	
4.0 **Workbook - Content**	☐ Does not apply	
4.1 Do the activities reinforce the lesson?	☐ 0 1 2 3 4 5	
4.2 Do the activities involve other communication modes?	☐ 0 1 2 3 4 5	
4.3 Do the activities encourage construction?	☐ 0 1 2 3 4 5	
4.4 How well do the questions cover these levels? 4.41 Literal	☐ 0 1 2 3 4 5	
4.42 Inferential	☐ 0 1 2 3 4 5	
4.43 Critical	☐ 0 1 2 3 4 5	
4.44 Creative	☐ 0 1 2 3 4 5	
4.5 Does it provide skill evaluation?	☐ 0 1 2 3 4 5	
4.6 Are the directions clear: 4.61 for teacher?	☐ 0 1 2 3 4 5	Avg.
4.62 for student?	☐ 0 1 2 3 4 5	
5.0 **Workbook - Format**	☐ Does not apply	
5.1 Are illustrations appropriate?	☐ 0 1 2 3 4 5	
5.2 Is the format repeated and varied effectively?	☐ 0 1 2 3 4 5	
5.3 Is the number of pages per story appropriate?	☐ 0 1 2 3 4 5	
5.4 Workbook 5.41 Are they durable?	☐ 0 1 2 3 4 5	Avg.
5.42 Perforated?	Yes/No	
6.0 **Tests - Content**	☐ Does not apply	
6.1 Within the experiential level of the children?	☐ 0 1 2 3 4 5	
6.2 Are the directions clear?	☐ 0 1 2 3 4 5	
6.3 Does it test what was taught?	☐ 0 1 2 3 4 5	
6.4 Questions? 6.41 Literal	☐ 0 1 2 3 4 5	
6.42 Inferential	☐ 0 1 2 3 4 5	
6.43 Critical	☐ 0 1 2 3 4 5	
6.44 Creative	☐ 0 1 2 3 4 5	
6.5 Can it be used as feedback to: 6.51 Pupils	☐ 0 1 2 3 4 5	
6.52 Parents	☐ 0 1 2 3 4 5	Avg.
6.53 Teachers	☐ 0 1 2 3 4 5	
7.0 **Tests - Format**	☐ Does not apply	
7.1 Is the print suitable?	☐ 0 1 2 3 4 5	
7.2 Are illustrations correlated with text?	☐ 0 1 2 3 4 5	
7.3 Are illustrations graphically clear?	☐ 0 1 2 3 4 5	
7.4 Is the format consistent with previous pupil experience in text?	☐ 0 1 2 3 4 5	
7.5 Is there statistical information on reliability and validity?	☐ 0 1 2 3 4 5	Avg.
7.6 Is there a placement test available?	Yes/No	

Figure 5.6 **A materials evaluation plan** (cont.)

EAST AREA-ANALYSIS OF READING MATERIAL

Rating

Instructions for rating:

☐	0 – 1	3 – 5
Does not apply	Omitted Seldom	Occasionally Consistently

INSTRUCTIONS: Circle ONLY ONE
rating for each category.

MANAGEMENT

	Rating	Comments
8.0 **Supplementary Material-Content**	☐ Does not apply	
8.1 Are they an integral part of the reading program?	☐ 0 1 2 3 4 5	
8.2 Are they at an appropriate experiential level?	☐ 0 1 2 3 4 5	
8.3 Do games have repeated and varied use?	☐ 0 1 2 3 4 5	
8.4 Can the materials be used independently?	☐ 0 1 2 3 4 5	
8.5 Do the stories have good literary quality?		
8.51 Distinctive literary style	☐ 0 1 2 3 4 5	
8.52 Sound characterization	☐ 0 1 2 3 4 5 Avg.	
8.53 Dialogue that flows naturally	☐ 0 1 2 3 4 5	
9.0 **Supplementary Materials - Format**	☐ Does not apply	
9.1 Are the materials easily stored?	☐ 0 1 2 3 4 5 Avg.	
9.2 Are the materials durable?	☐ 0 1 2 3 4 5	

Figure 5.6 **A materials evaluation plan** (cont.)

EAST AREA- ANALYSIS OF READING MATERIAL

Rating Scale

☐	0	—	1	3	—	5
Does not apply	Omitted	Seldom		Occasionally		Consistently

INSTRUCTIONS: Circle ONLY ONE rating for each category.

BALANCE - CONTENT		

1.0 Language Arts	Rating	Comments
1.1 Is there a variety of learning modes? 1.11 Speaking (drama-puppetry-oral intrepretation)	☐ Does not apply ☐ 0 1 2 3 4 5	
1.12 Listening (intrepretive, information gathering)	☐ 0 1 2 3 4 5	
1.13 Writing (creative, functional, narrative)	☐ 0 1 2 3 4 5	
1.14 Viewing (intrepretive, information gathering)	☐ 0 1 2 3 4 5 Avg.	
1.15 Designing (films, illustrating posters)	☐ 0 1 2 3 4 5	
2.0 Self and Others-Do the materials: 2.1 Provide for self-awareness?	☐ Does not apply ☐ 0 1 2 3 4 5	
2.2 Provide for awareness of a variety of jobs?	☐ 0 1 2 3 4 5	
2.3 Provide for value clarification and decision making?	☐ 0 1 2 3 4 5	
2.4 Provide for awareness of variety of life styles?	☐ 0 1 2 3 4 5	
2.5 Avoid stereotypes?	☐ 0 1 2 3 4 5	
2.6 Give equal representation to females and minorities (physical, religious, racial) in varied life situations?	☐ 0 1 2 3 4 5	
2.7 Avoid one-sided cultural representation?	☐ 0 1 2 3 4 5	
2.8 Provide group interaction?	☐ 0 1 2 3 4 5 Avg.	
2.9 Treat people with dignity regardless of age or economic position?	☐ 0 1 2 3 4 5	

SUMMARY COMMENTS

This model is just an example. Each teacher or teacher committee charged with evaluating materials must design a plan that is consistent with the needs and issues they have identified.

Estimating the readability of materials

A discussion of reading literacy—the ability to extract new information from a written message—normally focuses on the reader. But literacy is message specific. A reader may be literate with respect to one message but not to another. Reader factors that contribute to the level of literacy include the power of the reader's decoding and comprehension skills, his or her previous experience with the subject matter contained in the message, and his or her attitude toward reading and the specific message to be read.

Conversely, educators can examine the literacy issue by focusing on the materials. Teachers can help a student reader to be literate with respect to a message about a particular subject by carefully choosing the message. And different messages about the same subject will vary in their difficulty as vocabulary, sentence structure, and concept load are varied. Moreover, it is possible to distinguish between levels of difficulty of reading materials and thus to estimate the relative readability of a piece of material. There are two basic approaches to making such estimates: trained prediction and measurement.

Trained prediction can occur either through judgment or through specially designed comprehension tests. Several researchers have demonstrated that, on the basis of a reading of the material, people can be trained to make fairly accurate and reliable judgments of the readability of a message for a particular reader or group of fairly homogeneous readers. (See Klare, 1963; Schwartz, Sparkman, and Deese, 1970; Coke, 1973; and Carver, 1974). Although Klare (1974–1975) notes that such an approach becomes laborious with full-length books, Porter and Popp (1973) have demonstrated that it is feasible to train raters to judge as many as eighty books. However, Klare points out that this training of such raters becomes impractical as the situation becomes more complex. "Judgments can clearly be useful; but as the task becomes more complex, questions of reliability and validity—to say nothing of major additions of time and effort—become more serious. There is sometimes a further question of scale: Where does a piece of writing fit on a reading grade or reading age continuum?" (p. 65). He might have added that training all classroom teachers and librarians to be expert raters is a serious in-service problem.

Because trained raters can make good judgments of the relative difficulty of materials does not mean that untrained teachers can. Chall and Feldman (1966) found that teachers varied considerably in their ability to select reading materials that were of a suitable level of difficulty for students they were teaching. Jorgenson (1975) more recently confirmed that "elementary school teachers vary widely in their ability to judge accurately the difficulty level of paragraphs from various grades, and that a common sense of 'grade level' does not exist" (p. 73). He also found that urban teachers tended to rate the same material as more difficult than suburban teachers did. Clearly the rating of materials for difficulty is not practical without considerable training.

An alternative approach to trained prediction is through the administration of specially designed comprehension tests. Although standards and approaches for the use of such tests of selected material have been developed (see Ekwall and Henry, 1968), until recently they have been too expensive to develop and validate and laborious to administer, score, and interpret. Bormuth (1969), however, has developed a test of situational literacy based on the application of the cloze procedure to targeted reading material. According to the procedure, a teacher who wishes to determine how readable a particular book is for one or more readers randomly selects three or four seventy- to one-hundred-word passages from the book and deletes every fifth word in each passage, beginning with the sixth through the tenth word. (This initial word is selected following the first five words so that the reader has an uninterrupted lead-in to the passage.) Each word deleted is replaced with a blank. The student takes the test by attempting to supply the word that was deleted. Teacher help with spelling is permitted. When only an exact replacement is scored as a correct answer, Bormuth found that 35 percent correct is a minimal threshold of literacy, below which the student will not be able to gain much, if any, information. As the score rises above 35 percent, the student demonstrates increasing literacy with the material. A score of about 54 percent, Bormuth has found, demonstrates maximum comfort and challenge from the material. As performance on the material rises much above 54 percent, that material may become too easy.

Although fairly easy to develop and administer, this comprehension test of material readability is laborious to score. Clearly, some other alternative to trained prediction is required. That basic alternative is measurement through readability formulas.

Modern readability formulas began with the work in the late 1930s of Irving Lorge. Basically, these formulas provide quantitative estimates of the relative difficulty of written messages. Their intent is to estimate the probable success that a reader will have with a piece of material without requiring the reader to take a comprehension test based on the materials.

Klare (1963 and 1974–1975) has provided both a developmental history and a current review of modern readability formulas. We will not duplicate his effort here, but we will note that the Flesch, Dale-Chall, Fog, and Spache formulas are among the more traditional and accepted readability measurement tools. Recently, other researchers with strong linguistic backgrounds have developed formulas based on the cloze procedure and a fairly complex analysis of the linguistic, semantic, and rhetorical characteristics of written messages. Many of these formulas show a high positive correlation with the predictor variable (comprehension test score based on the same material), an improvement on older, more popular formulas. (Klare completely reviews both the traditional formulas and the newer developments.)

Although these formulas, particularly the more recent ones, are useful tools, they should not be used indiscriminately or without careful and cautious interpretation. For example, in the average seventh-grade classroom, the reading abilities of students may range from first grade to the equivalent of the second year in college. To select a book that grades out by formula at the seventh-grade level may be suitable for only a relatively small percentage of the students in the class. Also, a highly motivated student will often read material that grades out far higher than would seem reasonable for that student. Readability formulas are only gross predictors of the probability that a given student will be successful with a particular written message.

Biases in reading materials

As we noted earlier, one of the persistent concerns facing teachers is the presence of cultural and ethnic stereotyping and biasing in the materials they use. Many instructional materials, including materials for reading instruction, are biased against women, minority groups, and the socioeconomically poor. (Weitzman and Rizzo [1974] and Zimet [1972] review the research demonstrating such biasing rather conclusively.)

Although recent instructional materials show some progress in the attempt to provide a balanced picture of women, blacks, native Americans, Latinos, Asians, and other racial, ethnic, and social minorities, older material still in use is rampant with such stereotyping and biasing. Moreover, some of the newer material remedies one abuse, only to create another. Thus, teachers cannot assume that all recent material is fair in its portrayal of people. Clearly, teachers must be trained to analyze materials to be used in the classroom for two reasons. First, an analysis will promote the purchase of materials that show the least evidence of stereotyping or biasing. Second, it will allow the teacher to compensate for the inadequacies of existing materials by supplementing with other materials or by pointing out the stereotypes and biases at every opportunity and suggesting an alternative image or interpretation.

Detecting social or cultural stereotypes or biases requires more than good intentions. Products of white middle-class culture have been socialized to many of the ethnic and cultural injustices and thus completely overlook them. Unless educators are helped to break through their cultural shell by someone with alternative values and perceptions, they cannot by themselves detect the undesirable excesses. Some school systems have already begun in-service programs for teachers and administrators to sensitize them and equip them with the necessary tools to analyze instructional materials critically. The following criteria by Rosenberg (1973) for evaluating the treatment of minority groups and women in instructional materials are instructive to teachers or administrators attempting such an analysis:

Does this textbook or learning material in both its textual content and illustrations:

Yes   No

____ ____ 1. Evidence on the part of writers, artists, and editors a sensitivity to prejudice, to stereotypes, to the use of material which would be offensive to women or to any minority group?

____ ____ 2. Suggest, by omission or commission, or by overemphasis or underemphasis, that any sexual, racial, religious or ethnic segment of our population is more or less worthy, more or less capable, more or less important in the mainstream of American life?

____ ____ 3. Utilize numerous opportunities for full, fair, accurate, and balanced treatment of women and minority groups?

____ ____ 4. Provide abundant recognition for women and minority groups by placing them frequently in positions of leadership and centrality?

Yes   No

_____ _____ 5. Depict both male and female adult members of minority groups in situations which exhibit them as fine and worthy models to emulate?

_____ _____ 6. Present many instances of fully integrated human groupings and settings to indicate equal status and nonsegregated social relationships?

_____ _____ 7. Make clearly apparent the group representation of individuals—Caucasian, Afro-American, Indian, Chinese, Mexican American, etc.—and not seek to avoid identification by such means as smudging some color over Caucasian facial features?

_____ _____ 8. Give comprehensive, broadly ranging, and well-planned representation to women and minority groups—in art and science, in history and mathematics and literature, and in all other areas of life and culture?

_____ _____ 9. Delineate life in contemporary urban environments as well as in rural or suburban environments, so that today's city children can also find significant identification for themselves, their problems and challenges, and their potential for life, liberty, and the pursuit of happiness?

_____ _____ 10. Portray sexual, racial, religious, and ethnic groups in our society in such a way as to build positive images—mutual understanding and respect, full and unqualified acceptance, and commitment to ensure equal opportunity for all?

_____ _____ 11. Present social group differences in ways that will cause students to look upon the multi-cultural character of our nation as a value which we must esteem and treasure?

_____ _____ 12. Assist students to recognize clearly the basic similarities among all members of the human race, and the uniqueness of every single individual?

_____ _____ 13. Teach the great lesson that we must accept each other on the basis of individual worth, regardless of sex or race or religion or socioeconomic background?

_____ _____ 14. Help students appreciate the many important contributions to our civilization made by members of the various human groups, emphasizing that every human group has its list of achievers, thinkers, writers, artists, scientists, builders, and political leaders?

____ ____ 15. Supply an accurate and sound balance in the matter of historical perspective, making it perfectly clear that all racial and religious and ethnic groups have mixed heritages, which can well serve as sources of both group pride and group humility?

____ ____ 16. Clarify the true historical forces and conditions which in the past have operated to the disadvantage of women and minority groups?

____ ____ 17. Clarify the true contemporary forces and conditions which at present operate to the disadvantage of women and minority groups?

____ ____ 18. Analyze intergroup tension and conflict fairly, frankly, objectively, and with emphasis upon resolving our social problems in a spirit of fully implementing democratic values and goals in order to achieve the American dream for all Americans?

____ ____ 19. Seek to motivate students to examine their own attitudes and behaviors, and to comprehend their own duties and responsibilities as citizens in a pluralistic democracy—to demand freedom and justice and equal opportunity for every individual and for every group?

____ ____ 20. Help minority group (as well as majority group) students to identify more fully with the educational process by providing textual content and illustrations which give students many opportunities for building a more positive self-image, pride in their group, knowledge consistent with their experience; in sum, learning material which offers students meaningful and relevant learning worthy of their best efforts and energies?

Summary

Selecting materials for reading instruction is as important as many other decisions made about reading instruction. Among

123

many practitioners, a mystique has existed toward reading materials. We have attempted in this chapter to shatter that mystique. The decisions regarding materials must be made in the context of students, the reading curriculum, the skills and interests of the teaching staff, and the prevalent patterns of instructional organization. Such decisions are most effectively made at the individual school.

There are many kinds of materials and equipment to support reading programs and more are becoming available. Others, such as basal readers, have "changed" considerably in the past decade. An analysis of the kinds of materials currently available is provided in this chapter.

Finally, we have suggested a rational process for selecting reading materials. It begins with a product search, proceeds to the screening of available materials, and finally reaches the in-depth evaluation of promising materials. Materials evaluation should include an examination of the reading philosophy behind the materials, the reading curriculum presented through the materials, the readability of the material, the concept load, the cultural and ethnic balance, the organization and format, the durability, and the cost. In the last two sections of the chapter, we provided additional attention to readability theories and formulas and to detecting biases in reading material.

Bibliography

Bloom, Benjamin J., Thomas Hastings; and George F. Madaus. *Handbook on Formative and Summative Evaluation of Student Learning.* New York: McGraw-Hill, 1971.

Bloomfield, Leonard. *Language.* New York: Holt, Rinehart & Winston, 1963.

Bormuth, John R. *Development of Readability Analyses.* Final Report, Project No. 7-0052, Bureau of Research, U.S. Office of Education, 1969.

Carver, Ronald P. *Improving Reading Comprehension: Measuring Readability.* Final Report, Contract No. N00014-C0240, Office of Naval Research. Silver Spring, Maryland: American Institute for Research, May 14, 1974.

Chall, Jean, and S. Feldman. "First Grade Reading: An Analysis of the Interactions of Professed Methods, Teacher Implementation and Child Background." *The Reading Teacher* 19 (1966): 569–575.

Coke, Esther V. "Readability and Its Effects on Reading Rate, Subjective Judgments of Comprehensibility and Comprehen-

sion." Paper presented at the annual meeting of the American
Educational Research Association, New Orleans, Louisiana, February 1973.

Early, Margaret. "Important Research in Reading and Writing." *Phi Delta Kappan* 57, no. 5 (January 1976): 298–301.

Ekwall, E. E., and I. B. Henry. "How to Find Books Children Can Read." *The Reading Teacher* 22 (1968): 230–232.

Gagne, Robert M. "The Analysis of Instructional Objectives for the Design of Instruction." In R. Glaser (ed.), *Teaching Machines and Programmed Learning*, vol. 2: *Data and Directions*. Washington, D.C.: National Education Association, 1965, pp. 21–65.

Heilman, Arthur W. *Principles and Practices of Teaching Reading.* Columbus, Ohio: Charles E. Merrill, 1972.

Hubbard, Elaine. "Materials Selection Processes: Why and How?" Paper presented at the annual convention of the International Reading Association, Anaheim, California, 1976.

Jorgenson, Gerald W. "An Analysis of Teacher Judgments of Reading Level." *American Educational Research Journal* 12, no. 1 (Winter 1975): pp. 67–75.

Klare, George R. *The Measurement of Readability.* Ames, Iowa: Iowa State University Press, 1963.

———. "Assessing Readability." *Reading Research Quarterly* 10, no. 1 (1974–1975): 62–102.

Popham, W. James. *Criterion-Referenced Measurement.* Englewood Cliffs, N.J.: Educational Technology Publications, 1971.

Porter, Douglas, and Helen M. Popp. "An Alternative to Readability Measures: Judging the Difficulty of Children's Trade Books." Paper presented at the annual meeting of the American Educational Research Association, New Orleans, Louisiana, February 1973.

Rosenberg, Max. "Evaluate Your Textbooks for Racism, Sexism." *Educational Leadership* 31, no. 2 (November 1973): 107–109.

Schwartz, Deborah, John P. Sparkman, and James Deese. "The Process of Understanding and Judgments of Comprehensibility." *Journal of Verbal Learning and Verbal Behavior* 9 (February 1970): 87–93.

Smith, Richard J., and Dale D. Johnson. *Teaching Children to Read.* Reading, Mass.: Addison-Wesley, 1976.

Weitzman, Lenore J., and Diane Rizzo. *Biased Textbooks: A Research Perspective.* Washington, D.C.: The National Foundation for the Improvement of Education, 1974.

Zimet, Sara Goodman (ed.). *What Children Read in School: Critical Analysis of Primary Reading Textbooks.* New York: Grune and Stratton, 1972.

Chapter 6 Environments for reading instruction: Elementary, middle, and high schools

It is probably a truism that any reading program, successful or otherwise, occurs against the framework of some instructional environment. The students, materials, teacher energy, space, and instructional time must be organized logically for classroom instruction to take place. Some organizational patterns will provide considerable stability and structure for both teachers and students; others will emphasize flexibility. Some stress the efficient use of time and resources, and others stress student-teacher interpersonal relationships and teacher understanding of student needs. Some motivate the student; others tend to motivate the teacher. All models, however, impose different kinds of demands on a variety of communication patterns involving students, teachers, and parents.

There is no perfect organizational environment for reading instruction. Reading instruction is a system composed of a variety of interrelated parts; the instructional organization must be compatible with other parts in the system. The teacher's skills and attitudes, the students' expectations, the curriculum, the available materials, and the expectations of parents must be compatible with the selected instructional organization. Probably the most anyone can say about a given organizational environment is that it is good only if it works in a particular setting, and it is working in that setting only to the extent that all children are learning to read effectively.

In this chapter, we will outline the more popular environments for instruction at the elementary, middle, and high school levels and critique each one in terms of its facility for effectively supporting reading instruction.

Elementary school

Teaching reading is a primary mission of the elementary school. Thus, historically, considerable effort has been made to explore a variety of educational environments at the elementary level that support reading instruction. Each model has strengths and weaknesses.

SELF-CONTAINED, GRADED CLASSROOM

In spite of attempts during the last decade to introduce alternative structures, the *self-contained, graded classroom* remains the most popular instructional environment in elementary schools across the country. The model places twenty-five to thirty students with a single teacher, who is responsible for most (or all) of the instruction of those children in the basic curriculum areas (although specialists may be brought in to teach in such areas as art, music, and physical education). The basic curriculum taught will include reading, language arts, science, social studies, and mathematics (Snyder, 1960).

The self-contained classroom can be an effective environment for reading instruction. It is particularly important that children receive instruction appropriate to their needs. Teachers in this setting who attempt to implement a single reading series for all students often find that it is difficult to select such a series. Although most modern reading series permit different students to work at different points in the program, a teacher will often discover that a particular series is inadequately paced for certain students or contains an approach to word attack skill or comprehension skill acquisition that is inappropriate to the needs of others. Teachers confronted with that dilemma have turned increasingly within the self-contained classroom to multiple grouping of students and the use of more than one basal series.

The tribasal approach to reading instruction typically divides the self-contained classroom into three learning groups: slow, average, and rapid learners. Each group is assigned a basal series that is tailored to its needs. Theoretically the tribasal approach allows a teacher to move individual students between groups as their skills progress so that their needs can better be met in another group. However, these groupings can become a system of tracking with little movement of students between groups.

Advantages

The self-contained, graded classroom is generally thought to have the following advantages for reading instruction: First, children are supported in a secure, structured learning environment where they sense some logical order and sequence to the reading program. Second, because the classroom teacher is responsible

127

for most curriculum areas, it is relatively easy for that person to integrate both reading instruction and reinforcement into other curriculum areas. Third, because a strong child-centered relationship is fostered in the self-contained classroom, the teacher gains an in-depth knowledge of each student's reading needs. Fourth, the student senses warmth and community in his or her relationship with other students and with the teacher. Fifth, the fact that the self-contained classroom teacher knows the student well also contributes to the strength of the parent-teacher relationship. Because the parent has only one teacher to relate to for his or her child, there is a greater potential that the parent will work cooperatively with the teacher to support that student's reading program.

Disadvantages

The self-contained classroom also presents some disadvantages. First, a student who is assigned to a teacher inadequately or inappropriately trained in elementary reading instruction may be set back. Second, because the class is organized heterogeneously, the teacher may tend to teach to the average students in the class, completely boring gifted and accelerated students and bewildering slower-learning students with special educational needs. Third, the teacher may not communicate with other teachers in the school building. Such isolation can do much to fragment reading instruction within a grade and between grade levels.

JOPLIN PLAN

A variety of approaches have been utilized to reduce the strains placed on the classroom teacher by the heterogeneity of students in the self-contained classroom. Some schools have tried the *Joplin plan* or a modified Joplin plan. The Joplin plan reduces heterogeneity by homogeneously grouping students across grade levels for purposes of reading instruction only (Smith and Barrett, 1974). Thus, students who have identified needs for initial skill building in phonics might be grouped into the same class for reading instruction, irrespective of whether they are in grade 1, 2, or 3. For other instruction, they return to their heterogeneously grouped, self-contained classroom. The modified Joplin plan provides the same grouping potential within individual grade levels and is more likely to be utilized in a larger elementary school where each grade has several classroom sections.

Advantages

The Joplin or modified Joplin plan has the following advantages. First, homogeneous grouping into instructional units makes more efficient use of teachers' time for both planning and instruction because the teacher will not have to prepare for as wide a diversity of student needs. Second, if homogeneous grouping of students' needs has occurred, there is an increased likelihood that instruction is more appropriate to the needs of individual students. Third, the creation of reading sections by homogeneous grouping also allows teachers to be assigned to specific student groups where they (the teachers) are professionally strong.

Disadvantages

There are also disadvantages. First, identifying a student with a particular skill level group may impair that student's self-concept. Moreover, some programs become so rigid that a student is likely to be tracked in the same group throughout his or her elementary school career. Second, the use of homogeneous grouping for reading instruction tends to isolate the reading curriculum from other curriculum areas, thus preventing the natural integration of reading instruction with other areas. Third, a student is likely to have a teacher other than his or her self-contained classroom teacher for reading instruction. Because that teacher has the child only for reading, he or she is less likely either to get to know the student well or to feel any kind of primary accountability for the student's progress. Fourth, the Joplin plan can result in poorer communication patterns with parents, most of whom are used to communicating with the self-contained classroom teacher. Fifth, teachers, often lulled into believing that all the students of their homogeneous classes have the same instructional needs, may emphasize large-group instruction. Homogeneous grouping, however, suppresses only some individual differences; it can never adequately suppress all of those variables. Sixth, in some elementary schools, a stigma will be attached to teaching reading groups that are perceived as doing poorly. Because the assignments with the most status for teachers will be working with students who are reading well, often the experienced teacher with the best professional skills will be assigned to the reading group that perhaps is the easiest to teach; the new, inexperienced teacher must struggle along with students who are having difficulty learning to read.

129

DEPARTMENTALIZED

In a *departmentalized environment,* teachers specialize in one or
two curriculum areas which they teach to several sections of students. Most commonly, the students move back and forth among
the rooms of the teachers, although teachers can instead move
among the rooms of students. Departmentalization is quite rare
in kindergarten through grade 3. It is, however, found occasionally at grade 4 and above.

Within the departmentalized environment, reading is organized into a class taught by a teacher who specializes in reading
and who often has received extra training in the area. Homogeneous grouping is an additional twist that can be added to departmentalization. Under this arrangement, poorer readers work
with the reading specialist at the same time, as do average
readers and accelerated readers.

Advantages

The following are considered advantages of departmentalization.
First, departmentalization ensures that reading is taught, inas-
much as a teacher assigned that responsibility is specializing in
it. Second, because the teacher is working in an area of interest
and strength, the reading curriculum is more likely to be strong
and effective. Third, departmentalization, by allowing teachers to
specialize, makes more efficient use of a teacher's time and
talent.

Disadvantages

Balancing the advantages are a number of serious disadvantages.
First, the segregation of the instructional program may result in
little integration of reading into other curriculum areas, such as
science and social studies. Second, a teacher sees a child only an
hour or two a day and is less likely to get to know the child well
or to feel any responsibility for participating in the child's total
development. Third, departmentalization results in less effective
parent-teacher communication because the parent must interact
with several classroom teachers. Fourth, the individual student
feels less sense of community or group identity. Moreover, he or
she is less likely to perceive that there is an adult friend within
the school to whom he or she can go with reading problems.
Fifth, departmentalization and the specialization that it suggests
does not foster communication among staff members. Because

each teacher has become a specialist in one area, there is relatively little for elementary teachers to communicate about.

TEAM TEACHING

There are so many variations of *team teaching* that it is perhaps
inappropriate to think of it as a discrete organizational pattern in
the elementary school. When some teachers talk of team teaching, they really mean *turn teaching* or *turn planning*. Under a turn
teaching arrangement, one teacher will teach reading today, and
the next teacher teaches it tomorrow. A similar arrangement can
be applied to planning: "I'll plan the science unit this week; you
plan it next week."

Team teaching can be several teachers working simultaneously
in a classroom with a group of students. Perhaps a more sophisticated extension of this concept occurs when teachers team with
a variety of other personnel, including teacher aides and parent
volunteers.

It is difficult to assess the impact of team teaching of reading
instruction, since the term "team teaching" in the elementary
school makes no assumptions about how reading instruction is
organized. Moreover, the advantages and disadvantages of team
teaching are difficult to assess because of the many variations of
it used.

Advantages

Well-implemented team teaching should have a couple of advantages. First, the presence of other instructional persons in a
classroom for each student to interact with as reading instruction
is occurring should mean additional one-on-one instructional
minutes for each child and thus a richer reading program. Second, an appropriately developed team teaching structure can
maintain a sense of student community. That community,
though larger than the one to 30 normally encountered in the
self-contained classroom, can be maintained so that students
sense the security and structure attributed to the self-contained
classroom.

Disadvantages

There are also disadvantages to team teaching, particularly when
it is not effectively implemented: the organizational patterns are

normally more complex and confusing, particularly to young children, and there is a tendency for team teaching to stimulate specialization as different members of the team assume differentiated responsibilities for certain areas of the curriculum. This results in less integration of reading and other curriculum areas.

NONGRADED OR MULTIGRADED EDUCATION

The early one-room schoolhouse was the first experiment with *multigraded education.* Since one teacher would teach every grade from first through eighth, that teacher had to utilize a variety of approaches, including individualized instruction, small functional grouping and regrouping of students, and peer teaching. Often grades became blurred and students did not even know precisely what grade they were in, although they might know how many years they had been in school.

During the 1960s and 1970s, nongraded and multigraded organizations have reemerged and gained some popularity in elementary schools. The approaches have been brought about by combining team teaching and a more functional grouping and regrouping of students. The multiunit school developed by the Wisconsin Research and Development Center for Cognitive Learning represents an evolution of earlier nongraded concepts (Klausmeier et al., 1971). As the diagram in figure 6.1 suggests, a multiunit school may organize student groups around three or four units. Typically, these student groups are developed by a broad age grouping of students. It can also be done on the basis of the functional acquisition of skills (such as an initial skills unit, an intermediate skills unit, and an advanced skills unit). Each unit of 100 to 150 students is likely to be managed instructionally by a team that includes a unit leader, two or three staff teachers, a first-year teacher or teacher resident, a teacher aide, an instructional secretary, and an intern.

Advantages

There are several advantages to the nongraded or multigraded approach to reading instruction. First, students may forget about the graded system and their place in it. Much of the stigma attached to grade retention may also be lost. Second, nongraded and multigraded organizations also tend to increase the probability that teachers will individualize reading instruction. Third, teacher professional motivation and growth appears to be facilitated by interaction with peers. Fourth, making instructional decisions about the reading program in a team setting often results in a stronger program.

Figure 6.1 **An organizational chart of a multiunit school**

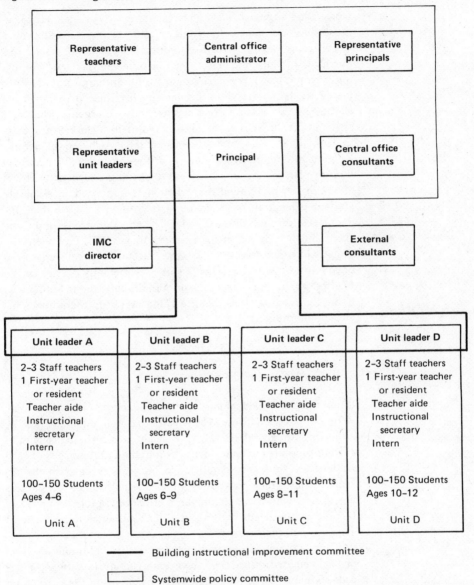

Source: Redrawn from Herbert J. Klausmeier, Mary R. Quilling, Juanita S. Sorenson, Russell S. Way, and George R. Glasrud, *Individually Guided Education and the Multiunit Elementary School* (Madison, Wisc.: Department of Research & Development, Madison Public Schools, 1971), p. 21.

Disadvantages

Nongraded approaches also have some disadvantages. First, because there are more adults and children to interact with and a looser, more flexible structure to attempt to relate to, many elementary students find these organizations complex and confusing. Second, teachers entering into a multiunit approach may not be adequately trained to implement it. They may not have learned how to relate to one another, how to organize time and space in a team setting, or how to maintain a close, warm relationship with individual students. Often, teachers are so busy keeping the organization going that they do not have adequate time to plan for the improvement of reading instruction. Third, although the nongraded organization is supposed to eliminate student perception of gradedness, it is often a facade that students see through immediately. Fourth, the presence in the classroom setting of many teachers makes it difficult for the parents to communicate with those teachers and feel some sense of community with the school. This is particularly critical for the reading program, because it is important that parents reinforce at home the reading skills that are being taught in the school's instructional program.

INDIVIDUALIZED INSTRUCTION

If there is one universal maxim that has emerged from over forty years of educational research, it is that no two students are alike either cognitively, affectively, physically, or psychologically. The current pressures to tailor instruction to the unique needs of each student are thus considerable. No one can argue with the research from which the notion of individual human differences emerges or with the logic that an instructional program uniquely tailored to the needs of the individual learner is more likely to succeed with that learner.

Thus, a variety of instructional approaches, all under the label of *individualized instruction,* have emerged during the past decade. Some of these programs begin by dividing the curriculum into a sequence of skills or bits of knowledge that are to be learned. Students move through the program at an individual rate, utilizing materials and such strategies as small groups and student learning guides.

Individually Guided Education (IGE) is representative of this approach to individualized instruction, according to Klausmeier et al. (1971):

IGE is a comprehensive system of education and instruction designed to produce higher educational achievements through providing well for differences among students in rate of learning, learning style, and other characteristics. Much instruction in the IGE system takes the form of a teacher instructing small groups of 8–20. There is also considerable independent, self-directed study in the instructional materials center by children who can read reasonably well and who have already acquired fundamental concepts. Self-instructional materials or systems are simply one important kind of material or medium to be used in instructional programming for the student. (p. 17)

The IGE approach to reading is a comprehensive skills program that provides a scope and sequence statement in six different skill areas: word attack, comprehension, study, self-directed reading, interpretive reading, and creative reading. Each area and each skill, respectively, contain broad, general objectives and discrete, behavioral objectives. In addition to such an explicit curriculum scope and sequence, the program includes instructional resources, assessment materials, and individual skill development records. The program operates not as a total curriculum for reading instruction but as a management system. The system would not preclude using a variety of materials from different sources, nor would it preclude the integration of reading instruction into the other content areas.

Advantages

There are several advantages to individualized instruction. First, children learn at their own rates. Second, the program provides for a convergence of human and material resources on the individual child. A child is not tied to a certain basal series because everybody in the class must use it. Third, individualized reading instruction helps each child learn personal independence and responsibility.

Disadvantages

There are also criticisms. First, individualized reading instruction generates a lot of information on each child that the teacher must collect, organize, and assimilate. This puts a considerable information burden on the teacher. Second, this program assumes that reading can be segmented and that integrating experiences are not nearly as important as molecular, incremental learning experiences. Third, individualized instruction requires

135

teachers to assume new roles and acquire new skills. Many times
teachers are not provided with adequate training in making the
transition to this type of instruction. Fourth, individualized instruction tends to look like the factory model to many critics. It
fosters little genuine sense of community and sharing of reading
experiences among students.

OPEN CLASSROOMS

Instruction in the open classroom is characterized by a changed
physical classroom arrangement, a more equitable distribution of
decision-making power between teacher and students, a curriculum that's likely to be organized around the current interests of
students, and a warm, open, informal, interpersonal climate.

In the typical open classroom, different students work on different learning tasks at the same time. The students with guidance from the classroom teacher, generally decide what they want
to work on and when they want to do it.

A variety of furniture—including tables, sofas, high-rise study
carrels, rugs, and other informal furniture—designed to make
the classroom less institutional and more of a unique learning
center is used. Though reading, arithmetic, language arts,
science, and other curriculum areas are taught, they may not be
immediately discernible because instruction is often focused
around a variety of learning centers within the room among
which students can move.

Learning in an open classroom proceeds from the current
needs and experiences of each individual child. For the open
classroom teacher, the "teachable moment" is most important
with the individual child. Most open classroom teachers suggest
that they are most interested in the total development of each
child.

Reading may take a variety of directions (Wiener, 1974), although an emphasis on language experience approaches and
more attention to the integration of reading with the other language arts activities is likely. This system does not mean that the
open classroom teacher does not use a basal series. However, if
one is used, the teacher will probably supplement it with a variety of other materials and will not hesitate to remove a student
from the program if he or she feels the program is not being appropriately beneficial.

Advantages

There are a number of advantages to open classroom instruction.
First, reading instruction is typically integrated into all of the

other curriculum activities. Second, the open classroom builds a strong sense of community among students and teacher that encourages students to share their reading experiences with one another. Third, instruction builds on natural student interests and curiosity and is thus more likely to build positive attitudes toward reading. Fourth, because the emphasis is placed on the development of the total child, attention is given to each student's self-concept and concept of his or her relationship with others. His or her confidence as a reader is enhanced. Fifth, the parent-teacher relationship in an open classroom is likely to be warm and open. The teacher and parent often operate as a team in helping the child with reading.

Disadvantages

The open classroom model has critics, particularly because the concept seems to treat the instruction of such basic and sequential skills as reading in a cavalier manner. First, an insufficient amount of curriculum structure in reading can lead teachers into an activity trap. Specific reading skills that are needed in order to develop reading power are often given insufficient attention. Second, in the open classroom, the teacher runs the risk of avoiding areas of instruction that are not of particular interest or for which that teacher has insufficient strength. Third, the program requires a sophisticated, sensitive teacher to implement it successfully. Fourth, because of the apparent lack of structure, some students can be overwhelmed and waste a considerable amount of time.

The middle grades

No issue has been more perplexing to educators during the last several decades than the issue of providing an appropriate instructional organization for children between ages eleven and fourteen. That age range, characterized by the onset of puberty and the emotional confusion inherent in shedding childhood roles and adopting adult roles, has not been consistently treated by educators. The plethora of organizational patterns used is not reassuring, for it suggests that educators are still searching for an appropriate instructional method for the early adolescent child. The school in the middle is still searching for an identity.

One of the more popular organizational patterns for this age range is the *junior high school,* which normally contains grades 7 and 8 or 7, 8, and 9 and which often has a high school–oriented

137

program. Another is the *extended elementary school,* which includes kindergarten through grade 8, so the early adolescent
child is in the same school building as the very young child. A
recent development has been the *middle school,* which can include
grades 4 through 8, 5 through 8, 6 through 8, or 7 and 8. It is normally developed to provide a transition between elementary and
high school. There are also a few programs that can be called *extended high schools,* which include grades 7 through 12.

The current dilemma over the organization of the middle
grades represents a basic philosophical struggle between the
child-centered and the curriculum-centered forces in education.
Reading instruction, like many other skill areas, is affected by
this clash of values, which has produced a plethora of organizational models and a wide variety of instructional environments.
Many of the elementary instructional patterns are extended into
the middle grades, especially if the program is attached to an elementary school. In some junior high school settings, the program
will be highly departmentalized and structured like a small high
school. We will not attempt to describe all the variations, but we
will review some of the more popular instructional environments.

DEPARTMENTALIZED

The departmentalized environment is characteristic of the traditional junior high school. Teachers are organized by their curriculum specialization, and an individual teacher teaches four or
five different classes in one or two subject areas to between 125
and 175 students per day. Teachers are organized into departments by content areas: English, social studies, mathematics,
science, music, art, and so on. In a departmentalized setting in
the middle grades, teachers will be trained for the secondary
level and more likely than not prefer the instructional style of the
high school.

Reading instruction is often neglected in the departmentalized
junior high school. When it is taught, it is generally the responsibility of the English teacher. If the English teacher has not been
trained in reading instruction, reading in that classroom is likely
to be defined as reading literature. Little emphasis is likely to be
given to the further application of reading skills. Often to
buttress these perceived weaknesses of the reading curriculum,
the program will include special classes and laboratories for students who need remedial reading help. Typically, these classes
and labs are managed by reading specialists.

We cannot identify any advantages for departmentalization in grades 4 through 8 except that it may be more efficient for classroom teachers. It has been our experience that the pattern of departmentalization is totally inappropriate to the reading needs of the early adolescent.

Disadvantages

First, the reading curriculum, when it exists, is often isolated from other curriculum areas. Second, a definable reading curriculum, philosophy, or program is usually missing. Third, teachers are most often inappropriately or not at all trained to teach reading. Fourth, reading instruction (when present) is often treated as a subject to be moved through in a linear fashion according to some preset time frame. It is not considered a processing tool to be taught through skill introduction and practice under a variety of situations. Fifth, often reading instruction is considered necessary only for the remedial reader and is defined as nothing more than the acquisition of word attack skills.

INTERDISCIPLINARY TEAMS

In an *interdisciplinary team,* several teachers, each of whom specializes in a different curriculum area, will form a multidisciplinary team and teach a large group of students. For example, an English teacher, social studies teacher, math teacher, and science teacher would work together to serve the instructional needs of a group of 100 to 150 students at one grade level. Or, an English teacher and a social studies teacher could team to meet the needs of similar groups of students.

Reading instruction often fares better in an interdisciplinary team environment than it does under strict departmentalization. Although reading will continue to be taught through the English class, the team may attempt to apply reading skills that are being taught in English class to other content areas. The teachers are also likely to attend to comprehension and critical reading skills.

Advantages

The interdisciplinary team offers a small improvement over departmentalization in the instruction of reading. First, often some attempt is made to extend reading instruction into the content areas. Second, an attempt is more likely to be made to provide a skill orientation to reading instruction. Third, reading is more likely to become part of the language arts, particularly if the language arts teacher does not have a strong high school orientation.

Disadvantages

The disadvantages of this approach are considerable. First, the interdisciplinary team is still more likely to provide a heavy content emphasis characteristic of departmentalization. Second, because teachers in a team are still discipline oriented, they are less likely to attend to the individualization of reading instruction. Third, like departmentalization, many interdisciplinary teams naturally gravitate toward homogeneously tracking the students. Thus, all the good readers are put in one class and problem readers in another one, where they are unable to learn from one another. Fourth, reading as skill acquisition can be neglected because of the heavy emphasis on content.

CORE CURRICULUM

The *core curriculum* organizational approach is an outgrowth of the progressive education movement of the 1940s in the newly conceptualized junior high school. It is characterized by one person teaching both language arts and social studies to the same students. Some variations have combined interdisciplinary teaming and the core curriculum (Vars, 1969). The intent of the core curriculum is to fuse or integrate concepts and skills from two or more curriculum areas into a single instructional program: for example, reading skills may be taught through social studies lessons, and English and social studies concepts may be integrated into a humanities type unit of instruction.

The core curriculum environment accords attention to the acquisition of reading skills and to the application of those skills to instruction in the other language arts and in social studies.

Advantages

First, the program tends to be more child centered. Second, because of the emphasis on skill development in the core curriculum, more attention is likely to be given to the reading program. Third, because the student is working with fewer teachers, both the teacher-student and teacher-parent relationships are strengthened. Fourth, reading in the other content areas is made more feasible by the fact that a single teacher is teaching those curriculum areas.

Disadvantages

The disadvantages are worth considering. First, the success of the core program is dependent upon the teacher's training. A social studies teacher, for example, may be uncomfortable teaching reading or the other language arts if he or she has had insufficient training. Second, even though there is more emphasis on skills, there may still be no reading curriculum as such. Third, even when one person teaches both language arts and social studies to the same children, he or she will very often teach the two areas in a separate and discrete fashion, without any attempt to create a core program.

SELF-CONTAINED ORGANIZATION

Self-contained organization in the middle grades is quite similar to that found in the elementary school. One person, usually elementary trained, will teach all of the basic curriculum areas, including language arts, reading, social studies, mathematics, science, and health. Specialists generally assist in teaching art, music, and physical education.

In the self-contained classroom, reading instruction, the teacher's responsibility, is likely to be integrated into the total language arts program. One danger is that it may be so totally integrated that it is not identifiable.

The advantages and disadvantages cited for self-contained classrooms in the elementary school section are equally applicable in the middle grades setting. One additional disadvantage is that very often the self-contained classroom teacher in these middle grades will lack sufficient sophistication and training in some curriculum areas to provide a suitable challenge to students who already have acquired basic concepts in those areas. If that lack of training or sophistication is in reading instruction, it can result in a decided problem for the acquisition of critical and creative reading skills.

High school

Of the three organizational levels in most school systems, the high school is least prepared to accommodate the need for reading

141

skill development during the adolescent years. High school teachers are content teachers, and they assume that students have already mastered the basic learning skills (such as reading). Adolescent nonreaders or disabled readers are tolerated in most high schools. As Smith (1972) notes,

> Although most students learn the basic reading skills in elementary school, a number continue to enter high school with extremely poor word attack and literal comprehension skills. These students are particularly troublesome to teachers and administrators. Individual remedial instruction for them is expensive and often unproductive because it amounts to too little, too late.

These students cannot cope with the high school's rigid and demanding instructional program. They have particular difficulty with humanities courses such as English and social studies, as well as the more demanding science classes. The general remedy that the high school has traditionally used is to isolate such students in remedial or adapted classes.

The average high school also makes no genuine commitment to further systematic instruction in the more complex critical and creative reading skills. Although some of those skills are indirectly emphasized through literature study or through the reading necessary for history or other social studies courses, few high schools can claim to have a systematic curriculum for the development of the more complex reading skills.

Some high schools have tried to accommodate the need for reading instruction, but, with rare exceptions, these organizational strategies have not been particularly successful. We will explore some of the more popular strategies.

HOMOGENEOUS GROUPING

Many high schools use *homogeneous grouping* of students in some form. Traditionally, in curriculum areas such as science, English, mathematics, or social studies, students are grouped into homogeneous classroom tracks on the basis of an IQ, verbal aptitude, or reading test. With the demise of IQ tests, there is a tendency to rely more and more on reading achievement scores derived from standardized tests administered at earlier grades.

To take the English curriculum in the high school as an example, students could be tracked by creating four separate sections: remedial English, basic English, college-bound English, and advanced-placement English. Through either the application of test score criteria and/or guidance counseling, students are directed into the level most suited to their abilities. In most cases the phrase "most suited to their abilities" refers to their reading ability. Within this kind of high school organizational structure, the curriculum for a particular class will be adapted to the abilities and needs of the students assigned to that level. Sometimes there may even be an attempt to teach reading skills to students in either basic or remedial English who exhibit a need.

More recently, some high schools, as a result of criticism of homogeneous grouping, have adopted an electives program in such curriculum areas as English and social studies, and students may choose from a variety of courses. In reality an electives program is a modern variation on the practice of homogeneous grouping. However, it is a somewhat more democratic process because students can select the educational experiences that they are to have. It also avoids the charge of student discrimination to which the courts have spoken.

Advantages

Homogeneous grouping has been generally discredited in modern high school education (Goldberg et al., 1966), although it offers some advantages. First, it reduces the amount of variability present among students in a high school class, thus making it easier for the average teacher to teach the same lesson to twenty-five or thirty different students. Second, the teacher may attempt to accommodate the reading instructional needs of poor readers.

Disadvantages

Unfortunately, there are considerably more disadvantages than advantages. First, classes designed for poor readers often become a victim of the adolescent status structure, and a stigma is attached to those assigned to the classes. Second, often teachers assigned to teach students homogeneously grouped into basic or remedial classes are not equipped to teach skills in those classes. Third, putting a large number of underachieving students in the same group results in unprecedented behavior problems for many teachers. Fourth, the lower professional status attached to teaching classes of slower students means that less experienced and less skilled teachers are often assigned to them.

REMEDIAL READING CLASSES

Remedial reading classes accommodate the needs of underachieving readers. When offered, they are usually a substitute for

English classes. They concentrate on providing gains in reading performance in one or two semesters by remediating the student's basic reading problems. Often these classes are taught by sympathetic high school English teachers. Occasionally, they are taught by reading specialists.

Advantages

First, remedial reading classes represent an attempt on the part of the high school to accommodate the reading needs of individual students. Second, the extent that such classes are likely to be substituted for regular English classes, they offer individual students a more helpful and enjoyable learning experience. Third, they sometimes provide trained reading teachers to work with the students.

Disadvantages

Though remedial reading classes often seem appealing to a high school staff, they have many disadvantages. First, because instruction in reading is isolated from the rest of the instructional program, it is often difficult for students to see any relationship between their learning to read and the demands that are being placed on them to read in other classes. Second, students assigned to such classes are stigmatized by the low regard that most high school students have for such classes. Third, often the curriculum in remedial reading classes is not sufficiently individualized to meet the unique needs of each student. Third, placement in such classes is often for no more than a year; such short-term experiences generally offer little learning reward. Fifth, these remedial classes are often too little, too late. Sixth, these classes also establish in the minds of most teachers, parents, and students the belief that only poor readers need instruction in reading skill development.

READING LABORATORIES

A high school *reading laboratory* is a diagnosis and treatment center for severely handicapped readers. In concept, it is often restricted to students who exhibit considerable intellectual ability but who have not learned to read well. The laboratories are generally staffed by reading specialists who work with five to seven students at a time. Students are programmed into such labs several times a week for individually prescribed work. The specialist diagnoses the individual student's reading problems, prescribes an instructional treatment to meet those problems, and directs the treatment process for each student.

The goal of the laboratory is to "cure" the students of their reading skill problems and return them to reading health in the regular instructional program. Reading laboratories usually contain a variety of machines and equipment: reading machines, workbooks, and remedial reading kits. Some laboratory teachers have also used the lab approach to help students with reading assignments in other classes and some have tried to use students to tutor their less able peers.

Advantages

There are at least two major advantages to the reading laboratory concept: Severely disabled readers with intellectual potential have the opportunity to work in a small group environment with reading specialists, and the reading laboratory teacher is likely to devote sympathetic attention to each student's unique reading problems, including their attitude toward reading and themselves as readers.

Disadvantages

The laboratory concept also has disadvantages. First, the "shot-in-the-arm" strategy prevails in reading laboratories. The work, unfortunately, may be too little, too late. Second, too often there is no link between the instruction in the reading laboratory and the reading demands being placed on the student in the rest of his or her instructional program. Third, the reading laboratory represents an extension of the medical model, which assumes that something is wrong with the student rather than with the high school instructional program. Fourth, like remedial reading classes, teenagers attach stigmas to assignment to reading laboratories. It is not a very prestigious place to be assigned to for instruction. Fifth, the concept tends to support the belief of teachers, parents, and students that average or better-than-average readers do not need systematic reading instruction at the high school level.

READING IN THE CONTENT AREAS

Some high schools have attempted to alter the mission of high school instruction by including reading skills instruction to all students. Generally, in this organizational approach to reading, the high school staff makes a commitment to teach reading skills within all reading-intensive curriculum areas. Thus, English, social studies, mathematics, and science teachers, as well as teachers in such applied areas as vocational arts and business education, attempt to build reading instruction into the everyday work in their content area. Often they are helped by a reading consultant who is assigned to work directly with the high school staff to provide considerable in-service education to content area teachers.

The school must also develop a reading skills curriculum to assist content area teachers in teaching comprehension, critical, and creative reading skills.

Advantages

First, reading skills are taught through reading content to which the student will be exposed. Second, all students, not just remedial or disabled readers, receive reading instruction commensurate with their needs. Third, generally there is a better attempt in this model to individualize content area curriculums to help meet the learning and reading needs of all students; teachers become especially sensitive to the readability of materials that they are placing in students' hands.

Disadvantages

First, teaching reading in the content areas often is not a decision made by the entire staff but rather by the administration. Under these circumstances, it is difficult to overcome teachers' negative attitudes and lack of any feeling of ownership for the idea. Second, the model requires a basic shift in the mission of the high school, something that few high schools have explored. Third, implementing the model can be expensive, since it may require considerable curriculum revision. If the appropriate released time and other resources cannot be made available, implementation may be difficult. Fourth, reading in the content areas is probably not a satisfactory strategy for helping teachers cope with students who have not acquired basic work attack skills.

Future directions

Predicting the future in American education is difficult. However, it may be useful to explore general trends that could influence future reading environments. It is not possible to predict specific environmental structures for reading instruction; however, it is possible to speak to specific trends that appear to be emerging.

The individualization of reading instruction will continue to be a strong professional trend. The trend will accelerate in the elementary grades, and it will also become a strong professional focus for curriculum reform in the middle grades. Future research will result in ever more sophisticated continuous progress skill-building programs in reading, which will individualize instruction and allow teachers to accommodate unique reading needs. More attempts will be made as well to provide alternative learning strategies in other content areas for each student. This individualization is a mixed blessing. On the one hand, it will help teachers to select learning experiences that are best suited to a wide range of readers and nonreaders. But it also runs the risk of reducing the amount of time that individual students spend practicing those reading skills they have already acquired.

The trend toward more organizational alternatives in education will also have an impact on reading instruction. The magnet school concept wherein a variety of schools is developed, each purporting to represent a different educational philosophy, is an exciting concept. However, the concept of many alternatives among which students and their parents can choose poses both problems and unique opportunities for those who must coordinate reading instruction. A close study must be made of each alternative to determine how reading instruction can best occur through that alternative. Attention must also be paid to a student's reading progress as he or she moves from one alternative to another.

A third trend is the growing competence of teachers. As both elementary and secondary trained teachers acquire a more sophisticated understanding of the reading process and of reading instruction, they will encourage the use of more sophisticated and effective organizational models for delivering this instruction.

Finally, we would like to suggest that the next ten years will bring a revolution in high school organization and instruction. There is growing disenchantment among parents, students, and educators with the relatively rigid mission and structure of the high school. Signs are emerging that high schools will come under ever more intense attacks in the years ahead and that considerable progress will be made in opening up high school instruction so that it can better accommodate the learning needs of high school age students, including their need to learn to read better.

147

Summary

As debate has occurred over reading materials, so too has it developed over the organization of instruction for reading. At the elementary level, the self-contained classroom remains by far the most popular organizational pattern for delivering reading instruction, although numerous other patterns are used. We have described and analyzed each organizational pattern.

For students ages eleven to fourteen, the story is less clear. The presence of junior highs, middle schools, K–8 elementary schools, and 7–12 high schools makes it difficult to suggest any prevalent approaches to reading instruction for this aged child. We have attempted to describe the confusion.

The high school is the wasteland of reading instruction. It is generally assumed in high school that students can read. Reading programs are designed almost exclusively to help the few students with serious reading problems. Thus, the emphasis is on reading labs and remedial reading classes.

Goldberg, Miriam, A. Harry Passow, and Joseph Justman. *The Effects of Ability Grouping.* New York: Teachers College Press, 1966.

Klausmeier, Herbert J., Mary R. Quilling, Juanita S. Sorenson, Russell S. Way, and George R. Glasrud. *Individually Guided Education and the Multiunit Elementary School.* Madison: Wisconsin Research and Development Center for Cognitive Learning, University of Wisconsin, 1971.

Smith, Richard J. "Reading in the Secondary School: Needs and Practices." *The Bulletin* (Spring 1972): 15–19.

————, and Thomas C. Barrett. *Teaching Reading in the Middle Grades.* Reading, Mass.: Addison-Wesley, 1974.

Snyder, Edith Roach (ed.). *The Self-Contained Classroom.* Washington, D.C.: Association for Supervision and Curriculum Development, 1960.

Vars, Gordon F. *Common Learnings: Core and Interdisciplinary Team Approaches.* Scranton, Penn.: International Textbook Company, 1969.

Wiener, Roberta. "A Look at Reading Practices in the Open Classroom." *The Reading Teacher* 27, no. 5 (February 1974): 438–442.

Chapter 7 Evaluating the student and the program

Typically, more efforts are made to evaluate reading instruction than any other curriculum area. In spite of these efforts, however, the evaluation of reading remains shrouded in misunderstanding and ministerpretation. Many attempts to evaluate reading programs and student reading achievement effectively have served only to confuse the issues further than to clarify them. There are several reasons for this dilemma.

Too often evaluation is set up as an afterthought; it is something that a teacher or administrator has been told to do. The evaluators thus have no "ownership" of the evaluation plan or the resulting data. They are evaluating to satisfy somebody else. Often nobody seems to know why the evaluation data were gathered.

Frequently evaluation is hampered by unclear objectives. Because little attention has been devoted to why the evaluation is occurring, it is unclear what is being evaluated. Is it an interest in knowing how well a particular student can read? If so, what is the definition of reading? And what will be evidence that the student can read? Perhaps, alternatively, educators are interested in how well the reading program is succeeding and how well students as a group are doing. But the problems remain the same: the definition of reading and the criterion of acceptable reading performance are not clear. What are the evaluation objectives?

Many teachers confuse evaluation and testing, although the terms are not synonymous. Testing, often further defined more narrowly as standardized testing, is but one evaluation strategy. Because teachers do not know why they are evaluating or what they are evaluating, they have not considered how they are going to evaluate. They limit themselves to one evaluation strategy, such as testing, although there are many others available.

Finally, because teachers have missed the opportunity to answer the "why," "what," and "how" of evaluation, they will often produce data or information that are harmful rather than helpful. Perhaps the result is test data that reach the newspapers and are misinterpreted by the community. Maybe it's a home-grown survey of reading attitudes with unknown reliability and questionable validity. Or it may be data from a test that bears no relationship to the reading program under question. They have not addressed the issue of how well they have evaluated.

We believe that carefully considered evaluation is an integral part of a good reading program. Moreover, we believe that reading evaluation has been carefully planned only when four questions have been systematically addressed: "Why are we evaluating?" "What are we evaluating?" "How are we evaluating?" and "How well are we evaluating?"

Why evaluate reading?

Too often reading evaluation is poorly conceived, misused, and rejected by teachers and administrators. But it will not be that way if everyone concerned has a better understanding of the purpose of evaluation.

DEFINING EVALUATION

Evaluation is the determination of the worth of something (Worthen and Sanders, 1973). It is an attempt to determine if some product, process, activity, or procedure is of value or is satisfactory. Included in evaluation is the act of asking questions about the issue to be evaluated, determining what is "valuable" or "of worth," gathering objective and reliable information about the issue, and assessing the worth of whatever is at issue.

In the context of a first-grade classroom reading program, for example, it could mean asking, "How well are the children learning their basic vowel sounds?" But before that question can be answered, another must be asked: "How well should they be learning their basic vowel sounds?" Perhaps the teacher has decided that all of the students at this point in the school year should have mastered long vowel sounds within monosyllabic words and 50 percent should have mastered short vowel sounds under the same circumstances. Now it is possible for the teacher to gather information that will answer the first question and evaluate the worth of the selected reading program for teaching vowel sounds.

151

If the second question ("How well should the students be doing?") is not addressed, the evaluation efforts will be impotent and of questionable value. Evaluation demands a standard against which data or information can be judged. Without it, no judgment of worth can be made. It is impossible for the teacher to determine whether the program is working, for he or she has not determined what the program should do.

Evaluation is not the same as research. Research is the process of uncovering new knowledge through controlled investigation, it is an attempt to secure powerful ideas that will help people better understand natural and human events. Unlike research, evaluation is immediate and pragmatic. It is a process that supports the day-to-day act of making instructional decisions. "Should Jane go on to the next primer?" "Has John mastered the concept of 'main idea'?" "Should we continue our language experience program with Title I students?" "Should the improvement of our school district reading program be a priority for the next three years?" "Are teachers implementing the reading program we designed last year?" "Were our in-service workshops effective?" These are the kinds of questions that demand evaluation. They are action-oriented questions, decision-laden questions, that demand immediate answers if good instructional decisions are to be made.

COMMON ATTITUDES TOWARD EVALUATION

Most teachers and administrators are interested in making the best possible instructional decisions to improve the reading program. Many like to believe that their decisions reflect the state of the art in reading instruction. However, whether teachers and administrators use evaluation to make better decisions is dependent upon their attitudes toward evaluation. Let's explore some of those attitudes.

Accountability has a bad connotation in education. Because it has come to be identified with some defined outcome (for example, "Your students will grow one grade level during the year") it has tended to make teachers defensive. Of course, no teacher can guarantee that every child will learn to read well or that a class of children will make the progress anticipated for them. There are too many uncontrollable variables. Because evaluation is often associated with accountability, it too has come to have a negative connotation. It is something the teacher or administrator must do to obtain some federal money, to satisfy the board of education, to mollify parents, or to maintain the confidence of taxpayers.

The concept of evaluation can be used to give accountability a more positive image. If to be accountable as teachers and administrators means demonstrating that you are in good faith making the best possible decisions about children and their reading instruction by using sound evaluation, then accountability has been redefined as a process. You are not being held responsible for the impossible: that all children will learn, whatever the circumstances. You are being held accountable for acting as rational, objective, responsible professionals. You are not being constrained from taking professional risks and failing; you are demonstrating, however, that you are learning from your successes and failures, and that is being accountable. You are evaluating to ensure that you are making professional decisions.

Why evaluate reading?

Many teachers and administrators, faced with the day-to-day load of correcting papers, preparing lessons, keeping records, disciplining, and instructing, consider evaluation a luxury that they cannot often afford to do. Their prevalent attitude is that they do not have the time and will evaluate only when outside pressure demands it.

Evaluation, however, is not a luxury; it is essential. It aids informed decision making in the classroom or school, and it contributes to the teacher's own learning. Many teachers forget that to be good teachers, they must first and foremost be good students. They must keep the spirit of personal inquiry alive and take an active interest in their own professional actions and observations. As Schaefer (1967) notes, "Teaching, more than any other vocation, perhaps ought both to permit and to encourage the pursuit of meaning beyond any current capacity to comprehend" (p. 59).

As educators we must treat our hunches, beliefs, and decisions as hypotheses to be tested by sound, objective information. We must proofread our own professional behavior, and having proofread, assume better hunches, beliefs, and possible decisions. We must model the ultimate intellectual behavior we expose for our students.

Finally, evaluation is lightly regarded by many teachers and administrators because they mistrust data. Some have been stung by data gathered by someone else. Many are confused by the jargon of the evaluator. Others are discouraged because past results often seem inconclusive. And others insist that because teaching reading is more an art than a science, it cannot be scientifically measured.

To analyze that attitude better, let's be philosophical. How do you "know" something (for example, if students are learning to read well)? Kerlinger (1964) suggests four ways; blind faith, authority, your own perceptions, and controlled investigation. *Blind*

153

faith seems self-explanatory; it is the stuff of religious conviction. *Authority*, the utterances of someone who should know, someone with credentials, is also fairly obvious.

Our own perceptions, however, needs more explanation. Perceptions are images taken in through the senses and filtered through previous experiences, prejudices, and the knowledge base in one's brain. Perceptions are personal interpretations of reality, but they are not to be confused with reality itself.

Controlled investigation also requires some explanation. It is an attempt to get to the truth of something by correcting for human biases and prejudices that cause people to misinfer or misjudge something that is happening. Many times controlled investigation confirms perceptions, blind faith, or authority. "That's just proving the obvious," we say. On other occasions, however, "Things are not what they seem."

A matrix may clarify the issue. Consider figure 7.1. Note that one side of the matrix moves from logically uncertain to logically certain; the other side moves from belief to experience. Blind faith, as a way of knowing, is "logically uncertain belief." St. Paul called it "the substance of things hoped for, the evidence of things not seen." Authority, though still tied largely to belief, carries more logical certainty. Perception carries the weight of experience but allows for considerable logical uncertainty (remember how perceptions are filtered). Only controlled investigation carries both the weight of experience and a stronger measure of certainty because it controls for natural biases.

This concept suggests that there are basically four ways of knowing if students are learning to read well. You can assume on blind faith that they are doing well. After all, you are honorable and well intentioned, attempting to do your best, using good techniques and materials. You can assume that students are

Figure 7.1 **A matrix of uncertain to certain and of belief to experience**

	Uncertain ◄─────────────────────────► Certain	
Belief ▲	Blind faith	Authority
Experience ▼	Perception	Controlled investigation

learning to read well because you are using a reading program or approach that some prominent authority endorses. Moreover, your experiences with your students, your perceptions, suggest they are learning to read well. ("After all, didn't little Johnny Morris, my best reader, start his fourth primer already and it's only January?")

These are all acceptable ways of knowing, but if you want to be certain you must evaluate through controlled investigation. You will gather some data, and you will show as much distrust for those other ways of knowing if your students can read as you often show for controlled investigation. The reason for evaluating is to become more confident that you "know."

In summary, reading evaluation is effective only when you affirm a need for objective, reliable information. If you need to be more confident of what you know about your reading instruction, if you desire to model the spirit of inquiry that you profess for your students, and if you require better information for professional decision making, then you need evaluation.

Evaluate "what" in reading?

Many teachers and administrators without negative or ambivalent feelings about evaluating reading are still put off by evaluation. They simply do not know where to begin. Although they sense why they should be evaluating; they are unable to translate philosophy into operation. Under those circumstances, an evaluation needs assessment can play an important role in getting started.

AN ASSESSMENT OF EVALUATION NEEDS

An *assessment of evaluation needs* is an attempt to identify whether additional information is required to support decisions currently being made about reading instruction. Perhaps defining a need will make the issue clearer. Gottman and Clasen (1972) define it as a discrepancy between some ideal goal or state and the reality of present circumstances. If the physician has a goal for you of good health, as measured among other indicators by a normal temperature of 98.6°, he will view with some alarm a temperature of 104°. There is clearly a discrepancy between your ideal and real state. You have an immediate health need, and he will suggest a curative intervention.

155

Similarly, you can determine if there is a discrepancy between the information required to make professional decisions and the information available. To do that, you must ask several questions:

1. What educational decisions do I make or help make?
2. What questions do I need answered to make those decisions?
3. Am I satisfied with the quality of the information that I am using to address questions?

Educational decisions

Classroom teachers, principals, and reading specialists all make, help to make, or influence many important decisions about the reading program. To assess your role in influencing decisions, respond to the following questions:

1. Do I determine if individual students are ready for reading instruction in my class or school? What decisions am I likely to make? (Readiness and screening.)
2. Do I determine what kind of reading instruction an individual student should receive? Do I ever change that instruction? What decisions am I likely to make? (Reading instruction.)
3. Do I communicate with parents about the quality of their child's progress in reading? What am I likely to report? (Parent reporting.)
4. Do I ever refer students with reading problems for special help? What decisions am I likely to make? (Diagnosis and remediation.)
5. Do I ever determine the reading curriculum that I will be using? What decisions am I likely to make? (Curriculum).
6. Do I ever select instructional materials for the reading program? (Instruction.)
7. Do I ever help to determine the resource level that my school or school district will devote to the reading program? (Management.)
8. What changes in the reading program am I currently helping to determine? (Improvement of instruction.)

By responding to each question, you will begin to identify important decisions. Take the first question as an example. A first-grade teacher might respond by noting that he or she decides if a student will begin to learn to read immediately or instead receive further readiness work. The teacher may also decide if the student will start at the beginning of the program or move into the program to his or her skill level. The teacher may find, too, that for a student who is not yet ready to start formal reading instruction, a decision must be made as to the nature of further readiness experiences.

Evaluate "what" in reading?

Remember that evaluation is useful to the extent that it supports or influences professional decisions. It may be a decision to do something new, to change something you are doing currently, to continue what you have been doing, or to do nothing. By responding to each of the questions above, as well as others, you will begin to identify decisions regarding reading that you make or influence.

Unanswered questions

As you face decisions, you will usually confront questions that clarify your options and constraints. Take, for example, the decision to begin formal reading instruction with Jenny. How will you decide if she is ready? The following questions come to mind.

1. What skills should Jenny have to begin formal reading instruction? Are those readiness skills specified in our curriculum? Why are these considered important readiness skills? What will happen if Jenny begins reading instruction without mastering these readiness skills?
2. How will I know if Jenny has acquired these skills? What level of mastery should she be able to demonstrate on each readiness skill? How will I determine mastery?
3. How does Jenny's previous background and experience prepare her for formal reading instruction?
4. Will one kind of reading program be more appropriate for Jenny than another as suggested by her readiness profile?
5. How does Jenny feel about learning to read?
6. If Jenny should not start formal reading instruction, what additional readiness instruction should she receive?
7. How will her parents feel about a decision to delay formal reading instruction? How will Jenny feel?
8. Is Jenny displaying any behavior that may significantly impede learning to read in the future?

Every teacher making a decision about a student must come to grips in some fashion with evaluation questions. To satisfy that question, the teacher will make a judgment, which must be based on some kind of information.

Information

The third step in your assessment of evaluation needs is to identify the information necessary to answer each question. Remember, there are four levels of being informed or of "knowing." For
each question, you must determine what you should know to answer that question and what you currently "know." Let's analyze
one of the questions regarding Jenny: "How will I 'know' if
Jenny has the necessary readiness skills to begin formal reading
instruction? What level of knowing is important?"

1. "She's ready. I just know it." (Blind faith.)
2. "The kindergarten teacher said she was ready." (Authority.)
3. "She is ready. Look at how eager she is. Besides, her mother
   has been buying her books since she was three." (Perception.)
4. "She is probably ready. I've administered our readiness battery to her and observed her behavior for the last two weeks
   using our readiness checklist. She has a few skill weaknesses,
   but none of these is serious and can be worked on within our
   language experience reading program." (Controlled investigation.)

An informational discrepancy

If you need to address the questions above about Jenny, then the
level of information available becomes critical. First, you must
determine which of the levels of information available above is
necessary for professional decisions. Then you must determine
the information you currently use. If your information is different from what you ideally need, there is a discrepancy. You
need better information and hence improved evaluation.

Not only must you make decisions about each student; you
must also make decisions about the reading program. Hence,
evaluation efforts must span more than individual children; they
must address questions and judgments of the reading program
itself. It may be timely at this point to discuss a blueprint for
evaluation.

AN EVALUATION BLUEPRINT

After you have assembled a list of evaluation needs in reading
instruction, you should prepare an *evaluation program* or a *blueprint*. A blueprint is helpful because some evaluation needs are

antecedents to others. If you set priorities for tackling evaluation needs without understanding that relationship, you may become frustrated if you hit a snag. For example, you will be unable to develop a test of reading behaviors until you have defined the reading act. Thus you probably should evaluate the utility of your curriculum first. Does the curriculum define reading carefully? But enough of this for now. What of the blueprint?

Evaluate "what" in reading?

There are many models for evaluation. Each is useful, and we do not necessarily champion one or another. Moreover, we will not review those models because the reviews are available elsewhere. (See Worthen and Sanders, 1973.) However, the application of one selected model here will assist in our attempt to blueprint evaluation needs. The CIPP model (Stufflebeam et al., 1971) has proven useful to us in helping teachers and administrators better understand evaluation. It postulates four different types of evaluation: context, input, process, and product. We will focus on program evaluation in discussing these concepts, but they can also be applied to individual students.

Context evaluation

Context evaluation is at the root of all evaluation efforts (Worthen and Sanders, 1973). It is an attempt to review and validate the underlying philosophy and goals of the reading program, determine the resulting objectives and standards of that program (statements that help you determine if the reading program is working well), and identify unmet needs for service, help, or improvement within the program.

To evaluate the context of your program of reading instruction for both the individual student and all students, you must answer some of the following questions:

1. How have I defined reading? Is it a clear, written statement to which all teachers subscribe?
2. What do I believe philosophically about the reading act and reading instruction? Are those beliefs documented and widely accepted by those who are part of the program? Are these beliefs supported by current theory and research?
3. Have I clearly stated the program objectives in terms of student development and growth?
4. Do I have a descriptive program statement? Does it include operational objectives (statements of how reading instruction will occur for different phases of the program)?
5. Does the program delineate subprograms for screening and readiness assessment, developmental reading, reading in the

159

content areas, recreational reading, corrective reading, diagnosis and remediation, accelerated reader programs, and adapted learning programs for disabled readers?

6. Do I have a systematic plan for evaluating the reading program? For identifying new and emerging needs for our reading program?

7. How does my program accommodate individual differences, needs, and patterns of growth in children? Do I have reading program articulation?

8. What needs do I have to improve my current reading program?

9. Is my program as defined compatible with the needs and characteristics of the students?

These are some of the questions that you must address as you evaluate the context of your reading program. They can be addressed for an individual student, a classroom, a school, or a school system. The response to each, whether it is on the basis of blind faith or controlled investigation, allows you to make decisions. How good those decisions are will depend on how valid the information is.

Input evaluation

The resources you will use to implement your reading program must also be decided. Those decisions precipitate evaluation questions that must be addressed as decisions are made. Input evaluation is a conscious attempt to determine if you have the resources that will be required to operate your reading program as defined.

To evaluate your resource capabilities, ask the following questions:

1. Are my reading program materials consistent with my reading philosophy and goals? (Even if you use a total commercial reading package or system, you must address this question.)

2. Do I have adequate materials for all phases of the program (developmental reading, remedial reading, recreational reading, etc.)?

3. Do the materials work? Are they interesting and stimulating? Easy for children to use? Durable? Cost-effective? Readily available?

4. Do the reading materials in our instructional materials center accommodate children with wide-ranging reading abilities?

5. Can children easily find materials that they can read?
6. Am I adequately trained to implement all phases of my reading program?
7. Are specialists available to help me with problems for which I am not trained (psychologist, reading consultants, diagnosis and remediation specialists, librarian, evaluator)?
8. Do I use parent volunteers or teacher aides in the reading program? Are their roles clearly defined? Do they have the necessary skills to do what is being asked of them?
9. Is the school building planned and equipped to support the reading program?
10. Do I have a record-keeping system that is complete, simple, and efficient?
11. How much of my time is spent in reading instruction with children? Individually? In small groups? Large groups?

Evaluate "what" in reading?

These are the evaluation questions that you must come to grips with as you make decisions about inputs or resources. How confident you wish to be of your answers will determine how carefully you evaluate.

Process evaluation

To understand better the full implications of process evaluation, you must distinguish between a plan and the implementation of that plan. For example, your reading curriculum is a plan by which instruction in reading will occur. Instruction itself is the actual instructing behavior of the teacher and the learning behavior of the child. Curriculum is the statement of your plans; instruction is the operational interpretation of those plans. Do not assume that because a plan has been developed, validated, and documented that it in fact is being implemented as designed. Process evaluation is necessary for three reasons: to maintain a record of instruction as it occurs, to detect flaws in the reading curriculum plan; and to aid in day-to-day decision making as you implement your reading program.

Process evaluation requires you to address such questions as:

1. Do I have a current record of my day-to-day activities in reading? Are those activities reflective of the program?
2. What is each child's current progress, instructional activities, and learning problems?
3. How much time do I devote daily to reading instruction? How is it divided?

161

4. Are my instructional decisions and activities generally consistent with those of other teachers who have a similar responsibility or who must also serve the needs of the children
I serve? Why or why not?
5. Are students making the progress I expect? How do I know?
6. Are the resources I had planned to use actually being used?
Do I need additional resources not previously planned for?
7. Is our in-service program for professional staff occurring as
planned? Is it meeting needs defined earlier?

Many reading evaluation efforts progress through context and
input evaluation but bog down when process evaluation is
reached. Teachers and administrators feel comfortable discussing
philosophy, goals, and materials but pale when evaluative efforts
turn to the day-to-day efforts of a classroom teacher. Such evaluation seems to smack of accountability, preclude individual
prerogatives, and challenge professional judgment. But it does
not have to.

If teachers operate in a spirit of personal inquiry about their
own instructional decisions, if they acknowledge the rights of
others on their professional team to know (but not to judge un-
fairly) what they are doing just as they have similar expectations
of others, if they see themselves as part of an instructional team
rather than an operator, and if they are dedicated to implementing and improving the total reading program for each child, then
they will not only tolerate process evaluation but demand it.

Product evaluation

Product evaluation, the final type in the CIPP model, is given the
most attention in efforts to evaluate reading. Product refers to the
outcomes of the program. In the context of a curriculum to teach
children to read, product evaluation is an attempt to determine if
the student objectives are being met. Is the program doing what
it was designed to do? Such evaluation can occur at the end of
the program (grade 12, for example) or at any checkpoint along
the way (the end of one organizational unit, such as elementary
school, the end of a developmental phase, such as instruction in
decoding, the end of a grade level, the end of a unit of instruction, or the end of an activity).

For product evaluation the questions to be asked will be determined by the objectives in the program statement. However,
some of the following may be useful:

1. Are children learning to read according to the program's definition of reading?

2. Do children value reading? Are they reading for pleasure? Do they read a variety of materials?

2. Do children value reading? Are they reading for pleasure? Do they read a variety of materials?
3. Do students continue to read after they leave school?
4. Is each student acquiring the necessary skills of the reading program? Is progress satisfactory?
5. Are students learning to read critically and creatively?
6. Are students reading well enough to learn by reading?
7. Do students use reading to solve their own problems or to acquire other kinds of skills? Do they view reading as having utility?
8. Do students have situational literacy: do they read well enough to handle everyday survival tasks and to meet personal and career goals?
9. Have students with reading disabilities compensated in a healthy and productive way?

Product evaluation must come to grips with such questions for both the individual child and children as a group.

Setting priorities and getting started

The final act in attempting to improve an evaluation of reading is to set some priorities. They can probably start anywhere—with an individual child, a group of students with similar needs or characteristics, or with the entire reading program. You can begin by trying to address your product questions, by grappling with what is actually happening in the classroom (by addressing the process questions), by taking an inventory of your inputs (are you using the best commercially available reading program?), or by using context evaluation (what is the reading program?). Wherever you begin, you will ultimately come back to the questions of context evaluation, for without a program philosophy, definition, goals, and objectives, it is difficult (and perhaps impossible) to answer many questions of input, process, and product.

Above all, if you are setting out to improve your evaluation of reading, set some priorities, but limit them to two or three. If several staff are involved, be sure you have consensus on those priorities before you address the question of "how" you will proceed.

Finally, before we move on to "how" to evaluate the reading program, we must respond to those readers who have by now accused us in this section of duplicity. We are actually suggesting more than just a strategy for determining "what" we will evaluate, you say; "We are providing a blueprint for reading program management and improvement." Yes, we must confess, that is probably true, but is that necessarily bad?

How to evaluate reading

The next question is, "How do I evaluate reading?" Obviously
your objectives provide guidelines as to what evaluation strategies are most appropriate. For example, a standardized test is an
inappropriate tool if your objective is to determine if students
can read well enough to handle everyday reading tasks. On the
other hand, it is very appropriate if you are seeking to determine
how well students in your school can read relative to some other
groups of students (for example, the national norming sample).
Obviously how you evaluate reading must be a logical extension
of what you wish to evaluate.

Because the evaluation strategies available for reading are extensive and complex, it is not possible to catalog all of them, even
in a cursory way. Besides, other authors have already provided
that service for the reader (see the suggested readings at the end
of this chapter). We suggest that teachers and administrators who
are attempting to evaluate reading consider working with an
evaluation consultant. Most large school systems, state departments of education, and universities have such resources available. An evaluation consultant can be particularly helpful if you
have already determined your reading evaluation needs, objectives, or questions.

We will discuss the major issues of how to evaluate reading.
In particular, attention will be given to basic controlling
ideas, testing and individual diagnosis, and reading attitude assessment.

BASIC CONTROLLING IDEAS

Evaluation of reading is an infant science. Much remains yet to
be learned about how to evaluate best the many complex components of the reading program. Already, however, some powerful
concepts are beginning to emerge.

Controlled investigation

Earlier we suggested that the purpose of evaluation is to make
judgments about the worth of something. We also suggested that
the manner of "knowing" about the phenomenon in question
will influence the confidence of our judgment. For example, you
should have less confidence in a judgment that children in your
reading program are learning to read well if that judgment is

based on blind faith or perception than if it is based on controlled investigation. The purpose of controlled investigation is to assist the evaluator in systematically and confidently eliminating competing answers for each evaluation question of interest. Take, for example, a principal's question, "How thoroughly have teachers implemented the reading curriculum?" If you were to trust your perceptions, you might casually observe that all materials and curriculum guides have been delivered to teachers' rooms and that briefing sessions have been held with each teacher. You might also visit briefly a couple of teachers during reading instruction on different occasions (teachers whose rooms are closest to the office). From your perceptions, you might infer that the program is being implemented well.

Consider the dangers inherent in your inference, however. Perhaps the materials are not being used. Maybe only the two teachers you visited are using the material well. And perhaps part of the program is not being implemented well or at all.

To make a sound judgment on the evaluation, you need to control your investigation. You need to establish a list of criteria of what is acceptable evidence of successful implementation of a particular program. You need to specify and then control your investigation of that question. For example, you might establish the following criteria:

1. All teachers using the program will be able to describe in their own words the objectives, scope and sequence, and operational guidelines of the program.
2. Visits to a random sample of teachers during a random sample of periods will find the reading program being used 80 percent of the time.
3. All materials in the program will show physical evidence of use.
4. During five visits to the classroom of each teacher, the observer (principal or a colleague) will find evidence that 80 percent of the events on a written checklist are occurring.

Your observations, though still somewhat informal, will be much more controlled if they are guided by the above (or other) criteria. What is being controlled is the propensity to see only what you want to see.

Assessing behavior

Often teachers and administrators will conflict with evaluation specialists over how to evaluate. More often than not, the source

165

of the conflict lies in the unwillingness or inability of practitioners to be specific. For example, perhaps they have asked the
question, "How well are our students comprehending what they
are reading?" The evaluation consultant will attempt to get the
client to specify what is meant by comprehension; the client may
resist and get frustrated.

Many teachers and administrators suffer, both in evaluation
efforts and in instruction, from what Mager (1972) calls "warm
fuzzies." Because they have not carefully enough defined their
goals of instruction, they are talking in warm fuzzies. An example is, "The student will learn to comprehend better." What is
"comprehension"? When have they learned? What is "better"?
Until these terms have been defined, it is not possible to know
how to evaluate the objective. The simple truth of pedagogy is
that the more carefully and concretely you can define the concepts, skills, and attitudes you are attempting to have children
learn, the greater is the likelihood that you can successfully teach
and evaluate these skills, concepts, and attitudes. Good evaluation of reading depends on how carefully and specifically you
have defined what is to be learned. Warm fuzzies, by their very
nature, cannot be evaluated with much confidence; statements of
expected behavior can be.

Converging measures

Webb and others (1966) have detailed the concepts of *converging
measures* and *unobtrusive evidence*. Traditionally, research design
has been built around the concept of a single, elegant measure,
usually a test of some sort. The concept of converging measures
has liberated evaluation from this confining tradition. If your intent in evaluating is to raise your level of confidence in the
knowledge you possess of some phenomenon, then it seems reasonable to gather several pieces of evidence, all of which converge on the issue.

For example, if you are to decide whether an entering first-
grade student should be placed in a language experience program
or a basal reading program, you might administer a diagnostic
test of language ability. That single piece of evidence may be
enough to make your decision. You can strengthen your confidence in your decision by also informally interviewing the child
and his or her parents, collecting and analyzing a tape-recorded
language sample, and observing the child in several instructional
and social settings. If all of the measures converge in agreement,
you will have more confidence in your decision; if they do not,
you may need to gather additional data before making the placement decision or treat the decision you do make as tentative.

Attendant to the concept of converging measures is the concept of unobtrusive evidence. Often when you get ready to evaluate you think of some special procedure, such as a test or a survey that is obtrusive and captures the attention of the student. Such a test or survey not only measures; it also changes the subject. For example, if you administer an attitude survey to determine if students enjoy reading, the act of administering may alter the students' attitudes. As an alternative to the survey or in addition to it, you might note over time how many students ask to go to the library or how many carry around something to read during their free time. You might even ask each student to keep a log of daily activities during certain randomly selected weeks. By counting the number of times the student notes that he or she is reading, you will be able to assess the degree to which he enjoys reading. (Note the implicit definition of "enjoyment" here, however.) Such an activity, though generally obtrusive, can be considered unobtrusive relative to the student's attitudes toward reading.

Sampling

One of the most powerful ideas in evaluation or research is sampling; however, many practitioners are suspicious of it and do not put much confidence in data that result from sampling techniques. Many practitioners do not realize that they are already using sampling procedures, though often inappropriately. For example, the principal who visited the classrooms of the two teachers closest to his office and concluded that all teachers must be implementing the new reading program was sampling. However, this procedure for selecting the sample had introduced an uncontrolled bias into the results and had thus jeopardized the truthfulness of the conclusions.

Sampling, used correctly, is a powerful tool for cutting the human and financial cost of evaluation. Its basic purpose is to allow the evaluator to generalize with some confidence from a subset of events to a larger class of events. That evaluator's confidence in his or her conclusion is directly dependent upon his or her confidence that the sample of events used is representative of the population of events to which he or she wishes to generalize. Fortunately, there are strategies that can be used to strengthen the probability that the sample is representative of the population (see Gottman and Clasen [1972], p. 352).

You probably think of sampling in terms of people; however, it is used in at least two other ways. For example, in building a test of reading achievement, you select items to make up that test. An item, such as a multiple choice item, is a single sample

167

of reading behavior from an extremely large population of such behaviors. A collection of fifty such items into a test is a sample of fifty behaviors from a large universe of such behaviors. Thus, when you infer from the score on a test that a student can't read, remember that you are inferring from a relatively small sample of reading behaviors to the total universe of such reading behaviors. The validity of your inference, as you can see, is strictly dependent upon how representative those fifty test items are of the total universe of test items from which they are drawn.

Second, when you record student behavior, either on a test or through observation, remember that that record is a sample from a large population of possible reading behaviors. For example, a score on a test is but one test administration given at one point in time from many that theoretically might have been given. The student's performance on that test will be controlled by factors other than the student's ability. Because you cannot test each student a large finite number of times under a variety of conditions, it is not possible to find his or her true score. You must be content with a single sample and all of the hidden biases that may be built into it. The student may have been distracted during the testing, preoccupied by family problems, or ill. These biases get built into the score. Thus, results for a single student must be interpreted with considerable caution, lest the test becomes tyrannical.

An incident involving the younger son of one of the authors is instructive in this regard. After doing a satisfactory job on a listening test and word analysis test, the third-grade student answered almost every item incorrectly on the reading comprehension test. When quizzed afterward, the boy responded, "I got tired, so I just marked them any old way to get done." A considerable mistake might have been made if the teacher had concluded from the score that the student had a reading comprehension problem.

TESTING OF READING

Reading instruction and testing are closely aligned. Indeed, more test development has occurred in reading than perhaps in any other single curriculum area. Tests are available for just about every dimension of reading instruction, including linguistic and psychomotor readiness, phonics, word analysis, vocabulary, literal and inferential comprehension, critical reading, literary style, and rate of speed. Tests have also been developed for screening, diagnosing, and assessing achievement. Farr (1969) has developed an illuminating and expansive review of this testing tradition in reading.

Most reading tests are based on norm-referenced measurement traditions spawned before and during World War II. A *norm-referenced* test judges the performance of an individual subject against the performance of the group of which he or she is a member. During the war, a large testing industry emerged as the armed forces sought a variety of test instruments to screen military recruits. After the war, this industry turned its attention to education. Reading was one of the primary beneficiaries. These measurement traditions made terms such as *norms, percentile rank, quartiles, test battery,* and *item analysis* commonplace among educators. Equally commonplace were such acronyms as ITBS (Iowa Test of Basic Skills), STEP (Sequential Test of Educational Progress), and SAT (Stanford Achievement Test), among many others. These are called *standardized tests* because the standards of the test's performance on some defined group of students have been prepared and documented.

Recently, however, another testing tradition has begun to emerge in education. Entitled *criterion-referenced testing,* this tradition has already begun to have a significant impact on measurement in reading instruction on a one-to-one basis.

Norm-referenced tests

To better understand norm-referenced or standardized tests of reading, it may be illuminating to review how such a test is constructed. Let's use a standardized test of reading comprehension as an example. First, you must develop a conceptual framework that represents a concrete definition of comprehension, since the term *comprehension* is too general by itself. In other words, you must map the term "comprehension." Comprehension has been one of the most controversial concepts in reading and no attempt will be made here to review the scholarly struggles that have occurred over the last thirty years. Nevertheless, every standardized test company that has developed a comprehension test over those years has had to adopt some definition of comprehension. For our purposes, assume that comprehension is

○ Knowledge of word meanings
○ Literal recall of information
○ Interpretation of contextual meaning of words
○ Selection of the main idea or thesis of the package
○ Inference of meanings not directly present in the passage
○ Detection of the intent, tone, and point of view of the author.

169

Next, determine the grade level or levels for which the test is
to be used and select or construct reading passages of anywhere
from one sentence to several paragraphs in length. These passages must be of suitable difficulty so that they challenge some
and are easy for others. In other words, the passages are deliberately chosen to discriminate among levels of reading comprehension within the group to be tested. A passage that everyone in
the target group can read well would be eliminated from consideration. Assume for discussion purposes that the test in question
is being constructed for students in grades 4, 5, and 6.

After passages have been selected, test items are constructed
for each passage. Some test items are developed for each concept
or skill in the comprehension skill list above. These test items are
usually multiple choice in format, with either four or five foils
(*foils* are the choices of answers following the question stem).
One foil will be the correct answer; the others will be distractors.

All test items are field tested on groups of fourth, fifth, and
sixth graders. Items that very few children answer correctly (extremely difficult items) or that most answer correctly (extremely
easy items) are either modified or eliminated. Test item distractors that attract no student responders or too many student responders are also altered or eliminated.

The intent of this process is to identify fifty or sixty test items
across the comprehension skill list that discriminate among students in the target group. Said another way, if everyone in the
target group were to consistently answer forty out of sixty items
correctly, the test would be a poor one indeed. The test is specifically developed to ensure a wide spread of scores from very few
right to almost all right, and the test maker manipulates test
items until he or she reaches that objective. This concept is critical to understanding and appropriately interpreting standardized
tests.

Upon final selection of passages and test items, the test is administered to a national sample of fourth, fifth, and sixth graders.
.Using these data, the test maker constructs statistical tables that
reference each raw score on the test (usually total number right)
against the percentage of students in the sample who had a score
lower than the one in question. Thus, if Johnny's score of 39 is at
the 57 percentile, his total number correct is equal to, or better
than, the scores obtained by 57 percent of the students in the national sample. One is not confined to using national samples. As
Prescott (1971) notes:

Interpretation of performance on standardized tests by comparing individual's scores with a norm based upon the perfor-

mance of many other individuals of the same age, grade, or
level of training has been standard procedure since the beginning of standardized tests. It involves comparing the score of
an individual with the distribution of scores made by a representative sample of other individuals in some way like the person tested. Thus, norms can be by age or grade; separate for
boys and girls; or if desired, for state, area, or local groups as
well as national. The choices are limitless, the selection depending upon the particular needs of the test user. (p. 348)

An understanding of the answers that standardized tests can
provide will put such tests in perspective and set the scene for
the discussion of criterion-referenced testing. Standardized reading tests measure a student's or group of students' performance
relative to some other group of students. The measure thus
suggests how well the student can read relative to other students.
The standardized reading test does not tell whether the student
can read well enough to handle everyday reading tasks, or
whether he or she has sufficient reading power to reach career
objectives. The score does not even tell whether the student can
comprehend the passages selected for the reading test in question, for as Bormuth (1970) has pointed out, a test of literacy with
respect to a certain passage requires that the entire universe of
test items for that passage has an equally probable chance of
being selected for the test. Put another way, the reading passage
in the test has a level of difficulty for the reader, which is
mapped by the total universe of available test items. Only a random sample of test items from that universe adequately reflects
the difficulty of the passage. The selection of items for standardized tests deliberately introduces biases that may not make the
items selected representative of the actual difficulty of the
passage.

Criterion-referenced tests

Although criterion-referenced measurement does not have the
long tradition of norm-referenced measurement, it has already
had a profound effect on both measurement and instruction in
reading.

A particular criterion-referenced test (CRT) of reading may appear to be no different from a standardized test. However, the
manner in which these tests are constructed and interpreted is
significantly different. Unlike standardized tests, which map the
reading act as a set of general factors such as literal comprehension, word analysis, and vocabulary, criterion-referenced tests

171

begin by analyzing the reading act into a more discrete and complex set of skills. Each reading skill may in turn be stated as a behavioral objective. Otto and others (1974) provide an example of
such a skills list.

After the reading process has been mapped as a series of skill
sets, criterion-referenced tests are constructed for each skill. Test
items are usually constructed according to the definition provided in the objective statement. Take, for example, this objective from Otto and others (1974): "The child identifies the letters
in the three letter blends, scr, shr, spl, str, thr, in real or nonsense words pronounced by the teacher" (p. 139). The test for
this objective might require the student to listen to a word and
then circle the correct three-letter blend from among several alternative letter blends. If the objective allows for the use of a multiple-choice recognition test items, such items could be used. For
many objectives, such as the following one (also from Otto and
others), test items that require the student to produce his or her
own unique answer are necessary: "Given facts, the child is able
to respond correctly to questions requiring that he make judgments and draw conclusions on the basis of the fact presented"
(p. 159).

Finally, for each objective, a test of several items is constructed. The items are selected primarily because they are reasonable measures of the objectives, not because they necessarily
discriminate among students in a particular group. A mastery
level is set for the test of the objective in question; perhaps it is
decided that the student has mastered the objective if he or she
answers eight out of ten correctly. Eight thus becomes the criterion or standard of measurement.

How, you may ask, is that standard set? Although criterion
test experts are working on more refined models, the teacher or
administrator who wants to use CRT is still pretty much confined
to selecting the figure arbitrarily. The dilemma of setting the criterion, however, is somewhat dependent upon the purpose for
which the test is used.

The most successful application of criterion-referenced reading tests to date has been as part of a program to individualize
reading skill development. Students are pretested on reading
skills. If they do not reach the mastery level, they receive instruction and are tested again. If they demonstrate mastery, they go
on to other objectives. If they do not reach mastery on the post-
test, they receive further instruction on that reading objective.
Within this kind of developmental model, it is apparent that a
reasonable criterion can be arbitrarily set and, if necessary, adjusted as teachers gain more experience with the program. Such

tests must be viewed as aiding teacher judgment, not as sup-
planting it.

Criterion-referenced tests of reading have also been used in
large-scale school systems and state and national assessments of
reading programs. When used as accountability measures, they
can present problems in public interpretation and understanding. If the question to be answered is, "Can Johnny read?"
the public is not satisfied to learn that students reached mastery
on thirty out of forty-five reading objectives. Another problem is
what the criterion should be and who should set it. Although
these are not insurmountable problems, they hamper present attempts to use criterion-referenced tests for accountability purposes. Clearly, other approaches to the assessment of reading
achievement are required and are being developed; unfortunately none has gained sufficient credibility to be promoted.
Hansen and Hesse (1973) have attempted to implement an alternative measure of reading literacy, and the National Assessment
of Educational Progress (1970) is also instructive in this regard.

ASSESSING ATTITUDES TOWARD READING

From time to time, we are asked to help teachers or administrators who wish to assess the attitudes of students toward reading
and reading-related activities. Many times when we are called,
an effort will already have been made to administer some sort of
attitude scale; now the practitioner wants us to help interpret the
meaning of the results. Often the survey is a home-grown effort
of unknown validity and insufficient reliability. Thus, some comment on the assessment of reading-related attitudes and values
would seem in order.

To begin with, there is no such phenomenon as an attitude or
value. An attitude is a label that the observer attaches to the behavior of someone else when the observer notes a consistency in
that behavior. If, for example, a student consistently selects mystery stories to read, the observer might infer that the student
likes mysteries. The only reality to point to in that situation is
that the student is selecting mysteries; the inference that he or
she likes them is an interpretation of reality, not reality itself.

Without gathering more data, the observer cannot be sure that
the student likes mysteries. He may be reading such stories for
other reasons: his parents, who like mysteries, think he should
be reading them; he does not like to read at all, but he dislikes
mysteries least, a mystery story was the first book he read completely, and he believes that mysteries are the only books he can

read successfully. The point is, attitudes and values are difficult to identify, and they (if they exist at all) need to be treated with respect and caution.

An attitude survey is no more infallible than observation; moreover, it gives no more information. It poses a situation and asks the student to behave, for example, to check a response to a statement or idea on a piece of paper. From that response, you will infer an attitude. When you make an inference, you take a risk. You may not be measuring what you think you are measuring; maybe the student, in marking the survey, is trying to please or punish you. Maybe he or she does not understand, and the marks are random noise. It is important to understand that your inferences are your judgments of the reality of some marks on a piece of paper.

We have spent this much time defining attitudes and their measurement not to scare readers off but to impress upon them that the assessment of reading-related attitudes is serious and cautious work. It will not work to put together a few statements like this one:

Reading is my favorite hobby.
strongly agree   agree   uncertain   disagree   strongly disagree

and claim to be assessing reading-related attitudes. This is no more acceptable than putting together three multiple-choice test items based on a short paragraph and claiming to be measuring reading ability.

A survey must be put together carefully with considerable attention given to various aspects of validity and reliability. For example, the survey must be long enough to be reliable and not so long as to be fatiguing for students. Items should be unambiguous and readable or understandable by the students responding to them. Items should relate to some central theme or concept.

After administering the survey, you can add across items to create a score which should measure the student's behavior toward that concept. Drawing a conclusion from a single item is useless, for that item by itself is unreliable; it is only as that item is combined with many others that a reliable survey may emerge.

Dulin and Chester (in press) have done considerable work on the measurement of attitudes of middle-grade students toward reading. Excerpts of their work are shown in figure 7.2 (pp. 176–177) and serve as one example of an attempt to measure attitudes.

A final note on assessing attitudes is essential. Young children are generally very trusting and open; they will, if you ask, generally share their legitimate feelings. They have not yet been taught to be defensive or protecting of their ego and of their integrity. As professionals, we must always be extremely protective of our human subjects. Attitudes are very personal and sensitive. If we probe them in defenseless children, we must treat the resulting data with respect and caution.

We could say much more about how to evaluate reading by elaborating on such issues as evaluation models, research designs, literacy assessments, statistical analysis, or interpretation and meaning of data. But in a single chapter, we can only go so far. The annotated references listed at the end of the chapter will allow the serious reader to read further.

How to evaluate well

Many teachers and administrators overcome negative attitudes toward the evaluation of reading, set some modest objectives, and try gathering some data. But the data can be discouraging: either they are too late, too little, or too unreliable. A typical question is, "Can we really believe what the data are telling us, especially if the results don't square with our perceptions or our beliefs?" The problem is the quality of the data.

The issue of quality control of evaluation is a critical issue. Like any other way of "knowing," controlled investigation (the heart of evaluation) can be tyrannical. Unless some quality has been built into the process, you may make erroneous judgments. Fortunately, there are criteria that can be used to assess the quality of evaluation efforts. Stufflebeam (1974) notes three kinds of quality control: technical adequacy, usefulness, and cost effectiveness. For our purposes, we will reduce these three indexes to two; tests of *integrity*, and tests of *consequence*, by including cost effectiveness as an issue of *consequence*. (The Stufflebeam essay gives an in-depth treatment of the issues surrounding quality control of evaluation. Readers comparing the two treatments will note that we have combined some of Stufflebeam's criteria and not included others.)

TESTS OF INTEGRITY

Tests of integrity ask one basic question: "How successful have you been in following the rules of controlled investigation?" Under that rubric come such issues as *validity, reliability, objectivity, security,* and *credibility.*

175

Figure 7.2 **Excerpt from Dulin-Chester reading attitude inventory**

II. Now, to take the next part of the inventory, you're to *grade* twenty statements in terms of how you feel about them. If you STRONGLY AGREE with a statement, give it an *A;* if you TEND TO AGREE with it, give it a *B;* if you feel FAIRLY NEUTRAL about it, give it a *C;* if you TEND TO DISAGREE with it, give it a *D;* and if you STRONGLY DISAGREE with it, give it an *E.* Be sure to read each statement carefully before you circle a grade for it, and be sure to grade *every* statement.

1. Reading is for learning but not for enjoyment.	A B C D E
2. Money spent on books is well spent.	A B C D E
3. There is nothing to be gained from reading books.	A B C D E
4. Books are a bore.	A B C D E
5. Reading is a good way to spend spare time.	A B C D E
6. Sharing books in class is a waste of time.	A B C D E
7. Reading turns me on.	A B C D E
8. Reading is only for grade grubbers.	A B C D E
9. Books aren't usually good enough to finish.	A B C D E
10. Reading is rewarding to me.	A B C D E
11. Reading becomes boring after about an hour.	A B C D E
12. Most books are too long and dull.	A B C D E
13. Free reading doesn't teach anything.	A B C D E
14. There should be more time for free reading during the school day.	A B C D E
15. There are many books which I hope to read.	A B C D E
16. Books should not be read except for class requirements.	A B C D E
17. Reading is something I can do without.	A B C D E
18. A certain amount of summer vacation should be set aside for reading.	A B C D E
19. Books make good presents.	A B C D E
20. Reading is dull.	A B C D E

III. This third part of the inventory calls for a bit of math ability. Your job this time is to *divide up 100 points* among the following ten things in terms of *how desirable* you feel they are as leisure activities. Remember, the total should come out to 100.

Figure 7.2 **Dulin-Chester reading attitude inventory** (cont.)

Activities	Points
Reading books	
Reading magazines and newspapers	
Watching television	
Playing musical instruments	
Doing craft and hobby work	
Listening to the radio	
Writing letters	
Listening to records	
Painting or drawing pictures	
Sleeping or napping	
Total	100

IV. And finally, to tell us a few things about *you* personally, please respond to the following three scales by circling the answer to each which *best describes you*.

1. Compared to other people your own age, about *how well* do you think that you read?

1	2	3	4	5
a good deal better than most	somewhat better than most	about as well as most	somewhat less well than most	a good deal less well than most

2. Compared to other people your own age, about how much do you feel you *like* to read?

1	2	3	4	5
a good deal better than most	somewhat better than most	about as well as most	somewhat less well than most	a good deal less well than most

3. And finally, compared to other people your own age, about how *much* reading do you feel you do?

1	2	3	4	5
a good deal more than most	somewhat more than most	about the amount as most	somewhat less than most	a good deal less than most

Thanks for your participation. Now please turn this in to your teacher.

Source: From Kenneth L. Dulin and Robert D. Chester, "Reading Attitude Inventory," in Orval G. Johnson (ed.), *Tests and Measurements in Child Development: A Handbook* (Boulder, Colo.: Child Measurement Project), in press.

Validity

Validity speaks to the quality of the evaluator's logic process and asks, "Have I evaluated what I thought I evaluated?" There are basically two validity issues: *internal* and *external*.

An evaluation effort is internally valid to the extent that the evaluator can be confident that the results are true. If the intent was to measure reading achievement, what confidence does the evaluator have that the data actually reflect a measure of reading achievement as opposed to intelligence or maturation? How similar are the results to the results of other evaluators who have investigated the same issue? If they are different, why are they different? Is the measurement based on a logically consistent theory? Have key terms been operationally defined? Is there a relationship among logically similar data? These questions address the care that the evaluator has taken in building the measurement of whatever is being evaluated.

External validity addresses the power of the evaluation results to be generalized to apply to other situations. External validity forces the evaluator to assess the extent to which he or she is able logically to reject alternative explanations of the data. For example, has a sample of students that have been tested been sufficiently controlled as to the representativeness of the sample to be generalized to the larger population?

In an earlier section, we spoke of the principal who visited the classes of two teachers close to the office in an effort to determine if a reading program was being implemented. The sample was small and had considerable bias built into it because the principal selected two rooms convenient to his office. He or she may be able to draw conclusions about the validity of those observations for the two teachers, but he or she will be unable to generalize to all of the teachers in the building who have the responsibility for implementing the program. Although the data may have internal validity, they definitely do not have external validity.

Evaluators may also wish to generalize across time. Thus, the principal observing those two teachers would, on the basis of one or two observations, probably wish to generalize to the entire year. Although it may be internally valid for him or her to suggest that on the two visits he or she did not observe appropriate implementation occurring, the biases built into both the small sample of visits and the unrepresentativeness of the timing of those visits would suggest that the observations do not have external validity. That is, it would not be valid to conclude that the two teachers were not in fact implementing the program. All that the principal could say is that they were not implementing the program on the two occasions of the visits. These evaluation efforts lacked external validity and may well have lacked internal validity as well. (See Campbell and Stanley [1963] and Kerlinger [1964] for a more thorough discussion of validity.)

Reliability

Reliability is the test of the accuracy of evaluation efforts. To be accurate, data must be both internally consistent and reproducible or stable. Internal consistency can be easily explained by the concept of converging measures. Earlier, we spoke of the need to use more than one measure in an attempt to get a sound and compelling evaluation of an issue. The extent to which those measures converged—that is, the extent to which they all signaled similar results—would make the evaluator confident about the accuracy of each measure.

The same concept operates in the development of a test. A test is internally consistent to the extent that all of the items that make up that test are converging in their measurement. For example, each item in a survey of students' attitudes toward reading should contribute to the assessment of the issue. Fortunately, there are various statistical tests that can be run on the test data to determine the extent to which items are internally consistent.

Internal consistency is not the only issue in reliability, however. The results also must be reproducible (identical) if the same measurement or observation were taken at two points in time under identical conditions. Psychometric discussions of reliability call reproducibility *test-retest reliability*. Although less attention is given today to test-retest reliability than to measures of internal consistency, it is still an important consideration when testing for the integrity of data.

If you cannot have faith that your results are stable and dependable, it will be difficult for you to believe that they are valid. This points up an important tautology between *validity and reliability*: Data that are not reliable cannot be valid; data that are reliable can still not be valid. A test may measure some phenomenon consistently, but be measuring something other than what you think you are measuring. For example, you may set up a system that allows you to count the number of books that students check out of the library as a measure of how much self-motivated reading students are doing. The measure may be very reliable, that is, the data reflect the number of books each student checks out. However, the students may not be reading the books at all but are checking them out and carrying them home to impress their

179

teachers and parents. The measure would be reliable, but it would not be a valid measure of how much self-motivated reading students are doing.

Considerable confusion surrounds the measurement of reliability, particularly as it refers to standardized tests. Many teachers and administrators who use standardized reading tests will observe in the testing manual that a particular test has a certain reliability; often it is above .90. That statistic, achieved by the test manufacturer, is useful only to the extent that the population of students with whom the teacher wishes to use the test is similar to the population of students that the test maker used to achieve the reliability figure. This is a commonly misunderstood issue and leads, in our opinion, to much misuse of tests and generation of unreliable information. Many times standardized tests are used with underachieving students for the purposes of identifying them for special programs. Before teachers or administrators put much faith in the data, they should determine the specific reliability of that test for the particular group of students with whom they are using it. The test may be unreliable for this group.

Objectivity

Everyone has biases. Rarely does a teacher, administrator, or evaluator set out to evaluate without having some idea about what the data will show. For example, you may be investigating the extent to which a new individualized reading program is effective in teaching children to read. If you believe strongly in that program (you have invested a lot of money in the program or convinced the community of the programs perhaps), you may desire the data to be positive. It is a short step from that kind of posture to the process of "stacking the deck" of the study so that the outcomes are favorable to your original position.

The issue has nothing to do with ethics. At a conscious level, you may make every effort to be as fair as possible in your design and conduct of evaluation. However, your posture as an evaluator will cause you to make decisions, unwittingly perhaps, that are positively responsive to the outcome you desire. When that happens you are not being objective.

To deal with the issue of objectivity, you must examine your own attitudes, values, and resulting behaviors. Be conscious of the impact of your decision about your evaluation design and the resulting data. If you begin your evaluation effort from a posture of subjectivity, it is less likely that your efforts will have integrity.

Unlike the tests of validity and reliability, which can be addressed logically, the test of credibility is a subjective one. Credibility relates to how much faith you are willing to place in your results, how trusting you are of them, how valid you feel they are. It is possible for evaluators intellectually to accept data for the purposes of evaluation without emotionally owning that data. If the results of the controlled investigation conflict with alternative belief systems (e.g., perception, blind faith, or authority), the issue becomes which belief system is most trustworthy.

If, as a teacher, your perception is that you are doing a good job of teaching students how to read, and you administer a variety of measures that indicate that you are not doing well, which belief system are you going to place most faith in? The issue is obviously a complex one because it will touch on your values, ego, and, if others are observing, professional credibility. Research and evaluation experts often use the term *face validity* when they are speaking of the issue of credibility.

When an evaluator is providing a service to someone else—for example, a teacher, administrator or a community—the issue of credibility is also bound up in the extent to which clients are willing to trust the evaluator. Unfortunately, many people, both professional and lay, still mistrust not only data but those who prepare the data. In the face of such mistrust, it is not unusual for the client to demand to know how the results were arrived at: what measurement processes, research procedures, and statistical tests were used. Hence, credibility is often enhanced by keeping the design, the analysis, and the reporting of results simple and easy to understand. This, of course, is not as easy as it sounds, for such guidelines often prevent evaluators from using powerful measurement and statistical tools that would otherwise be available. However, if the data are not credible, they will not be of much consequence.

TESTS OF CONSEQUENCE

The American Heritage Dictionary of the English Language (1969) defines consequence as "that which logically or naturally follows from an action or condition" (p. 283). Consequence is an effect or result. If an evaluation of reading and reading programs is to be more than just a game that teachers and administrators play with themselves, each other, and the community, then that evaluation must have a consequence. Unlike research, which is often undertaken for the sheer joy of discovery, evaluation is by definition

181

immediately purposeful. To be purposeful, it must be of consequence. Important tests of consequence are utility, timeliness, ownership, and cost effectiveness.

Utility

Utility is a straightforward issue. It basically asks, "What happened to the data?" "What did those data affect?" "How did they affect?" and "Whom did they affect?" A number of issues bear on the issue of utility.

First, were the data relevant to the issue? If, to answer the question "Can Johnny read?" you administer a standardized test, you may generate data that are not relevant to the question. The problem may be that you have not spent enough time analyzing the question. If in fact the question is, "How well can Johnny read material that he will reasonably be expected to read as a successful adult?" it is hardly likely that standardized test results will address that question.

A second test of the utility of the evaluation deals with the scope of the data. Is it equal to the magnitude of issues that are being addressed? If, for example, a school system is intent upon evaluating the quality of its remedial reading program, it would hardly be sufficient to administer a diagnostic reading test to a handful of students. The effort would not have sufficient scope to be of much value in assisting that school district in its evaluation.

Concomitant with the scope of the data is the issue of the power of the data. Contrary to what some purists may think, reading evaluation is a political process, whether that evaluation is being undertaken by an individual teacher or whether it is a process being undertaken for an entire school system. There are already forces and stresses at work in the environment in which the evaluation is occurring that will control decision making. If evaluative data are to have any impact at all, on the decision or even the opinion of others, they must be powerful enough to compete with the other stresses and forces.

Finally, the utility of the evaluation relates to how pervasive the data have been. Was the evaluation used widely? Did it reach its primary audience? Did that primary audience use the data as they were intended? Did the data reach any secondary audiences? If so, what was the impact on those audiences? Utility, then, depends on relevance, scope, power and pervasiveness.

Timeliness

Altogether too often in education, evaluative data are gathered after the fact. Evaluation becomes an afterthought, it occurs too

late with too little planning and attention to be effective or helpful. The time to consider evaluation is at the beginning of the
planning process, not at the end of the implementation process.

Bloom, Hastings, and Madaus (1971) have distinguished between formative and summative evaluation. *Formative evaluation*
occurs during the process of planning, development, and implementation. *Summative evaluation* is basically product evaluation;
it is undertaken more for the purpose of accountability. In the
context of the CIPP model introduced earlier, context, input, and
process evaluation are generally formative; they help to make the
many decisions that result in achievement or learning. Product
evaluation, basically summative, asks, "Was it all worthwhile?"

Both kinds of evaluation are important. If evaluation is to be
timely and helpful, it must be an integral part of the plans as they
are being developed and implemented. Professionals must force
themselves to analyze their decisions and ask themselves what
evaluative information will be required to make good decisions.

Ownership

Data that are not owned are not used. Ownership identifies for
whom the data were gathered and with whom they are being
used. Altogether too much evaluation occurs to please others, not
to help teachers and administrators do a better job. If teachers
and administrators themselves are not involved in the evaluation
process and do not have legitimate ownership of the data, it is
unlikely that the data will have a profound effect on professional
decision making.

Cost effectiveness

Very often educators newly committed to evaluation want to
evaluate everything. Like almost anything else, it is possible
with evaluation to have too much of a good thing. In fact, we are
distressed by the penchant for often measuring the "molehills"
and ignoring the "mountains." For example, often a school system will evaluate an alternative high school program serving 50
students and ignore the need to evaluate a regular high school
serving 2,000 students.

If the data are not used, then the cost is prohibitive whatever
it is. Above and beyond that, however, we must judge the cost of
data relative to the impact that those data can make. In some situations, it may be equally as reasonable to make a decision without the data, since the consequences of being wrong are fairly
small. In other cases, the data will be vital. Cost effectiveness is
not an easy problem to address, but it is vital to the test of consequence.

183

Some final thoughts

The evaluation of reading for both the student and the program
is a prominent ingredient in maintaining a quality reading program. Although educational evaluation is still an infant science,
it is having a profound effect on reading and reading instruction.
Intense debates are raging within the reading research community over the needs for reading evaluation, the strategies for
reading evaluation, and the control of the quality of reading evaluation.

Missing, to date, is the widespread involvement of teachers
and administrators in these efforts and debates. Because preparation in evaluation has not been part of the practitioner's training,
he or she is burdened with a negative attitude, insufficient skills,
or both. Evaluation of reading efforts is the business of all of us.

Several annotated readings follow, which will help you as a
teacher or administrator get started. But remember that the best
way to learn about evaluation is to do it. The list is not exhaus-
tive; it is rather carefully selected and annotated to get the reader
started.

Summary

Too often evaluation is set up as an afterthought: something that
a teacher or administrator is directed to do. But reading evaluation is most effective when teachers or administrators own it,
when they see the relationship of evaluation to program decision
making and program development. To build that ownership,
teachers and administrators should ask four sets of questions. (1)
"Why am I evaluating at all?" "What are my motives for evaluating?" "What needs do I have for data?" (2) "What are my objectives for a specific evaluation activity?" "What do I hope to
learn?" "What questions do I need answered?" "How will certain
alternative outcomes influence my thinking and my decisions?"
(3) "How will I obtain those data?" "Which of several alternative
strategies will give me the most useful data for the questions I am
asking?" (4) "Have I evaluated it well?" "Have I met the tests of
good evaluation so that I may have confidence in my data?"

Suggested readings

Agnew, Neil M., and Sandra W. Pyke. *The Science Game: An Introduction to Research in the Behavioral Sciences.* Englewood
Cliffs, N.J.: Prentice-Hall, 1969. This common-sense critique

of the scientific method debunks much of the magic surrounding science. Although the book is at times critical of science and the scientific method, it provides an excellent and easily understandable discussion of the critical issues that must be addressed whenever educators are utilizing controlled investigation.

Amos, Jimmy R., Foster Lloyd Brown, and Oscar J. Mink. *Statistical Concepts: A Basic Program.* New York: Harper and Row, 1965. This volume, a basic introduction to statistics, presents the material in a simple, straightforward manner using a programmed format. A diagnostic test and alphabetical index are included to help students assess their strengths and weaknesses after having finished the program or as an initial exercise before moving into the material.

Bormuth, John R. *On the Theory of Achievement Test Items.* Chicago: University of Chicago Press, 1970. Although this book is not for the novice, it makes several profound statements about the measurement of achievement that has a direct bearing on reading. Chapter 2, "Adequacy of Current Test Construction Methods," is particularly good. A complete understanding of subsequent chapters will require some elementary understanding of contemporary English grammar systems.

Gottman, John M., and Robert E. Clasen. *Evaluation in Education: A Practitioner's Guide.* Itasca, Ill.: F. E. Peacock, 1972. Gottman and Clasen have assembled a practical and easy-to-use manual for evaluation that any practitioner can use and benefit from. We recommend it as early reading for anyone who wishes to explore evaluation.

Hively, Wells (ed.). *Domain-Referenced Testing.* Englewood Cliffs, N.J; Educational Technology Publications, 1974. For practitioners interested in criterion-referenced testing, this volume presents an approach that is an alternative to the use of behavioral objectives. It may be particularly appealing to practitioners of reading instruction programs.

Kerlinger, Fred N. *Foundations of Behavioral Research* 2d ed. New York: Holt, Rinehart and Winston, 1973. This book represents a sound, in-depth presentation of the basic concepts of controlled investigation. One of the foremost volumes on behavioral research methodology, it deserves a close and careful reading by anyone who is seriously interested in research and evaluation.

Mager, Robert F. *Goal Analysis.* Belmont, Cal.: Fearon Publishers, 1972. Although its subject is not evaluation, this book presents a usable strategy for helping practitioners to get more planning efforts beyond the stage of "warm fuzzies."

Popham, W. James (ed.). *Criterion-Referenced Measurement: An*

Introduction. Englewood Cliffs, N.J.: Educational Technology Publications, 1971. This early book-length treatise on criterion-referenced measurement has become a classic. It is essential reading for any practitioner who is interested in the concept.

――――. *Evaluation in Education: Current Applications.* Berkeley, Cal.: McCutchan Publishing Corporation, 1974. This scholarly volume on evaluation presents a series of essays on concepts and issues important to the process of evaluation in education. All of the chapters are worthy of careful reading, but we especially recommend chapter 5, "The Use of Standardized Tests in Evaluation," chapter 6, "Criterion-Referenced Measurement," and chapter 9, "Formative Evaluation of Instruction."

Slonim, Morris James. *Sampling.* New York: Simon & Schuster, 1960. This straightforward, practical guide to the statistics of sampling is essential reading for all students of educational evaluation.

Webb, Edward, Donald T. Campbell, Richard D. Schwartz, and Lawrence Sechrest. *Unobtrusive Measures: Nonreactive Research in Social Sciences.* Chicago, Ill.: Rand, McNally, 1966. This volume on unobtrusive measures has had a profound impact on both research and evaluation in the social sciences. A careful reading of the concepts presented will provide both evaluators and practitioners with entirely new insights into research and evaluation.

Worthen, Blaine R., and James R. Sanders. *Educational Evaluation: Theory and Practice.* Worthington, Ohio: Charles A. Jones Publishing, 1973. This current and fairly comprehensive review of the theories emerging in the field of educational evaluation should be read by all students of the evaluation process.

Bibliography

The American Heritage Dictionary of the English Language. Boston: Houghton Mifflin, 1969.

Barrett, Thomas C. (ed.) *The Evaluation of Children's Reading Achievement.* Newark, Del. International Reading Association, 1967.

Bloom, Benjamin S., J. Thomas Hastings, and George F. Madaus. *Handbook on Formative and Summative Evaluation of Student Learning.* New York: McGraw-Hill, 1971.

Bormuth, John R. *On the Theory of Achievement Test Items.* Chicago: University of Chicago Press, 1970.

Campbell, Donald T., and Julian C. Stanley. *Experimental and Quasi-Experimental Designs for Research.* Chicago: Rand McNally, 1963.

Carver, Ronald P. "Reading as Reasoning: Implications for Measurement." In *Assessment Problems in Reading*. Newark, Del.: International Reading Association, 1973.

Davis, Frederick B. "Research in Comprehension in Reading." *Reading Research Quarterly* (Summer 1968): 499–545.

Dulin, Kenneth L., and Robert D. Chester. "Reading Attitude Inventory." In Orval G. Johnson (ed.), *Tests and Measurements in Child Development: A Handbook*. Boulder, Col.: Child Measurement Project. In press.

Farr, Roger. *Reading: What Can Be Measured*. Newark, Del.: International Reading Association Research Fund, 1969.

Gottman, John M., and Robert E. Clasen. *Evaluation in Education: A Practitioner's Guide*. Itasca, Ill.: F. E. Peacock, 1972.

Hansen, Lee H., and Karl D. Hesse. *An Assessment of Student Reading Literacy*. Madison: Research and Development Department, Madison, Wisconsin, Public Schools, March 1974.

Hoffmeister, Georgia (ed.). "Taxonomy of Evaluation Techniques for Reading Programs." Bloomington: Measurement and Evaluation Center in Reading Education, Indiana University, 1969. Unpublished ms.

Kerlinger, Fred N. *Foundations of Behavioral Research*. New York: Holt, Rinehart, and Winston, 1964.

Mager, Robert F. *Goal Analysis*. Belmont, Cal.: Fearon Publishers, 1972.

National Assessment of Educational Progress: Reading Objectives. Denver, Col.: National Assessment of Educational Progress, 1970.

Otto, Wayne, Robert Chester, John McNeil, and Shirley Myers. *Focused Reading Instruction*. Reading, Mass.: Addison-Wesley, 1974.

Popham, W. James (ed.). *Evaluation in Education: Current Applications*. Berkeley, Cal.: McCutchen, 1974.

Prescott, George A. "Criterion-Referenced Test Interpretation in Reading" *The Reading Teacher*, 24 (January 1971): 347–354.

Schaefer, Robert J. *The School as a Center of Inquiry*. New York: Harper and Row, 1967.

Stufflebeam, Daniel L. *Meta-Evaluation: Paper No. 3*. Occasional Paper Series. Kalamazoo: Evaluation Center, College of Education, Western Michigan University, 1974.

———, W. J. Folen, W. J. Gephart, E. G. Guba, R. L. Hammond, H. O. Merriman, and M. M. Provus. *Educational Evaluation and Decision-Making in Education*. Itasca, Ill.: F. E. Peacock, 1971.

Webb, Edward, Donald T. Campbell, Richard D. Schwartz, and Lawrence Sechrest. *Unobtrusive Measures: Nonreactive Research in the Social Sciences*. Chicago, Ill.: Rand McNally, 1966.

Worthen, Blaine R., and James R. Sanders. *Educational Evaluation: Theory and Practice*. Worthington, Ohio: Charles A. Jones, 1973.

Chapter 8 Prevention, correction, and remediation of reading problems

Reading problems have been a concern of educators, parents, and politicians for as long as the ability to read has been perceived as a prerequisite for being successful. Yet, regardless of the resources expended to eliminate them, reading problems persist for some students at all academic levels and for some into their adult lives. The elimination of reading disability appears to be either an unrealistic national goal or one that is far more difficult to attain than many people think it is, or at least at one time thought it was. There is no reliable program that has been shown to produce substantial gains in the national race to give all citizens a better life by teaching them to read. Despite efforts in this area, many people do not read well enough to use print for information and recreation as easily and as productively as they use other media.

The elimination of reading problems at the national level will require a broader base of attack than instructional programs within the school setting can provide. Reading retardation can be traced to social conditions beyond the boundaries of the school curriculum, and these conditions must be improved if national literacy goals are to be attained. An instructional program can undo only part of the mischief caused by inadequate medical care, poor living conditions, family instability and a host of other out-of-school factors that bear heavily upon children's learning to read. Even a strong instructional program cannot by itself eliminate reading problems. Some of the social conditions that encourage reading retardation must be eliminated by professionals other than teachers before teachers can do the job that they are trained to do—teach reading to children who are intellectually, emotionally, and physically able to learn that complex process.

School programs are only one force in the national effort to teach reading to all students who are not seriously handicapped intellectually, emotionally, or physically. Working in consort with other professionals, teachers can play a significant role in attaining national literacy goals. However, to place the entire burden on school programs is unrealistic.

A number of good remedial reading textbooks are on the market, and most of them discuss the diagnosis and treatment of reading disabilities thoroughly and well. Therefore, we will focus our discussion in this chapter upon the development of school programs or facilitative environments within which good diagnosis, correction, and remediation can be implemented. We will also discuss the importance of preventing reading problems in the school setting.

Preventing reading problems

Because many students are victims of social conditions that seriously interfere with their ability to learn to read, an effort to prevent reading problems would begin with good prenatal medical care for mothers and include the provision of a continuing environment that fosters intellectual development and maintains good emotional and physical health. But since the focus of the discussion in this chapter is upon school programs, we will discuss what we believe to be key factors in the prevention of school-related reading problems.

READINESS

The individual nature of child growth and development is a generally known and accepted concept. However, most parents think that children must begin formal reading instruction at the chronological age of six or upon the first day of their entry into first grade or very shortly thereafter. Teachers and administrators are also eager to start the learning-to-read process and feel pressured to get to the business of teaching reading quickly. Consequently, children who lack the necessary readiness abilities (such as attention span, auditory discrimination, ability to deal with abstractions) may be introduced to formal reading instruction too soon. The result for the children will be anticipation, confusion, apprehension, and failure, in that order.

Schools must introduce students to reading instruction carefully. The failure that results from trying to learn to read before the necessary readiness abilities are present often leaves permanent damage. When the readiness abilities do appear, students are often fearful, resentful, self-conscious, and unwilling to attend to the instruction they need to make them readers.

Formal reading readiness tests should be administered and informal assessments made before children are introduced to reading instruction. For children who are not ready, formal instruction should be postponed and an extended period of readiness training provided. Teachers, administrators, and parents must be educated about the advisability of postponing reading instruction until the child is ready to profit from it. Proper timing in regard to initiating reading instruction is one of the major preventatives of reading disability. Obviously the task is not easy. Changing attitudes and expectations takes time and skillful education. In addition to a good public relations effort and educational program for parents, teachers, and administrators, many schools need to develop a high-quality reading readiness curriculum.

PACING

Some children learn more slowly than others. They need to practice the basic reading skills more than other children do. Or they need more teaching to understand what they are supposed to do when they encounter an unfamiliar word or fail to comprehend a sentence. Proper pacing in the reading program is a major factor in preventing reading problems. Students who are paced too slowly become bored, and students who are paced too fast become confused, overwhelmed, and superficial readers. They never quite rise above the level of struggling with the mechanics of decoding materials that are more difficult than materials they are able to read comfortably, and they never fully understand the messages they must decode so laboriously.

Because it is so easy for classroom teachers to lose their perspective in regard to pacing, school districts should build a monitoring system into their reading programs designed to ascertain whether students are being paced properly. Any of the following methods can be used.

1. Reading specialists who observe classroom teachers teaching reading, watching carefully to be sure students are being taught at the proper instructional level.
2. Video or audio tapes of the teacher teaching reading for the teacher to listen to or view.
3. Informal assessments of each child's reading of the material he or she is being instructed with. The child should be asked

to read orally, skipping any unfamiliar words, until the material can be determined to be at the instructional or frustration level for oral reading. The child should also be asked to read approximately a hundred words silently and to tell, without prompting, what he or she recalls from the experience. Both oral and silent reading assessments will tell teachers whether their students are working with material that is too difficult.

The idea is that instructional materials should be at a level of difficulty consistent with the students' reading ability. Students who stumble through materials or who must be prompted frequently are reading material that is too difficult for them to use to improve their reading. Reading growth is facilitated only with materials and tasks at a level of difficulty that allows students to read them and respond to them correctly with a minimum of teacher assistance.

Parents need to be educated about the serious damage to a child's skill development and to his or her attitude toward reading that can occur if he or she is pushed too fast. Teachers, administrators, and parents must realize that a child cannot learn to read from a book that is too difficult. Much practice at each progressive level of difficulty is indicated for many children who would develop serious reading problems if less practice were given for the sake of "keeping them moving" or "keeping them challenged."

PRACTICE EXERCISES

Many reading problems could be prevented if students were given more assistance with the skill development practice exercises they are assigned. The importance of doing practice exercises correctly cannot be overemphasized. Students who aren't sure of what they are doing or who don't understand why they are completing exercises are likely to become confused and uncertain about the nature of the reading process. In addition, they may develop some thinking strategies and some attitudes toward learning to read that hinder their growth as good readers. Students need practice to master skills, but the practice must reinforce the correct reading-thinking strategies. There is no benefit derived from doing exercises incorrectly.

Too many students leave an instructional session with their teacher without understanding what they have been trying to learn. They find the seatwork which should support the lesson, confusing and difficult. Consequently, what is intended to enrich

191

the learning experience with the teacher actually in a sense undermines it. Teachers must be certain that the practice exercises they assign can be done correctly by the students to whom they are assigned.

Careful monitoring of seatwork activities is important. A student should be stopped from making a mistake before he or she makes it, if that is possible. Students should never be permitted to continue responding incorrectly to items on a worksheet or in a practice book. Those who respond incorrectly to an item should receive immediate clarification and additional instruction if it is needed. Too many seatwork activities amount to evaluations of students' knowledge rather than instruction, and too many of the evaluations find the students lacking.

Teachers should stay with their students long enough to ascertain that they are doing their practice exercises correctly. Discovering students' failings after school or the following day is too late. Teachers should try to schedule their instructional programs so that they are watching their students and available to help them as they begin their seatwork. Teacher aides or parent volunteers can be used very effectively to monitor and help students with this practice work, thereby preventing the development of reading problems.

ANXIETY INTERFERENCE

A major factor in the development of reading problems is anxiety interference. Therefore, administrators and teachers should do everything possible to help children and their parents avoid or overcome the detrimental effects of anxiety about learning to read because the ability to learn to read breaks down rapidly under emotional stress.

Perhaps the best way to avoid stress interference is to acknowledge the fact that some people have more trouble learning to read than others. Differences in reading aptitude are as obvious to teachers (and to some parents) as are differences in aptitudes for other endeavors. Much of the anxiety surrounding slow reading development arises from the notion that everyone should be equally good readers and with proper effort and good instruction would be. Unfortunately, that is not the case. Some students at all academic levels will continue to outperform their fellow students in reading and reading-related tasks. Parents, teachers, and administrators must realize that there are other things to be good at besides reading.

A major source of anxiety is concern about whether the student is prepared to succeed at the next academic level. Parents of elementary school children who are poor readers frequently say, "But how will he pass his subjects in junior high school?" One high school student said, "How can I get married and raise a family if I can't read?"

School systems must teach students how to read whenever they are ready to profit from it and for however long they need help. Furthermore, teachers must learn how to educate poor readers without relying so heavily upon printed materials. In our technological society, there is no need to deprive students of an education because they are poor readers. When parents, teachers, and students realize that reading is only one of many human abilities and that print is only one of many media for information and recreation, the hysteria surrounding the area of reading disability may be dissipated and many anxiety-caused reading problems prevented.

TEACHING PRACTICES

Because teachers have many responsibilities and duties, their methods of presenting information, making assignments, asking questions, correcting students' errors, and performing other tasks may not always be faultless. Unless they receive ongoing in-service education, their teaching skills may not reach or remain at the level of quality necessary to prevent reading problems from developing in certain students.

A periodic supervision of teachers is important. As part of the in-service education of teachers, it should be perceived as an opportunity, not an autocratic or threatening imposition. The efforts expended to improve teaching skills without offending or intimidating teachers and without trespassing on their professional autonomy may have deprived them of a simple but effective source of teaching improvement, supervision.

A reading specialist was observing a first-grade teacher teaching a middle-ability reading group the sound of f in initial position. The teacher asked his students, "Who can tell me a word that sounds like 'fish'?" The time allotted for reading instruction was running out, and the low-ability group had not yet had its turn with the teacher. So the teacher asked the question again, with a note of impatience in his voice. Three or four hands began to wave, some more certainly than the others. The hands of three students didn't move at all, in keeping with the blank looks on their faces. To save time, the teacher called on the student most likely to be able to supply a correct answer.

"Fireman," Sally responded.

"Correct!" the teacher said as one or two other students

193

brought their hands down slowly, after being ready to answer, in all probability, with the word "dish." The teacher then sent the group to their seats to complete some exercises requiring them to match words with the same initial consonant sounds.

Certainly many students learn in spite of the lack of precision illustrated in the example. How many students develop reading problems because of it is difficult to estimate. Later the teacher was told that he might have confused the children. He was surprised and indicated that he was unaware of what might have been happening in the minds of his students. He was also grateful for being informed about a communication problem that could cause major reading problems for some students. The likelihood that this weakness in teaching technique could have been corrected by typical in-service programs seems slight. Someone else had to be in the room to notice it and call it to the attention of the teacher so he could correct it. Many other faulty or imprecise teaching techniques might well be detected and corrected by on-the-spot supervision, observation, visitation, or consultation.

Certainly there are other ways to improve faulty or weak teaching practices and maintain effective ones. One is in-service education, which we discuss in Chapter 10. Another is the development and maintenance of a strong developmental reading program. We believe, along with other reading specialists, that many reading problems are caused by teaching practices and instructional materials that for any number of reasons do not provide students with the quantity and/or quality of reading instruction they need to avoid reading problems. Johnson and Kress (1968) say, "Another great concern about programs for disabled readers has been the degree to which, at least in some schools, they have taken precedence over the normal developmental program. All too often the basic instructional program of the school has gone unchanged while special reading teacher after special reading teacher has been added to the staff to correct reading disabilities. The result has been that a never-ending and sometimes steadily increasing supply of retarded readers has been guaranteed."

In addition to the classroom teacher, the principal and a reading specialist are important for a strong developmental reading program. Working with teachers, the principal and a reading specialist can effect nearly any kind of curriculum improvement desired. A capable principal who takes on the leadership role in reading curriculum development promotes an effective reading program. Principals and reading specialists who help teachers stay informed and who insist upon high-quality teaching performances are likely to inspire classroom reading programs that prevent many reading problems. We cannot emphasize enough the importance of such effective cooperation among school personnel.

Correcting reading problems

Describing corrective readers and suggesting instructional reading programs for them is considerably easier than actually identifying and teaching them. Often it is difficult to distinguish between students who have reading problems that can be corrected in the regular classroom and those who require remediation in an out-of-classroom environment. Nonetheless, the distinction is important and helpful to classroom teachers, principals, reading specialists, and, most importantly, the students.

Otto, McMenemy, and Smith (1973) describe corrective instruction as follows:

> Corrective instruction can be differentiated from strictly remedial instruction in two ways. First, corrective instruction is given within the framework of the regular classroom, whereas remedial instruction is offered apart from the regular classroom instruction. Most corrective instruction is typically offered by the classroom teacher, but it is becoming increasingly common to make subject matter specialists who are skilled in diagnostic and remedial techniques available to school staffs. Such persons often spend part of their time providing traditional remedial instruction and part of their time consulting with classroom teachers and actually offering some corrective instruction by way of demonstration lessons, teaching particular skills, etc. This appears to be an important step toward breaking down a barrier in communication that sometimes exists between classroom teachers and remedial specialists. Second, corrective instruction is given when it is found that (1) an entire class is deficient in a particular skill or skills and/or (2) a class or a group within the class is not achieving up to expectation in a subject matter area. For example, if it were observed that all the members of a class appeared to be deficient in their mastery of the basic rules of punctuation, the teacher might then begin a sequence of corrective instruction designed to improve the class level of mastery. Or, if it were found that, say, five or ten children within a class were having more than normal difficulty in understanding the process of long division, the decision might be to offer corrective instruction in multiplication in

195

order to prepare the way for the more advanced under-standings required by long division. Corrective instruction is provided when the nature and the degree of disability are not such as to appear to demand intensive remedial instruction. (p. 34)

Dangers and difficulties are, of course, inherent in establishing categories and assigning students to them. Guidelines we suggest for identifying corrective readers should be used only for initial identification. Decisions based upon them should be tentative and subject to revocation if other evidence that is obtained at the time of initial screening or as the instructional program progresses suggests the need for a different kind of program. Furthermore, students identified as corrective readers may respond well to corrective instruction and show no further need for it. Or their reading problems may worsen to the point that remedial instruction is indicated. In either case, they should be reassigned to a program more suitable to their needs.

On the basis of our experience, we offer the following guidelines for the identification of corrective readers.

1. Corrective readers are making progress in the classroom developmental program but at a slower rate than that of the majority of students.
2. The reading skills deficiencies of corrective readers can be diagnosed specifically enough to permit straightforward teaching to strengthen the weaknesses. The skill weaknesses are not masked by emotional or psychological problems. The skill area(s) in which additional instruction is needed is (are) clear.
3. The ability of corrective readers to recall and to discuss selections read to them is better than their ability to recall and discuss selections they have read to themselves. Their observed ability to learn from nonprint media is better than their ability to learn from printed material.
4. Corrective readers have some independence in reading. They are able to engage in "practice reading" without the constant and direct assistance of their teachers.
5. Corrective readers' attitudes toward improving their reading are more positive than negative. They do not require constant and sophisticated motivational appeals.
6. Their reading skills can be strengthened with additional teaching and practice exercises using supplementary instructional materials. They don't require an entirely different approach from that being used in the classroom.

Corrective readers generally have trouble with more than one skill, and they often need additional help throughout most of their elementary schooling. Correcting reading problems requires more than taking a student aside for a few minutes once or twice a week. These students need additional help on a daily basis if they are to maintain enough progress with skills development to continue receiving their reading instruction in their regular classroom by their classroom teachers, perhaps with some assistance from a reading specialist or an aide.

USING READING SPECIALISTS

Increasingly teaching specialists are being made available to classroom teachers to assist in providing programs for students with special needs. The trend should help teachers to individualize their instruction to meet a wide range and variety of needs in the regular classroom. The concept of *mainstreaming* students with serious intellectual, emotional, or learning problems, (arranging for them to spend at least part of their school day in a regular classroom) will surely reinforce the trend toward using reading specialists.

A reading specialist can help to identify the students who need and are likely to profit from corrective instruction. The identification process, a cooperative effort between the specialist and the teacher, should be made after the teacher has made some informal assessments. The teacher's perceptions can be shared with the specialist, who should also observe the students and support or question the teacher's assessments. The teacher and the specialist might together evaluate each tentatively identified student using the guidelines presented earlier. Some informal testing and/or teaching might be done by the specialist when more information is needed. With a second opinion the classroom teacher will feel more confident about his or her identifications of corrective readers.

When the students to receive corrective instruction have been identified, the reading specialist may do all of the diagnostic testing or share this task with the classroom teacher. Both informal and formal diagnostic assessments will help to pinpoint the specific strengths and weaknesses of these students.

The actual instruction of the corrective readers might proceed in a number of ways. The specialist might supplement the teacher's work with the corrective readers while the teacher teaches another group. Or the specialist might help the teacher plan instruction and seatwork for the corrective readers. Still another approach would be for the specialist to teach some of the

197

other groups so that the teacher can spend more time with the corrective readers.

In schools where homogeneous ability grouping is employed, all of the corrective readers might be placed in one class. The reading specialist would accordingly assist the teacher in conducting the entire class by performing essentially the same tasks suggested above.

USING TEACHER AIDES

Teacher aides are used most effectively if they have been employed for a specified purpose—perhaps freeing a teacher to enable him or her to spend more time instructing corrective readers, monitoring the seatwork of more able students, listening to students read, discussing stories with them, or performing other relatively nonsophisticated teaching tasks. Aides should not be responsible for teaching reading to the corrective readers, who need the expertise and personality of the trained teacher. If aides are to be used for giving instruction, it should be with students who learn most easily. Obviously, aides should be used sparingly for instructional purposes and only under the direct supervision of the teacher.

In schools where homogeneous ability grouping is employed, instructional aides would be used in essentially the same ways, but with the entire class. They would not be used to correct the skills weaknesses of students except in an assisting way.

CORRECTIVE READING IN THE SECONDARY SCHOOL

Corrective reading programs in secondary schools are likely to take the form of classes, grouped homogeneously according to ability, or reading laboratories, which often are essentially classes where students work at learning stations according to individually prescribed reading improvement programs. In either case the teachers in these classes and laboratories are likely to be reading specialists. A specialist or a more-specialized consultant, could help diagnose students' problems and perhaps plan and implement some special learning activities that require more than one teacher to be maximally successful. They could also help to identify corrective readers for the reading classes or laboratories; and if the classes and laboratories serve heterogeneous ability groups, the specialists would perform the same responsibilities as specialists working at the elementary school level.

Content area teachers can do a great deal to help corrective readers understand their assignments and, as a by-product, improve their basic reading skills. The following suggestions will be helpful to secondary school content area teachers who want to help corrective readers and to reading specialists:

1. Know the reading abilities of the students to whom reading assignments are made. Make realistic assignments in terms of how much material is assigned and the difficulty level of the material. Nothing is to be gained by assigning material students cannot or will not read.
2. Prepare students for the assigned selections. Define difficult vocabulary words. Explain and discuss unfamiliar or difficult concepts presented in the material. Explain the purpose for reading the material.
3. Try to interest students in reading the assigned selections. Raise some provocative questions. Ask students to make some predictions about what arguments the author will make, what points of view will be given, or what factual information will be presented. Let the students know what you enjoyed, appreciated, or found interesting about the assignment when you read it.
4. Have students read the assignment in chunks, pausing at specified transitional spots to answer assigned questions, make predictions about what they're going to read next, or reflect upon what they've just read.
5. Have students write two or three sentences immediately after finishing a reading assignment that summarize the selection, raise questions about the ideas in the selection, or paraphrase some major ideas presented in the selection. Use these sentences for postreading discussion.
6. Organize small (three to five students) discussion groups for postreading discussions of questions or issues that require more divergent than convergent thinking (for example, "What probably would have happened if the United States had maintained neutrality and not entered World War II when it did?").
7. Tape-record the most important and/or difficult-to-read material and encourage corrective readers to listen to the recordings and follow along in their books. Multiple copies of these recordings can be made and stored in the instructional materials center or the library for students to use. Members of high school speech, drama, and English classes are good sources for volunteer readers. Community members and faculty members who are good oral readers could help also.

Providing instruction and reading assistance for corrective readers is an important responsibility for administrators, teachers, and reading specialists in elementary and secondary schools. The special help these mildly disabled readers receive may enable them to avoid the need for remedial reading instruction, which is more costly in terms of the school's resources and the students' personal resources.

EXAMPLES OF CORRECTIVE READING PROGRAMS

The corrective reading program at one elementary school will serve as a good example of a special program for corrective readers. At this school the principal was familiarized by one of the school district's reading specialists with the concept of corrective readers and asked to participate in developing an experimental program to help students in grades 1 through 6 who could be identified as corrective readers. The plan (which had been tested in another elementary school in the same school district) was to hire and train teacher aides to assist in teaching students without problems, thereby freeing the classroom teacher (who would also be given special training) to spend more time teaching the corrective readers. The principal liked the idea and agreed to use some of his budget for the additional aides if his staff agreed to the plan.

The plan was explained to the staff at an in-service meeting, and, after many questions and with some apprehension, all of the teachers agreed to participate. The students had already been assigned to classrooms on a random basis, so each class contained students with a wide range of reading ability. Aides were hired for four hours a day, and the reading block of time was scheduled so that each aide could spend an hour a day with three different teachers while they were teaching reading. The additional hour was for preparing and planning with the teachers.

A six-hour in-service program was held for the aides. The program directors were a central office reading specialist from the district, the principal, and the school's reading resource teacher. The aides were given some basic information about the school's reading program and were familiarized with their roles in the corrective reading program, the materials they would be using, and the kinds of activities they would engage in. They were also taught how to administer and score the Stanford Diagnostic Reading Test, Levels I and II (Harcourt, Brace and Jovanovich Publishing Co.).

Approximately six hours of in-service training were given to the teaching staff in grades 1 through 6. The teachers were taught the guidelines for identifying corrective readers presented earlier in this chapter, how to administer, score, and interpret the Stanford Diagnostic Reading Test, how to use their aides, and what materials and techniques to use with students who have trouble mastering basic reading skills.

For the first several weeks of the corrective reading program, the central office reading specialist spent her mornings at the school to answer questions and help aides and teachers. At the end of the first year of the program, test results indicated a more than normal improvement in reading skills development and attitudes toward reading by the students. The teachers' perceptions and the principal's assessment were extremely positive (Benn, 1973).

Examples of secondary school corrective reading programs are not hard to find. At one senior high school (with approximately two thousand students in grades 9 through 12), courses in reading improvement and developmental reading are available to students on a voluntary basis. Students with less serious problems are taught in the former and those with more serious problems in the latter. Students are often referred to the classes by content area teachers who have been trained to detect reading problems and to estimate the extent of a student's problem. The teachers also practice the suggestions presented earlier in this chapter for helping students read content area assignments.

In the reading classes, students practice skill development exercises and read and discuss recreational materials. They also receive help with their reading assignments from other classes. Each class usually has about twenty students, one teacher who is a reading specialist, and no aides. University students who are training to be reading specialists often assist the teachers as a field experience.

A smaller high school (approximately six hundred students in grades 9 through 12) has a reading laboratory. Interested students—with reading skill development that ranges from poor to excellent—are encouraged to visit the laboratory for diagnosis and for work with prescribed exercises to improve or maintain their reading ability. The laboratory is open before school, during study periods, during lunch breaks, and after school. Interested students take some diagnostic tests and then discuss the results of the tests with a specialist. Those who need and want some work in the laboratory are given a prescription for improving and maintaining reading ability and are shown how to use the appropriate materials. Periodic conferences with the reading specialist in charge of the laboratory are scheduled,

201

sometimes on an individual basis and sometimes with small groups.

Because poor, average, and good readers use the facility, no stigma is attached to those who are being helped. At any one time, the mixture of reading abilities among the students in the laboratory is substantial.

Another good feature of the reading laboratory was that staff members are invited to visit the lab during their preparation periods to assist the reading specialist and thereby learn how to teach reading skills to high school students. One of the English teachers became so interested and knowledgeable that she spent several days teaching in the reading lab, and the specialist taught one of her classes. The teachers who spend some time in the lab learned a great deal about correcting reading problems. A close tie between the library and the reading lab has also been established. Students who are working in the lab learn the importance of practice reading with interesting materials at an appropriate level of difficulty. The librarian visits the lab, gets to know the students' interests and abilities, and personally helps many of them find the kind of reading material they need.

At the secondary school level, we believe classes and laboratories for correcting reading problems should be voluntary. Too many excellent opportunities for high school students to correct their reading problems are ruined because of disruptive or lethargic behavior. No one can make a student improve his or her reading. Unless he or she can be motivated with reasonable effort to devote the time and energy necessary to do the job, the experience will be wasteful. Corrective readers in the high school are good candidates for special instruction only if they cooperate and take advantage of the instruction offered them. Each student's responsibilities must be clearly spelled out so that the student can make some important decisions about his or her willingness to learn to be a better reader and to refrain from any behavior that would interfere with other students' rights to do the same.

Remediating reading problems

Probably no area of the school curriculum has generated as much publicity, controversy, and emotion as remedial reading has. Unfortunately, there still are no definitive answers regarding the remediation of serious reading problems or even their cause. Diagnosing and treating reading disabilities that are severe enough to require out-of-the-regular-classroom attention by a specialist in remedial teaching are difficult because each seriously disabled reader presents highly individual characteristics and potential. No two are quite alike.

In this subsection we will not discuss how to diagnose and treat remedial readers. There are many good remedial reading textbooks that treat these subjects. Instead, we will describe and comment upon the characteristics of programs that can be used to implement diagnostic and remedial teaching techniques.

THE FULL-TIME REMEDIAL READING TEACHER IN ONE SCHOOL

Probably the most prevalent approach to remediating reading problems in both elementary and secondary schools is to hire one or more full-time remedial reading teachers for one school and to establish a special room where the teacher works and to which students in need of remedial reading instruction are referred. Some important points need to be considered before establishing this kind of program.

First, *have the staff been prepared for their participation in the program?* Sometimes the administrative and/or regular classroom teaching staff in a school do not expect to be involved with the remedial program. In fact they will (or at least should) be called upon (1) to assist in identifying students who need this instruction, (2) to coordinate classroom reading instruction with remedial instruction, and (3) to modify instruction in other curriculum areas so it does not conflict with the remedial program.

Second, *is the regular developmental program being monitored to detect weaknesses that cause or at least do not prevent reading problems?* We refer again to Johnson and Kress (1968): "Another great concern about programs for disabled readers has been the degree to which, at least in some schools, they have taken precedence over the normal developmental program. All too often the basic instructional program of the school has gone unchanged while special reading teacher after special reading teacher has been added to the staff to correct reading disabilities. The result has been that a never-ending and sometimes steadily increasing supply of retarded readers has been guaranteed."

Third, *have enrollment limitations for remedial reading instruction been established to avoid unrealistic demands upon the remedial teacher?* Most remedial reading teachers are able to work efficiently with no more than three or four students at a time, and some students require one-to-one instruction. In addition, remedial reading teachers need considerable planning time for each

203

student. Therefore, priorities for students who need remediation must be established and adhered to.

Fourth, *have guidelines for the identification of remedial readers been established to avoid consuming the remedial teacher's time with students who are unlikely to benefit substantially from remedial teaching?* Mentally retarded students (intelligence scores below 80 on an individually administered IQ test), severely emotionally disturbed students, and students with extremely poor motivation to improve their reading are usually poor candidates as are students who have a high rate of absenteeism.

Fifth, *are the physical facilities for remedial instruction attractive?* Students and remedial teachers are justifiably reluctant to work in a setting that adds to the stigma of being a disabled reader or a teacher of disabled readers. Unfortunately, such stigmata exist in some schools.

Sixth, *are sufficient and varied instructional materials available?* Reading materials should include functional and recreational reading materials, as well as skill development materials: paperbacks, menus, road maps, catalogs, greeting cards, filmstrips with captions, newspapers, magazines, hobby and recreation journals, play books, and TV guides, among others. Moffett (1968) says,

> Conventionally . . . poor readers whose problems go beyond decoding . . . are made to undergo the sort of dull, mechanical course that actually requires the "most" motivation, confidence and maturity to get through. They submit to "practice readers," "word study" workbooks, "skill builders," "spellers," and so on. Remediation that consists of relentless drills and comprehension questions is based on a false assumption that the underlying problems are reading problems, whereas the problems are ones that "manifest" themselves in reading as elsewhere. For these children reading should be more, not less, fun than for others. (p. 112)

Seventh, *is the school schedule flexible enough to allow the students who need remedial instruction to get as much as they need in the most efficacious time blocks for as long as they need it?* Too often scheduling difficulties interfere with remedial programs. Students miss art or physical education to go to remedial reading, or they must stay with the remedial teacher for an entire hour when twenty minutes would be a better block of time, or they are allowed only two years of remedial help to make room for other students, when, after two years, the remedial program is just beginning to produce good results for them.

Eighth, *are special in-service educational opportunities available to the remedial reading teacher?* Remedial reading teachers need continuing education just as classroom teachers do. Opportunities to discuss problems with other remedial reading teachers, to read, to confer with university and central office personnel, to be observed and evaluated, and to have special sessions at professional meetings are important to maintaining remedial teaching skills at a high level.

There are several advantages to having a full-time remedial reading teacher in one school. First, the teacher is likely to be well qualified academically and personally. Schools that spend the time, effort, and money to establish a good remedial reading program are likely to look very carefully for a competent specialist. Second, the normal reading curriculum may derive many benefits from curriculum modifications, classroom teachers' contacts with a special reading teacher, and a greater awareness of the need for ongoing reading curriculum development. Third, students who are severely reading disabled can receive the help they need as part of their regular school program. Problems of transporting students to different locations with the concomitant unsettling effects upon students and their parents are avoided. It is also easier for students to return to the regular classroom program when they have not left their building for remedial reading. The communication among the remedial teachers, classroom teachers, administrators, and parents is likely to be better when all are or can be closely involved with the program. And finally, the full-time remedial teacher assigned to one school has an opportunity to become involved with remedial readers' parents and their out-of-school community lives. Remedial reading teachers are not and should not try to be family counselors, and/or social workers. Nevertheless, home and community contacts on behalf of one, many, or all remedial readers in a school often pay big dividends. Full-time remedial teachers are in a good position to make the needed contacts.

This approach to the remedial reading teacher has some disadvantages. The seven conditions described earlier (staff preparation, flexible school schedule, enrollment limitations, and so forth) are difficult to achieve. Therefore, the effectiveness of the remedial program is often less than it would be under ideal conditions. Sometimes just one adverse condition—for example, lack of staff preparation for participating in a remedial program—can result in a program that is more wasteful than productive.

Another key factor in the success of this approach is the remedial teacher. A remedial teacher working full time in one school may have a negative as well as a positive effect on the entire school program and on the students themselves. Without the necessary personal and academic qualifications for the job, the

205

effect of the person's work may be more negative than positive. (We discuss personal and academic qualifications for reading specialists in chapter 9.) Thus schools implementing a full-time remedial reading teacher in one school approach need a highly qualified remedial teacher.

Some schools are using remedial reading teachers to work as resource teachers for classroom teachers or as reading consultants, as well as remedial teachers. In schools that have no other access to a reading specialist, this approach may be important in regard to preventing reading problems. However, excellent remedial reading teachers are not necessarily good resource persons for classroom teachers or good consultants. Therefore, care must be taken to ensure that good remedial teachers are not pressed into doing a job for which they are not qualified personally and/or academically.

REMEDIAL READING TEACHERS SERVING
MORE THAN ONE SCHOOL

Another fairly common approach to providing remedial reading instruction is to assign one or each remedial teacher to two or more schools. The approach is used when school districts don't have enough money for full-time remedial teachers in all schools or when certain schools do not have enough students with serious reading problems to warrant the employment of a full-time remedial teacher.

This approach is generally a compromise. Schools would prefer a full-time teacher if the budget allowed it, but at least they have access to a remedial teacher on a regular, though part-time, basis.

There are several pitfalls of programs in which schools share one remedial reading teacher. Essentially, in trying to do "at least something" for more than one school, the teacher may end up doing nothing substantial for any school. Although the evidence obtained from evaluating remedial reading programs is sketchy, the need for seriously disabled readers to have long-term daily instruction seems important—if not essential.

Remedial reading instruction should be coordinated with classroom instruction. The coordination for remedial teachers who are full-time staff members is difficult, it is more so for part-time teachers. Just scheduling remedial readers for special instruction when the remedial teacher is available is often a major problem. Furthermore, the part-time remedial teacher is sometimes perceived as more of a nuisance than a support and resource person. Administrators, classroom teachers, students, and the remedial teachers often end up dutifully going through their paces and acting out their roles halfheartedly. When the program remains in this condition or deteriorates to it, the likelihood of helping seriously disabled readers is slight. However, with good administrative leadership, energetic remedial teachers, and well-prepared classroom teachers, these problems can be worked out.

REMEDIAL READING CLINICS

Professionals other than teachers have historically participated in the attack upon reading disability. Their participation continues, more in some communities than in others. Some of the most popular teaching theories, methods, and materials are the products of neurologists, linguists, speech therapists, psychologists, pediatricians, and other professionals whose major training is not in education. In public school, university, and hospital settings, these professionals join with remedial teachers and form multidisciplinary teams, which always diagnose and sometimes prescribe programs for or treat disabled readers.

The reason for the formation of these interdisciplinary teams or clinics is that specific reading disability (often termed "dyslexia" in clinics in medical settings) may be caused by or related to factors not related to education, such as delayed speech development, emotional distress, neurological dysfunction, general physical debility, or poor motor control, which may need therapy before or in conjunction with remedial reading training. Typically, the disabled reader is diagnosed by each member of the team and their diagnostic findings are pooled at a meeting to determine whether the poor reader needs highly specialized treatment. Typically parents are counseled, reports are written, and an instructional program is prescribed. Often the program prescribed is one favored by most or all of the members of the team, the Gillingham-Stillman (1968) program, for example. The program can be administered in the clinic if the clinic has a school, in the student's regular school by a specially trained teacher, or by a private tutor or private practitioner. If medication, exercises, or other therapy is needed, that too is prescribed and given by the clinicians.

One of these authors has been a member of a hospital-based learning disabilities clinic for six years. In his judgment, the major service performed by that multidisciplinary team is the identification of the likely causes of the problem and the elimination of related physical and/or emotional problems that may be exacerbating the reading problem. The teachers who work with the reading problems, then, have the assurance that all possible factors have been investigated and that related problems have been or are being attended to. Some of the major benefits derived from the services of a multidisciplinary team are realized by the disabled reader's parents, who are frequently confused, fearful, and sometimes guilty about their children's disability. The complete diagnosis done by the team members, the careful explanation of the findings, and the recommendations of the team, who in combination can address themselves to nearly every possible area of human growth and development, often put parents' minds at ease, thereby eliminating one of the factors that has in all probability been aggravating the learning problem.

One of the less desirable aspects of remedial reading clinics is that students need to be transported to them, often at considerable expenditure of time and money. Another problem is the communication gaps that may occur among parents, the student's regular school personnel, and the clinicians. Professionals in different disciplines generally use a different vocabulary and often approach and discuss the same problem differently. Still another problem is the difficulty in coordinating the student's remedial program with the regular school program. Distance, terminology, and different perceptions and philosophies all work against effective coordination. Finally, remedial reading clinics are often very expensive, and there are not many of them. They are, therefore, available to only a small percentage of the total population of seriously disabled readers. Perhaps this last problem should not be perceived as a weakness in clinical programs. However, this fact of exclusivity can lead to a distorted view by clinicians of the vast majority of disabled readers. In other words, clinicians who repeatedly see a select sample from the total population may develop diagnostic instruments, instructional programs, and recommendations for identifying and treating seriously disabled readers who do not typify the actual population (poor readers from poor socioeconomic backgrounds, for example).

SUMMER PROGRAMS

Summer programs for remedial readers continue to be quite popular. They are generally organized and directed by an administrator or a reading specialist for students in one school, a cluster of schools, or the entire district. They select a site, procure tests and instructional materials, hire teachers, find students through teacher referrals and perhaps some screening procedures. These summer programs have several advantages:

1. Students who are receiving remedial instruction during the school year can have the special help they need continued through the summer. Harris (1968) says, "Studies tend to show that remedial reading can have very favorable outcomes but that the gains may be lost if the remediation is stopped too soon. Even a very occasional contact may help a pupil to maintain his momentum."
2. Students who have no or almost no pleasant association with reading during the school year may be able to derive some pleasure from reading or a reading-related activity during a summer program.
3. The summer program may result in a more thorough diagnosis of the student's reading strengths and weaknesses than was possible to obtain during the school year.

However, there are some negative aspects to many summer remedial reading programs:

1. The teachers in the program are often regular classroom teachers who are not necessarily remedial teachers.
2. The duration and timing of most programs amounts to too little too late.
3. Attendance is often poor because of family vacations and competing recreational opportunities.
4. Students resent attending school during the time they perceive to be vacation time they have earned or have a right to. Some programs stress that attendance is voluntary, but considerable subtle (or not so subtle) coercion is usually involved.
5. There is still some stigma attached to attending summer school, although it seems to be lessening.
6. The students referred to the programs may be too seriously disabled to profit from the kind of help available in the summer programs.

All things considered, summer remedial reading programs are of questionable value. Some school districts decide that the money spent on them might be used more wisely on assistance during the regular school year.

UNIVERSITY TEACHER-TRAINING PROGRAMS

University courses that are primarily or that include supervised teaching experiences with disabled readers are often a good source of help for remedial readers. Communities that are located near universities that train reading specialists are in a good position to obtain some inexpensive, high-quality, temporary teachers. There is, however, no guarantee that all university programs provide high-quality help for students in the public schools. Some university programs may upon close inspection do more harm than good. School districts should assist in the planning and implementation of all such programs to ensure good instruction for both the university students and the public school students. The following criteria should be insisted upon:

1. The disabled readers should receive enough instruction. Two thirty-to-forty-minute sessions a week is the minimum.
2. Excellent supervision of all student teachers by a qualified person should be provided. Supervision 75 percent of the time student teachers are working is important.
3. Time for planning and coordinating classroom and remedial programs should be a regularly scheduled part of the program. At least fifteen minutes a week is the minimal amount of time for the classroom teacher and the student teacher to confer.
4. Provisions for keeping disabled readers in the program for as long as they need special help should be part of the program.
5. Every student teacher should provide the school with a written report at the end of the supervised teaching experience. The report should include instructional objectives, tests and materials used, major instructional activities, an evaluation of the work done, and written reports of all conferences with parents.

VOLUNTEER TUTOR AND TEACHER AIDE PROGRAMS

Volunteers who work with disabled readers come from all walks of life: housewives, senior citizens, members of university societies, Future Teachers of America club members, retired teachers, and others. Some participate on an individual basis, some do through structured programs, such as "Youth Tutoring Youth." Often they have little, if any, special training for remedial teaching.

These volunteers and aides can be extremely helpful in working with able readers and perhaps helping students who have very minor problems, but they may do more damage than good if they try to remediate seriously disabled readers. Too often, sincere but untrained persons do little more for seriously disabled readers than keep them occupied. Therefore, untrained or minimally trained personnel should be used to help students who don't have problems and for clerical or administrative tasks, thereby giving classroom and remedial reading teachers more time to teach students with learning problems.

SOME GENERAL CONSIDERATIONS

The line between students with learning disabilities and those with reading problems is fuzzy and at this writing becoming fuzzier. In some schools, especially in districts that are reimbursed by the state for a large part of learning disabilities teachers' salaries, these teachers spend most of their time remediating reading problems. In Wisconsin, for example, 70 percent of learning disabilities teachers' salaries is state reimbursed. Obviously for economic reasons school administrators are hiring LD specialists to remediate reading problems. A major shortcoming in the arrangement is that these specialists may be much better trained to diagnose and teach students with general behavior problems, mental retardation, severe emotional disturbances, and other problems that are not specific reading problems. Or their approach to reading remediation may be so different from that taken by the classroom teachers that serious communication and coordination problems occur. The solution seems to lie in a fairly straightforward policy: any learning disabilities specialists who diagnose and treat serious reading problems should also be well trained in the diagnosis and treatment of reading problems.

A number of schools use federally allocated funds under Title I of the Elementary and Secondary Education Act for special programs for students who are "educationally disadvantaged." The special programs must be in addition to regular classroom programs. Often the most obvious educational disadvantage identified is reading. Unfortunately, not all teachers in Title I programs that emphasize remedial reading are qualified remedial reading teachers. In addition, the government's guidelines on evaluation, proposals, and other program-related matters may not work in the best interests of particular instructional programs. Therefore, whenever possible, school districts should establish their own remedial reading programs so that the Title I programs can be truly supplementary. Where this is impossible, administrators of Title I programs must insist that any teacher who works with remedial readers be qualified to do so.

Remedial reading specialists generally agree that the earlier one begins remedial reading instruction with students who give evidence of unusual difficulty, the better the results. Thus, the major remedial reading thrust should be in the primary grades. Remediating serious reading problems becomes increasingly difficult as students progress through the grades. No one would deny secondary students access to remedial reading instruction, but a wholesale attack on reading problems at the high school level is misplaced. We recommend the following guidelines for offering remedial reading instruction to secondary school students who have never had it before or who had it with no or little noticeable improvement:

1. The program should be voluntary for students. No one can force secondary school students to learn to read or convince them against their will that reading is important for them.
2. Instruction should be available at least three times a week for at least forty minutes each time.
3. The teacher should be highly qualified personally and academically for teaching secondary school students.
4. The students should agree to spend at least an additional thirty minutes a day, seven days a week reading or doing developmental reading activities.

Finally, a poor remedial reading program may be worse than none. The frustration and disenchantment resulting from a poorly administered or poorly taught program are devastating to students, parents, teachers, and administrators. There is no merit to starting and maintaining programs that don't have all of the components necessary to be effective. Too much money and personal energies have been wasted on poor quality programs that have done little more than occupy time and space and exist to assure the public that a program is available.

Summary

The most efficient way to eliminate reading problems is to prevent as many as possible from occurring. Good reading readiness programs, proper pacing, careful instruction, and the elimination of anxiety that interferes with learning are all factors in preventative teaching. Schools should be able to identify the measures they are taking to prevent reading problems.

Schools should also be able to identify the special measures they are taking to give students who develop relatively minor reading problems the special help they need in their regular classroom settings. Slower instruction, more practice exercises, and special materials are some provisions teachers can make to help corrective readers from becoming more seriously disabled.

Some students develop serious reading problems in spite of the best efforts to prevent and correct problems. These remedial readers need out-of-the-classroom diagnosis and instruction by a teacher with special training in this area. Occasionally specialists from disciplines other than education (such as neurologists and psychiatrists) are needed to contribute to the diagnostic or remediation process. Schools have a responsibility to develop high-quality remedial programs that provide for the identification of remedial readers, the diagnosis of their problems, and remedial instruction by a specially trained teacher.

Bibliography

Benn, Alice. "The Effects of Implementing a Corrective Reading Program on the Attitudes of the Teaching Staff and on the Reading Skills of Selected Pupils." Master's thesis, University of Wisconsin-Madison, 1973.

Gillingham, A., and B. Stillman. *Remedial Training for Children with Specific Disability in Reading, Spelling and Penmanship.* Cambridge, Mass.: Educator's Publishing Service, 1968.

Harris, Albert J. "Diagnosis and Remedial Instruction in Reading." In *Innovation and Change in Reading Instruction,* NSSE Yearbook, edited by Helen Robinson. Chicago: University of Chicago Press, 1968, pp. 159–193.

Johnson, Marjorie S., and Roy Kress. "Programs for Disabled Readers." *The Reading Teacher* 21 (May 1968): 706.

Moffett, James. *A Student-Centered Language Arts Curriculum, Grades K–6: A Handbook for Teachers.* Boston: Houghton Mifflin, 1968.

Otto, Wayne, Richard A. McMenemy, and Richard J. Smith. *Corrective and Remedial Teaching.* Boston: Houghton Mifflin, 1973.

Chapter 9 Specialized reading personnel

The emphasis that American schools put on teaching children to read and the practice of using printed material in the content areas to help teachers teach specific subjects place considerable responsibility to teach reading on teachers at all academic levels. Although primary school teachers start the reading process, no other teacher is exempt from continuing the development of the students' reading abilities. One would think, then, that all teachers and principals would have studied and had field experiences in reading pedagogy and the supervision and administration of reading programs. This is not the case. Nearly all classroom teachers and principals say that they need more training in the teaching of reading and in administering and supervising reading programs.

Part of this need stems from a long history of insufficient attention to the training of teachers and administrators in teaching reading and developing reading programs. The first Harvard-Carnegie reading study, undertaken to determine how well prospective teachers were being prepared to teach reading, revealed that the pre-service education of elementary school teachers was shockingly inadequate in this area. Austin and Morrison (1963) summarized the findings of their study:

> . . . (1) Three per cent of the colleges and universities do not require prospective elementary school teachers to enroll in any course work devoted to the teaching of reading as a requirement for graduation (2) when reading is taught with other related subjects in a single course (for example, language arts), as is done in 50 per cent of the colleges, actual class hours devoted to reading average only 8, (3) when time is a factor, intermediate grade study skills will usually be omitted from the course, or, if included, will be treated so cursorily as to be of little benefit to the prospective intermediate grade teacher, (4) little preparation is offered that will help beginning teachers to

recognize, diagnose, or treat reading difficulties, and (5) little, if any, guidance is offered in reading research. (p. 164)

A second study was initiated to answer some questions raised by the first, including the role principals play in improving reading instruction in their schools. Austin and Morrison (1963) concluded, "There is evidence that some principals are reluctant to accept major responsibility for instructional improvement because they are unfamiliar with curriculum matters, particularly those relating to the reading program" (p. 204).

Prospective secondary school teachers have even less training in teaching reading than elementary school teachers have. Burnett (1966) assessed the pre-service education of secondary teachers and judged that the training they received for teaching reading was often nonexistent and at best exceedingly general and superficial. Moore (1961) has described the feelings of secondary school teachers about teaching reading:

> One reason why teachers have failed to embrace the notion that "all teachers are teachers of reading" is that they have not been clear as to why they should be. They have not seen reading related to the basic purpose of the content fields in such a fashion as to make clear the significance of reading problems, nor what they, as content teachers, may do to assist in solving such problems.

Certainly the fact that many teachers and principals have not received sufficient education in reading pedagogy is at least partly responsible for the weaknesses of reading programs. As late as 1963 the situation seemed dismal. Austin and Morrison (1963) reported:

> . . . after visits to fifty-one school systems in the original study and fourteen in the supplementary study, observations in about two thousand classrooms, and interviews with approximately twenty-five hundred school personnel, the staff concluded that present day reading programs were mediocre at best and not currently designed to produce a future society of mature readers. (p. 2)

Without doubt, conditions have improved greatly since these studies were reported. Teacher preparation institutions have revised their curriculums to include more and better courses in the teaching of reading and in the development of school reading programs. Some states have made certification requirements

215

more demanding in regard to preparation for teaching reading. In a number of states, for example, all secondary school teachers are required to complete at least one reading methods course; and it seems likely that more, and perhaps all, states will follow suit. Large sums of federal money have been spent on teachers, instructional materials, and in-service education to improve reading instruction for educationally disadvantaged students. Many school districts, realizing their reading curriculum needs, have hired specially trained reading teachers and consultants. Workshops, lecturers, conferences, and other kinds of in-service education in reading have been made increasingly available to teachers and administrators.

The studies done in the 1960s resulted in calls for action, which are being met in a number of ways. Therefore, the theme running throughout this chapter is a positive one: reading specialists are needed in schools to advance the work in reading program improvement that is already well begun. We are not unmindful of the work remaining to be done in teacher-training institutions, as well as in public schools. However, in this chapter, we will emphasize the role of public school reading specialists working for the continual improvement of reading instruction, kindergarten through grade twelve.

Qualifications of reading specialists

Although many state certification agencies and teacher training institutions have established criteria for reading specialist certificates, licenses, or degrees, these criteria vary widely from state to state and from institution to institution. Austin (1968) says, "In reviewing the requirements for teacher certification in reading, the lack of agreement among states concerning operational definitions of 'reading teacher,' 'remedial reading personnel' and 'reading consultants' is evident" (p. 372). In regard to university programs for training reading specialists, she comments:

> In many instances, their preparation has been too meager to enable them to meet the demands placed upon them. In fact, the availability of those persons who possess the requisite skills is limited, and their training frequently is incomplete or impractical. Consequently, universities should design special programs for training teachers to become qualified, knowledgeable reading consultants. (p. 380)

Because university programs and state certification requirements vary and change frequently, the specific differences among them will not be presented here. The minimal educational qualifications suggested by the International Reading Association (1968), however, we believe are representative of those required by universities, state agencies, and sometimes individual school districts that have established educational requirements for reading specialists:

Special Teacher of Reading   Complete a planned program for the master's degree from an accredited institution to include:

1. A minimum of 12 semester hours in graduate level reading courses with at least one course in each of the following:
   a. Foundations or survey of reading. A basic course whose content is related exclusively to reading instruction or the psychology of reading. Such a course ordinarily would be first in a sequence of reading courses.
   b. Diagnosis and correction of reading disabilities. The content of this course or courses includes the following: causes of reading disabilities; observation and interview procedures; diagnostic instruments; standard and informal tests; report writing; materials and methods of instruction.
   c. Clinical or laboratory practicum in reading. A clinical or laboratory experience which might be an integral part of a course or courses in the diagnosis and correction of reading disabilities. Students diagnose and treat reading disability cases under supervision.
2. Complete, at undergraduate or graduate level, study in each of the following areas:
   a. Measurement and/or evaluation.
   b. Child and/or adolescent psychology.
   c. Psychology, including such aspects as personality, cognition and learning behaviors.
   d. Literature for children and/or adolescents.
3. Fulfill remaining portions of the program from related areas of study.

Reading Clinician   Meet the qualifications as stipulated for the Special Teacher of Reading and, in addition, complete a sixth year of graduate work to include:

1. An advanced course or courses in the diagnosis and remediation of reading and learning problems.
2. A course or courses in individual testing.

217

3. An advanced clinical or laboratory practicum in the diagnosis and remediation of reading difficulties.
4. Field experiences under the direction of a qualified Reading Clinician.

Reading Consultant Meet the qualifications as stipulated for the Special Teacher of Reading and, in addition, complete a sixth year of graduate work to include:

1. An advanced course in the remediation and diagnosis of reading and learning problems.
2. An advanced course in the developmental aspects of a reading program.
3. A course or courses in curriculum development and supervision.
4. A course and/or experience in public relations.
5. Field experiences under a qualified Reading Consultant or Supervisor in a school setting.

Reading Supervisor Meet the qualifications as stipulated for the Special Teacher of Reading and, in addition, complete a sixth year of graduate work to include:

1. Courses listed as 1, 2, 3, and 4 under Reading Consultant.
2. A course or courses in administrative procedures.
3. Field experiences under a qualified Reading Supervisor.

We do not believe that a national standardization of state certification policies or of university programs for specialized reading personnel is advisable. Different states have different needs and resources, and different universities should have the right to structure their programs according to their philosophies, their students' needs, and their resources. In addition, individual school districts have created positions for "specialists" in reading that were not formerly conceived of and that are so varied and changing, in kind and level of specialized training needed, that establishing criteria for qualifications is no longer realistic except at the individual school level. Suffice it to say that the designation "reading specialist" is so broad in meaning that one can only respond to the designation by asking what the specialist does and what training he or she has or needs. In our judgment this condition reflects an individualization and diversification that are healthy and important for the employment of specialists to work with a phenomenon as dynamic and varied as reading curriculum. The concept of accountability has probably done more to ensure the placing of qualified people in specialized positions than national or state course work requirements ever did.

This is not an argument for the abolition of the International Reading Association recommendations. These guidelines and similar ones are welcome so long as they do not stifle the creation of new positions and training programs for people who are hired to fill them.

Different states and different school districts generate positions that allow professionals to work for reading improvement in a variety of ways that are different from the work of teaching reading in classroom settings. These "specialists" (we use the term broadly rather than as a designation of some level of academic achievement) should determine the nature and amount of training necessary to do the job well. For example, a group of classroom teachers given some released time each week to assist their principals in conferring with other classroom teachers, ordering materials, or performing other services related to reading instruction need a far different kind of training from that needed by a secondary school consultant whose total responsibility is helping content area teachers incorporate reading instruction into their daily teaching.

PERSONAL QUALIFICATIONS

Personal qualifications are as important as educational qualifications to the effectiveness of reading specialists. It is important that the student, teacher, or administrator who receives help and the specialist who gives it emerge from the exchange with a desire to work together again.

Anyone who has worked as a specialist knows that people who are most in need of specialized help are often also most reluctant to receive it. Therefore, the reading specialist frequently has to initiate the communication with teachers and administrators. Thus, only those who can initiate and maintain communication in a nonthreatening manner will be successful in changing the behavior of the recipients of the specialized help.

Patience is an important personal characteristic for a reading specialist. Teaching concepts and changing behavior are slow processes, so the specialist must be prepared for the long periods of time required by others to assimilate concepts relative to grouping students, diagnosing problems, evaluating programs, developing positive attitudes toward reading, and other complex aspects of teaching reading. Helping them modify their behavior takes even more time. One of us worked with a school principal for nearly a year before he understood that referring students to remedial teachers solely on the evidence of standardization reading tests scores was a poor practice. It took another year before more sophisticated referral practices were instituted.

219

Reading specialists must also be able to accept defeat and not be defeated. Ideally, all conditions can be structured and controlled to contribute maximally to each student's reading development. But not everyone can be helped. Realistically, there are always inept or uncooperative people, shortages of funds, lack of space, community pressure groups, lack of enlightening research, and other obstacles. Unfortunately, rebuffs are still part of educational specialists' work lives. Some teachers and even students may resent the specialists and look upon their attempts to improve instruction as interfering, imposing personal values, or making a living the easy way. Specialists must realize that negative attitudes exist and will be manifested in mild rebuffs and occasional open hostility and meet these attitudes with calmness and a refusal to do battle. Reading specialists who are not prepared for some resistance to their efforts to change behavior may be shattered personally before the reading program is improved.

Finally, reading specialists have to be able to maintain objectivity while working with people. They must empathize with many different personality types, establish rapport, be sensitive to people with a variety of problems, and offer advice according to their appraisal of the individual to whom they are speaking. This work demands a personal involvement that is physically and emotionally draining. Specialists need to acknowledge the personalities with whom they work without losing their own identity and without losing sight of their job.

The same qualifications are necessary for specialists who work with adults or with children in need of specialized reading instruction. Specialists who are unable to establish good personal relationships with children can rarely communicate effectively with adults about matters that are ultimately concerned with teaching reading to children.

EXPERIENCE QUALIFICATIONS

No one should become a reading specialist without having had successful classroom teaching experience. Teachers and principals are much more willing to work with specialists who have been successful teachers. In addition, specialists who have been classroom teachers are more likely to know the problems of classroom teachers and to offer practical advice. "When I was teaching . . ." are often the words that open minds and classroom doors when they are injected by a reading specialist into conferences with teachers and principals. In addition, reading specialists need a background of teaching experience with students at as many different ability levels and from as many different cultural backgrounds as possible. For this reason it is good for them to have taught in a variety of schools serving students with various abilities and various cultural differences.

Because of the differences between elementary and secondary schools, it is advisable for a reading specialist to have had previous successful teaching experience at the level he or she is working at. Those who work at both levels should have had teaching experience at one level and have thoroughly studied reading instruction in the other. Elementary school teachers tend to feel that secondary school teachers know very little about teaching in the elementary school, and secondary teachers think that elementary teachers don't fully understand the jobs of secondary teachers. These feelings are probably valid because of the major differences in the pre-service education of elementary and secondary teachers.

Classroom teaching experience is also important for the specialist who works directly with students. Because students who receive special instruction attend regular classroom settings, coordinating special programs with classroom programs is vital. Specialists who haven't had this kind of experience can have difficulty in communicating with classroom teachers and in planning coordinated programs for their students. How much teaching experience is necessary seems to be a highly individual matter. Wisconsin requires two years of teaching experience for certification as either a reading teacher or a reading specialist. However, that figure was probably set more arbitrarily than scientifically.

Typical roles of specialists

Reading specialists generally function either as teachers of students with special needs or as consultants to administrators and classroom teachers. Figure 9.1 shows how personnel in a school district with reading specialists in the central office and reading specialists (consultants and teachers) in schools might be organized. It also shows the positions for which reading specialists are most frequently employed. Not all school districts have or need all of the different reading specialists included in the figure (although some do) and some employ specialists that serve different roles from those in the figure.

READING COORDINATOR

Reading coordinators are farther away from the actual business of teaching students than other reading specialists are. Typically

Figure 9.1 **Organization of reading specialists within a school
district's central office and within schools**

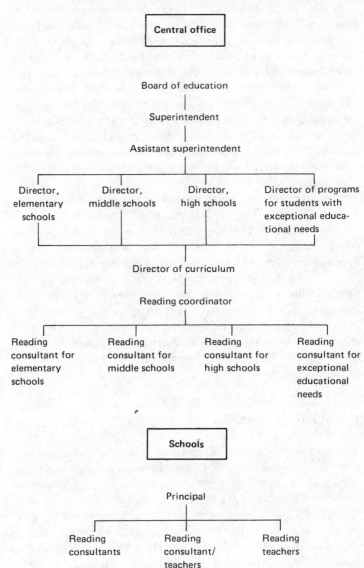

Central office

Board of education

Superintendent

Assistant superintendent

Director,
elementary
schools

Director,
middle schools

Director,
high schools

Director of programs
for students with
exceptional educa-
tional needs

Director of curriculum

Reading coordinator

Reading
consultant for
elementary
schools

Reading
consultant for
middle schools

Reading
consultant for
high schools

Reading
consultant for
exceptional
educational
needs

Schools

Principal

Reading
consultants

Reading
consultant/
teachers

Reading
teachers

they are not hired in small districts that do not also have a relatively large central office staff or do not have a number of other
reading specialists. The following position description indicates
a reading coordinator's duties and the desired qualifications:

Reading Coordinator

Reports to: Director of curriculum development.

Supervises: Central office reading consultants and reading
teachers.

Required experience and training: Master's degree in remedial
and/or developmental reading; at least six years of successful
teaching experience in the areas of remedial and developmental reading; successful experience in leadership roles with
teacher groups.

Desired additional experience and training: Ph.D., Ed.D., or
reading specialist degree or certificate with emphasis in reading curriculum and instruction; successful experience with research.

Desired personal characteristics: Creativity; leadership qualities;
ability to work cooperatively with teachers, principals, and
central staff personnel; ability to communicate orally and in
writing at a high level of proficiency.

Position responsibilities:

Designs and directs new development in the instructional
reading program, K–12.

Provides in-service education for central office reading consultants, teachers, and administrators.

Interprets the reading program to the board of education and
community groups.

Assists in developing systemwide testing procedures relevant
to the reading program.

Advises and cooperates with nearby universities in teacher
education and research relative to reading.

Aids in the recruitment, interviewing, and selection of reading program personnel.

Designs and directs reading research.

Attends and participates in meetings relevant to the school
system's reading programs.

Disseminates information regarding reading program development throughout the school system at the local, state,
and national levels.

Visits classrooms with the approval of school principals to assist in evaluating teachers and improving their capabilities
in the area of reading instruction.

223

Assists the director of curriculum development in the preparation of course outlines and teaching guides.

Assists in the evaluation and selection of textbooks and other resource materials.

Works with the central office reading consultants to coordinate the reading curriculum from kindergarten to grade 12.

CENTRAL OFFICE READING CONSULTANT

The following example of a position description for a reading consultant working out of a central office should illustrate the role that person might play and the academic and personal characteristics needed for successful performance.

Central Office Reading Consultant

Reports to: Reading coordinator. (If the school district does not employ a reading coordinator, reports to curriculum director, assistant superintendent or superintendent).

Supervises: Reading teachers assigned to individual schools.

Required experience and training: Master's degree with an emphasis in reading; successful teaching experience at the academic level assigned.

Desired additional experience and training: Ph.D., Ed.D., or reading specialist degree or active engagement in an academic program leading to one of the above; successful experience in teacher education and in leadership roles with teacher groups.

Desired personal characteristics: Ability to work cooperatively with teachers, principals, and central office personnel; leadership ability; ability to communicate orally at a high level of proficiency; good sense of organization.

Position responsibilities:

Aids school staffs in developing objectives for reading instruction in the schools assigned.

Organizes and conducts in-service education programs for classroom teachers and for reading teachers assigned to individual schools.

Aids the reading coordinator in research relative to the reading programs being conducted in the schools assigned.

Investigates materials for the academic level assigned and recommends their purchase to teachers and principals.

Aids the reading teacher and the principal in developing and evaluating special instructional programs.

Aids the reading teachers in a continual evaluation of each
school's reading program.

Studies the latest writings and research on reading instruction
at the academic level assigned and communicates this information to teachers and administrators.

Works with reading teachers for initiating projects that will
benefit from a temporary team approach.

Diagnoses and prescribes instruction for seriously disabled
readers.

Communicates frequently with central office reading consultants assigned to other schools and other academic levels.

Works with the reading coordinator and other central office
reading consultants to coordinate the reading curriculum
from kindergarten to grade 12.

Supervises reading teachers in their work with teachers and
students.

Introduces innovative reading programs and materials to the
schools assigned.

Serves on textbook and other committees that affect reading in
the schools assigned.

Gives classroom demonstrations for teachers.

Conducts in-service meetings and classes for reading teachers,
classroom teachers, administrators, and parent groups.

BUILDING CONSULTANT/TEACHER (SECONDARY SCHOOL)

Building consultants are much more likely to be assigned to secondary than elementary schools. In addition, small secondary
schools (fewer than one thousand students) are less likely than
larger schools to employ a full-time consultant. This is not to say
that small schools do not need help with staff development by a
reading specialist, but many times part-time consultants from
nearby colleges, universities, or larger public school districts can
help meet their needs.

Many secondary schools, and in increasing numbers elementary schools, hire a reading specialist who works as a consultant
and as a teacher. These consultant/teachers or teacher/consultants,
depending on the emphasis, work with both students and staff.
In most schools, the use of this dual role appears to be a good
way to establish a reading specialist in a building. Although a
full-time specialist working as a consultant may promote reading
growth for a greater number of students by working through all
teachers rather than directly with students, misunderstandings
about the role and opposition to it may occur on the parts of both

225

parents and teachers. An increasing number of schools are discovering that a reading specialist must first develop a reputation as a good teacher who is immediately concerned with and attending to the needs of poor readers before parents and teachers become satisfied with this expenditure of money and become willing to seek consultation about their own roles in improving reading ability.

The following position description is an example of one that might be developed for a secondary school consultant/teacher. Omitting consultant responsibilities would result in a position description for a full-time special reading teacher.

Consultant/Teacher (Secondary School)

Reports to: The principal.
Supervises: No one.

Required experience and training: Master's degree or enrollment in a program leading to a master's degree with an emphasis in reading; course work in developmental reading in the secondary school, remedial reading, principles of appraisal and measurement, supervised teaching of students in a secondary school instructional reading program; successful teaching experience in a content area in a secondary school.

Desired additional experience and training: Reading specialist degree or certification beyond the master's degree; successful teaching experience in more than one content area in a secondary school.

Desired personal characteristics: Ability to establish and maintain good interpersonal relationships with high school students, teachers, parents, and administrators; leadership abilities; ability to communicate orally at a high level of proficiency; good sense of organization.

Position responsibilities:
Develops and maintains, with the help of central office reading consultants, a systematic developmental reading program residing in the content areas by helping content area teachers incorporate the teaching of reading into their curriculums. This help may be in the form of in-service meetings, demonstrations, individual conferences, or team teaching.
Develops and teaches special classes, seminars, and workshops, and supervises individualized study projects for

students with special reading needs, which may be remedial, corrective, or accelerated. These special instructional programs should be closely related to the work being done in the content area classes and sometimes conducted in conjunction with a particular unit of study.

Advises the principal and central office reading consultants regarding desired reading program development.

Implements, with the help of central office reading consultants and guidance counselors, a testing program and communicates information regarding students' reading abilities to their content area teachers.

Administers diagnostic reading tests to specially referred students and on the basis of the test results recommends special materials, assignments, and achievement expectancies to their teachers.

Teams with reading teachers in other schools and with central office reading consultants to conduct short-term projects or in-service work in another school.

The role of the reading teacher in the secondary school is much more clear-cut and much better accepted by teachers than the role of reading consultant. Most secondary teachers know that some, perhaps many, of their students cannot read the assigned materials. Consequently, they generally welcome the reading specialist, who should make their jobs as content area teachers simpler and more effective. In addition, these difficult-to-teach students will be the responsibility of someone else.

It is a shock when the specialist announces his or her intention to help the teachers, not the students. Furthermore, the specialist insists that even the good students in their classes could improve their reading if the content area teachers taught them how to read the material they assigned. Instead of simplifying the teachers' jobs, the specialist appears to be complicating them by asking teachers to individualize assignments, use materials other than the textbook, introduce vocabulary, provide purposes for reading, give shorter reading assignments, ask questions at higher cognitive levels, use informal reading inventories, and ascertain each student's instructional reading level.

The teachers may complain: "If I wanted to teach reading, I'd be an elementary teacher." "I thought someone was finally going to teach these poor kids how to read." "I don't know a vowel from a consonant, and I'm supposed to teach reading. Who's the reading specialist, anyway?" "Why doesn't the elementary school just go back to teaching phonics?" "I can't cover my courses now. How am I going to teach reading too?"

227

Unquestionably, secondary school reading consultants will continue to have their work cut out for them, until the preservice education of secondary teachers persuades them that part of their responsibility is to teach their students how to read the material they assign. Many secondary teachers lack both the knowledge and the willingness necessary for incorporating the teaching of reading into their content area teaching. They are not convinced that helping students learn to read is part of their jobs. Secondary school reading consultants must be diplomats, as well as specialists, in teaching reading in content areas. The slogan "Every teacher is a teacher of reading," although intended to help communication, may have worked to separate specialists and teachers even further. Consultants should not convey the idea that they want to teach content area teachers to be reading teachers. Rather, they should explain that they want to give some suggestions to help content area teachers help their students read their assignments more efficiently and with better comprehension.

READING TEACHER (ELEMENTARY SCHOOL)

Reading specialists assigned to elementary schools (sometimes serving two or more schools) typically teach poor readers who are referred to them according to established guidelines or criteria. The following position description might be written for an elementary school reading teacher.

Special reading teacher (elementary school)

Reports to: The principal.
Supervises: No one.

Required experience and training: Bachelor's degree with an emphasis in elementary education; graduate courses in developmental reading in the elementary school, remedial reading, and principles of appraisal and measurement; supervised experience with diagnosis, remediation, and evaluation of disabled readers in the elementary school; successful teaching experience in the elementary school.

Desired additional experience and training: Master's degree or reading specialist degree or certification; successful teaching experience in both primary and intermediate grades.

Desired personal characteristics: Ability to establish and maintain good interpersonal relationships with children, teachers, parents, and administrators; leadership ability; ability to communicate orally at a high level of proficiency.

Position responsibilities:

Organizes a systematic plan of referral and instruction for disabled readers likely to profit from individual or near-individual teaching.

Diagnoses and gives remedial instruction to students with reading disabilities.

Acts as a resource person for the principal and teachers in reading to the employment of materials, methods, etc., for reading instruction.

Diagnoses and prescribes corrective programs for mildly disabled students likely to profit from corrective help by their classroom teacher.

Confers with central office reading consultants regarding systemwide reading program development in the elementary school.

To conclude this discussion of typical roles of reading specialists, we feel that specialized reading personnel would be more effective in improving reading instruction if they were given more realistic and more clearly defined assignments than they typically receive. Currently many spend too much time and energy attacking overwhelming numbers of problems or deciding which problems fall within their domain and which do not. A reading specialist who is responsible for systemwide testing programs, materials evaluation and selection, in-service education for classroom teachers, and other duties does not have the time to administer diagnostic tests to individual students, confer with parents, give remedial instruction, refer students to special reading laboratories or classes, and so on. The key to the effective utilization of specialized personnel is specific, realistic job descriptions. If the number of specialists available is too limited to accomplish the many tasks that need doing, then task priorities have to be set and clearly communicated throughout the school system.

Our position descriptions include more responsibilities than most specialists should be expected to perform. Our purpose was not to list actual descriptions but rather to provide an idea of what information might be included in them and some ideas about the different kinds of specialists. The specifics of how to accomplish the kind of improvement desired are best left to individual schools or school districts.

Innovative roles for reading specialists

Two innovative programs that utilize the regular teaching staff to improve reading instruction are the reading resource teacher program and the reading research teacher program. The teachers who participate in these programs can be defined as reading specialists if the term is defined broadly enough to include classroom teachers who have special training and released time from classroom duties to perform special services for improving reading instruction. Our examples, which describe programs in Madison, Wisconsin, can be replicated in school districts with similar characteristics or modified for school districts with quite different needs and resources.

READING RESOURCE TEACHERS

The reading resource teacher program was established in the Madison, Wisconsin, public schools as a means of helping elementary school principals fulfill their instructional leadership responsibilities in the area of reading curriculum development. Volunteer classroom teachers were given a twenty-hour in-service training program in reading and, at the beginning of the program, one-half day a week released time from their classroom duties to assist their principals in developing good instructional reading programs. These teachers are now released one day a week. The program is designed to give principals easy access to a person with a special interest and special training in a major curriculum area. The specifics of the Madison program have been reported in detail by Smith (1969).

One important factor in determining the roles of the resource teachers has been the effectiveness of the principals and these teachers in gaining staff understanding and acceptance of the reading resource teacher concept. Some principals have effectively established their reading resource teachers as consultants to other teachers in their buildings. In schools where their role as consultants has been accepted by the teachers, reading resource teachers spend most of their released time conferring with individual classroom teachers about grouping, materials, diagnostic procedures, and other common concerns. In schools where the consultant role has not been emphasized, the reading resource teachers work more directly with students, to diagnose reading problems, establish tutorial programs, and teach students who have special needs.

One important role of all reading resource teachers has been to help maintain a liaison between central office staff and teachers in the individual elementary schools. At periodic meetings between the central office staff and small groups of reading resource teachers the teachers can discuss their problems, share their satisfactions, and become acquainted with central office activities in reading curriculum development. Central office personnel, in turn, become familiarized with classroom problems and with program development.

Reading resource teachers are first and foremost classroom teachers. However, their title, special training, and accomplishments have given them some extra prestige among administrators, other classroom teachers, and parents. Their expertise in reading instruction is generally acknowledged throughout the community. Consequently, they are often called upon to support teachers' requests to principals on matters related to the teaching of reading and to help convey teachers' judgments regarding individual students to the students' parents. It is not unusual for reading resource teachers to work cooperatively with other teachers to prepare for parent-teacher or principal-teacher conferences and sometimes participate in these conferences.

Principals, parents, teachers, students, central office staff, and reading resource teachers have expressed satisfaction with the program, which must be attributed to the voluntary and flexible nature of the program that permits participating schools to determine the roles of these reading resource teachers. Few schools have left the program, and only a few reading resource teachers have asked to be replaced. When a reading resource teacher does request a replacement, volunteers are generally available.

Currently the only major dissatisfaction appears to be the shortage of released time available for reading resource teachers to perform the many services they are capable of performing. It has been necessary to caution these teachers not to overburden themselves but to be satisfied to give service in accord with the limitations of the amount of their released time.

READING RESEARCH TEACHERS

Another innovative program for identifying and training classroom teachers to serve specialized roles in middle school reading curriculum development was implemented in the Madison, Wisconsin, district. The principals of three middle schools (grades 6, 7, and 8) were consulted by a district reading consultant and a professor from the University of Wisconsin about recruiting several classroom teachers to conduct research with their own students that might be helpful in discovering ways to improve the reading of students in the middle grades.

Eleven teachers from three different content areas and one learning disabilities teacher, who were interested in hearing more about the proposal before committing themselves, met with the program directors to hear the proposal. The plan was for the reading consultant and the university professor to help the teachers identify research questions relative to their students' reading and for the reading consultant, the university professor, and the district coordinator for research and testing to help the teachers design studies to answer their questions. The teachers were to be given released time to meet three or four times a year as a group and individually in their schools to receive the help they needed. The twelve teachers agreed to participate with the understanding that they could terminate their participation at any time. As it turned out, none took advantage of the option to terminate. As the program progressed, apprehension disappeared and enthusiasm increased.

The questions identified by the reading research teachers were directly related to the improvement of reading instruction for middle-grade students. Group meetings were held to discuss common concerns, keep each other informed about the progress of individual studies, and to study research design, simple statistical procedures, and methodology for the research. Studies reported in professional journals were read and discussed as models for the reading research teachers to follow.

Each research teacher was visited in his or her school by the reading consultant, the university professor, and the coordinator for research and testing upon request. The teachers were helped to find or construct instruments for measuring student growth and helped with typical problems in collecting data, establishing treatment groups, and planning for data analyses. The educational significance of the studies was discussed frequently, and the reading consultant and the university professor had many opportunities to talk with the teachers about the teaching of reading.

The first studies were concerned with the following aspects of teaching reading in the middle grades:

○ Reading interests
○ Student-teacher conferences about books
○ Reading to students
○ Teaching poetic devices (such as metaphors and personification)
○ Using audio visual aids as prereading organizers

- Establishing the effect of time of day on comprehension of science material
- Using recipes to teach following directions
- Teaching strategies for improving comprehension of short stories
- Contracting for practice reading at home
- Evaluating subjectively versus using standardized tests
- Listening to social studies materials versus reading them

When the studies were concluded, a group meeting was held to decide the best method of disseminating the results and the instructional implications of the studies to other middle grades teachers. The decision was to publish the studies in a journal format and make them available to interested teachers and administrators. In addition, the group decided to hold in-service meetings with other teachers and administrators throughout the district so they could present their studies and communicate their enthusiasm for engaging in reading curriculum development.

After the first group of reading research teachers had accomplished its goals, a new group was formed. Several teachers from the first group are now working with the new group to help get it started. All of the teachers in the original group have indicated an interest in continued participation in various kinds of curriculum development activities in their individual schools.

Employing a reading specialist

The role of the reading specialist is often misunderstood and almost always difficult to establish. If the specialist is a remedial teacher, expectations may be unrealistic, and coordinating remedial instruction with classroom instruction is always difficult to accomplish. If the specialist is a teacher of college-bound, secondary school students, the position may be perceived as a frill or a "soft touch." Reading coordinators or consultants working out of the central office may be looked upon by teachers and principals as outsiders who would be better employed teaching poor readers than teaching teachers and developing curriculum, a process difficult to describe to those who haven't done it. Specialists who act as building consultants may be seen as interfering and not doing their fair share in the instructional program because they don't spend all of their time teaching students. The misperceptions and communication gaps that can develop around the roles of reading specialists are very real obstacles to their effectiveness and job satisfactions.

However, careful and cooperative planning can reduce and perhaps even eliminate the misperceptions and communication gaps that frequently interfere with the work of reading specialists. School districts that hire reading specialists should know what aspect of their reading curriculum is most in need of attention. For example, schools with increasing numbers of linguistically diverse students may need to add one or more teachers with an expertise in teaching beginning reading to these children. Districts that discover through one kind of needs assessment or another (usually standardized test administration) an unexpected number of students with serious reading problems may want a specially trained remedial reading teacher. A high school that enrolls a high percentage of students who go to college may want someone to teach speed reading or classes in reading improvement for college-bound seniors. Still another high school might discover that students are reading their content area assignments with poor comprehension and want to hire a consultant to help content area teachers teach their students to read assigned material with better comprehension. The point is that different schools have students with different needs, and specialists should be hired first of all to help students with special needs, whatever those needs might be.

In most school districts, the results of a student-needs assessment must be used to establish priorities on the most urgent needs. From a very practical standpoint, the assessment is usually necessary to persuade administrators that hiring a reading specialist is a needed expenditure.

The student-needs assessment, which can include standardized testing, student surveys, parent surveys, and teacher surveys, should be followed by the formation of a reading curriculum advisory committee. This committee should be responsible for analyzing the results of the student-needs assessment, deciding the qualifications (personal as well as academic) of the reading specialist that is needed, and writing a job description for the desired specialist. It is good procedure to allow some flexibility in the job description: people and job descriptions are rarely perfect matches, and when someone with the essential qualifications is hired, it is good to let that person assist in writing a more permanent job description.

Administrators, district reading specialists, classroom teachers, parents, and, if the specialist is to work at the high school level, students, should be represented on the advisory committee. If committee members feel the need for some guidance by a person who can maintain an objective attitude or for some kind of expertise committee members themselves do not possess, someone experienced in reading curriculum development who is not regularly employed by the district should be hired to assist the committee. Universities and other school districts are good resources for finding such a person.

Since the members of the reading advisory committee are representing different groups with which the reading specialist being hired will have to work, they will need to talk with the people they represent either through informal contacts or formal surveys. Staff meetings might be devoted to sharing the work of the committee and soliciting information and perceptions from teachers. A similar strategy might be used by the parent representative at a meeting of the parents' association and by the student representative at a student council meeting. Most school districts have regular meetings for administrators or an administrative council where the committee work can be discussed. Probably the most difficult people to involve in the decision-making process are secondary school classroom teachers. The size of the group and the diversity of backgrounds and interests make obtaining information and perceptions from them difficult, especially if the school is a large one.

Hesse and Smith (1973) constructed and used an instrument for discovering secondary school content area teachers' perceptions and preferences regarding the role played by reading specialists in their schools. With modifications, this instrument might be used effectively by the reading curriculum advisory committee for obtaining information from elementary as well as secondary teachers, administrators, and perhaps even parent and student groups. The instrument is designed to elicit a response of "very important," "important," "undecided," "not too important," or "unimportant" to each of the forty-two items below.

How important is it for a reading specialist to do each of the following?
1. Help measure the ability of each of your students to read the material you assign.
2. Administer diagnostic reading tests to students identified as having problems in reading.
3. Help plan instruction that teaches students to infer ideas that are not directly stated in the material read.
4. Compile and interpret profiles of standardized reading test scores for your class.
5. Aid in constructing questions that will lead students to comprehend, analyze and evaluate materials you assign.

235

6. Teach, in various subject area classes, sequences of appropriate reading lessons that are based on the materials assigned in those classes.
7. Discuss with you ways to use oral reading in your class so that the best interests of both good and poor readers are served.
8. Conduct inservice sessions that will give all teachers a better understanding of the reading process and how to teach reading.
9. Sit in on classes and help determine the effectiveness of your teaching of reading in your subject area.
10. Teach, in various subject area classes, sequences of appropriate reading lessons through use of commercial reading workbooks and kits.
11. Discuss with you the reasons why certain students appear to remain poor readers in spite of extra help they have received.
12. Offer classes in efficient reading for teachers so they might improve their reading speed.
13. Teach word analysis and basic comprehension skills to classes of low level readers.
14. Provide teachers with workbooks, kits and other instructional material that students can work through independently to improve their general vocabulary and comprehension.
15. Offer suggestions for individualizing your reading assignments according to students' abilities and interests.
16. Conduct short lecture-discussion sessions at staff meetings on the topic of "helping students who have reading problems."
17. Aid in setting up classroom situations in which students can work together in pairs or small groups on reading skills used to read materials you assign.
18. Help find readings more suited to certain students' abilities than the textbook.
19. Provide classes in reading for teachers, so they might improve their own critical reading skills.
20. Team with a committee of teachers, department heads and the principal in setting the goals of the school reading program.
21. Teach reading classes for college preparatory students and students with good basic skill development.
22. Set up and operate a study skills center where students can get individual help with their reading assignments.
23. Assist in selecting and sequencing class activities related

to reading that will aid the student in developing the concepts of the course.

24. Present to regular classes techniques students can use to improve the reading skills needed in those classes.
25. Help plan instructional practices that cause students to note the logical organization of the reading material you assign.
26. Set priorities of the reading program in your school without assistance from teachers and administrators.
27. Assist in creating learning situations in which students can apply the reading skills taught in the language arts classes.
28. Provide two or three hours of instruction in reading per week to various individuals or small groups who have been identified as seriously disabled readers.
29. Team with you in your unit planning to help you incorporate reading instruction into your content teaching.
30. Help you organize a program of voluntary reading that is related to the objectives of your course.
31. Work with the librarian in ordering a wide range of materials for recreational reading.
32. Aid you in helping students see the relationship between their listening and their reading.
33. Help you to teach your students how to read for specific purposes.
34. Plan and supervise an attractive area loaded with paperback books where students can come and read for pleasure.
35. Give you suggestions for helping students master the vocabulary they encounter in the reading you assign.
36. Help you locate or construct phonograph records, audiotapes, pictures, filmstrips that will give poor readers the information they need without requiring them to read.
37. Help you construct exercises that teach students to vary their rates of reading according to the material you assign and their purposes for reading it.
38. Work with you in developing ways to help students utilize their background experiences to understand what they read.
39. Assist in setting up writing assignments, such as summarizing, that will cause students to attend to the organization of the material read to aid comprehension and retention.
40. Identify and list the reading skills that students will need to have if they are to be successful in the various subject area classes.

41. Work with students in classroom settings to develop their abilities to function effectively in small groups.
42. Provide instruction in speed reading for good students.

The final task for the reading curriculum advisory committee is to write a job description that is in tune with the greatest needs of the students, that allows the specialist to work effectively, and that reflects the needs of the people for whom the specialist will serve as a resource person. The job description should allow for some adjustments so that it can also reflect the special characteristics and preferences of the specialist who is hired. All, or at least some, of the committee members should be part of the interview team when candidates are considered.

Getting started

Reading consultants sometimes have difficulty establishing themselves as members of the school staff and starting their work. Those who work directly with students generally have no difficulty setting up a referral system and beginning to teach individual students, small groups, or classes. Although they must coordinate their work with classroom teachers and other specialists who may also be working with the same students, their role as a teacher is more clear-cut and more easily accomplished than acting as a consultant. Beginning consultants—and perhaps experienced ones—may find these suggestions helpful:

1. Meet informally and, if possible, individually with as many principals as possible to discuss their satisfactions and dissatisfactions with the existing instructional program and their perceptions of your role in their schools.
2. Do a needs assessment (formally or informally) to determine teacher satisfactions and dissatisfactions with the existing reading program, as well as their perceptions on how you can be most helpful to their needs.
3. Assist central office administrators or other responsible persons in developing your job description. Be responsive to the information provided by the principals and the teachers in this task.
4. Establish your credibility as a good and experienced reading teacher (by helping a beginning teacher organize his or her class, working with a group of students with special needs, conferring with one or more teachers individually or in small groups about their favorite projects or objectives).

5. Identify one or more classroom teachers who are willing to keep you posted on their needs and perceptions and to offer suggestions as you develop your role.
6. Attempt to start a modest curriculum development project. Be certain to have specific objectives and evaluation procedures carefully planned. For example, help a team of history teachers introduce their reading assignments so that students are reading for specific purposes. Help them also to design good reading comprehension tests for the material they assign.
7. Find or establish some vehicle for disseminating information about your work specifically and reading curriculum development generally. Highlight the efforts of teachers and administrators in the district. Arrange for all or selected information to reach the general community. Be explicit about your desire to receive reactions and suggestions on any and all aspects of reading curriculum development. Many districts already have newsletters whose editors welcome regular contributions.
8. Assess your personal characteristics, resources, and development periodically. You may wish to enlist the aid of others in these assessments.
9. Move slowly, listen carefully, and be prepared for negative as well as positive reinforcement for your best efforts.
10. Know your personal philosophy of reading instruction and share it with the teachers, but don't try to force it upon them.
11. Be aware of the power of group dynamics and utilize various techniques for staff development (reading together, small-group discussions, study groups, brainstorming sessions, creative writing, decision making about hypothetical but common situations focused upon the personal element in schooling).
12. Develop, project, and take refuge in a sense of humor. Take yourself and your job seriously, but not too seriously. Good consultants need to share enthusiasm and optimism as well as knowledge with the teachers, administrators, and students they serve.

Summary

Reading program development is an ongoing process in all school districts. In the effort to help all students achieve the highest level of reading growth they are capable of achieving, researchers, methods professors, school administrators, classroom teachers, and parents are searching for, finding, evaluating, keeping, modifying, or discarding instructional materials and strategies designed to teach students to read as well as each is able. Reading specialists are needed to help direct and coordinate these efforts, as well as to teach children with special needs.

Different schools have different needs and different expectations for reading specialists. Therefore, job responsibilities vary from school to school. Some reading specialists teach children with special instructional needs, some help teachers improve the teaching of reading in their classrooms, some are employed both as specialists and as classroom teachers. Regardless of the roles they play, reading specialists have become important persons on many school staffs.

All signs are that activity in the area of reading program development will increase or at least be maintained. Therefore, it is likely that reading specialists, who already have proved themselves valuable resources, will be increasingly called upon to work with administrators, teachers, and parents in building better reading programs from kindergarten through grade twelve and beyond. Furthermore the reading specialist's job will become increasingly complex and demanding as reading programs become more complex and parents and students make more demands upon school reading programs.

Because reading specialists are being employed for increasingly complex and demanding jobs, the level of training and the personal qualifications of the people who are hired for the jobs must be of the highest quality. People responsible for programs for training reading specialists must work diligently to recruit good students and develop high-quality programs for preparing them. Only people who are well equipped personally and well prepared academically will bring what is needed to the job of reading specialist and will take from their work the satisfactions that are there for the right people.

Bibliography

Austin, Mary C. "Professional Training of Personnel." In *Innovation and Change in Reading Instruction* edited by Helen M. Robinson. Chicago: University of Chicago Press, 1968, pp. 357–396.
———, and Coleman Morrison. *The First R.* New York: Macmillan, 1963.
Burnett, Richard W. "Reading in the Secondary School: Issues and Innovations." *Journal of Reading* 9 (1966): 322–328.

Hesse, Karl D., and Richard J. Smith, with Aileen Nettleton. "Content Teachers Consider the Role of the Reading Consultant." *Journal of Reading* 17 (December 1973): 210–215.

Moore, Walter J. "Every Teacher Is a Teacher of Reading." *University of Kansas Bulletin of Education* 15 (1961): 85–92.

"Roles, Responsibilities and Qualifications of Reading Specialists." *Journal of Reading* 2 (1968): 60–63.

Smith, Richard J. "A Reading Resource Teacher for the Elementary School." *The Reading Teacher* 22 (May 1969): 696–701.

Chapter 10 In-service education: Guidelines and examples

There is widespread agreement that the pre-service preparation of both elementary and secondary teachers to teach reading has been inadequate.[1] Critics of teacher training point at what they see as the outcome of inadequate training: rampant reading problems in inner-city schools, large numbers of functionally illiterate adults, and decreasing reading achievement scores in some areas. Teacher trainers have responded in a number of ways, but the most salient response to date has been to require more pre-service reading courses for teacher certification. Some say that the result thus far has been more quantity without more quality, but the promise of improved pre-service training is still positive. Nevertheless, in-service education is necessary for any major impact in terms of better reading programs, improved teaching of reading, and increased reading ability. The programs are in the schools and the problems are in the schools, so ultimately the improvements and the solutions must be in the schools.

Unfortunately, both teachers and administrators are generally disenchanted with in-service education as a vehicle for improving students' performance in reading. They ought to be, because most of them have experienced in-service programs that were dull, totally useless, inspiring but not informative, too general to be very useful, or too specific to be worthwhile. In-service programs have suffered from uninspired direction, lack of planning, inadequate commitment and support, inappropriate format, and absence of follow-up activities. The picture is bleak, but the outlook is better because in-service programs can be improved.

Although we present guidelines for planning and implementing in-service programs and offer some examples of successful programs, we are not suggesting that there is a universal way to handle in-service programs. Local variables will always be prime determiners of what works in local in-service programs. So study

[1]Much of the material in this chapter is adapted from Otto and Erickson (1973) with permission of the International Reading Association.

the guidelines and examine the examples, but be prepared to make adaptions.

The problem and
a plan

The problem and a plan

The Music Man said that in order to do a successful job of selling, "You've got to know the territory!" That's good advice for salesmen and equally good for anyone who will plan, present, or participate in in-service programs. The major flaw of many in-service programs that have failed was their lack of focus: no clearly identified goal, no explicit audience, no acceptance of responsibility by key personnel, no provision for action outcomes. Focus comes, in major part, from knowing the territory.

THE NEED FOR IN-SERVICE TRAINING: A CLOSER LOOK

The need for in-service work in reading is quite clear: as many as one-third of the schoolchildren in the United States do not read well enough to meet the demands of school and society. One problem may be that unquestioned needs tend to be met with unquestioning solutions. Many of the frenzied activities that have come about in response to the national Right to Read effort are a case in point. As often as not, they seem to be designed more to give visibility to their directors than to accomplish any well-conceived goal.

We can take for granted the need to improve reading achievement and the notion that in-service education is a proper vehicle for responding to the need. The unmet—and often unrecognized—need is to devise ways of dealing with the challenge of offering worthwhile, productive in-service programs. One step in the right direction is to examine some of the factors that have a powerful effect on in-service efforts. Those factors are part of the territory.

Attitudes toward in-service education in general

Much evidence is available documenting the inadequacies of teachers' pre-service education. Nevertheless, educators and laymen tend to think that a teacher with a bachelor's degree and several years of teaching experience is a finished product. The fact is that the product is never finished. There is already too much to know about children and how to teach them to be

243

learned in a lifetime. It would seem, then, that in-service education would be as highly regarded by administrators, teachers,
and the general public as pre-service education. But that's not
always the case. In-service education has gained considerable re-
spectability in the last several years, but it is still sometimes regarded as something of a nuisance and definitely as something
extra rather than a basic component of teacher education. The
four years a prospective teacher spends taking university courses
and the relatively short amount of time given to student teaching
are considered by most to be the heart of his preparation, regardless of the number of years spent in the classroom subsequently.

The heavy stress placed on a teacher's pre-service education
has been one factor in causing the apathetic response to in-service education. Until the notion that the college graduation cere-
mony is the final step in training is discarded, in-service education is likely to remain a promising but not very productive
enterprise. The professors who train teachers must emphasize
the limited role they are able to play in the education of a
teacher. They must present their courses and pre-service field experiences as the beginning, not the end, of a teacher's instruction
in how to teach; they must develop in prospective teachers positive attitudes toward in-service education. Hiring officials must
maintain these positive attitudes by telling new teachers that in-
service education is highly regarded in their school system's
operation and that active participation in the in-service opportunities provided is a necessary part of the teaching contract.

Attitudes toward in-service education in reading

Attitudes toward in-service education in reading present special
problems in both elementary and secondary schools.

In the elementary school, teaching reading is considered the
most important task of teachers at all grade levels. It is the curriculum area that most concerns parents and therefore the area
about which teachers are likely to be the most defensive. Elementary school teachers rarely admit to any deficiencies in teaching
reading. Because they think their ability to teach this important
subject should be unquestioned, they hesitate to show much interest in any program that is designed to improve their teaching.

In the secondary school the special problems related to in-service education in reading arise from the feeling of most content
area specialists that teaching reading is not their concern. In this
respect, the basic problem in the secondary school is the an-
tithesis of that in the elementary school. The pre-service education of secondary teachers has not convinced them of their responsibility to teach reading as well as subject matter. Some

content area teachers are offended by suggestions that they have some responsibility for teaching certain reading skills because they consider this area to be the job of special reading teachers. The argument that all high school students can profit from reading instruction and that the job is too large for special reading teachers tends to fall on deaf ears. Teachers who do accept the argument may be willing to incorporate some simple techniques into their teaching, but most are reluctant to make major changes in materials or the pace of instruction.

Attitudes toward in-service education in general can probably be changed more easily than attitudes toward in-service education in reading. So long as in-service efforts are seen as a threat by elementary teachers or as an intrusion by secondary subject matter specialists, attitudes are likely to remain negative. One very basic in-service need, then, is to deal realistically with the causes for the negative attitudes in planning in-service sessions on reading.

Resistance to change

Change is what in-service education ultimately is all about: changed teacher behavior in the classroom. Change tends to be difficult and painful, and it is likely to be resisted. One view of the forces for and against change in the schools is summarized in figure 10.1, which shows how teacher behavior is affected by four different pressures.

The model explains why in-service programs run the risk of changing teacher behavior very little. Ignoring the inhibiting forces dooms the chances for changed behavior. With the model as a guide, in-service plans may include some extrinsic rewards to counteract the hard work required. Or released time may be required to allow teachers to bring fresh energy to the in-service task. A social activity may balance the fact that better teaching procedures cannot be guaranteed. The halo effect from mass media publicity may also help overcome a lack of productivity or extrinsic rewards.

Change is difficult. In-service programs designed to bring about change must be planned with that fact prominently in mind.

Involvement and commitment

Although the operation of schools is far more democratic than it once was, the board of education and the administrators are still the major determiners of policy. *Line officers* are the administrators who allocate the budget and who ultimately make the decisions that determine the goals of a school and how they will be

245

Figure 10.1 **The dynamics of curriculum change**

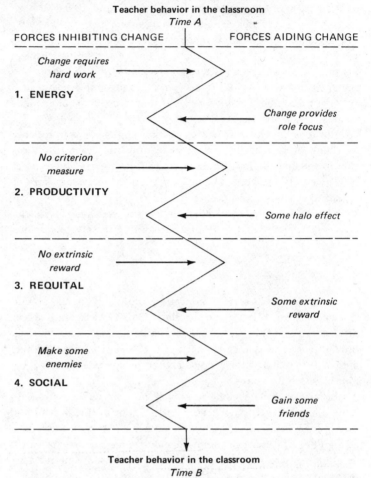

Teacher behavior in the classroom
Time A

FORCES INHIBITING CHANGE | FORCES AIDING CHANGE

Change requires
hard work

1. ENERGY

Change provides
role focus

No criterion
measure

2. PRODUCTIVITY

Some halo effect

No extrinsic
reward

3. REQUITAL

Some extrinsic
reward

Make some
enemies

4. SOCIAL

Gain some
friends

Teacher behavior in the classroom
Time B

Source: Adapted from J. M. Lipham, "Dynamics of Curriculum Change,"
Department of Education Administration, University of Wisconsin, Madison, 1972, and from Wayne Otto and L. Erickson, *Inservice Education to
Improve Reading Instruction* (Newark, Del.: International Reading Association, 1973). Reprinted with permission of the authors and the International Reading Association.

achieved. People in *staff positions* function according to line decisions. Since line officers hire and evaluate staff, staff people are
generally responsive to the desires of line officers. In simple
terms, central office staff members follow the direction of the superintendent of schools, and teachers follow the direction of their
principals.

Although much has been said about improving reading education and considerable money and other resources have been

expended for in-service education to effect changes, certain administrative problems persist. Almost a decade ago, Martin (1969) investigated the effect of federal aid programs on the establishment or improvement of secondary school reading programs in Minnesota, Wisconsin, Iowa, and North and South Dakota. Although he saw some positive effects, he failed to note any major progress:

> It must be noted that schools of the Upper Midwest have not in the course of the past five years achieved a theoretically sound reading program. Schools today report their major problem in developing reading programs is the lack of qualified reading teachers. The area of staffing is the one most in need of federal assistance. Budget deficits are a second problem in all strata. These same two concerns were also paramount five years ago.

That schools continue to cite the lack of qualified reading teachers and budget deficits as the major obstacles to improving reading education is instructive. Because neither need can be satisfied through in-service education, these programs are often perceived by administrators as a compromise to use until funds to hire special reading teachers become available.

To note how administrators use qualified reading teachers and money when these two resources are available is revealing. In the elementary schools, administrators who can afford it are likely to change from one instructional system to another in their basic reading program and to purchase more and newer materials for their supplementary program. This is the case even though there is considerable evidence that it is the teaching, not the particular system or materials, that contributes most to children's success in reading. A qualified reading teacher is more often assigned to work full time with the most seriously disabled readers in the school than to devote at least some time to helping classroom teachers with grouping, questioning techniques, pacing, and other instructional practices. In the secondary school, administrators furnish and staff reading laboratories, schedule remedial reading classes, require a special unit in developmental reading in all tenth-grade English classes, and support other special reading programs that have never been shown to be effective in eliminating secondary reading problems.

The expenditure of money and the utilization of staff for special reading programs, different methods, or new materials instead of for in-service education to improve teachers' instructional practices indicates either a complaisant satisfaction with current conditions or a lack of confidence in the ability of in-service education to improve them. The fact is that administrators

That's a nice sentence, but it doesn't support the fact that in-service would do any good —

have been committed to using budget and specialized personnel to apply bigger and brighter patches instead of tackling problems at their source. The slow progress in improving reading programs must be attributed in large part to a lack of administrative commitment to changing the instructional practices of classroom teachers from kindergarten through grade 12.

Basic changes made in teachers' instructional practices to accommodate team teaching, modular scheduling, nongradedness, independent study, and other innovations have been successful where there was administrative commitment to the vigorous expenditure of time and money and productive in-service education.

Says who?

Teachers have joined with boards of education and administrators to help bring about specially designed school buildings, effective organizational patterns, and, most important, improved instructional programs. Unfortunately this kind of commitment to reading program improvement has been rare. In-service education in reading generally suffers from a lack of the kind of administrative zeal enjoyed by certain other programs. If line officers were as vigorous in their support of reading program development as they are in supporting other kinds of development, in-service education in reading would be sought after, attended to, and productive of better instructional practices in the classroom.

I really believe all this, but saying it doesn't make it so.

Negative attitudes, resistance to change, and a lack of commitment are significant and powerful forces in the planning and implementation of worthwhile in-service reading programs. Any one of them can cripple a program, and in the aggregate they virtually ensure failure. A basic need in in-service efforts, then, is to recognize and to deal with these negative forces.

THE PROMISE OF IN-SERVICE

Considering the complex forces that tend to retard improvements and the conditions and actions that appear necessary to facilitate changes, the task of improving reading instruction demands considerable expertise, hard work, ideal conditions, and a little bit of luck. But the in-service efforts to improve reading instruction appear to be well worth the effort. In-service efforts can bring about significant results:

1. In-service programs can unify and motivate educators to work toward common goals. Too often teachers work alone and receive little stimulating feedback. When teachers and administrators work together and identify common interests,

248

the results can be electrifying. These common areas can become the nucleus of worthwhile in-service programs.

2. In-service programs can help school staffs to develop total reading programs in which teachers become aware of the overall reading plan. Knowing where each bit fits into the scheme clarifies teachers' roles and permits them to individualize their instruction on a continuum rather than to conceptualize their teaching efforts as having a definite starting and ending point for any individual.

3. In-service programs can clarify problems and suggest solutions. Often problems in teaching reading appear to have no alternatives or solutions. The result is low morale, lack of motivation, and a poor learning environment. In-service programs can reduce major problems into manageable questions and offer alternative solutions. When failure is defined as a lack of alternatives, teachers cannot ignore efforts that yield viable alternative approaches to improving reading instruction.

4. In-service programs can introduce and help to implement new ideas and procedures. New practices need to be tested, ideas modified, and well-known, proven practices continued. In-service programs help to ensure that reading instruction remains lively and dynamic.

5. In-service programs can improve accountability procedures by enabling teachers to diagnose individual needs and to prescribe activities for individuals or small groups of students with common needs.

6. In-service programs that involve parents and others from the community can increase public support for education. Providing people outside the schools with a better understanding of the reading process, and demonstrating the variety of teaching strategies necessary in order to try to teach all children to read, can increase public support for schools.

Perhaps in-service can do these things, but I've never seen it do these things.

THE MISTAKES OF IN-SERVICE

Harris and Bessent (1969) have identified three serious mistakes that are often made in planning and implementing in-service programs.

Failure to relate staff participants' needs

Practice often violates the common-sense expectation that in-service efforts should focus on the needs of teachers and other staff.

249

*But involving
teachers by
letting them
make decisions(?)
after 4:00 is
poor involvement*

Programs dictated by the school board or by the administration rarely serve the group for whom they are intended. Those based on superficial surveys ostensibly reflecting teacher interests are likely to be of little real value. Even when true interests are identified, programs are more often designed for uniform presentation than to meet teachers' individual differences, differences that are as great as those among students. Finally, a careful evaluation to determine the degree to which needs are met and/or the extent to which other needs have been identified as a result of the program is seldom undertaken.

Failure to select appropriate activities

Adults (just like children) learn best when activities are diverse, paced according to participants' progress, and flexible enough to respond to individual needs. Too often in-service activities take stereotyped forms—lecture followed by discussion, film followed by buzz session, a series of topical meetings—with no real consideration given to the purpose to be served by the activities.

Failure to assure effectiveness by using sufficient staff and other resources

As Harris and Bessent point out, "In-service education involves costs in terms of time and money for staff, materials, and facilities." Brief afterschool sessions are not sufficient for in-service education. Staff members must be freed for a few hours, a day, a week, a month, or a year as necessary. In-service leadership must be assumed or assigned and given high priority status, and budgets must provide for adequate released time, resource people, and materials.

Successful in-service programs must be carefully planned to discover the genuine needs of proposed participants, select activities that are most appropriate to the purpose or goal, and commit sufficient resources to assure effective implementation and adequate follow-up.

AN IN-SERVICE PLANNING GUIDE

The girls in *Gypsy* said that "you gotta have a gimmick," and sometimes in the more sedate business of education that's still good advice. But the fact is that in in-service education—and, no doubt, in certain other endeavors—content is the basic ingredient. Take away the content and all the gimmicks in the world will not bring about change. Now, having said that, we propose to devote the rest of this chapter not to the content, but to the *process* of in-service education. We do so by design. The *content* of in-service programs in reading can be specified only as the *process* is implemented. We can deal with the process in the present context, but the content must be identified to meet specific needs. Six steps in the process of in-service education are summarized in figure 10.2.

Other sets of guidelines for planning in-service education have been suggested. One example is Draba's (1975) "Guidelines for Viable Inservice Education." They are: emphasize benefits, secure voluntary participation, limit group size, identify problems, set feasible goals, share the planning, plan divergent activities, enlist administrative support, arrange for release time, provide evaluation, make adjustments, make in-service continuous. Note that the process implicit in the list parallels the six-step planning guide shown earlier. The main difference is that Draba's list offers specific suggestions that go beyond our guide points.

Figure 10.2 **An in-service planning guide**

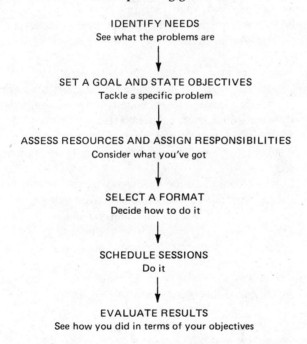

IDENTIFY NEEDS
See what the problems are

SET A GOAL AND STATE OBJECTIVES
Tackle a specific problem

ASSESS RESOURCES AND ASSIGN RESPONSIBILITIES
Consider what you've got

SELECT A FORMAT
Decide how to do it

SCHEDULE SESSIONS
Do it

EVALUATE RESULTS
See how you did in terms of your objectives

Identify needs

The identification of significant in-service needs is no simple
matter because, in our experience, the real needs are often hidden behind a façade of apparent but trivial concerns. Teachers
are less reluctant, for example, to indicate an interest in learning
about a new instructional program than to admit that they have
misgivings about their ability to teach comprehension skills. In
the scheme of things the former is utterly trivial when compared
to the latter. Yet in-service programs must never be planned
without the active involvement of those who will participate in
and, ultimately, benefit from the efforts. Of course leadership
must be provided to stimulate interest and to seek out and identify significant needs.

ONE APPROACH TO ASSESSING NEEDS

Smith, Otto, and Harty (1970) have described an approach to
identify in-service needs. They went directly to a sample of
308 classroom teachers in order to discover the teachers'
attitudes toward the pre-service preparation for teaching reading
that they had received, their perceptions about personal needs
for additional information, and their preferences for certain approaches to in-service education.

1. How well do you feel your preservice education prepared
   you to teach reading in your first regular teaching assignment? (Response choices ranged from *Very Adequately* to
   Very Inadequately on a 5-point scale.)
2. Please rank order the following in terms of when you feel
   instruction in reading is most valuable to elementary
   teachers.
   _____ before the student teaching experience
   _____ during the student teaching experience
   _____ after the student teaching experience, but before
           beginning the regular teaching assignment
   _____ after beginning the first regular teaching assign-
           ment
3. Check the specific areas of reading instruction about
   which you currently feel a need for information.
   _____ grouping students
   _____ diagnosing individual instructional needs
   _____ using basal materials
   _____ using supplementary materials

_____ different methods for teaching reading (ITA, pro-
       gramed)
_____ developing word attack skills
_____ developing comprehension skills
_____ providing for the disabled reader in the classroom
_____ differentiating instruction for different groups
_____ providing for the superior reader
_____ using the library or IMC
_____ using writing, speaking, and listening in reading
       instruction

4. Please rank order the following according to your preference for the ways in which in-service education may be
presented.

_____ Television programs produced and presented by
       personnel in your school system.

_____ Television programs produced and presented by
       personnel who are not regular employees in your
       school system.

_____ Films or video tapes viewed by teachers individ-
       ually or by the staff of one school.

_____ Classes offered for professional improvement (but
       no university credit) for teachers of specified
       grades.

_____ One to one conferences with a reading specialist
       at your request and in your own school.

_____ Presentations by a reading specialist at one or
       more staff meetings at your school during the
       school year.

_____ Classes or workshops offered at a nearby univer-
       sity for university credit either during the regular
       school year or the summer session.

This approach which ensures anonymity in responding, will
evoke more realistic answers than alternatives that require, in effect, that respondents admit to deficiencies. The questionnaire
can be adapted to a variety of situations by changing the response choices, but it should retain three general characteristics:

○ Pay attention to attitudes toward alternatives. Every situation
offers an array of alternatives for dealing with identified needs.
The alternatives ought to be known even as needs are identified so that respondents can indicate preferences and/or attitudes. When such information is incorporated into planning,
the positive appeal of any resultant programs is likely to be
enhanced.

○ Offer an array of concrete choices of topics rather than open-ended response type items.
○ Seek preferences for types of presentations that could be made available.

SPECIAL CONCERNS AT THE SECONDARY LEVEL

In-service reading programs in secondary schools present special problems:

1. With some exceptions, secondary teachers want to teach content, not reading.
2. Teaching reading tends to equate secondary teachers with elementary teachers, who are sometimes perceived as having less prestige than secondary teachers.
3. Many secondary teachers think of reading ability in terms of word recognition and word analysis; they think a student either can or cannot read.
4. Many secondary teachers don't require much more than factual recall and literal comprehension from their students.
5. Most secondary teachers consider themselves as teachers of a particular subject matter and prefer to become more proficient in that field than to become more skillful in teaching learning skills.
6. Some secondary teachers see only the need for remedial reading in the secondary school, and they have an unwarranted faith in the ability of remedial reading teachers to help poor readers.
7. Secondary teachers are often limited in their access to appropriate materials at the ability levels of their students and are consequently using materials that are too difficult for their students to read independently.

For these and other reasons, in-service reading programs are often condescendingly tolerated rather than enthusiastically welcomed by secondary school teachers. Until their pre-service education convinces them that teaching reading at their academic level is both necessary and exciting, in-service reading programs will be more difficult to conduct in secondary schools than in elementary schools.

The following practices are helpful in conducting in-service programs with secondary school teachers:

1. Work with teachers in content area groupings. Teachers tend to think that their teaching and their problems are different

from those of teachers in other disciplines. Consequently, meetings with teachers from different content areas often seem to be irrelevant to certain teachers.

2. Discuss both the limitations of remedial reading in the secondary school and the legitimacy and nature of an adapted curriculum for students who will probably never learn much from reading.

3. Present reading as a thinking process that must function in special ways to enable readers to master content with a particular structure.

4. Demonstrate instructional procedures to improve reading by using materials currently being assigned to students.

5. Have samples of materials that are below grade level difficulty, related to the teachers' content, and not embarrassing for secondary students to read.

6. Assure the teachers that teaching reading is not an esoteric enterprise reserved for elementary teachers and specialists but is good teaching practice used to improve skills that never reach their ultimate level of sophistication.

7. Take time, usually at the beginning of the session, to answer truthfully and sincerely the inevitable questions about readability formulas, speed reading, reading machines, and other interesting aspects of reading pedagogy about which teachers are generally curious and often misinformed.

8. Respond to questions with information whenever possible and admit without being defensive any lack of knowledge.

9. Present reading program development as something to be tailored to the unique needs and resources of each secondary school.

10. Approach the development of the reading program as an experiment to be tried and evaluated, be specific about how the evaluation will be conducted.

A consideration of these special concerns can be useful in preparing the kind of questionnaire discussed previously.

THE FIRST STEP

The identification of in-service needs, the first step in the process, requires and deserves as much attention as any other aspect of designing and carrying out good in-service programs. Some significant in-service needs are:

○ Elementary school teachers need help in selecting new instructional materials

o Teachers need assistance in devising more efficient ways of grouping pupils for instruction
o The entire staff of a school building needs help on the details of implementing a new instructional program
o Secondary teachers need to become acquainted with specifics of an all-school approach to reading instruction and what each one can do about the teaching of reading

Leadership is essential to identify needs, and careful planning is required to meet them. The planning process is focused by goals and objectives.

Set a goal and state objectives

In many in-service efforts, activities are initiated and carried out, but little attention is given to the outcome: the form of improved instruction, more positive attitudes, and so forth. Without sufficient attention to these outcomes, the in-service efforts are almost certain to be ineffectual. Thus, specific goals and objectives must be identified.

TRANSLATING NEEDS TO GOALS AND OBJECTIVES

Once a significant need has been identified, a realistic goal, an outcome that responds to the need, must be set. (For an example of the translation of a need into a goal see the end of this section.)

A specific goal is best tackled by pursuing even more specific goal-related objectives. Worthwhile objectives are stated in performance, or behavioral, terms, terms that describe what a participant ought to be able to do upon completion of the program. Objectives help to identify learning activities and to give substance to desired outcomes. Consider the contrast between the following objectives that are stated in performance terms and those that are not.

Not Stated in Behavioral Terms	*Stated in Behavioral Terms*
To understand the philosophies that underlie different approaches to phonics instruction	To contrast analytic with synthetic approaches to phonics instruction

To know how to interpret checklists in the evaluation of materials	To identify or devise checklists to be used in evaluating materials	Set a goal and state objectives
To understand the function of readability formulas in the preparation of materials for reading instruction	To apply readability formulas to selections from basal readers	

The performance objectives prescribe tangible, observable acts; the others simply point in a direction. The former can be attained; the latter can only be pursued.

So far, the in-service process requires that:

o An in-service need be identified
o The need be translated into a goal for a complete in-service program
o The goal be broken into more specific performance objectives

Harris and Bessent (1969) have observed that activities are too often confused with objectives: "It is not unusual to find an in-service program in which the only indentifiable objective is to have an in-service program." In-service programs without goals and objectives will not produce worthwhile results.

AN EXAMPLE

The sequence that moves from need to goal to objectives could proceed as follows.

1. Identify a need. *Elementary school teachers need help in selecting new instructional materials.* Such a need could be identified through the use of a questionnaire similar to that described earlier.
2. Set a goal. The need in the example is so broad that it could call for an endless series of sessions—ranging from diagnosis to child development to library science—that would burden the budget, exhaust the resources, and try the patience of the participants. Therefore, a goal must be set that is realistic in terms of resources required and of the participants' needs. The latter can best be determined by surveying their interests through more specific questioning and by assessing their existing knowledge through formal and/or informal pretesting.

257

After this focusing, a somewhat restricted but attainable goal might be stated in this way: *to improve teachers' ability to apply objective criteria in selecting materials for reading instruction.* With such a goal, it becomes possible to state objectives that lead to the goal in a reasonably direct way.

3. State objectives. It is easy, even with restricted goals, to devise an extensive array of related objectives. Therefore, in setting final objectives, consideration should be given to the resources available, including the total time available, the background of the participants, and, of course, the ultimate, or terminal, goal.

The examples of objectives stated in performance terms that are related to the present goal are: to contrast analytic with synthetic approaches to phonics instruction, to identify or devise checklists to be used in evaluating materials, and to apply readability formulas to selections from basal readers. Each concerns quite different aspects of the total process of selecting instructional materials, yet each is relevant to the overall goal. In effect, the objectives serve to define the goal.

Assess resources and assign responsibilities

A realistic assessment of available resources and a careful consideration of the roles and responsibilities of all personnel are as essential to the success of in-service efforts as sensible goals and objectives.

CLEARING THE WAY FOR CHANGE

Realistic resource assessment involves considering all of the components in an educational organization that must be adjusted to provide support for altering an existing reading program or implementing a new one. For example, significant changes in reading instruction, such as starting an objective-based approach, may take two or three years and require substantial organizational changes. An in-service effort that ignores these elements is likely to run out of momentum before the important goals are attained. Some components that may need attention in order to accommodate the changes are grading and reporting practices, planning time, physical facilities, personnel allocations, differentiated staffing, and (of course) budget. Others that are crucial to

educational change but are too often ignored are the encouragement, stimulation, and morale-building forces that can sustain
personnel during conflict induced by change. Because planners
of in-service programs have a responsibility to consider all of the
components that may need adjusting, those involved must "include someone who is influential enough in the organization to
bring about needed changes" (Harris and Bessent, 1969).

A checklist will help to assess the resources and prepare the
way for changed behavior.

1. Demonstrate the need. Have provisions been made to evaluate present practice? Are the major concerns of the teachers
   regarding the present reading program and their suggestions
   for improvement known and understood by the in-service
   planners?
2. Gather data. Do existing policies and procedures conflict
   with the goal of the in-service program? Is there evidence
   available in the form of research results or personal testimony
   that the proposed program will be productive?
3. Consider personnel. Will there be a preplanning session,
   prior to the in-service program, with key reading people,
   supervisory staff, and administrators? Has a key person been
   selected to coordinate the program? Lead in-service instruction? Act as a local consultant? Has a target population been
   identified? Is there a need for social activities following
   workshop sessions?
4. Determine a budget. Have provisions for funding been made
   to cover released time for participants, consultant fees, cost of
   materials, facility rental, equipment purchase and maintenance, and clerical supplies?
5. Plan a time line. Have definite dates been established, and
   are facilities available for the in-service sessions? Has adequate time been allowed for implementing the proposed program?
6. Expand communication. Are people within and outside the
   organization aware of how the outcomes will affect their responsibilities?
7. Check facilities. Will remodeling of facilities, new facilities,
   and/or new furnishings be required?

Of course, no sample checklist can be comprehensive. Local
realities will dictate more specific concerns to be considered by
persons responsible for planning and carrying out in-service education to improve reading instruction.

ROLES AND RESPONSIBILITIES OF PERSONNEL ·

Because so much depends upon the purposes of the in-service
program, the resources available, and the needs and abilities of
the participants, we cannot offer an explicit description of the
roles of the participants. We can, however, make some general
statements about the rights and responsibilities of teachers and
the leadership roles of principals, superintendents, instructional
supervisors, outside consultants, and reading consultants within
the system. The descriptions of roles and responsibilities are neither complete nor mutually exclusive. Overlap is the rule rather
than the exception.

Teachers

Because teachers are responsible to the administrative hierarchy
in most school organizations and because in-service programs
often represent attempts to change teacher behavior in some
way, both the rights and the responsibilities of teachers must be
considered. This means that each teacher has a right to expect
basic considerations from the school officials who expect a
change in behavior. In fact, changed teacher behavior may be facilitated by changed administrator or supervisor behavior. Also,
changes in teacher behavior will probably occur only when their
own expectancies for change are seriously provided for in the in-
service effort. Teachers have a right to expect:

○ That they will have an adequate chance to express their feelings about changes and innovations
○ That in-service programs will be carefully planned, with consideration for factors of time, energy, reward, and social needs
○ That administrative or supervisory behavior will change in
  proportion to the change expected from teachers (provided that
  changes in both roles are warranted)

At the same time, they have these responsibilities:

○ To communicate to the program leaders their concerns about
  reading, including specific proposals as to what the in-service
  program should accomplish and the kinds of activities that are
  needed
○ To participate in planning in-service programs when opportunities for active involvement are offered
○ To prepare for meetings to ensure full benefit from the program

- To remain receptive to new ideas presented at the sessions
- To cooperate with other teachers and program leaders in trying out new ideas before accepting or rejecting possible new practices
- To evaluate both existing practices and new ideas in a continuing attempt to improve reading instruction

Principals

In most school systems, the principal is responsible for the reading program in the school building. He or she must know the elements of an effective reading program, be able to provide competent supervision, and have more than a superficial knowledge of essential reading skills, the sequence from level to level, ways to deal with individual differences, and the effectiveness of the total program. The principal who accepts his or her responsibility for the reading program:

- Builds a background of understanding about what constitutes a good reading program and seeks to increase his or her understanding of reading
- Initiates action to improve the reading program in the school when the need is demonstrated
- Utilizes his or her authority and organizational expertise to involve the appropriate reading personnel and to arrange for substitutes, released time, materials, and the host of components necessary for productive in-service programming
- Takes an active part in the program and shows that he or she is committed to changing his or her administrative/supervisory behavior

Superintendents

As the most influential educational leader in the school district, the superintendent's leadership in improving reading instruction is crucial. His or her interest, involvement, and commitment to in-service education in reading is directly related to the quality of the school district reading program. The superintendent must personally accept or delegate responsibility for:

- An accountability arrangement consisting of written policies that charge specific personnel with specific responsibilities for the district reading program

261

- Selecting a qualified, adequate number of staff to carry out the program
- Insuring that budgeted funds are available to support the continuing in-service program
- Two-way communication between the superintendent's office and line staff on efforts to improve reading
- Demonstrating support for worthwhile activities by allowing in-service activities during the school day, by participating when possible, by reviewing research, and by suggesting further in-service study

Supervisors

Many school districts employ instructional supervisors whose job is to provide help for teachers in all areas of the elementary and secondary curriculum. In many instances so much is expected of these general consultants that they cannot possibly do everything that everyone thinks they should. Fortunately, many instructional supervisors have developed a good background of knowledge in the area of reading and are in an excellent position to assume leadership roles in reading improvement programs.

The general supervisor who takes an active part in reading in-service programs has many important responsibilities:

- To develop a knowledge and understanding of the elements of a good reading program, as well as the necessary methods and materials to carry out the program
- To act as a liaison between the superintendent and the individual schools involved in the in-service program, attempting to keep the superintendent as actively involved as possible
- To help principals and teachers recognize the areas of need for in-service activity by pinpointing them with the results of valid surveys and tests
- To become involved in in-service reading programs by effectively demonstrating methods and materials, by encouraging and aiding teachers to assume in-service leadership roles, by securing appropriate materials for the participants, and by arranging for consultants from outside the system when such expertise is needed

The general instructional supervisor in school systems that lack a reading consultant may have to assume specific and far-ranging responsibilities in the area of reading instruction. A supervisor must be able to recognize his or her personal weaknesses and know when to call for outside help.

Consultants from outside the system

Outside consultants can make valuable contributions to in-service programs provided they meet the specific needs of the particular program. To invite an expert for the sake of having a well-known authority may be a waste of everyone's time. Before an outsider is hired, the specific goals, possible activities, and tentative follow-up plans for him or her should be established. Outside consultants should not be invited unless they can do something more effectively than anyone within the system. For instance, most are not as effective as group leaders as are local people familiar with local problems. On the other hand, change can be aided by pressures from outside the system; that is, suggestions from outsiders sometimes carry more weight than those from friends. If a consultant is hired, he or she must:

○ Insist on knowing what the participants want and how this activity fits into the total in-service design
○ Refuse an invitation if he or she cannot effectively do what is requested
○ Refuse an invitation if the local in-service leaders will not prepare the groundwork for his presentation or plan for systematic follow-up
○ Talk to school in-service leaders about the program prior to his or her direct involvement
○ Learn as much as possible about the present practice of reading instruction in the schools prior to presenting his or her portion of the program
○ Prepare and present his or her activity in a manner consistent with the purposes of the program

Reading consultants

The reading consultant is fast becoming a very desirable component of the school district reading program. The duties vary from district to district. Some consultants test and teach children with reading disabilities, and others work only with the administrators and teachers. Because specific responsibilities vary from position to position, the best way to discuss the consultant's role is to study those functions that relate directly to in-service activities: acting as observer, resource person, leader, and catalyst.

Observer Reading consultants must regularly spend a portion of their time observing reading instruction. Without this direct contact, he or she will quickly lose the ability to empathize with the children and teachers. Furthermore, discussing daily successes

263

and failures with teachers and principals is one of the consultant's most important functions.

The responsibility can best be met by spending extended periods of time—a week or two—in one school. Visitations must be worked out with the principal and staff beforehand. With careful preplanning the reading consultant can communicate effectively with the staff by visiting classrooms (preferably by invitation), examining and evaluating materials, testing children, and conferring with teachers individually and in groups.

This extended exposure to and interaction with the teachers and principals will enhance the credibility of the reading consultant in the role of resource person, leader, and catalyst.

Resource person The reading consultant is most valuable when he or she helps select reading materials for classroom use. Because of the consultant's expertise regarding instructional materials in reading, administrators should count heavily on their recommendations. Bypassing the consultant or ignoring his or her expert opinion can be a serious administrative oversight.

The consultant must have access to a wide range of materials and must have the authority to introduce new materials to teachers, as well as the ability to shift materials from school to school. New materials can stimulate and support improved reading instruction. Involving teachers in evaluating and trying out new materials is one way to stimulate change.

A more personal—and possibly the most important—role of the consultant is to respond to the needs of individuals and groups of teachers who are seeking help. He or she must be organized, free from paperwork chores, able to come when needed, and able to provide useful solutions to urgent teacher or school needs.

Leader The reading consultant should be a leader in developing professional and public understanding of the reading process and reading instruction. To do so, he or she must take some initiative in bringing ideas to the teachers, a job that can be best done by spending time in classrooms with teachers and principals. The rapport that should develop through the sharing of classroom concerns can enable the consultant to suggest changes in a tactful, nonthreatening manner.

In another role the consultant can increase understanding by acting as a bridge between the administration and the classroom when philosophies and policies on reading instruction are formulated.

Catalyst Ideally, the reading consultant should have a relationship with teachers and administrators that allows him or her to challenge them to try different materials and techniques in a search for improved reading instruction. These attempts must be honest efforts to meet recognized and defined needs.

Select a format

The success of an in-service reading program will be determined by the marriage between the specific goals and objectives and the actual activity engaged in by the participants. More than twenty years ago Thelen (1954) made a basic point: activities can be used effectively or disastrously. A buzz session with nothing to talk about is embarrassing, a panel of reading experts whose expertise is not relevant to the needs of the teachers is maddening, and role playing at the wrong time with the wrong participants can be ghastly. Thelen warned that cautious selection is called for when in-service activities are planned and offered four guide questions for matching activities with objectives:

1. What main objective is the activity supposed to accomplish?
2. Under what conditions does the activity actually work successfully?
3. What undesirable things does the activity produce?
4. What part of the activity is fixed and what can be modified to fit a particular situation?

We will describe and analyze some of the formats or basic activities of in-service programs to serve as a resource for in-service leaders. The activities cannot be matched hastily with an objective to produce an automatic successful in-service effort. Careful attention must be paid to subtle differences in activities. Each activity is not necessarily a format in itself. A series of similar activities or a combination of different activities carefully put together can result in a program that reaches specific objectives and satisfies the variety of different purposes that are apparent in the usual school in-service effort.

LECTURE

Probably the most used and most misused in-service activity is the lecture. It is an excellent vehicle for providing one-way, controlled dissemination of information. But it is relatively low on

265

the scale of experience impact because the learner is usually passive, the content is controlled by the speaker, and perception is limited to listening, although visual aids such as charts, slides, overhead transparencies, and filmstrips can improve listener comprehension.

The chief value of the lecture is that it is an efficient, straightforward, and simple way to arrange for in-service participants to receive specific information: basic facts, definitions of terms, a framework from which to move to higher-order objectives, and so forth.

Often too much is expected from the lecture format. If the objective of an in-service program is to change values, attitudes, or instructional techniques, calling upon the most dynamic speaker of outstanding authority may begin but will not complete the process of change. The lecture should not be abandoned. It is a sound activity, if the specific objective calls for a controlled input of information to commence, sustain, or summarize a portion of a program.

In the final section of this chapter a number of examples of in-service reading programs call for an input of basic information. In one example, a lecture would be appropriate for defining the terms and presenting examples of analytic and synthetic approaches to phonics instruction. In another session, aimed at identifying or devising checklists to be used in evaluating reading materials, a most appropriate activity is a brief lecture which presents the scope and sequence of such lists. Or, in a program showing teachers how to apply readability formulas to selections from basal readers, a lecture containing an overview of a number of formulas, as well as their uses and limitations, would be desirable.

DEMONSTRATION

In this basic activity the participants witness a real or simulated teaching activity in a setting that usually includes procedures, materials, equipment, and techniques actually employed. Demonstrations have a relatively low experience impact because the content is tightly controlled, the observer is generally passive, and, unless immediate follow-up activities are included, communication is most often one way.

A demonstration is used to portray an active process being carried out. It provides teachers with models of specific behavior and helps to answer specific questions. The specificity necessary for a worthwhile demonstration calls for a relatively narrow topic. Harris and Bessent (1969) have listed the following steps Select a format that stress the need for narrow demonstration activity goals and tight planning.

1. Expect one demonstration to cover only a limited purpose. Plan separate demonstrations when a number of purposes are intended.
2. Select a demonstrator who has considerable skill and knowledge of the specifics being presented.
3. If possible, stage a practice with a few observers to suggest refinements.
4. Prepare a detailed demonstration plan, which includes a time schedule and follow-up activities.
5. Prepare a packet of materials for the participants to use before, during, or after the demonstration. The packet should include an agenda, background information, resources, and a writing activity that encourages note taking.
6. Maximize visual presentations and use listening as a supporting element. Generous explanations should be used only if they fit the situation.
7. Try to limit the participants to those who are interested or have expressed or diagnosed need. Use principals, supervisors, and department heads to assist in follow-up activities.
8. Avoid lengthy introductions and move into the demonstration quickly, saving explanations and discussion for the follow-up session.
9. Take advantage of immediate interest by having follow-up activities while impressions are still clear. Use the demonstrator in the follow-up but have someone else take the major responsibility.
10. Allow maximum viewing and listening for the observers and minimize technical difficulties by selecting a properly equipped staging area.

Tight planning and specificity may increase the clarity of the presentation, but they also create the most serious limitation of a demonstration activity. Because teachers realize that many reasonable alternatives actually exist, there is a tendency for them to reject modeling behavior. For example, a demonstration that attempts to show how a teacher-student conference can motivate a child to read more library books runs the risk of rejection by a teacher who thinks, "That isn't what I would say." To counterbalance this tendency, immediate feedback in the follow-up activity should be planned to allow teachers to react. Another way to increase teacher acceptance is to limit demonstrations to situations where specific skills are to be copied, such as learning how

to administer a standardized reading test or operate a specific
audiovisual device.

There are three important points to remember: although detailed planning and a dry run may be useful, try to avoid over-
staging the demonstration and keep the behavior spontaneous
and natural; demonstrations can provide information and understanding, but don't expect them to result in skill development;
and try to see the demonstration from the observers' viewpoint
and always include a follow-up activity that permits them to
review the purposes and verbalize their perceptions of what they
have witnessed.

OBSERVATION

Observations provide participants with opportunities to view
teaching activities in actual classroom situations. The rationale
for this activity is simply to show how to do something.

Observations like lectures and demonstrations, have a relatively low experience impact because there is no control over the
content other than the original selection of the observable activity. If the observation takes place in a classroom, there is usually
little chance for communication between the observers or between the teacher and the observers. A few schools have one-
way observation windows, including sound systems, which
solve the problem of interruptions and allow observers to share
comments. But in most, the observer is cautioned to be passive,
and communication is most often one-way unless time arrangements, previous planning, or the activity allow the observers to
ask questions.

Because of the unpredictability of the classroom and the
usually unavoidable lack of detailed planning between the visitors and the school, the content of the observation is not as focused as it is in a demonstration. Therefore, observations must
be limited to rather general objectives. A better plan (although it
doesn't work for groups of teachers) is to observe a specific skill
lesson over a period of time (for example, a week).

Because observations are limited in experience impact, somewhat unpredictable in content, and often too brief, they are probably overused in the name of in-service activity. For example,
there will probably be little change in teaching behavior among a
faculty that observes a model reading program in the next
county. On the other hand, if there was a need to observe a different reading program, and if the observers were prepared in
advance to seek definite ideas and to act on what they had seen,

the experience could stimulate change or answer practical ques- Select a format
tions.

Some guidelines for planning, arranging, and carrying out observations indicate the need for careful planning in order to obtain maximum impact from observing actual classroom instruction.

Guidelines for observers
1. Decide what activities must be seen to meet the objectives of
   the in-service program.
2. Investigate several possible places and select the situation
   that best fits your stated objectives.
3. Communicate with the proper administrator well in advance
   of the proposed visit.
4. When inquiring about the proposed observation, tell the
   purpose of the visit and describe the type of activity you
   wish to observe.
5. To help in your preobservation preparation, ask for a witness
   description of the program. Also try to obtain information
   about the location of the school, the names of the administrators and teachers, the room numbers, and a time schedule.
6. At the school, check in at the office before looking for the
   location of the observation and inquire about the rules of observing.
7. Always try to arrange a time to talk to the teacher about what
   you observed. Observations almost always raise many questions that need answering in order to clarify perceptions.
8. Try to take notes to facilitate remembering the key points you
   wish to consider when you return.
9. When you return, carry out follow-up activities while impressions are fresh and interest is high. Try to answer the
   question, "What are the implications for our instructional
   program?"

Guidelines for schools that receive observers
Note: Although the following guidelines represent a change in
   viewpoint they are offered with the intent of improving observation as an in-service activity.
1. If visitors continually (every week) request permission to observe specific activities, set aside a time for observations.
   Teachers will know what to expect, the interruption will be
   less disruptive, the numbers of people can be controlled, and
   there will be smoother overall administration.
2. Prepare a brief visitor data sheet, which states the goals of
   the program, general student information, and instructions
   on interruptions.

3. Determine an advance notification period. A good practice is to notify teachers on Friday of the visitors for the coming week.
4. When a request is received, determine the intent of the visit and pass this information to the teacher(s).
5. Refuse to allow mass visitation to pass for in-service education. Ask visitors what their intent is and if they have planned a follow-up activity.
6. Because observations have a limited usefulness in the first place, reserve the right to turn down requests. A good rule of thumb is simply that the students' and teachers' needs have precedence over the visitors' needs.

If observations are to achieve any worthwhile goal, they require detailed planning prior to the visit to coordinate the needs of the observers with the actual instruction observed. Follow-up activities are imperative to determine what, if any, implications there are for changing reading instruction.

INTERVIEWING

Interviewing includes both the *personal interview* or individual conference examined in terms of its implications for changing teacher behavior, and the *group interview,* an efficient method of communicating a wide variety of ideas to large groups of in-service participants.

Personal interview

This person-to-person interaction activity is basic to education and consumes a great deal of time for many educators. Usually the objective of this activity in terms of in-service education is to exchange information with another person in order to effect changes in either one or both persons' behavior. For example, a principal may wish to give a teacher some information about his or her performance. The intent is that the teacher will understand his or her own performance better, accept the principal's viewpoints, and, if necessary, change future behavior. Whether behavior changes occur depends upon many factors, one of which is the role of the interviewer. Harris and Bessent (1969), who deal extensively and quite sensibly with the personal interview, point out how the outcomes of an interview are controlled in part by the following three examples of interviewer behavior (in these examples, as in most school situations, the interviewer is the principal or supervisor and the other participant is the teacher):

1. *Directive, critical.* The interviewer is the expert and knows the problems. He or she tells the teacher what is wrong and gives specific instructions on how to improve. The problem is faced squarely with no compliments offered. If the teacher resists, threats are used to indicate the serious need for change.
2. *Laissez faire.* The interviewer is easygoing and wants to seek a solution without causing difficulty. A cordial relationship is intended, and compliments and positive comments flow. A problem is implied and the supervisor assures the teacher, "I have faith that you will do a good job."
3. *Nondirective, constructive.* The interviewer acts as a counselor by acknowledging the problem but seeking clarification and asking for suggested solutions. He or she offers assistance but clearly indicates that the teacher is responsible for taking the initiative.

Participants react quite differently to these three interview situations, and different persons may react in different ways to the same interview. But extensive experience with the three modes suggests the following generalizations:

1. If a principal or supervisor desires a positive response toward improvement, the critical and laissez-faire approaches are often less effective than the nondirective.
2. When negative side effects can be tolerated, the critical approach may be effective in obtaining acceptance of suggestions.
3. The nondirective constructive approach gives the supervisor/principal insight into the teacher's perception of the problem and may allow him or her to be truly helpful.
4. The direct, critical approach puts the principal or supervisor in a role of expert and tends to rule out the use of other resources.
5. The laissez-faire approach may build false confidence on the part of the teacher and may not evoke any suggestions for improvement.

Because the interview or conference offers some predictable outcomes, supervisors and principals should keep in mind that no one type of superordinate behavior is bad or undesirable under all conditions. In some situations, any one of the three approaches is appropriate and, in fact, necessary. Too often, little thought is given to the mode of the conference and the necessary outcome. Most often the tendency is to keep peace and harmony

271

when the need for change far outweighs the side effects of a direct, critical approach. There is also a tendency for people to use only one method. The interview should vary according to the situation. By giving more thought to the need for changed behavior and less thought to the need for harmonious personal relationships, principals and supervisors can use the interview activity as an effective format for improving reading instruction.

Group interview

This activity consists of a situation where one person interviews several others. The intent is not to change personal behavior. The format is appropriate in problem-solving meetings because it allows several resource people to respond to the same concern in a structured manner.

Usually the interviewer has a list of questions developed by the in-service participants, and each expert responds to the same question. Thelen (1954) points out that the panel should be told to respond only with ideas that have not already been given. An example of a group interview is a report on the results of a number of buzz group sessions. Each group sends a reporter to be interviewed in front of all the participants. Another example is to examine a proposed reading program by interviewing a panel of selected people who are thoroughly familiar and competent with respect to the program under consideration.

In summary, the personal interview is an efficient way to attempt to bring about changes in specific behavior. The interviewer matches his or her approach with the desired outcome. Group interviews appear to be an efficient technique for sharing expert opinion or small group ideas with a larger audience.

BRAINSTORMING

Although in-service programs use brainstorming sessions to stimulate ideas, inform people of other ideas, suggest alternative solutions, and enhance positive attitudes toward alternative solutions, this activity has essentially one narrow purpose: to allow ideas to surface. To obtain this result, special care must be taken to avoid criticism, analysis, and discussion of ideas. The usual procedure is to select a topic and then to inform the participants of the special procedures necessary to allow ideas to be generated. The rules, sometimes posted, should include the following:

1. All ideas related to the topic in any direct way are desired.
2. A maximum number of related ideas is desired.

3. One idea may be modified or adapted and expressed as another idea.
4. Ideas should be expressed as clearly and concisely as possible.
5. No discussion and no criticism of ideas should be attempted.

Select a format

Brainstorming can use a group leader for small groups or a recorder and/or an assistant leader for large groups. As few as two people on groups as large as sixty or seventy (provided that two or three leaders are available to receive ideas at the same time and to record them) can brainstorm. A chalkboard, overhead projector, or large sheets of paper are useful for writing down ideas. A microphone used with a "man in the audience" technique may help to gather a maximum number of ideas. Some practical suggestions for conducting brainstorming sessions include:

1. Establish a time limit based on the size of the group and the issue.
2. Encourage and stimulate without being too directive.
3. Restate ideas, but also let silence prevail for up to a minute to allow for thinking time.
4. Record each idea so that all participants can refer to them during the session.
5. Let ideas flow informally with a minimum use of formal recognition of people.
6. When interest wavers, terminate the session with a brief resumé to let the participants see their productiveness.

Follow-up activities such as group discussions or buzz sessions should analyze, criticize, edit, revise, and suggest implementation procedures for all of the ideas.

Brainstorming should be used only to solve problems and only if there is a need for many new ideas. If the group senses that their ideas will not be used, the brainstorming session may end in painful silence. If only two alternatives are possible, brainstorming is not appropriate. But, if a fresh approach is needed, and there are no restrictions on the possibility of a new method, go ahead and brainstorm.

BUZZ SESSION

In this basic, small group activity, temporary groups are formed to discuss a specific topic. The activity is characterized by a maximum of critical interaction and a minimum of structure. There is relatively high experience impact because participants are active,

273

they contribute to the content, and they make immediate voiced value judgments of other people's ideas. Buzz sessions are designed to focus on a specific topic in order to promote verbal interaction among the participants. They should stimulate interest and commitment to change as the groups identify points of agreement and conflict. Some of the necessary procedures include:

1. A minimum time limit of ten to fifteen minutes is necessary; an hour or more may be needed for a complex subject.
2. To facilitate feedback, recorders for each group are necessary. They should be instructed to keep their notes brief.
3. Group leaders may be appointed or may be selected by the group. The point to keep in mind is that full discussion is encouraged, including disagreement and alternative suggestions.
4. Leaders should circulate among the buzz groups but should not participate to allow them to get a sense of general direction and at the same time let the participants feel they are not left completely alone.
5. The ideal buzz group size is five to nine members.
6. Round tables or circles or chairs with no head position, separated enough to avoid interference between groups, are important.
7. Leaders normally need only to act in a general fashion, but the recorders should be able to screen ideas, digest, synthesize, and analyze.
8. Because buzz group participants need to be familiar with each other, name tags are useful.
9. A follow-up activity is always necessary to analyze the ideas generated. The recorder, a discussion group, or consultants should review the ideas for the participants.
10. Buzz sessions should be used only after some prior activity. Participants must be interested in the topic, have some knowledge about it, and have definite ideas to express.
11. Buzz sessions should not be used when opinions are not crucial in approaching the problem or when only one solution is available. The exception to this is the situation where the intent is to get reactions to a solution that seems apparent.

An example of an effective use of the buzz session would be in an in-service program where the objective is to get junior high school teachers to teach reading in their content areas. Once the teachers agree that many students do not comprehend their textbooks very well, they could form buzz groups to seek solutions to this problem. The follow-up activities would be to organize and Select a format analyze solutions and to arrive at some tentative plans.

Finally, if the buzz group activity is properly carried out, it can change a meeting from a passive session into an active, alert, action-oriented meeting. The buzz session is easy to use and highly flexible, and it appears to be well suited to the needs of groups of teachers who need to engage in purposeful activity.

GROUP DISCUSSION

Small group activity usually centers on a problem and is intended to rely on organized interaction to arrive at either a common decision or a clearly defined disagreement. Groups share information, analyze alternatives, develop understandings of complex problems, and arrive at carefully considered decisions. Variations of discussions include the buzz session, the case analysis, and the leaderless group.

The *case analysis* is a group discussion structured around a real problem. Many parts of a complex situation are presented in narrative form with a minimum of irrelevant information. The leader should stimulate the participants to interpret the significant variables of the case. Sometimes, though not always, the leader already knows these variables. This factor determines to a great extent the amount of structure the leader provides. When only a few alternatives are relevant, more structure is usually necessary; when several alternatives are available, the discussion can be much less structured.

The *leaderless discussion* is intended to increase the involvement of the participants. This concept assumes that group assumption of responsibility is more important than seeking a solution to a problem. Seeking a leader is discouraged. Usually the group is observed by persons who are responsible for its conception, and sometimes a skilled leader should assist the group in overcoming obstacles and withdraw to allow the participants to begin again.

The participants must be interested in the problem, need to discuss the topic, and have pertinent information about it. The group must also project a plan and timetable for carrying out its purposes. A record of the outcomes of the discussion should be kept and distributed to each discussant before any subsequent session. Follow-up activities—and often they aren't necessary— could include a brief published report or an action research project to develop and evaluate the ideas generated.

Groups must be large enough to carry out their work and

small enough to allow considerable personal interaction. The optimal size usually ranges from seven to fifteen people. The meetings should be held in a quiet, comfortable setting where the participants can see each other. Sometimes it is better to let the leader be designated by behavior rather than by "the chair" position at the table. Group discussions have some limitations:

1. Group leaders must be trained to be effective. Don't assume that the personable, eager person can always be effective.
2. Avoid letting a discussion become a recitation of questions and answers. It is better to share diverse opinions with open-ended questions that stimulate a variety of responses.
3. Avoid the tendency to call on each person systematically, and don't be afraid of silence. Let people feel the need to say something but also prevent some from dominating the interaction.
4. Don't organize a discussion to support what is already decided and don't involve people in a discussion of "your" problem. Most people will see through these types of manipulation and will resent wasting their time.

Finally, there is more to a group discussion than getting a group of people together. There must be a need, an objective, some careful planning, and usually some result or follow-up activity.

ROLE PLAYING

In this activity one or more people assume roles and spontaneously act out a specified problem in an attempt to act and feel as they might in the real situation. The object is to understand the feelings of other people and to develop skill in spontaneous verbal interaction.

The general procedure is to establish rapport, identify a situation, assign roles, adhere to the roles, and stop at the appropriate time. Because of the high intensity of involvement, it is important that the participants feel comfortable with the role. The role playing should be directed to a very specific problem, and role assignments must be explicit so the participant knows what is expected. Activity leaders must caution participants to adhere to their assigned role and must terminate the play before involvement becomes emotionally embarrassing.

Follow-up activities must be carried out to seek the reactions of both the actors and the audience. Follow-up group discussions, an expert's analysis, or switching roles (provided additional time is spent contrasting the two situations) are good follow-up activities. With small groups of ten to fifteen members, each participant can observe two actors, carry out discussions, and have a chance to role play. Larger groups may require buzz sessions to carry out follow-up activities.

The leaders must be sensitive to the feelings of actors. By displaying a friendly, permissive, and constructive attitude toward role players, embarrassment can be overcome.

One instance of a role playing session in a reading in-service session is when teachers act out a conference between a parent and a teacher where the teacher wishes to convince the reluctant parent that the child might benefit from a summer remedial reading program. Role playing may also be useful in situations where truly changed behavior is desired. For this reason improved reading instruction may result when teachers have opportunities to feel the need for a change.

SUMMARY AND APPLICATIONS

A wide range of formats will allow in-service leaders to select activities that best suit the objectives of their programs. The lecture is an effective way to permit participants to receive information. Demonstrations provide a useful method for viewing specific teacher and/or pupil behavior. Observation shows how others handle activities. Interviewing is a way to communicate individually and in large groups. Brainstorming is a useful method for generating ideas; so is intense group interaction on a specific topic. Group discussions of various sorts can be used too. Finally, role playing is a technique in which participants act out a real situation.

If in-service activities are to have any lasting effect, they must have some impact on each individual participant. Harris and Bessent (1969) present an analysis of the experience impact of a variety of activities which is summarized in figure 10.3. The range of activities that can be employed in in-service sessions is given in the column on the left. The next three columns show variables that control the experience impact of activities. Note that the activities that give participants some degree of control over content, are open to multisensory presentations, and permit interaction and feedback through two-way communication have the highest potential for experience impact. For example, a film

277

Figure 10.3 **Experience impact of activities**

ACTIVITIES	Control of content	Multisensory	Two-way communication
Lecture	*		
Illustrated lecture	*	*	
Demonstration		*	
Observation		*	
Interviewing	*		*
Brainstorming	*		*
Group discussions	*		*
Buzz sessions	*		*
Role playing	*	*	*
Guided practice	*	*	*

Low experience impact

↑

↓

High experience impact

Source: Ben M. Harris, Wailand Bessent, *In-Service Education: A Guide to Better Practice*, © 1969, p. 35. Reprinted by permission of Prentice-Hall, Inc., Englewood Cliffs, New Jersey.

or demonstration of a reading specialist administering a diagnostic test will not have as much experience impact as a guided practice session in which participants actually administer the test.

Harris and Bessent offer another analysis for choosing appropriate activities. In figure 10.4, activities are listed in the column on the left; each of the remaining columns gives a type of objective. Note that the objectives range from the cognitive type (for example, to learn about objective-based reading instruction), to the broad spectrum type (such as to demonstrate the effect of differentiated instruction on teachers' efficiency), to the affective type (such as to determine the effect of individualized instruction on pupils' attitude toward reading). By analyzing the impact of activities and by relating activities to objectives, educators can help ensure the degree of involvement that is needed to obtain desired outcomes.

Schedule sessions

The matter of scheduling in-service sessions may seem a bit mundane after a discussion of needs, goals, resources, and formats, but this facet usually turns out to be an important factor in the success of the program. Too often the nature of the program is dictated by the time available. Otherwise well-planned in-service programs are hastily thrown in the day or two before school starts—when most teachers would prefer to be getting their rooms and their thoughts ready for the arrival of the children. Or they are tacked onto busy school days when the thoughts of even the most conscientious teachers are elsewhere. If in-service programs are worth careful planning, they are also worth the time required for implementation.

Scheduling depends on the availability of local budgetary support, negotiated contracts, the availability of relevant resources, and the flexibility of the local organization. But whatever the constraints, in-service plans should include the provision of released time and/or paid (or contracted) supplementary time for participation in the activities. If only limited time can be made available, the activities must be limited to fit the time. No sensible newscaster would attempt to fit thirty minutes of news into a fifteen-minute time slot; no intelligent in-service planner should attempt to jam twenty hours of work into two or three one-hour sessions.

Some school systems provide a number of in-service days throughout the school year. The children are dismissed, and the day is available for whatever work needs to be done. The idea is sound, and the plan is workable so long as the days do not become catchalls for administrative tasks or deteriorate to grab bag sessions where a variety of speakers is brought in to amuse, delight, and inspire the assembled throng. Some schools provide

Figure 10.4 **An in-service design grid**

ACTIVITIES	OBJECTIVES					
	Knowledge	Comprehension	Applications	Synthesis	Values & attitudes	Adjustment
Lecture						
Illustrated lecture	Cognitive objectives					
Demonstration						
Observation						
Interviewing		Broad-spectrum objectives				
Brainstorming						
Group discussions						
Buzz sessions						
Role playing				Affective objectives		
Guided practice						

Source: Ben M. Harris, Wailand Bessent, *In-Service Education: A Guide to Better Practice*, © 1969, p. 37. Reprinted by permission of Prentice-Hall, Inc., Englewood Cliffs, New Jersey.

for released time during the school day to enable committees and work groups to meet. Released time can also make possible visits to other schools or facilities to observe relevant programs. Time can be made available during the summer break. This option is especially desirable because relatively long, uninterrupted blocks can be scheduled and collaborative programs can more readily be worked out with nearby colleges and universities.

Remember that work always expands to fill the available time. Therefore, it is not very sensible to make the time available and then try to figure out what to do. Tackle it the other way around: figure out what needs to be done and how to do it, and then schedule the time.

Evaluate results

The last step in the process is to evaluate results to ensure that in-service efforts are effective. In this age of accountability, without evaluation there can be no accounting for the expenditure of time and money required for in-service programs.

Objectives that are stated in behavioral terms greatly facilitate evaluation by serving as the criterion referents in assessing the impact of the activities. That is, each activity can be evaluated in terms of the objectives that served to set it up in the first place. For example, take an objective we considered earlier: to identify or devise checklists to be used in evaluating materials. The assessment of sessions devoted to such an objective becomes a relatively simple, straightforward matter of observing the output from the sessions. More content-dependent objectives might call for paper-and-pencil testing to determine whether basic facts and/or concepts have been mastered.

Once an objective sets a criterion referent, evaluation can be done in a number of ways. Observation of the outcomes is the most natural, and perhaps paper-and-pencil testing is most objective. But work samples (the checklists devised in the activities just discussed) and performance tests (seeing whether the checklists are actually used properly) can also be used.

When in-service sessions are evaluated in terms of their contribution to an objective, decisions can be made regarding the specific activities employed and their contribution to progress toward the overall goal. Perhaps additional input will be required in order to meet a given objective, or a different type of activity may seem more appropriate after careful evaluation of a session. On the other hand, experience may suggest that the objective itself or the ultimate goal ought to be modified. Objectives and goals should be reconsidered if experience shows that they are unrealistic in terms of expectations and/or available resources.

Moberg (1974) offers a useful discussion of specific approaches to research relating to in-service programs. He observes, "Reduced to its most basic components, research dealing with inservice programs involves the measured effectiveness of the program's activities (the independent variable)" (p. 33). And that, of course, is exactly what in-service education in reading is all about. He also discusses some of the factors that complicate research and evaluation efforts in the area.

Examples of in-service programs

In the pages that follow we present some examples of in-service programs that have been implemented in a variety of settings. They are examples, not models to be implemented in other settings without regard for local considerations. Some additional ideas regarding in-service programs in reading are put forth in recent journal articles by Criscuolo (1975) and Olson (1975), and in the International Reading Association publication *Modular Preparation for Teaching* (Sartain and Stanton, 1974).

In-service programs may be offered at the building level, where some or all of the teachers in a given school participate, at the district level, or at the state or regional level. Examples of programs at each of these levels are given. Each example is presented with regard for the critical factors in the in-service process identified in the earlier section of this chapter. Our comments are given parenthetically.

BUILDING-CENTERED PROGRAMS

In-service programs that focus on the needs of the teachers and staff of a specific school come closest to dealing with grass-roots concerns. At the building level, one or two teachers may get together to study a problem that perplexes them, a group may decide to pursue a common interest, or the entire building staff may work toward improving the overall reading program. The whole range of options should be available at all times to permit staff members to tackle problems in the most straightforward manner possible. Two examples of interest group programs and an example of a buildingwide program follow.

281

Interest groups

Example 1: Interest group

NEED Following a districtwide closed-circuit television presentation on developing students' ability to think creatively about certain reading selections, the primary grade teachers in one building requested more information on how to teach creative reading.

GOAL To help elementary teachers be more systematic and precise in teaching their pupils to think creatively about certain reading selections. (*Comment:* The goal was identified and stated by a reading consultant for the entire district. Although this method is somewhat at odds with our recommendations about the identification of needs and statement of goals, the preliminary activity did lead to the identification of need at the building level.)

OBJECTIVE To help teachers improve their teaching of creative reading. (*Comment:* This objective is not stated in behavioral terms. Is it possible to state a prescriptive objective when the topic is creative reading? If not, what is to be done about evaluation?)

ACTIVITIES A single late-afternoon session was arranged with the district consultant who had been responsible for the initial television presentation. Since the television programs had been recorded on audiotape, the teachers could listen again to the definition of creative reading and the characteristics of questions designed to stimulate thinking at the cognitive level of creativity. In addition, the written reactions to the television programs submitted by teachers throughout the school system had been used to construct questions for teachers to ask:

1. Do your good readers often have their hands raised before you finish asking your question about a story? It was apparent from the television demonstration that the participating students frequently raised their hands to answer a question before it was completely asked. Information received from teachers who viewed the programs indicated that this is typical behavior of good readers. Premature hand raising suggests that students are conditioned to expect questions about their reading that do not require higher-level thinking.
2. Do your students understand how to adjust their thinking when you change the cognitive level of your questions about a story? During the programs, the demonstrating teacher had to clarify precisely the limits of the response being solicited before the students took advantage of the freedom available

to them. The students tested the limits to which they might go with their answers. As the teacher reacted to their responses, they learned the rules for working at the cognitive level of creativity.

3. Are you uncomfortable when your questions about a story are met with silence? A number of teachers who responded to the TV programs commented on the lack of time available for teaching creative reading. Teachers who have a positive attitude toward teaching creative thinking will not be uncomfortable about taking the time necessary to permit students to answer high-level questions about their reading.

4. Do you find yourself answering some of the best questions you ask about a story? When teachers do ask questions that call for creative thinking, they often wait too short a time for students to do effective thinking before answering the questions. Students become used to this pattern and wait for the teacher to answer hard questions.

5. Do you feel a twinge of conscience if you don't tell a student that his or her response to a question about a story is either right or wrong? Teachers are accustomed to rewarding correct responses and withholding rewards for incorrect responses. In the television programs, the demonstrating teacher had difficulty finding language patterns that accepted students' responses without evaluating them as correct or incorrect. Teachers who teach creative reading effectively are likely to have a ready supply of accepting but nonevaluating responses.

EVALUATION The questions and the audiotape were left with the teachers to improve their teaching of reading. (*Comment:* Could anything more have been done by way of evaluation? Remember, there was no prescriptive objective.)

Example 2: Interest group

NEED All of the secondary school teachers in the district were invited to take a course on how to improve their reading ability. Nineteen people enrolled in the classes that were designed to improve their vocabulary, rate, and comprehension.

GOAL No overall goal was stated.

OBJECTIVE To help secondary school teachers develop positive attitudes toward incorporating the teaching of reading into their content area classes and to teach them specific instructional practices to use with their students. (*Comment:* Neither the need nor the objective is stated in terms of the participants' perceptions.

283

The program described here was instigated by the district reading consultant to accomplish a secondary purpose: to change the participants' attitudes by working with them on improving their personal reading skills.)

ACTIVITIES A personal reading improvement course of seven two-hour sessions. It was hoped that the participating teachers would inductively learn some techniques to use with their own students and would develop positive attitudes toward incorporating these techniques into their teaching. The inductive approach was adopted to avoid the negative attitudes that sometimes result when a specialist tells teachers how they should teach.

EVALUATION In addition to improving reading rate and comprehension, a survey questionnaire indicated that this particular in-service approach had desirable effects on attitudes and teaching. On the questionnaire, thirteen of the nineteen subjects responded that because of the course they felt better able to improve their students' reading; eleven said that they were more willing to make reading instruction part of their classes; and seven commented that they were already teaching their students some reading improvement techniques they had learned in the course.

Buildingwide program

Example 3: Program development

This program was devised to meet the contractual agreement for a reading development course between a school board and the local teachers' organization. The clause in the contract provided:

> A joint committee of three members appointed by the Superintendent of Schools and three by the President of the Association is created to study and establish a course or courses in reading development for all District teachers and administrators. All District teachers and administrators shall be required to take this course within a four year period following January 1975 unless such a course is in evidence on their credit transcript no earlier than 1969.

The program was carried out in one middle school building (grades 5–8).

NEED The general need for improved reading instruction was underscored by the negotiated contract. The specific need was to translate the contractual clause into a worthwhile in-service program for the building teachers.

GOAL The goal was to establish a viable reading program for the middle school.

OBJECTIVES

1. Teachers will define a reading program to fit the needs of the middle school philosophy.
2. Teachers will participate in study, group work, and discussion to discover the processes of reading suggested by reading authorities.
3. Teachers will establish a sequential skill list as a basis for individual assessment.
4. Teachers will develop a profile for individual assessment and progress to follow the child through middle school.
5. Teachers will write objectives for using the reading skills across content areas.
6. Teachers will index reading materials that meet the needs of individual students.
7. Teachers will show how reading is related to the communications process.
8. Teachers will plan an individualized program.
9. Teachers will write terminal goals for middle school students.
10. Teachers will complete a reading program to meet our needs at the middle school.

ACTIVITIES A series of weekly, after-school sessions was held. Six major topics provided a focus for the sessions: the reading process, reading in the content areas, reading in the communication process, skills essential to successful reading performance in the middle school, individualizing the teaching of reading, and an overall reading program for the middle school. Multiple sessions were devoted, as needed, to each topic. For each topic, relevant resource materials and/or people were identified, related objectives were stated, and performance criteria were established. Background information was gained mainly from presentations and discussions led by resource people and work study sessions, with subsequent sharing among the subgroups. Participants spent much of their time in work-type activities—for example, identifying essential reading skills, writing instructional objectives, devising plans for individualizing instruction—working individually, in small groups, and, finally, as a total group. (*Comment:* Where could brainstorming and buzz sessions have been employed to good advantage? Would systematic observations have been useful?)

EVALUATION The program was evaluated in terms of the following objectives:

1. Teachers will write lesson plans using skills, games, strategies, and techniques discussed in the in-service sessions.
2. Teachers will discuss reading in relation to the communication process.
3. Students will be involved in programs that start where the students' needs begin and meet their individual needs.
4. When a teacher is observed presenting a reading lesson, he or she will be preparing students for the lesson they will be working on.
5. There will be a continuous growth in student use of supplementary materials.
6. Students will check out more books for recreational reading.
7. In a random sampling of students concerning their feelings about reading there should be a noticeable improvement in positive attitudes toward reading.

(*Comment:* Are the objectives for evaluation sufficiently prescriptive to permit a straightforward evaluation of the program? Which ones are and which ones are not? Look back at the clause in the contract and decide whether the in-service program described meets the spirit of the requirement. If you think it does not, what would you change?)

DISTRICTWIDE PROGRAMS

Certain types of in-service programs can be handled most effectively and efficiently on a districtwide basis. Programs aimed specifically at principals, for example, would necessarily involve representatives from a number of school buildings. Other examples are programs designed to meet the unique needs of staff members in a particular attendance area within the district (dealing with the language development problems of certain cultural or economic groups), to bring together the teachers in one content area (teaching the requisite reading skills in the context of a secondary social studies class) or at a given age/grade level (coping with children who have difficulty in making the transition from kindergarten to first grade), or to prepare personnel for the implementation of a new approach to instruction (an objective-based approach to reading skill development). The entire range of options should be available so that programs can be devised to meet unique needs. Some examples of these programs follow.

Special interest groups

Example 4: Program for principals

NEED A survey (conducted by the district reading coordinator) of elementary school principals in the district disclosed that the principals felt they were not adequately prepared to administer the reading program for the primary grades. They responded favorably to an invitation to attend five two-hour classes entitled "Administering the Primary Grades Reading Program" and taught by two central office reading consultants.

GOAL No overall goal was stated. (*Comment:* In practice, even well-conceived and carefully planned in-service programs that are designed for a specific purpose may not be related to a long-range, overall goal. Is this a serious flaw? How could the practice best be changed?)

OBJECTIVE To help principals administer the primary grades reading program in their schools. (*Comment:* Is this a useful objective?)

ACTIVITIES The classes were held twice a week from 9:00 A.M. to 11:00 A.M. They were held early in May when the principals were hiring teachers, planning their instructional programs, and ordering materials for the following school year.

The first meeting was devoted to a consideration of the following organizational plans for teaching reading: three groups in one heterogeneous classroom taught by the homeroom teacher; completely individualized teaching; team teaching; homogeneous grouping for reading within one grade; homogeneous grouping for reading between two or among three grades. The principals were given handouts with diagrams and explanations of the various schemes and asked to list the advantages and disadvantages of each approach. Small group discussion followed.

The third, fourth, and fifth meetings provided the principals with information about evaluating the total reading program, evaluating a teacher's performance in the classroom, and using financial resources and specialized personnel. All meetings began with a short presentation by one of the instructors and included time for questions and discussion. (*Comment:* What other activities discussed in this chapter might have been profitably implemented?)

EVALUATION No formal evaluation was done. (*Comment:* Open discussion was employed in each session. Do you think a formal evaluation was needed?)

Example 5: Program for primary teachers

NEED A new junior primary program to provide a transition year between kindergarten and first grade was instituted for students who lack readiness for reading instruction. The participating teachers expressed their need for some readiness training before the new program began.

GOAL To help teachers understand basic differences between the junior primary program, the kindergarten program, and the first-grade program.

OBJECTIVE To help teachers understand the objectives of the program in regard to reading instruction. (*Comment:* Unfortunately, no explicit objectives were ever stated for the program.)

ACTIVITIES The participating teachers were released from their teaching responsibilities for two full days to meet with central office coordinators of mathematics, science, social studies, and reading. The final two and one-half hours were devoted to a group discussion between the reading coordinator and the teachers.

As a follow-up procedure, the reading coordinator sent a memo to each teacher several days after the end of the program. She had used this technique following other in-service meetings and found it effective in summing up group discussions and reminding teachers of the plans that were made during meetings. A carefully written, follow-up memo often communicates ideas better than they are communicated in oral discussion. The oral summing up at the end of a spirited two-and one-half-hour meeting is often done imprecisely and at a time when fatigue is interfering with concentration.

The following paragraphs are excerpts from the memo each junior primary teacher received when he or she returned to the classroom after two days of in-service meetings:

To: All junior primary teachers
From [name], Reading Coordinator

The recent in-service meeting we shared was a good learning experience for me. The group discussion brought to my awareness the many fine things being accomplished in our junior primary classes, as well as some of the administrative and instructional problems that accompany the program.

I think we all agree that many children who have completed kindergarten but seem to be lacking in readiness for a structured reading program need the junior primary program. These students apparently fall into two categories: those with serious and complex readiness deficits and those with relatively minor readiness deficits. The question seems to be for which of these students junior primary classes are most needed or perhaps whether one junior primary class should service the readiness needs of students from both categories. How a particular school answers this question seems important not so much in terms of whether certain students will benefit—it seems obvious that students in either category will profit from the special advantages the program offers—but rather in terms of the expectancies of parents and future teachers regarding the junior primary graduate's ability to read. The need for precise communication regarding the kind or kinds of students a particular junior primary program services is important. The instructional program and our evaluation of the effects of the instructional program must consider the seriousness of the student's disability when he or she enters the program.

Unfortunately, our present methods of predicting a child's reading readiness are not as reliable as we would like. Some children who are judged to have serious readiness deficits may prove to be less seriously deficient. In these cases, the junior primary teacher should begin in the instructional reading process when the child evidences readiness, or in rare cases the child may be transferred to a first grade class.

However, I believe that junior primary teachers should not feel that getting all of the children—or any of their children if they teach the seriously deficient—started in a formal reading program is their responsibility. The junior primary program, I feel, should be a thirty-eight-week language readiness program, not an instructional reading program that begins in February, instead of September. It is true that given the conditions present in most junior primary classes some children who would not respond to formal instruction in a first grade class can be taught to respond to print. These responses, however, may be short-lived and unproductive of the thinking processes that engage a mature reader.

There is evidence that reading ability correlates positively and highly to general language ability. The sole function of the junior primary program might be to provide children who have speaking and listening deficiencies with many and varied speaking and listening experiences. Motor coordination development might also be an appropriate objective for some children. Getting a child started in a reading program should be an objective that may emerge as the junior primary program progresses.

Rhythm and rhyming games, creative dramatics, listening to and telling stories, talking about shared experiences, music, and art are representative of activities that may be varied and presented at different levels of sophistication for an entire school year without boring most children and without formal reading instruction. If these activities are presented correctly, children may inductively learn much about reading that will in the long run serve them better than some formal experiences with decoding the language.

It was apparent during our in-service discussion that opinions and procedures regarding the role of reading instruction in the junior primary program vary. This is consistent with our philosophy that every school should have the kind of instructional program it needs. It was also apparent that the nature and objectives of each school's program need to be communicated to that school's entire faculty and to parents whose children are in the program.

The ideas stated in this memo are certainly subject to discussion and argument. They are ideas which I formed during our first meeting. Perhaps they could serve as a base for discussion at future in-service meetings.

EVALUATION No formal evaluation was done. (*Comment:* What might have been done? Could anything sensible have been done since there were no stated objectives for the program and no prescriptive objective for the in-service sessions?)

New programs

Example 6: Teacher aide program

NEED The district was instituting a new program to provide aides for primary teachers to assist particularly with the teaching of beginning reading. The teachers and the newly selected aides requested a program to help them understand their new roles and responsibilities.

GOAL To improve the teaching of beginning reading.

OBJECTIVE To introduce newly appointed teacher aides to the concepts and techniques of beginning reading instruction. (*Comment:* Note that a specific objective could be stated for each of the five two-hour sessions.)

ACTIVITIES The following excerpt is from the proposal for the in-service program that was offered.

Proposed in-service program

General texts

1. Ekwall, Eldon E. *Locating and Correcting Reading Difficulties.* Columbus, Ohio: Charles E. Merrill, 1970.

2. Rauch, Sidney J. *Handbook for the Volunteer Tutor*. Newark, Delaware: International Reading Association, 1969.

Session 1 A GENERAL INTRODUCTION TO READING AND READING INSTRUCTION

If a teacher aide is to function effectively and harmoniously in assisting her teacher-supervisor, they must both share the same overall mental model of the reading process. The opening session will be devoted to offering alternative definitions of reading, presenting briefly the four major approaches to the teaching of reading that have arisen out of these varying definitions, and then comparing and contrasting the four in terms of the underlying rationale, the implicit organizational and curricular patterns, and the instructional, enrichment, and evaluatory procedures. Sample instructional materials representative of each approach will be shown and demonstrated, and a summary examination will be administered, corrected, and discussed.

Suggested follow-up readings
1. Kerfoot, James F. (ed.). *First Grade Reading Programs*. Newark, Del.: International Reading Association, 1965.
2. Spache, George D., and Evelyn B. Spache. *Reading in the Elementary School,* 2d ed. Boston: Allyn and Bacon, 1969, chaps. 1, 3, 4, 5, 6.

Session 2 THE TEACHING OF WORD RECOGNITION AND WORD COMPREHENSION SKILLS

This session will deal with reading at the "word" level: the building of sight vocabulary, the teaching and reinforcement of word-attack skills, and the role of decoding skills in reading generally. Various "essential" word lists will be presented, compared, and discussed. In particular, the usefulness of the Dolch and Fry lists, both instructionally and as diagnostic tools, will be stressed. Next, the various contextual clues and phonic "rules" used by more advanced primary readers will be presented and demonstrated. The emphasis throughout this section will be upon reading—even at the word level—as a thinking process. As in session 1, a summary quiz—corrected and discussed immediately afterward—will culminate the session.

Suggested follow-up readings

1. Gray, William S. *On Their Own in Reading,* rev. ed. Chicago: Scott, Foresman, 1960.
2. Wallen, Carl J. *Word Attack Skills in Reading.* Columbus, Ohio: Charles E. Merrill, 1969.
3. Wilson, Robert M., and Maryanne Hall. *Programmed Word Attack for Teachers.* Columbus, Ohio: Charles E. Merrill, 1968.

Session 3 READING AS THINKING: TEACHING THE COMPREHENSION SKILLS

This session will be divided into two major parts: identifying the major comprehension skills in reading and discussing specific ways to promote and enhance them.

During part one, various lists of skills drawn together by reading authorities will be presented and discussed, with relative priorities, or timetables, developed for their attainment by young readers. During part two, the crucial role of questioning will be discussed, with Bloom's and Sander's taxonomies presented as possible models.

Both oral questioning and the creating of written questions for study guides and lesson activities will be covered. As an application level activity, the participants will be divided into small groups, given representative sample instructional material, and charged with the creating of questions appropriate to both situations.

Suggested follow-up readings

1. Spache, George D., and Evelyn B. Spache. *Reading in the Elementary School,* 2d ed. Boston: Allyn and Bacon, 1969, chaps. 9, 13, 14.
2. Stauffer, Russell G. *Directing the Reading-Thinking Process.* New York: Harper and Row, 1975, chaps. 2, 4, 5.

Session 4 DIAGNOSTIC, CORRECTIVE, AND REMEDIAL TECHNIQUES IN READING

This session, too, will have two parts: a theory section and a practice period. Part one will consist of a lecture-discussion period—pitched at a general level—dealing with the overall major causes of reading retardation in young readers and how these problems can best be avoided or mitigated. Part two will focus upon specific, concrete diagnostic and remedial tools and techniques available to the classroom teacher or teacher aide. Among these will be the Quick Test of IQ, the Dolch Word List Test, the Gilmore Oral Reading Test, and the Informal Reading Inventory. The session will conclude with a practice period during which participants will record, analyze, and interpret a young reader's taped oral reading.

Suggested follow-up readings
1. Johnson, Marjorie S., and Roy A. Kress. *Informal Reading Inventories.* Newark, Del.: International Reading Association, 1965.
2. Otto, Wayne, Richard A. McMenemy, and Richard J. Smith. *Corrective and Remedial Teaching*, 2d ed. Boston: Houghton Mifflin, 1973, chaps. 1, 2, 3, 5, 6, 7, 8, 9, 15.
3. Zintz, Miles. *Corrective Reading*, 2d ed. Dubuque, Iowa: William C. Brown, 1971.

Session 5 SUMMARY SESSION: MEETING THE NEEDS OF ALL READERS

This final session will attempt to draw together what has been covered so far and at least touch upon any areas not yet dealt with: meeting the needs of better readers with particularly high potential, selecting teaching-learning materials appropriate to all levels of readers, and discussing the problems of articulating reading instruction with the content areas of the elementary-school curriculum. An open-ended kind of format will prevail during this session, and participants will be able to voice questions, problems, and feelings generated throughout the series.

EVALUATION A paper-and-pencil examination and a course evaluation sheet were given to each participant. The examination was checked and discussed at the final session. Note, too, that some type of evaluation was proposed for each session.

Example 7: Extension course

NEED District administrators, using information provided by consultants and representative teachers, decided to adapt an objective-based approach to the teaching of reading in the district elementary schools. Because the approach requires an understanding of instructional objectives, criterion-referenced testing, the concept of accountability, record keeping, and techniques for focusing instruction, a request for a course designed to deal with these topics was directed to the extension division of a nearby university.

293

GOAL To improve the teaching of reading in the elementary schools of the district.

OBJECTIVE To acquaint staff members (teachers, aides, principals, and local curriculum consultants) with the basic concepts required to implement an objective-based approach to reading skill development. (*Comment:* One or more specific prescriptive objectives could have been stated for each weekly session.)

ACTIVITIES A course, "Workshop in School Program Development: Objective Based Reading Instruction," was arranged through extension. It carried three hours of university credit and was staffed by a professor and five project staff members from the university. The course content was planned in collaboration with representatives from the school district, and the six university people assumed responsibility for instruction and leadership on the basis of their particular expertise. Thirteen three-hour weekly sessions were held in the early evening. Thirty-nine persons from throughout the district enrolled in the course; there was at least one representative from each elementary school building.

The following topics provided a focus for the thirteen sessions:

1. Organization of the workshop; overview of an objective-based approach to reading skill development.
2. Instructional objectives, their nature and function.
3. Assessment: criterion-referenced tests and techniques for criterion-referenced testing.
4-5. Word attack skills: specific objectives, record keeping, organizing for instruction.
6. Focusing instruction in an objective-based program: diagnosis, continuous progress, grouping, scheduling.
7. The overall developmental reading program. (*Comment:* The purpose was to show how the objective-based skill development program complements the total developmental reading program.)
8-9. Study skills: specific objectives, record keeping, organizing for instruction.
10-11. Comprehension skills: specific objectives, record keeping, organizing for instruction.
12. Self-directed, interpretive, and creative reading: expressive or open objectives, record keeping, organizing for instruction.
13. Discussion, summary, and evaluation of the workshop.

During each session there was time for basic informational input from the instructor for the session and follow-up activities as needed. Participants had opportunities to identify essential skills, to state related objectives, to identify instructional activities and materials related to the objectives, and to work through the specifics of implementing the objective-based approach.

EVALUATION Plans were made for the local reading consultant to analyze and evaluate the implementation effort during and after the first year of the program's operation.

STATE AND REGIONAL PROGRAMS

The Right to Read campaign of the 1970s has given much impetus to efforts to improve reading instruction at the state level. Plans have been developed in several states to provide leadership, coordination, and resources for a wide variety of in-service activities, ranging from volunteer tutor programs to programs for teachers who deal with children with severe learning disabilities. Although the specifics of such efforts may not differ significantly from those at the district level, when efforts are pooled and coordinated, additional budgetary and other resources may be made available to meet persistent and even very specialized in-service needs. Everything we have said about planning and carrying out in-service programs applies at this level. In fact, the identification of needs and the focusing of activities ought to be done with special care because of the additional distance between the grassroots participants and the planners. Too many well-funded statewide efforts have been dissipated when the programs offered miss the groups for whom they are intended.

The main reason for offering programs on a regional basis is that by pooling money and talent, better programs can be offered. Local educators ought to be aware of regional mechanisms that exist either within or across states because they can help to expedite local in-service efforts. In Wisconsin, for example, the Cooperative Education Service Agencies each serve several counties. In Texas, education service centers serve different regions of the state. Many comparable public and private agencies exist. They are a resource that ought to be considered when in-service efforts are planned.

At the national level, the in-service activities associated with the product dissemination efforts of research and development centers and educational laboratories are good examples of in-service efforts on a large scale. Educational products—materials for teaching reading, systems for assessment—are being offered by various public and private laboratories and centers in increasing numbers. The successful implementation of these products at the local level requires substantial in-service input. The labs and

295

centers are beginning to tackle the staff development job with reasonable success. Local school people ought to become aware of such offerings and to participate when appropriate.

Summary

We have discussed the problems associated with in-service efforts related to reading improvement and examined teachers' attitudes toward in-service education; some common mistakes that contribute to negative perceptions of in-service programs have been described. Our emphasis has been that in-service education ought not to be a negative, passive business but a positive, active one that involves teachers in working toward self-improvement.

We have offered a six-step in-service planning guide elaborated with examples and have enumerated these steps toward planning viable in-service programs as follows: (1) identify needs, (2) set a goal and state objectives, (3) assess resources and assign responsibilities, (4) select a format, (5) schedule sessions, and (6) evaluate results. In essence the process means, first, focusing on worthwhile goals through thoughtful needs assessment and identification of objectives, and then carrying out a program in a format that makes full use of available resources, at the same time recognizing the local limitations that may exist. Our examples of objective-based in-service sessions and programs have shown the process in action.

Bibliography

Criscuolo, N. P. "Strategies for Developing a Dynamic Reading Program." *Peabody Journal of Education* 52 (1975): 155–159.

Draba, R. E. "Guidelines for Viable Inservice Education." *Journal of Reading* 18 (1975): 368–371.

Harris, B. W., and Bessent, W. *Inservice Education: A Guide to Better Practice.* Englewood Cliffs, N.J.: Prentice-Hall, 1969.

Lipham, J. M. "Dynamics of Curriculum Change." Unpublished manuscript, University of Wisconsin-Madison, 1972.

Martin, W. R. "A New Look at Secondary Reading Programs in the Upper Midwest." *Journal of Reading* 12 (1969): 467–470.

Moberg, L. G. *Inservice Teacher Training in Reading.* Newark, Del.: International Reading Association, 1972.

Olson, J. H. "In-Service with an Impact." *Elementary English* 52 (1975): 708–710.

Otto, Wayne, and Erickson, L. *Inservice Education to Improve Reading Instruction.* Newark, Del.: International Reading Association, 1973.

Sartain, H. S., and P. E. Stanton (eds.). *Modular Preparation for Teaching Reading.* Newark, Del.: International Reading Association, 1974.

Smith, Richard J., Wayne Otto, and Kathleen Harty. "Elementary Teachers' Preferences for Preservice and Inservice Training in the Teaching of Reading." *The Journal of Educational Research* 63 (July–August 1970): 445–449.

Thelen, H. A. *Dynamics of Groups at Work.* Chicago: University of Chicago Press, 1954.

Chapter 11 The role of research in improving the teaching of reading

The topic of the May–June 1974 issue of *The Journal of Educational Research* was "Research in Reading as Reviewed in the Journal of Educational Research, 1933–73. Almost five thousand studies related to reading were summarized in the journal over the forty-one years covered. Otto and Smith (1975) put the volume of research in perspective:

> Research in reading has proved to be an enterprise that is both persistent and pervasive. For years researchers have been examining the complex process that is reading, and each year for the past four decades the number of studies reported has been substantial. Now the pace appears to be accelerating. At the same time, the trend has been for researchers from a broader range of disciplines to focus on readers and the reading process. A few of the studies have turned out to be classics, some have proved worthwhile for their heuristic value, others have had their effect on practices in the classroom, and many have been quickly and justly forgotten. Through it all, reading researchers and reading teachers have had to do their best to sort out the good and throw out the bad.

Russell and Fea (1963) agree that the sheer volume of research related to reading is virtually overwhelming: "Research on reading instruction comprises more material than does any other part of the curriculum" (p. 865). Even two decades ago, according to Gray (1960), more than four thousand careful, scientific reading-related studies plus twice that many interpretive and descriptive reports, were available. Since then the pace of production has continued to increase. One of the major tasks of practitioners interested in improving the teaching of reading is, indeed, to sort out the good (or, perhaps more properly, the *useful for their specific purposes*) and to throw out the rest. A second major task is to participate in the process of research related to reading to ensure that the outcomes do in fact contribute to improving the teaching of reading.

We will not attempt to review the research literature related to reading here. Such an undertaking would be beyond the scope of the chapter and outside the mainstream of interests of most practitioners. General research reviews are available from such sources as the current *Second Handbook of Research on Teaching* (Della-Piana and Endo, 1973), the annual reviews in the *Reading Research Quarterly*, a journal of the International Reading Association, *Elementary English*, a journal of the National Council of Teachers of English, and the ERIC Clearinghouse on Reading and Communication Skills (ERIC/RCS).[1] Instead we will offer guidelines for locating and sorting out the good and the useful and suggest an approach to reading research that involves researchers, developers, and practitioners.[2]

A viewer's guide to the literature

The literature related to reading offers a rich resource for improving the teaching of reading. Empirical research reports plus descriptive and interpretive pieces can be useful in solving some problems, in identifying important issues, and in setting directions for development and practice. The answers to many questions are available in the current extensive literature. Yet a word of caution is in order: Because the literature is vast and varied, some believe that it offers explicit answers to most of their ques-

---

[1] Funded by the National Institute of Education, ERIC/RCS is located on the University of Illinois campus, 1111 Kenyon Road, Urbana, Illinois 61801.
[2] Current reviews of research in reading offered by Agin (1975), Maliphant, Supramaniam, and Saroga (1974), and Cooper (1974) are particularly worth perusing because they demonstrate the wide range of audiences addressed by reviewers—from classroom teachers to basic researchers—as well as the wide range in competence of the reviewers themselves. Cooper's review is especially relevant to the focus of this chapter.
  A recent publication of the International Reading Association, *Searching the Professional Literature in Reading* (Curry and Morris, 1975), offers explicit suggestions for exploring, searching, and keeping abreast of the vast literature related to reading. The suggestions are sensible and very much worthwhile, even for the fairly sophisticated consumer of research reports. *Help for the Reading Teacher: New Directions in Research* (Page, 1975), sponsored by the National Conference on Research in English and ERIC/RCS, is, according to the Foreword, "designed to be a bridge between teachers and research in such topics as the cloze procedure, readability formulas, miscue analysis, reading strategies, informal reading inventories, and concepts and reading in the content areas." The two books are particularly good examples of efforts by professional organizations to facilitate communication between researchers and practitioners.

tions and specific solutions for most of their problems. The fact is
that as often as not, the literature will offer only direction at best,
not definitive answers or explicit solutions. Those who use the
literature must be prepared always to interpret and to extrapolate
and sometimes to find nothing or to find more questions and
problems than answers or solutions. This is not to suggest that
the literature is a vast wasteland; it must be viewed critically and
realistically and with perspective and common sense. In this section we will offer guidelines for personal evaluation of research
reports and interpretive/descriptive pieces.

EMPIRICAL RESEARCH REPORTS

An adequately written report of empirical research includes five
essential parts: statement of the problem, description of the
method, summary of results, discussion of results, and a succinctly stated summary of the entire study.

The problem

A research activity begins with the identification and statement
of a problem. Sophisticated methodology and esoteric statistical
treatment can do little to salvage a study in which inadequate attention has been given to these parts. Although there is no single
procedure for finding and sufficiently defining a problem, one
requirement is that the problem must be placed within the context of existing knowledge; that is, new hypotheses or questions
should be generated in view of past research through empirical
study and/or in terms of what seems reasonable on the basis of
logical analysis and experience. Thus an adequate introduction to
a research report includes a brief review of the related literature
and/or thinking. The review is important because it clarifies the
rationale for the study and also precludes efforts that would be
merely repetitive or tangential to a straightforward line of inquiry.

Problems are usually best explicated and laid open to objective
scrutiny through the statement of hypotheses. Once the identification and definition of a significant problem have set the
stage for inquiry, the statement of one or more hypotheses can
provide the stage directions that guide the research activity. Hypotheses, possible explanations of conditions or events, are
based upon and include facts, but they transcend known facts
because they are carefully considered guesses about unknown
conditions. A well-stated hypothesis is plausible in terms of
what is already known, and it is testable in terms of resources

The hypothesis provides the re-

that can be brought to bear. The hypothesis provides the researcher with a framework for designing a study and gathering the information that will be the basis for its support or rejection. Three key questions should be in mind when the problem is evaluated:

1. Is the general problem unambiguously stated, and is it defensible in view of related facts and explanations? Objectivity in answering this question may be clouded by personal feelings about the importance of the problem. Teachers may tend to reject problems that do not appear to be relevant to practice in the classroom; theoreticians, may reject action-oriented problems as premature, not adequately based on demonstrated facts. The point is simply that a problem should be examined for its merits, not on the basis of the viewer's biases.
2. Has there been an adequate review of the literature, and is the review coherently summarized? All of the literature directly relevant to the variables being investigated should be cited. Equally important, sound judgments on the technical adequacy and the justifiable conclusions of the studies cited should be given.
3. Is the specific hypothesis (or hypotheses) so stated as to be testable and useful in solving the problem? Although the statement of formal hypotheses is desirable, many published studies have tested no formal hypotheses. More informal questions or the statement of the problem itself may be the sole basis for the study. If this is so, look for questions that are answerable and problems that can be solved.

The method

The methodology section is a detailed description of the approach the researcher took in attacking the problem. Since each problem is unique, the method of attack must be unique. (To provide some degree of focus, this discussion is limited to a consideration of experimental studies.)

An adequate description of method must be so clearly and thoroughly presented that another researcher would be able to replicate the procedures and, theoretically, obtain the same results. If this requirement is not met, the reader can only guess what actually was done, and any attempt at further critical analyses is reduced to whimsical speculation.

When the reader is given an accurate description of how the experiment was conducted, a number of considerations merit particular attention:

1. Were the subjects selected in such a way as to avoid systematic bias? For example, if the intent is to compare the performance of good and poor readers on a particular task, some means to ensure that the two groups were comparable in general ability is required. Without such a precaution the comparison may in fact be between bright and dull pupils rather than good and poor readers.

2. Were the variables not under consideration or control randomized? For example, in a study comparing the results of two distinct instructional treatments, the preferred procedure is to assign pupils from a large pool of pupils to the two treatment groups randomly. This procedure is much sounder than assigning pupils from one school or classroom to one treatment and pupils from another school or classroom to the other treatment. Expediency may be served in this way, but the result is a seriously flawed study. Many factors that may produce systematic biases in the results remain intact when existing groups are assigned to treatments.

3. Was the possibility of a confounding effect considered or at least recognized? Take, for example, a study designed to compare the reading achievement of pupils who scored high on a test of visual perception with pupils who scored low on the same test. Perhaps the two groups differed as much—or more—in ability, socioeconomic indexes, exposure to instruction, and so forth as they did in visual perception. Of course, it is not always possible or even desirable to "randomize away" the related factors. The point here is that the possibility of confounding effects should be considered in the rationale for the study and at least acknowledged in the method section. Another example is a study designed to compare the effects of two methods of instruction. Unless extreme care is exercised, many factors other than method can influence the outcome of such a study. We can specify a few: If two different teachers taught the two methods, any difference in results might be attributable to the teacher rather than to the method. Uncontrolled factors might raise the motivation level in one group but not in the other. The time of day at which instruction is given, the physical setup of the classroom, the format of the materials used, and so forth might work more favorably for one group than the other.

4. Was sufficient care taken to standardize procedures and to control the subjects' experiences during their participation in the study? When two or more groups are involved, small variations in procedure can inadvertently provide subtle cues or additional information to the advantage of a single group.

Subjects tested early in an experiment can pass on information to subjects tested later. In some studies, rest periods may become rehearsal time unless precautions are taken. Seemingly trivial variations and breaks in routine can scramble the results of an otherwise well-executed study.

5. Were the directions to the subjects clear enough to be understood by each person? A worthwhile practice is to pilot directions, particularly when working with children, to see that the directions do in fact evoke the desired behavior, or at least an attempt to behave in the desired manner. The directions given to the subjects should be stated in the method section.

6. Were any tests and measures used in the study clearly identified or described? Were they chosen from among the best available, and were they appropriate for all the subjects (for example, was the range of behavior sampled sufficiently great)? If judgments were required, were the judges qualified, and were the intra- and inter-judge reliabilities reported?

7. Was the design of the study cleared described? Were the assumptions underlying the statistical techniques met? In many instances, an adequate answer to the second question would require a great deal of statistical sophistication, and even then sophisticated statisticians might not agree. Our advice to the statistically unsophisticated reader is to accept the judgment of the editors of the journal in which the study is published. The credibility of a journal is established by its editorial policies, its consulting editors, and its performance. As always, consider your source.

Although this list of general questions is not comprehensive, it should be clear that logical analysis and common sense are useful in reacting to the method section of a research report.

Presentation and discussion of results

A research report may include separate sections or a single combined section for reporting the results and for discussing them. When separate sections are given, the former is devoted to a straightforward presentation of the results of the study—the data obtained and analyses of the data. The latter includes a consideration of the hypotheses in the light of the results obtained, a discussion of the problem in terms of the confirmation or rejection of the hypotheses, and a statement of the limitations and the

implications of the study. When the sections are combined, results are presented and discussed in a systematic way, commonly
in the order in which the hypotheses were initially stated.

Keep the following questions in mind when you evaluate a
presentation of results:

1. Are the results presented in an orderly and logical sequence?
   Perhaps the order that is the most straightforward is dictated
   by the arrangement of hypotheses or questions in the introduction to the study. In some instances, however, the tests
   of more than one hypothesis will be inherent in a single
   analysis—say, in an analysis of variance with several pertinent main effects. In that case, it is imperative that the relevant findings be sorted out and directed back to the appropriate hypothesis.
2. Are the data presented completely, concisely, and clearly?
   There is seldom a need to report raw data; measures of central tendency, standard deviations, ranges, and so on, ordinarily suffice. The presentation should be sufficiently complete, however, to lay a solid groundwork for all conclusions
   reached on the basis of the data. Graphs, charts, and similar
   devices should supplement tables when they can help clarify
   the presentation.
3. If the results of post hoc tests are reported, has the researcher
   mentioned their use and the reason for their use? Post hoc
   tests are used in after-the-fact examinations of data. Sometimes their use is very straightforward, for example, when
   three or more means occurring within a significant main effect are compared. But in other instances, both the tests and
   the explanations derived from the results are purely oppor-
   tunistic. There is nothing wrong with post hoc reasoning so
   long as it is recognized and labeled as such.

The following are some guide questions to consider in evaluating a discussion of results:

1. Do the results discussed relate to the hypothesis posed in the
   study? The requirement here is that each hypothesis be accepted or rejected on the basis of results of the study. Sometimes the results will support a hypothesis only partially.
   This fact should be noted in the discussion.
2. Is a solution to the original problem suggested? Sometimes
   the data seem to point in a direction that is tangential to the
   original problem. In such cases, no clear resolution to the
   problem is likely to emerge. Even in this case, the discussion

should focus on the original problem before it moves on to alternatives or redefinitions.

3. Are suggested conclusions limited to the results actually demonstrated in the study?
4. Are limitations noted?
5. Are implications for practice and/or further research noted?

Summary of an entire study

A well-written summary to a research report is a succinctly stated review of the purpose, method, and results. In recent years, the practice of including a brief abstract at the beginning of each article has been adopted by most journals. The abstract serves the same function as the traditional summary and therefore supersedes it. Abstracts are commonly limited by editorial policy to a maximum of 120 to 150 words. Very often the abstract does not serve the function of an adequate summary, so the reader must skim the entire article.

DESCRIPTIVE/INTERPRETIVE PIECES

Included here are descriptions of programs and practices, discussions of issues and procedures, and reviews of research and/or theory. These presentations are apt to be quite subjective because the format and the language are not so explicitly prescribed as they are for research reports. Nevertheless, we can offer some general criteria for evaluating descriptive articles, although all of them will not always be relevant.

1. The article should clearly state its purpose. A review of existing research, for example, may be written either to extract immediate implications for practice or to seek inferences for theory development and/or further research. Unless the purpose of the article is made clear early, the reader may easily get lost in the shuffle. An author should also make clear his or her purpose in writing a description of, say, an existing program of instruction. He or she may be suggesting that it serve as a model, that it be modified on the basis of the observations, or that it be replicated only under certain conditions. This point is so basic that it seems trivial. But for a reader to be left wondering why an article was written is disconcerting—and may indicate that the author never bothered to come to grips with that basic question.

305

2. Sufficient detail should be provided in the article to accomplish the stated purpose. An example is a description of
an all-school reading program: If the purpose is to provide a
model, then sufficient details must be given to permit repli-
cation. Too many writers do not provide enough information
for readers to act upon the writer's suggestions.

3. References should be cited when they are available and pertinent. Because articles in this category often turn out to be
distillations of many ideas from diverse sources, they need to
be backed up by references to primary sources. General discussions do serve an integrative function; in fact, more efforts to pull together and interrelate research results and
thinking in the many areas related to reading are very much
needed. The integrative effect is most clear when at least the
key sources are identified.

4. Through writing as well as the use of references and/or behavior descriptions, the writer should clearly indicate
whether he or she is citing facts or is guessing.

5. A personal evaluation of a descriptive article is, of course,
often influenced by the relevance of its content to the concerns of the reader. A person interested in basic research is
likely to find relevance and value in articles that practitioners
view as too esoteric. Practitioners may find great relevance in
articles that basic researchers would reject as irrelevant to the
development of theory or a line of research. The point here is
that relevance is likely to be a critical factor in a personal
evaluation, but it is not an absolute criterion for judging the
competency of an article.

IMPLICATIONS VERSUS INFERENCES

We will make just one point about drawing inferences from the
literature: be skeptical. Too much is often done too soon simply
because a tentative finding is aggressively pushed for profit or
prestige. Certainly we need to be flexible and open-minded. But
at a time when many innovations in ideas and practices are
being offered, there is a particular need to proceed with caution.

Can we get there from here?

Remember the story about the city slicker who stopped his car
and asked the farmer how to get to Crivitz? The farmer talked
and then he pointed and then he drew a map in the dust. Finally,

in disgust, he wiped out the map and said, "Sonny, you can't get there from here!" Direction is what was needed.

Can we get there from here?

In reading research we are at a point where a great deal already exists. Now we would like to be at a point where we would have definitive answers to questions about how to teach reading efficiently and effectively. Whether we can get there from here depends very much on whether we can figure out where we are and then move forward with direction. Two attempts to do just that are a fairly recent special issue of the *Journal of Educational Research* and a conference on reading sponsored by the National Institute of Education.

THE JOURNAL OF EDUCATIONAL RESEARCH

The final paragraph from the editor's foreword to the special May–June 1974 issue of *The Journal of Educational Research* set the purpose:

In this issue of *The Journal of Educational Research,* the editor and four contributors have prepared a general overview and specific overviews of the four main categories of research reviewed over the four decades: sociology of reading, physiology of reading, psychology of reading, and the teaching of reading. The overviews are offered to workers in reading education for their historical and heuristic value. Together with the forty-one annual reviews the overviews amount to a comprehensive coverage of the research related to reading as it was viewed from year to year. To a student who wants to get a feel for developing lines of research, we offer a look back at what has been done. What has been done can, if it is viewed with sensitivity and a bit of empathetic appreciation, be very useful in bringing direction and purpose to what is yet to be. We are confident that the historical purpose will be served. We can only hope that there will be an impact on future research as well.

Forty-one years of research

Each year from 1933 through 1973 the *Journal* carried an annual summary and review of research related to reading. The special issue for 1974 was an overview of the entire forty-one year span. Otto's introduction to the issue (1974) demonstrates trends in the volume of research over the entire time and identifies the journals in which research reports have appeared. The supporting tables provide direction for reviews of the literature.

One can hardly look back over forty-one years of anything without some nostalgic feelings. The summary and review articles are no exception. In the 1945 review, for example, Professor Gray noted a decrease in the number of studies related to reading and he attributed it to the fact that resources were being channeled into the war effort. That year he also noted that most of the studies he reviewed had been done by people in higher education, not public school people, and he predicted that this would continue to be so. Anyone who lived through World War II will remember the rationing, the shifted priorities, and the reallocation of resources. And anyone who looks at the research after 1945 will see that Gray's prediction was valid: the bulk of the research continues to be done by people in or associated with higher education. Yet the involvement of public school people has been persistent and, particularly in the last decade or so, increasing. The very next year, in 1946, Professor Gray observed that the studies he reviewed ". . . were more carefully planned and the findings more valid than has been true generally in the past." Perhaps that was a totally objective observation; perhaps it was only a bit of post-war optimism.

But so much for the nostalgic view. Let each reader take his own trip backward and let each one ponder the past in his own way. In the remainder of this chapter we offer summary information, mainly limited to the last dozen or so years, about certain aspects of the annual reviews. We have resisted the enormous appeal of the current trivia craze and we offer only information that ought to be useful to students of reading who are interested in reviewing the research.

The number of studies reviewed each year, 1933 through 1973, is given in Table 1; and totals are given for each of the last four decades. The most recent decade shows a marked increase in the number of studies reviewed. This increase is even more significnt in view of the fact that prior to 1962 the reviews were not confined predominantly to studies reported in journals; other reports, reviews, and books were more commonly cited. While the summary and review has always been somewhat selective regarding the studies included, the trend toward greater research activity in recent years seems quite clear. The period covered by the 1973 summary and review shows a particular surge in the number of studies related to reading, with 324 studies cited. Those studies were judged to be most clearly relevant to reading from more than 900 that had been tentatively identified.

A list of all the journals cited in the reviews from 1962

through 1973 is given in Table 2. A total of 141 journals was cited. Following the name of each journal the number of years the journal was cited and the total number of studies cited are given in parentheses. Thus, the notation (12/120) after *The Journal of Educational Research* means that the journal was cited in each of the twelve years covered and that a total of 120 studies was cited. The list should be useful for two main reasons: First, it includes the full range of journals that have carried reports of empirical research in reading for the last dozen years. Second, it identifies those journals which have most consistently carried reports of research related to reading. The five journals that were cited each year and carried the greatest number of studies were as follows: *The Reading Teacher*, 246 studies; *The Journal of Reading*, 137 studies; *The Journal of Educational Research*, 120 studies; *Perceptual and Motor Skills*, 109 studies; and *Elementary English*, 91 studies. More than half (60 percent) of the journals listed carried only five or fewer studies over the period covered. The numbers of different journals cited each year are given in Table 3.

Table 4 is a composite listing of the ten most frequently cited journals for each year, 1962 through 1973. (Note that for some years only nine or more than ten journals are listed. This is due to tied rankings.) The information will have limited usefulness in directing people who are reviewing the literature to the most frequently cited journals for each year. The fact is that these journals account for only a relatively small percentage of the studies cited each year. The majority of studies in each

Can we get there from here?

Table 1 **Number of studies reviewed 1933 through 1973**

Year	Studies	Year	Studies	Year	Studies	Year	Studies
1933	118	1944	110	1954	123	1964	188
1934	94	1945	54	1955	84	1965	139
1935	95	1946	70	1956	91	1966	115
1936	112	1947	72	1957	116	1967	143
1937	100	1948	80	1958	96	1968	165
1938	95	1949	89	1959	118	1969	153
1939	98	1950	92	1960	120	1970	122
1940	126	1951	98	1961	101	1971	179
1941	119	1952	94	1962	148	1972	223
1942	114	1953	91	1963	112	1973	324
1943	114						
Decade Total	1067		850		1109		1751

Total Studies Reviewed: 4895.

Table 2 **Journals cited (years cited/total citations)—1962 to 1973**

Acta Psychologica (1/2)
Acta Sociologica (1/1)
A–V Communication Review (7/12)
Adult Leadership (1/1)
Alberta J. of Educational Research (6/13)
Am. Educational Research J. (9/26)
Am. Annals of the Deaf (7/10)
Am. Biology Teacher (1/1)
Am. J. of Mental Deficiency (7/24)
Am. J. of Ophthalmology (2/3)
Am. J. of Optometry & Archives of the Am. Academy of Optometry (2/2)
Am. J. of Psychology (9/15)
Am. J. of Orthopsychiatry (9/14)
Annals of Otology, Rhinology & Laryngology (1/1)
Archives of Neurology (3/3)
Archives of Ophthalmology (1/1)
Arithmetic Teacher (4/5)
Australian J. of Education (3/3)
British J. of Educational Psychology (9/31)
British J. of Psychology (7/15)
Bulletin of the School of Education (Indiana University) (1/1)
California J. of Educational Research (9/19)
Canadian Education & Research Digest (1/1)
Canadian J. of Psychology (8/14)
Chicago Schools Bulletin (2/2)
Child Development (11/32)
Clearing House (2/2)
Cognitive Psychology (1/1)
College Composition & Communication (1/1)
College English (1/1)
Developmental Psychology (1/5)
Editor and Publisher (1/2)
Education (6/11)
Educational Administration & Supervision (1/1)
Educational & Psychological Measurement (8/12)
Educational Leadership (2/5)
Educational Records Bulletin (3/6)
Educational Research (10/24)
Educational Review (1/1)
Elementary English (11/91)
Elementary School J. (12/63)
English J. (5/6)
Exceptional Children (10/26)
Genetic Psychology Monographs (4/5)

Harvard Education Review (1/1)
High Points (1/1)
High School J. (3/3)
International J. of Adult & Youth Education (1/1)
J. of Abnormal Psychology (formerly J. of Abnormal & Social Psychology) (6/20)
J. of Applied Behavioral Analysis (1/1)
J. of Applied Psychology (11/17)
J. of Clinical Psychology (7/11)
J. of Communication (9/20)
J. of Comparative & Physiological Psychology (2/2)
J. of Consulting and Clinical Psychology (6/7)
J. of Counseling Psychology (1/1)
J. of Education (1/1)
J. of Educational Measurement (4/10)
J. of Educational Psychology (12/84)
J. of Educational Research (12/120)
J. of Experimental Analysis of Behavior (1/1)
J. of Experimental Child Psychology (5/12)
J. of Experimental Education (11/45)
J. of Experimental Psychology (8/34)
J. of Experimental Social Psychology (1/1)
J. of General Psychology (5/7)
J. of Genetic Psychology (9/14)
J. of Learning Disabilities (5/42)
J. of Mental Deficiency Research (1/1)
J. of Negro Education (6/13)
J. of Neurological Neurosurgical Psychiatry (1/1)
J. of Pediatrics (1/1)
J. of Personality and Social Psychology (4/5)
J. of Personality Assessment (formerly J. of Projective Techniques & Personality Assessment) (1/1)
J. of Psychology (9/15)
J. of Reading (formerly J. of Developmental Reading) (12/137)
J. of Reading Behavior (4/36)
J. of School Psychology (3/5)
J. of Social Psychology (4/6)
J. of Special Education (3/5)
J. of Speech & Hearing Disorders (2/2)
J. of Speech and Hearing Research (6/16)
J. of Teacher Education (2/2)
J. of the Am. Medical Association (1/1)
J. of Am. Optometric Association (1/1)

Table 2 **(cont.)**

J. of Verbal Learning & Verbal Behavior (9/35)	Quarterly J. of Experimental Psychology (5/12)
Junior College J. (3/3)	Quarterly J. of Speech (1/1)
Journalism Quarterly (12/79)	Reading (3/6)
Language Learning (1/3)	Reading Horizons (1/1)
Library Quarterly (5/6)	Reading Improvement (4/8)
Mathematics Teacher (1/1)	Reading Newsletter (1/1)
Mental Hygiene (1/1)	Reading Research Quarterly (6/24)
Merrill–Palmer Quarterly (1/1)	Reading Teacher (12/246)
Michigan Educational J. (2/3)	Reading World (formerly J. of the Reading Specialist) (6/27)
Modern Language J. (3/3)	Research in Teaching English (4/7)
National Association of Secondary School Principal's Bulletin (2/2)	School & Community (2/2)
NCEA Bulletin (1/1)	School & Society (1/2)
New Era in Home & School (1/1)	School Review (1/1)
Ontario J. of Educational Research (3/5)	School, Science & Mathematics (3/3)
Peabody J. of Education (4/5)	Science (1/1)
Pediatrics (1/1)	Science Education (4/5)
Perception & Psychophysics (1/8)	Sight Saving Review (1/1)
Perceptual & Motor Skills (12/109)	Sociology & Social Research (1/1)
Personnel & Guidance J. (4/8)	Sociometry (1/1)
Personnel Psychology (2/2)	Speech Monographs (2/2)
Psychiatria et Neurologia (1/1)	Theory into Practice (1/3)
Psychological Monographs (1/1)	Today's Education (1/1)
Psychological Record (4/5)	Training School Bulletin (6/7)
Psychological Reports (9/33)	University of Kansas Bulletin on Education (1/1)
Psychological Review (1/1)	University of Washington College of Education Record (1/1)
Psychology in the Schools (7/32)	Vocational & Guidance Quarterly (4/5)
Psychonomic Science—Human Section (5/54)	Wisconsin English J. (1/1)
Public Opinion Quarterly (5/10)	

Table 3 **Number of different journals cited by year**

J.E.R. Issue	*Number*
February, 1962	51
February, 1963	40
February, 1964	61
February, 1965	45
February, 1966	38
March, 1967	37
February, 1968	43
March, 1969	35
March, 1970	41
February, 1971	52
February, 1972	50
April, 1973	70

Table 4 **Journals cited most frequently—1962 to 1973**

Journal	1962	1963	1964	1965	1966	1967	1968	1969	1970	1971	1972	1973
Alberta J. of Educational Research	4[a]											
American J. of Mental Deficiency							1		4	5		
American J. of Psychology									4			
British J. of Educational Psychology	4	4		4	5							
Canadian J. of Psychology					5				5			
Child Development		3										
Education												
Educational Research								4		4		18
Elementary English	4	10	11	13	6	8	9	5		4		
Elementary School J.	6		11	10	6	7		4				
Exceptional Children				5			5					
J. of Abnormal Psychology[b]	4	3	6						5			
J. of Communication												
J. of Educational Psychology	8	4	7	9	6	6	6	8	6	15	6	15
J. of Educational Research	16	7	21		11	17		9	4			14
J. of Experimental Education			7	6					4		6	11
J. of Experimental Psychology							5	5		8	6	14
J. of Learning Disabilities								28	5	11	8	
J. of Reading[c]	9	18	8	10	10	9	8	8			10	
J. of Reading Behavior							6			8	11	14
J. of Verbal Learning & Verbal Behavior							12				12	10
Journalism Quarterly	13	9	15	18	9	4						
Perceptual and Motor Skills						10	14	8	7	12	15	23
Personnel and Guidance J.				4								
Psychological Reports			7			4						
Psychology in the Schools					5	6	8		5	4		
Psychonomic Science (Human Section)												
Reading Research Quarterly						4				7	7	
Reading Teacher	13	12	17	18	8	36	38	33	23	20	35	13
Reading World[d]							5	12			18	10

[a] Number of articles contributed during those years when Journal placed in the top ten.
[b] Formerly J. of Abnormal and Social Psychology until 1965.
[c] Formerly J. of Developmental Reading until 1964.
[d] Formerly J. of the Reading Specialist until 1971.

Table 5 **Number of studies by area**

Year	Sociology	Psychology	Physiology	Teaching	Total
1962	26 (17.6)[a]	51 (34.5)	6 (4.0)	65 (43.9)	148
1963	18 (11.2)	47 (42.0)	7 (6.3)	40 (35.7)	112
1964	40 (21.3)	47 (25.0)	11 (5.9)	90 (47.9)	188
1965	33 (23.7)	49 (35.3)	7 (5.0)	50 (36.0)	139
1966	12 (10.4)	48 (41.7)	9 (7.8)	46 (40.0)	115
1967	17 (11.9)	53 (37.1)	5 (3.5)	68 (47.6)	143
1968	17 (10.3)	68 (41.2)	9 (5.5)	71 (43.0)	165
1969	10 (6.5)	61 (39.9)	5 (3.3)	77 (50.3)	153
1970	8 (6.6)	62 (50.8)	11 (9.0)	41 (33.6)	122
1971	24 (13.4)	99 (55.3)	6 (3.4)	50 (27.9)	179
1972	22 (9.9)	125 (56.1)	22 (9.9)	54 (24.2)	223
1973	48 (14.8)	109 (33.6)	54 (16.7)	113 (34.9)	324
Total	275 (13.7)	819 (40.7)	152 (7.6)	765 (38.0)	2011

[a] Percentage of year's studies in the area.

Table 6 **Top five journals by area, 1966–1973**

Journal	Sociology	Psychology	Physiology	Teaching
Elementary English	14[a]			32
Elementary School J.				23
Exceptional Children			9	
J. of Educational Psychology		51		
J. of Educational Research	8			32
J. of Experimental Psychology			8	
J. of Learning Disabilities			10	
J. of Negro Education	9			
J. of Reading				67
J. of Verbal Learning & Verbal Behavior		31		
Journalism Quarterly	19			
Perceptual and Motor Skills		51	25	
Psychonomic Science (Human Section)		48		
Reading Teacher	17	29	7	133

[a] Total number of articles contributed.

year's review are carried by journals that are cited only once or twice. The implicit point is that a thorough search of the literature must, of necessity, cover a wide range of different journals.

As already pointed out, the studies reviewed since the late 1950's have been classified each year into the four main categories of sociology, psychology, physiology, and the teaching of reading. The number of studies classified in each main category in 1962 through 1973 is shown in Table 5. Clearly the majority of studies has been in psychology and the teaching of reading. Since 1966 the annual reviews have included a separate list of references for each area rather than a composite list for the entire review. A list of the five journals most frequently cited for each area since 1966 is given in Table 6 along with the total number of studies carried in each area. *The Reading Teacher* shows the best balance by placing among the top five journals in all areas. The information in Tables 5 and 6 should be useful when the purpose is to track down studies in a given area.

Researchers in reading have been prolific in their output. In fact most critics would agree that the quantity of research has surpassed the quality. Yet there is no questioning the fact that out of it all has come a better focus, a better sense of what holds promise, and a development of methodology that will permit us to move farther in the next four decades than we did in the last.

Progress and prospect

The special issue of the *Journal* also includes summary reviews for each of the four major research categories identified in the annual reviews: sociology, physiology, psychology and teaching. We will present here the concluding statements by the reviewers for each area. Each reviewer offers a brief statement regarding the present status of the research in the area and some promising directions for the future.

Sociology of reading The review was prepared by Dulin (1974).

In this reviewer's opinion . . . we *don't* need any more studies to convince us that children deep in the culture of poverty don't read nearly so well as do children from affluent, middle to upper class homes, nor do we need to have any more evidence of how poorly these children perform on standardized psychosensory and academic-achievement batteries. Instead, it would be much more useful, in this reviewer's opinion, to hear of developmental and remedial programs developed for this audience and the ways in which these programs do or don't work.

We probably don't need any more studies (sometimes reported in this area and at other times reported under the heading of Physiology of Reading) to show us that deaf children, mentally-retarded children, and children with gross speech de-

Can we get there from here?

fects have severe reading and reading-related language problems, even if at times these problems are somehow culture-related. By now this area, too, has been well enough documented that it's time to move on to trying out, and then reporting on, new approaches to amelioration and rehabilitation.

As for research we *do* need, several avenues, some new but most of them old, appear promising. In terms of content-analyses and the role of printed materials in creating, sustaining, and/or changing attitudes, for example, the newly-emerging women's identity movement shows much evidence of stimulating a good deal of interesting research.

Also, now that Americans seem finally to have accepted the reality of the existence of social classes in America, a good deal of interesting research on instrumental reading and its role in social stability and/or mobility could be done. In addition, the very ubiquity of non-print public-information and public-education media in America today suggests possibilities for many comparative studies. Marshall McLuhan has clearly sounded the challenge to print as a preferred medium of communicating across and within social strata, and reading researchers should certainly be responding.

Then finally, the whole range of affective response to reading, particularly the reading of persuasive writing, is still in need of further exploration. If America is ever to become a truly universally-literate nation, and the research in the Sociology of Reading over this past forty years suggests that, at least, in the true sense of the term, it has not so far, these mature applications of reading ability need to become as important to the theoreticians and practitioners of reading as are the basic skills. Someone once said, "The man who doesn't read isn't much better off than the man who can't." This reviewer would only add that in some cases he may even be *worse* off, if his eduction hasn't equipped him to read carefully, critically, and well. (p. 396)

Physiology of reading The review was prepared by Smith (1974).

Persons who observe the extreme difficulty certain students have in vocalizing the sounds that letters and words represent and the difficulty they have in extracting meaning from print cannot avoid suspecting some physiological condition as being responsible for the problem. The instruction that gives students with similar outward characteristics the power to read is often wasteful or even harmful when it is given to students

315

who eventually take on the labels of dyslexic or learning disabled. Therefore, the conclusion or at least suspicion that the
problem is caused by some endogenous or genetic condition
in the organism is difficult to escape. The conclusion or suspicion of a physiological causative agent is especially tempting
for professionals in the various fields of medicine who see a
select clientele and who approach their clients from a physiological orientation.

Unfortunately, the research activity regarding physiology
and reading that was reviewed throughout the past forty-one
years has been more productive of hypotheses than conclusions. This is not to say that conclusions were not drawn, for
they were indeed; but they were often based upon questionable data or were in conflict with the conclusions of similar
studies. The reports of many studies ended cautiously with the
major conclusion being that more research was needed with a
more suitable population, a better research design and/or more
precise instruments. In conclusion, it appears that in forty-one
years researchers in this area have asked more interesting
questions than they have found definitive answers, at least in
terms of answers that lead to a direct attack upon reading disability in the way that poliomyelitis and small pox have been
attacked. We have learned that approaching reading from a
physiological orientation is every bit as complicated and as
fraught with obstacles to clear-cut findings as approaching it
from other orientations.

If that lesson has been learned well from the research activities of forty-one years, the resources that have been expended
in that effort will prove to be a wise investment. Future researchers will construct more reliable instruments and adopt
more rigorous research designs. And practitioners in school,
office, and clinical settings will cease looking for clear-cut solutions to the problem of reading disability. Furthermore, fewer
and fewer parents, teachers, and disabled readers themselves
will be taken in by those who advertise a simple solution for
what has proved to be a complex problem to trace to its cause,
let alone to solve. (p. 402)

Psychology of reading The review was prepared by Chester (1974).

. . . the area of psychology is rather nebulous and many
studies are classified under this heading by default, rather than
by design. The pragmatics of a review such as this necessitate
the arbitrary omission of many studies and areas which have

obvious importance to many educators. Topics such as paired-associate learning, home-environmental influences, and innovative research techniques all have relevance to the psychological aspects of reading, but have not been reviewed because for the most part, they are integrated with other topics which have been covered.

Can we get there from here?

A review of the last forty years of research in the psychology of reading leads one to mixed conclusions. Although the research in intelligence has amounted to doing the same thing over and over, it has resulted in more realistic interpretation of the relationship of intelligence and reading. Research in hygiene of reading is rapidly declining, but other areas of research such as cognitive style, language, and personality are emerging as major centers of interest. Research in readability and comprehension has changed dramatically over the last two decades with more attention now being given to the syntactic and semantic variables, but unfortunately, the findings have not yet been translated into materials and instructional techniques appropriate for classroom use.

The question of whether or not research has grown better or worse over the last forty years appears less relevant than the question of whether or not it adequately deals with current problems in reading education. And quite possibly of even greater importance is the question of whether today's research is initiated by real or manufactured problems. With some exceptions, the answer to the latter question appears to be that the problems are real. However, this question can ultimately only be answered when research results in meaningful contributions to the needs of students and teachers. (p. 411)

Teaching of reading The review was prepared by Johnson (1974).

During the four decades of research reviewed in *The Journal of Educational Research,* the Teaching of Reading was of major interest to large numbers of reading researchers. Much of the research was of doubtful quality because of research design and methodological problems. Until the past decade the Review has contained little information pertaining to sample size, control group procedures, and statistical treatment, making an evaluation of the studies difficult. Despite problems with design, the obvious interest in understanding problems related to the teaching of reading has been commendable.

Though perhaps the majority of the research investigations conducted during these decades involved comparisons of organizational plans and instructional methodologies, remedial

317

reading, and the status of reading achievement, few such studies had significant impact on educational practice. The areas in which it is evident that educational change developed from reading research were reading readiness, instructional materials, word attack, vocabulary, and teacher training. In these areas in particular, things *are* being done differently today than they were years ago, and it is likely that certain key studies contributed to this change. Reading materials are more relevant and more varied today than at any time in our history. Reading readiness programs are more sensible and widespread. Decoding skills are being more adequately taught. The quality and quantity of children's vocabularies are more accurately and definitively known. Most important, teachers of reading are being better prepared. The improved status of reading instruction today is in many ways a result of the efforts of reading researchers during the past four decades. (p. 420)

THE NIE CONFERENCE ON STUDIES IN READING

The National Institute of Education (NIE) sponsored the Conference on Studies in Reading in August 1974. Smith (1974) explains the purpose and intent of the conference:

The impetus for the Conference stemmed from a number of concerns about the state of Federal funding of research and development in education. Four concerns stood out in particular for reading.

1. Research in the field of reading was fragmented and non-cumulative.
2. The Federal Government was not making constructive use of the state of knowledge in the field in their decisions to fund new research and development.
3. There was a lack of positive and firm coordination between the Federal Government and the professional research and practitioner organizations around the country.
4. A large number of scientists in a variety of disciplines carry out research with relevance to reading. We considered it important to attract these scientists to work in the applied areas of educational research.

The Conference itself was a step in meeting these concerns. During the past year, the NIE has been developing plans for funding research and development in reading for the next two years. Suggestions from the Conference have played an important role in this process. But planning is an ongoing process and we hope by publishing and widely disseminating the reports from the Conference to stimulate discussion of the reports, of research and development in the field of reading, and, indirectly, of the plans of the Institute.

To some extent the format for the Conference was influenced by three other similar efforts of the Federal Government. In the area of health research, the conferences leading to the National Cancer Plan and the National Heart and Lung Institute Plan served as partial models. Within NIE, the Teaching Division had held a major planning effort in the area of teaching research during the early summer of 1974. The intent in each of these efforts was to develop a coherent set of documents that would be responsive to the needs of the American public and to knowledge in the field.

We felt it necessary to structure the Conference in two important ways. First, after extensive consultation with scientists and practitioners in the field we arrived at the conclusion that major efforts in the past had often ignored or down-played the critical importance of the stage of reading called "reading comprehension." Although we realized the impossibility of actually separating out "reading comprehension" from the earlier stage of learning to read—which requires the learner to be able to translate written letters and words into speech—our advice suggested that the comprehension or "reading for meaning" stage required far more attention than it had received in the past. Consequently, seven of the ten panels focused on problems in this area. Second, to direct the focus of the panels to planning future research we requested the panelists to organize their ideas into general *approaches* within the problem area, within the approaches to suggest *programs* for research, and, finally, when possible to specify particular research or development *projects*.

The seven panels addressing problems in comprehension spanned a wide range of concerns. The first three panels focused on basic research issues. Their panel reports are titled: *Semantics, Concepts, and Culture; The Structure and Use of Language;* and *Attention and Motivation.* The fourth panel was asked to consider the problem of *Modeling the Reading Process.* The fifth panel directed its attention to the issue of measuring how well people read and its report is titled *Assessment of Reading Comprehension.* The sixth and seventh reports directed themselves respectively at the practical problems of

319

the *Application of Existing Reading Comprehension Research*
and *Reading Comprehension and the High School Graduate*.
The final three panels directed their attention to three pressing
concerns in early reading: *Learning and Motivation in Early
Reading; Reading Strategies for Different Cultural and Linguistic Groups;* and *Essential Skills and Skill Hierarchies in Reading.* (Preface)

The NIE conference was an attempt to proceed from our
present status through careful planning, with subsequent funding of related activities by a federal agency. Many questions
could and should be raised about both the stragegy and the plan,
but at least the conference offered a view of the present and a
vision of the future. Certainly it represents a significant attempt
to move forward.

Seeking answers to the problems that come up when practitioners attempt to improve the teaching of reading ordinarily
does not entail reviewing four decades of research or planning a
major research thrust. Often answers to very specific questions
for application in very specific contexts are needed to move forward. We have attempted to present a broad view of the status
and direction of research in reading in order to establish a context for more highly focused inquiries.

There is reason to be optimistic about the future of research in
reading. Much remains to be done, but there are some reasonably clear directions for moving forward. Some of the things that
have been learned have had a positive effect on some teaching
methods. And, perhaps more important, educators now have a
better understanding of their problems and—because of ad-
vances in research technology—better ways to tackle them than
previously.

An approach to research in reading

Different people are likely to expect somewhat different things
from well-directed research in reading. Some will look to the
substance of the research itself; others will expect direction for
the development of techniques and materials, and still others will
demand nothing short of direct applications for the classroom.
Yet the very fact that researchers, developers, and practitioners
focus on different aspects of the process of improving the teaching of reading bespeaks the need for all three groups to work

together. Otto (1975) discussed that need and suggested a response to it in a paper presented at the 1975 annual meeting of the International Reading Association. The paper, a very personal statement, deals with an approach that could prove quite useful to educators concerned with improving the teaching of reading.

A pragmatic empirical approach

I'm not a theoretician. So I do not propose to deliver a treatise on *what* research in reading ought to be like. I'm certainly neither a statistician nor a methodoligst. So I'm not about to tell you *how to do* research in reading. I *am* a realist. I believe that man's grasp ought to be about equal to his reach. So I tend to be a pragmatist. I'm incined to say, "If it works, do it." I have profound respect for common sense—so profound, in fact, that I can accept the common sense observation that common sense often suggests a number of equally plausible alternatives. Common sense told everybody that the world was flat until somebody had the common sense to find out that it isn't! So I do believe that common sense notions need to be reality tested. And that, I guess, makes me an empiricist. A pragmatic-empiricist.

What I'd like to do, then, is tell you how I—by my own definition a pragmatic-empiricist—am inclined to approach research in reading. That may appear to be an ego trip on my part, because what I propose to do is simply to tell you what I do. But that may be less egotistical than for *me* to say what I think *you* ought to be thinking and doing and how you ought to be going about doing it. . . . A pragmatic-empiricist would *never* be so presumptuous as that!

THE RESEARCH-DEVELOPMENT DILEMMA

First I'd like to share with you some thoughts expressed by David R. Krathwohl in his 1974 Presidential Address to the Division of Educational Psychology of the American Psychological Association.[1] He titled his address "Perceived Ineffectiveness of Educational Research." I'm inclined to say that

---

[1] The quotations used in this chapter are from a revised version of the speech that was published in the *Educational Psychologist* (Krathwohl, 1974).

"perceived" could have been dropped from the title, making it a stark "Ineffectiveness of Educational Research." The latter would *not* have described Professor Krathwohl's message. But it most assuredly would have summed up a conclusion that I—with extreme reluctance, I must add—have come to: The preponderance of what is and has been passing for and published as educational research is both ineffectual and ineffective. Of course we can identify certain research that has had profound effects on both educational theory and educational practice. But the preponderance tends to be pure twaddle and I think almost everybody who thinks about it knows it. In our field, much of what is published as research related to reading is related to reading only in the most obtuse way and it has no real importance to anyone—except perhaps the researchers and their immediate families.

Professor Krathwohl was trying to deal constructively with a problem. He spoke about one aspect of the problem as follows:

> There is continual pressure to shorten the initial stages of [the research and development] process which is resisted by the true empiricist. He is troubled by missing and/or too markedly abbreviating the confirmatory steps, for he fears users will base their actions on research which later will be invalidated. Indeed, even if no harm were done to the consumer by use of a product later found to be invalid, such an occurrence gives research a bad image. Potentially it could sour the public on support of research. For similar reasons, he may be equally dismayed when work in incomplete stages of development is put to use and fails. It then reflects badly on the developers and the processes they used. (p. 78)

The research-and-development dilemma is well known to anyone who has ever tried to engage in that process, which looks so beautifully simple and logical when it is described on paper. Make your move too soon and you become the object of ridicule and scorn when what seemed to work perfectly in its pristine state falls flat in a real world tryout. But make it too late and you find yourself talking to an empty auditorium.

Professor Krathwohl pointed out another aspect of the same problem:

> But the process [of research and development] is a very long one for practitioners faced with the daily press of problems that research is supposed to help alleviate. It operates in a time frame which is a world apart from the one in which he must operate. And the fact that the process sometimes is

*extended because the developer will not release a product
until it is engineered into a "teacher proof" package makes
the user doubly resentful, first because of the period the
produce is withheld from use and, second, because of his
implied incompetence which results in the need to "teacher
proof" products. (p. 78)*

So there you have the problem that has been experienced by
many practitioners who have gone skipping down the yellow
brick road of research and development. The road turns out to
be long, it gets rocky, and it is beset by witches!

THE WONDERFUL WIZARD OF OZ

Now if we can squeeze that metaphor a little bit more, I sup-
pose we couldn't blame a sensible practitioner for making any
deal he had to just to get back to Kansas. Trouble with that is
he may already have decided that Kansas *isn't* where he wants
to be! So . . . how can he get to see the Wonderful Wizard
of Oz?

Professor Krathwohl suggested several ways to improve perceptions of educational research. Two of them seem most relevant to resolving the research-development dilemma we've
identified. Both have to do with bridging the gap between researcher and user, *especially* the practitioner-teacher.

First, researchers can begin to think of themselves not so
much as knowledge producers as producers of findings to be
confirmed in practice. Speaking for the researchers, Krathwohl
says:

*. . . . rather than presenting our findings as proven, our
presentations should make clear the tentative nature of our
findings and routinely seek the help of practitioners in further
validating or invalidating these findings, suggesting the
simplest possible methods for doing so. (p. 83)*

The big change would be that instead of being content merely
to point out "implications for further research" to others of his
own ilk, the researcher would be inviting practitioners to participate in testing the validity of his findings. Such a change
could be very significant. Ultimately it could lead us to ask a
researcher *not* "How many articles have you published?" but
"What impact has your research had on practice?" Equally important, it could also establish a solid base for the validation
efforts of practitioners. It's time that practitioners stopped flitting endlessly from one innovative flower to the next without
even thinking about the possibility of changing the flowers!

Second, developers can consider modifying their model, particularly with regard to the extended time lines and the production of "teacher proof" products. Krathwohl put it this way:

> . . . developers may wish to research the most appropriate level of development relative to "teacher proofness" in terms of teachers, schools, and instructional goals. If materials can be put on the field at earlier stages of development, this would both reduce the time and expense of development, as well as give teachers more of the creative and intellectual challenge which many of them want as growing professionals. (p. 84)

Or, better still, developers can consider teachers full partners from the outset and focus as much or more on the *process* as on the *product* of development.

How can we—researchers, developers, practitioners—get to see the Wizard? The answer is simple, but it isn't easy: We all skip down the yellow brick road together. If we work together toward a common goal, we can all get where we want to be. And remember—getting to *see* the Wizard is the hardest part.

PRAGMATIC-EMPIRICISM IN PRACTICE

We went on that little excursion because I think that the pragmatic-empirical approach to research in reading offers a way to deal with the research-development dilemma in our area. It offers us a chance to see the Wizard! But I said at the outset that *I* would tell you what I do—rather than what I think *you* should do—to put the approach into practice.

The good news and the bad news

In the first place, it should be clear that in most of the work I'm currently involved with I find myself in between the hard line researcher on the one hand and the soft line practitioner on the other. Let me explain. Most of the people who I consider real "researchers" are what I would call hard liners: if it comes to choosing between elegant design and rigorous methodology on the right hand and a common sense approach to a practical problem on the left, they'll *always* go for the right. The good news is that their results are impeccable in terms of clarity and probability. The bad news is that they tend to tell us more and more about less and less. Most of the people who I consider *real* practitioners—teachers—are what I would call soft liners: if it comes to making a choice between a practice or product that has known flaws but could be improved and possibly greatly enhance children's learning on the right hand and a practice or product that nobody really understands but seems to work okay on the left, they'll *usually* go for the left. The good news is that they keep school. The bad news is that it never gets any better.

What's needed, of course, is what lots of people have been saying for a long time is needed: something or somebody to bridge the gap between the hard line researchers and the soft line practitioners. That's where pragmatic-empiricism comes in.

How it goes

Now this is going to sound a lot simpler than it really is. And it's also going to appear to be a lot more egocentric than it turns out to be because there are lots of check points in the application. Also lots of people involved. What we do is this. We listen to the practitioners tell us what they can do and what they need. We listen to the researchers tell us what they know and what they think they might be able to do. Next we pick out one of the practitioners' needs and we come up with one common sense alternative—one that reflects all the research results we can handle—for responding to it. For a while we put all our eggs in a single basket and we develop the alternative we have chosen—with continuous input from practitioners and input as needed from researchers—until it is as good as we can get it. And then we try it out, first on a very limited scale with lots of support. If it seems to work, we try to find out why because ultimately it has to work without more support from the developers. If it bogs down, we try to find out why. If we find a problem, we revise. If we see a gap, we add on. We do a hard line study when we think we know enough to plan one. We do a soft line tryout when we need to feel our way. If we're dealing with a product that's used in the classroom we look at it in at least two ways. We find out how *teachers* perceive it, whether they are using it as we thought they would, and whether they want to continue. And we find out how kids perceive it, whether they can handle it as it comes to them, and whether it makes any difference in terms of achievement or anything else.

Some problems

That's it. The pragmatic-empirical approach in practice. I *told* you it was going to sound simple. But I also said it sounds a lot simpler than it really is. These are some of the things that complicate the approach in practice.

1. Remember that *I* said *I* was going to tell you what *I* do as a pragmatic-empiricist? But did you notice that all the while I was telling you, I *never* said I. *We* was the world. That's not modesty . . . that's a fact. In practice, the approach requires the collaborative efforts of—or at least substantial input from— researchers, developers and practitioners. Try to do it all yourself and you're spread too thin to get anything significant accomplished. Cut out or soft pedal input from any one of the sources and you wind up with an end result that (a) doesn't make sense, (b) doesn't work, (c) nobody wants, or (d) all of the above. The hard part, of course, is to strike a working balance.

2. The working balance is important. The hard line researcher will insist that he needs at least two more decades before he feels he can release his findings. The practitioner will insist that he needs the product tomorrow because the Board of Education wants *everybody* to read at grade level by next week. The developer will say that he needs something that (a) has the unequivocal backing of research and theory, (b) is consistent with current trends in curriculum development, (c) is universally appealing to teachers, administrators, children, the public, the funding agencies, (d) shows no bias with regard to race, religion, sex, handicapping conditions, or anything else that the human mind might at some future time imagine and/or choose to interpret, (e) is not harmful to the environment, (f) cannot conceivably be harmful to anybody under any conditions, even when taken internally, (g) can be packaged neatly, (h) doesn't cost much, and (i) will be attractive to a publisher. The balance can be struck, but *everybody* has to give a little. And common sense helps a lot.

3. The process is time consuming, so there must be a continuing commitment from all concerned. If we start with what we know in terms of research results and what we need in terms of practitioners' perceptions, we know from the start that some excursions are likely to be needed. Additional research to clarify a point. Corrections when data fail to support a common sense observation. Major revisions if tryouts fail to yield positive results. Participation in such a process is difficult and sometimes discouraging, particularly with the on-again, off-again funding we've come to know in recent times. But the alternatives can't be very appealing: either making do with what we've got, with no attention paid to trying to improve it, or flitting forever from one alternative to the next in an endless quest for the best.

4. If time is important, *timing* is equally so. Some reasonable balance must be struck between the empiricists' demand

for rigor on the one hand and the pragmatists' demand for action on the other. One thing we've done is to put out a "developmental edition" of certain products. That means a product has had limited tryout but there are still basic problems and major revisions continuing. At the same time we feel that the product is as good or better than the alternatives that are available. The problem is that it is disconcerting to some practitioners to know that a product will change substantially in the relatively near future. But the alternatives are either to keep a product that is already "workable" and reasonably effective on the shelf or to stop development short of an attainable goal.

I see no reason to continue the list. The point is that the pragmatic-empirical approach must be implemented with a pragmatic-empirical attitude on the part of all who participate. That means we roll with the punches.

A last word

The pragmatic-empirical approach amounts to taking what we've got and then tinkering with it—on the basis of good solid data—to make it better. This is an enterprise, we are convinced, that calls for much more mutual concern, and *respect,* among researchers, developers and practitioners than has commonly been evident in the past. The role of research *in improving the teaching of reading,* then, is to provide not only a basis for improved development and practice but also continuous direction for positive change. This is a much broader view of the role of research than the traditional one that simply looks for implications for the classroom or tries to "translate" research results into practice.

Perhaps what we have been advocating sounds difficult or esoteric. It isn't, but you'll have to try it for yourself. Meanwhile, be assured by the following passage from *Zen and the Art of Motorcycle Maintenance:*

> If you want to build a factory, or fix a motorcycle, or set a nation right without getting stuck, then classical, structured, dualistic subject-object knowledge, although necessary, isn't enough. You have to have some feeling for the quality of the work. You have to have a sense of what's good. That is what carries you forward. This sense isn't just something you're born with, although you are born with it. It's also something you can develop. It's the direct result of contact with basic reality, quality, which dualistic reason has in the past tried to conceal.

327

*It all sounds so far out and esoteric when it's put like that
it comes as a shock to discover that it is one of the most
homespun, down-to-earth views of reality you can have.
Harry Truman, of all people, comes to mind, when he said,
concerning his administration's programs, "We'll just try
them . . . and if they don't work . . . why then we'll just try
something else." That may not be an exact quote, but it's
close. (Pirsig, 1974, p. 284)*

Summary

The volume of research related to reading is virtually overwhelming. And, perhaps more important, practitioners who seek research-based solutions to their problems are likely to be disappointed by the quality and the specificity of the research that exists. The purpose of the chapter, then, has been to deal with the latter, rather than to attempt even a cursory overview of the research. We have offered guidelines for locating and sorting out the good and the useful and suggested an approach to reading research that involves not only researchers but also developers and practitioners.

Bibliography

Agin, A. P. "An Overview of Recent Research in Reading." *Elementary English* 52 (1975): 370–375.

Chester, Robert D. "The Psychology of Reading." *Journal of Educational Research* 67 (1974): 403–411.

Cooper, C. R. "Doing Research/Reading Research." *English Journal* 63 (1974): 94–99.

Curry, J. F., and W. P. Morris. *Searching the Professional Literature in Reading.* Reading Aids Series, International Reading Association. Newark, Del.: International Reading Association, 1975.

Della-Piana, G. M. and G. T. Endo. "Reading Research." In R. M. W. Travers (ed.), *Second Handbook of Research on Teaching.* Chicago: Rand McNally, 1973, pp. 883–925.

Dulin, Kenneth L. "The Sociology of Reading." *Journal of Educational Research* 67 (1974): 392–396.

Gray, W. S. "Reading." In C. W. Harris (ed.). *Encyclopedia of Educational Research,* 3d ed. New York: Macmillan, 1960, pp. 1086–1135.

Johnson, D. D. "The Teaching of Reading." *Journal of Educational Research* 67 (1974): 412–420.

Krathwohl, David R. "Perceived Ineffectiveness of Educational Research." *Educational Psychologist* 11 (1974): 73–86.

Maliphant, R., S. Supramaniam, and E. Saroga. "Acquiring Skill in Reading: A Review of Experimental Research." *Journal of Child Psychology and Psychiatry* 15 (1974): 175–185.

Otto, Wayne. "A Pragmatic-Empirical Approach to Research in Reading." Paper presented at the annual convention of the International Reading Association. New York City, 1975.

———. Introduction. *Journal of Educational Research* 67 (1974): 387–391.

———, and K. Koenke. *Remedial Teaching: Research and Comment.* Boston: Houghton Mifflin, 1969.

———, and K. M. Smith. Foreword. *Journal of Educational Research* 67 (1974).

Page, W. D. (ed.) *Help for the Reading Teacher: New Directions in Research.* National Conference on Research in English Bulletin Series. Urbana, Ill.: ERIC Clearinghouse on Reading and Communication Skills, 1975.

Pirsig, R. M. *Zen and the Art of Motorcycle Maintenance.* New York: William Morrow, 1974.

Russell, D. H., and H. R. Fea. "Research on Teaching Reading." In N. L. Gage (ed.) *Handbook of Research on Teaching.* Chicago: Rand McNally, 1973, pp. 865–928.

Smith, M. S. Preface. In report of Panel 1, *Semantics, Concepts and Culture,* NIE Conference on Studies in Reading. Washington, D.C.: National Institute of Education, 1975.

Smith, Richard J. "The Physiology of Reading." *Journal of Educational Research* 67 (1974): 397–402.

Chapter 12 Problems for discussion

The discussions in the preceding chapters have been addressed to both the theoretical and practical aspects of improving reading instruction. This chapter gives problems that can be used to test the readers' preparedness to respond to situations that can arise when reading specialists, teachers, and administrators are engaged in reading curriculum development.

All of the problems are drawn from the real world of curriculum development. The problems described could happen, and, in many cases, they have happened. Talking about them will give a further sense of reality to the material in this book and give students and professors in classes using this book an opportunity to focus their thinking upon the kinds of problems that occur when people work to improve reading instruction. A response to each problem that follows is given later in the chapter. Although the solutions to the problems are not clear-cut, readers may enjoy and profit from comparing their judgments with ours.

Problem 1

When tackling problem 1, you may want to refer to chapters 9 and 10.

Providing in-service education in reading for classroom teachers is a major responsibility of reading specialists and administrators. Smith, Otto, and Harty (1970) surveyed teachers in seventeen elementary schools in Madison, Wisconsin, to discover how well primary grades (1–3) and intermediate grades (4–6) teachers felt their pre-service education had prepared them to teach reading, for which aspects of teaching reading these teachers would feel the greatest need for more information, and which selected approaches to in-service education would be most appealing to them.

A. Would you expect primary and intermediate grades teachers
to differ in regard to their evaluation of their pre-service education to teach reading? Would you expect years of teaching experience (1, 2–5, 6–10, 11+) to make a difference in regard to teachers' evaluations of their pre-service training?
B. For which of the following aspects of teaching reading would you expect elementary teachers to feel most in need of additional information?
   ○ Grouping students
   ○ Diagnosing individual instructional needs
   ○ Using basal materials
   ○ Using supplementary materials
   ○ Different methods for teaching beginning reading (ITA, programmed, linguistic, etc.)
   ○ Developing word attack skills
   ○ Developing comprehension skills
   ○ Providing for disabled readers in the classroom
   ○ Differentiating instruction for different ability groups
   ○ Providing for the superior reader
   ○ Using the library or IMC properly
   ○ Using writing, speaking and listening in the reading program

Would you expect differences between primary and intermediate grades teachers? Would you expect differences among teachers with different numbers of years of teaching experience (1, 2–5, 6–10, 11+)?
C. Of the following approaches to in-service education in reading, which would you expect to be most and which least appealing to elementary teachers?
   ○ Television programs produced and presented by personnel in your school system
   ○ Television programs produced and presented by personnel who are not regular employees in your school system
   ○ Films or video tapes viewed by teachers individually or by the staff of one school
   ○ Classes offered for professional advancement on the district salary schedule (but no university credit) for volunteer teachers at specific grade levels
   ○ One to one conferences with a reading specialist at your request and in your school
   ○ Presentations by reading specialists at one or more staff meetings at your school during the school year
   ○ Classes or workshops offered at a nearby university for university credit

See response 1 for the results of the survey.

Problem 2

When tackling problem 2, you may want to refer to chapters 6, 7, 8, and 9.

Read the short monologue that follows. Then respond to the three questions following it.

Good morning, reading consultant

I faced my own students for the first time. They were high school juniors and I was fresh out of college. Not much difference in our ages, really. They were good kids, and I was a trained teacher with good grades in all of my college course work, subject matter and methods courses both. I knew what I wanted to do and I knew how to do what I wanted. But I was licked before I got started. My plans called for my students to read as I had read to learn the subject matter in my field. And in just two weeks I knew my students either wouldn't or couldn't read the material that I had planned to rely heavily upon to help me reach my instructional objectives. No one had prepared me for this. I assumed that kids who had completed ten years of school could read. I guess my professors had assumed that too. What had their grade school teachers done with these kids? Why hadn't they been given remedial reading? They needed to learn how to read more than they needed to learn about the Civil War. So I went to see my principal to find out how to get a good lot of my students signed up for remedial reading. I would be willing, I told him, to let those kids in my classes who couldn't read the material go to remedial reading class instead of my class until they learned to read well enough to understand the material I assigned. Well, I was told that we didn't have remedial reading classes or even a remedial reading teacher. We had a reading consultant! Big deal! So I stopped in to see our reading consultant!

1. What are the different aspects of the problem with which the reading consultant will be faced?
2. Could the problem or certain aspects of the problem have been avoided?
3. What recommendations would you make in regard to how the reading consultant should deal with the problem?

See response 2 for our answers to the three questions.

When tackling problem 3, you may want to refer to chapters 9 and 10.

Read the sketch below. Then respond to the questions following it.

An almost finished, short play in one scene

Characters

A personnel director in charge of interviewing candidates for elementary teaching positions in a metropolitan area.

A beginning teacher applying for a teaching position as an elementary teacher in a metropolitan area.

Setting

The office of the personnel director.

As the play begins, the teacher and the personnel director have just concluded the exchange of pleasantries that typically precedes the more-to-the-point dialogue between an interviewer and a candidate. Both characters are trying to effect an appearance of informality and nonchalance. The personnel director is being more successful in striking the desired appearance than the candidate.

Personnel Director:

Thinks: I like the looks of this fellow. We need more men in our elementary school. I wonder if he knows anything about teaching.

Says: In looking over your transcript I was favorably impressed by your excellent grades in reading methods courses. Reading is the most important subject in our elementary school.

Teacher Candidate:

Thinks: I'll bet. Next to discipline.

Says: There's no doubt about it. If kids can't read, they're in trouble. You really can't get very far in today's world if you can't read. I'm glad to hear you consider reading to be so important. I do too.

Personnel Director:

Thinks: This kid's quick. I think he's trying to psych me out. I'll find out where he's really at.

Says: Teachers have some freedom in our schools in regard to how they teach reading. How would you teach reading if we hired you and assigned you to a class of first graders?

Teacher Candidate:

Thinks: Oh, oh. I wonder what she wants to hear. Well, here goes nothing. Let's see. What did Professor Johnson used to say?

Says: I think the language experience approach is the best beginning reading approach for all children.

Personnel Director:

Thinks: Oh, boy. Another one. Must have had Johnson for reading methods.

Says: That's very interesting. Tell me, how does the approach work?

Teacher Candidate:

Thinks: I wish I had read that handout more carefully. Why did I cut that class?

Says: Well, I've never really used that approach because in my student teaching I had to use a basal series. But in language experience the kids write their own material and learn to read from that.

Personnel Director:

Thinks: I think I'll see how this fellow operates under pressure.

Says: Sounds like we could save a lot of money on books. Is that really how you would teach reading?

Teacher Candidate:

Thinks: Of all the classes to cut!

Says: Well if money is saved on books, I'd like to have it spent for an aide to help me record the students' stories and to help them read their stories. But I'll need books too. The language experience stories are used only to introduce the students to reading.

Personnel Director:

Thinks: Good. He seems like a nice fellow. And capable. I wonder how honest he is and how self-confident he feels.

Says: Let me ask a very direct question? Do you feel competent to step into a classroom with twenty-five first graders and teach them how to read?

Teacher Candidate:

Thinks: Wow! I don't know. I cut a couple of classes, but I passed the exams okay. I think I know how. But no professor ever told me exactly what to do—I mean step by step. All I ever heard was theory. And in my practice teaching, I only helped my cooperating teacher. And she used a basal series.

Says: (With sincerity): I don't really know exactly. I mean, I have to find out. I think I can do the job, but honestly I'm a little scared.

Personnel Director:

Thinks: Well, honesty is the best policy. Reminds me of how I felt when I took my first job.

Says: Scared? You earned an A in developmental reading in the elementary school, an A in remedial reading. Both from a good university. I suspect you're being modest.

Teacher Candidate:

Thinks: What do I say now? The thought of trying to teach twenty-five first graders to read petrifies me. Maybe I should give up the whole idea of being a teacher. Why didn't at least one of my professors tell me exactly what to do for a class of twenty-five first graders.

Says: I think I can do the job. I certainly want an opportunity to try. And I do have good grades. But in spite of my grades, I must honestly say, I'm a little nervous about taking full responsibility for a whole class, especially first graders.

Curtain descends.

1. Is the play believable?
2. The candidate is obviously not completely self-confident about his ability to teach reading. Is this attitude typical at his state of professional growth?
3. Who, if anyone, should be chastised for the candidate's feelings of insecurity?
4. Add one or more speeches to this play.

See response 3 for our replies to the four questions.

Problem 4

When tackling problem 4, you may want to refer to chapter 8.

As a central office reading consultant, you are frequently on

the firing line regarding students with reading problems within
the district. One day a week you are in your office to receive
phone calls and confer personally with people who have various
concerns regarding students with reading problems.

How would you respond to the following people?

1. A first-grade teacher in her first year of teaching who wants
   to use a language experience approach with her students instead of the adopted basal because she has been assigned a
   low-ability class and her students aren't doing well with the
   basal materials.
2. A concerned parent who is upset because her first grader is
   reading stories he dictates instead of stories in the attractive
   books being used in other schools. She thinks he is not making enough progress, and she is also concerned because his
   stories aren't "corrected" before they are typed for him to
   read. She wonders if he is being given a program designed
   for children who aren't expected to become good readers.
3. A principal from an inner-city school who wants suggestions
   for writing a proposal for federal funds to bring his students'
   standardized test scores up to the same level as those of students in more affluent areas of the district.
4. A distressed parent who knows that children can be taught to
   read in kindergarten and whose kindergartner is given only
   nonreading activities.
5. A school board member who heard a professor from a well-
   known university say recently that students wouldn't need
   remedial reading if reading were taught correctly in the first
   place. Why then are you requesting allocations for more remedial teachers?
6. The director of secondary education for the district who is
   angry that she is not being allocated remedial reading
   teachers in proportion to those being assigned to elementary
   schools. After all, she argues, senior high school is the last
   opportunity to get to these kids, and many of them can't read
   more than second or third grade level material.
7. A pediatric neurologist who wants to start a learning disabilities center based in one of the city hospitals and wants the
   district to supply a remedial reading specialist to serve on a
   multidisciplinary team.
8. A member of a service club who feels that kids have trouble
   in school mostly because they are behind in reading. His organization wants to give the kids in his neighborhood some
   help with reading before they eat the hot breakfasts the service club has been providing for them. What will you do to
   help?

9. An eye specialist who is forming a group to insist upon eye examinations by vision specialists for all children entering first grade as a major step in eliminating reading disability. She wants your support.

10. An alderperson from a low socioeconomic area who insists upon a return to phonics and discarding the "look-say" method, which never did work, as the key to bringing kids in her ward up to grade level in reading.

11. A senior high school science teacher who wants to know why the elementary school isn't doing its job in teaching reading. Most of her students are doing poor work because they can't read the materials she assigns.

12. An undergraduate student in a reading methods course who is writing a paper on the major cause of reading disability in the country and wants your opinion on what it is and how to eliminate it.

13. A school psychologist who thinks Jimmy Brown should not have to take remedial reading because he has a severe case of dyslexia, borne out by lateral dominance tests and by investigations that found neither his grandfather nor his father could learn to read even though they attended school to the sixth and tenth grades, respectively.

14. A school psychologist who just returned from a conference that stressed the importance of perceptual-motor skills on reading development. He is recommending that all remedial readers receive perceptual motor training as a major part of their programs.

15. A first grade teacher who believes that the irregularities of the English language are the major cause of reading disability. He wants the initial teaching alphabet used in all first grades to cut down on reading problems.

16. A nursery school teacher who has been trying to teach phonics to four year olds to give them a head start. They don't seem to be learning what she's teaching. What can she do to improve her teaching?

17. A pediatrician who wants to know what percentage of students in the district are suffering from dyslexia and what is being done to help them.

18. A salesperson from a publishing company reporting that the use of their new program has just about solved the reading disability problem in certain school districts in Pennsylvania and California.

19. A remedial reading teacher who wants some advice for a fourth grader who has had remedial instruction for two years with no apparent gain. She suspects a neurological maturational lag.

20. An English teacher who suspects that if more emphasis were
    given to teaching kids to write, their reading problems
    would diminish.

See response 4 for our responses to the twenty situations above.

Problem 5

When tackling problem 5, you may want to refer to chapters 3, 6,
and 8.

Elementary school organizational plans for reading instruction
do not in themselves help students to be better readers. The
function of any organizational plan is to facilitate the teacher's
opportunities to give children the reading experiences they need.
The following five assertions are arguments against the practice
of assigning students to teachers or classes for reading instruction on the basis of their reading achievement. The assertions are
arguments for giving reading instruction in self-contained
classrooms with the full range of reading abilities represented. In
other words, they are arguments against interclass grouping for
reading instruction.

Offer a counterargument for each of the five assertions and
write a concluding statement indicating your preference for interclass or intraclass grouping for reading instruction.

1. Poor readers are extremely difficult to work with and require
   more individual attention than good readers. Asking a
   teacher to do a good job with an entire classroom full of poor
   readers does not seem realistic. Although the range of reading ability in terms of vocabulary, rate, and comprehension
   is decreased by assigning all poor readers to one class for
   reading instruction, the actual number of specific skills problems for the teacher to deal with is greatly increased for the
   teacher of that class.
2. Any organizational plan should facilitate the movement of a
   child from group to group. It may be more upsetting to
   change a child to a different room and a different teacher for
   reading instruction than to change him or her to a different
   group within the same room and with the same teacher.
3. When an entire class consists of poor readers, both students
   and teachers are deprived of good models.
4. With intraclass grouping, teachers have opportunities to
   group students homogeneously for skills instruction and heterogeneously for interest-based reading about a selected
   theme.

5. Teachers who teach reading, social studies, math, science, and other subjects to the same students are better able to incorporate the teaching of reading into their content area teaching and more aware of the need for differentiating reading assignments in the content areas than are teachers who do not teach reading to the same students whom they teach in the content areas.

See response 5 for our counterarguments and concluding statement.

Problem 6

When tackling problem 6, you may want to refer to chapter 9.

Score the following suggestions for reading consultants in terms of their potential for helping elementary classroom teachers to improve their teaching. Then score them again in terms of their potential for helping secondary teachers to improve their teaching. For each suggestion use the following scale.

1	2	3	4	5
No				Excellent
potential				potential

1. At the beginning of the school year, devote an entire staff meeting to some discussion about improving the school's reading program. Set some definite objectives (for example, better teaching of reading in the content areas, establishment of functional and recreational reading groups, better use of diagnostic information). Let the staff set the objectives and suggest ways in which the reading consultant can be most helpful. Decide also when and how the objectives will be evaluated.
2. Send out a biweekly newsletter listing consultant activities performed during the past two weeks. Include some excerpts from the professional literature that are relative to reading program development.
3. Set up a display of instructional materials and offer to discuss any that look appealing with interested teachers.
4. Ask to team with one or more teachers to experiment with new materials or a new instructional practice (such as getting students to read for purpose by making predictions about the content of a selection on the basis of its title).
5. Conduct some action research and analyze the results (for example, look at the effects of assigning creative and noncreative writing assignments relative to a reading selection on

students' comprehension; look at the effects of summary writing on students' comprehension).

6. Form a committee of teachers and the principal to meet on a regular basis to discuss reading program improvement and suggest priorities for your services.

7. Form a study group with one or more interested teachers to study one aspect of teaching reading (such as teaching contextual analysis word attack skills) and present a short panel discussion at a staff meeting.

8. Team with a central office supervisor and one or more teachers to videotape some demonstration teaching for use throughout the school district.

9. Work with a group of corrective readers in the classroom while the classroom teacher does some enrichment activities with accelerated students in the same room.

10. Offer to help teachers administer informal inventories and establish reading groups at the beginning of the year.

11. Ask teachers to listen to audio tapes of your work with their remedial readers and suggest ways for coordinating their teaching with yours.

12. Establish an interschool newsletter highlighting interesting reading projects in other schools. Include teachers' evaluations of the materials they are using.

13. Survey teachers to discover their greatest areas of concern about the school's reading program. Discuss the results with the principal.

14. Meet with principals and reading consultants from other schools to share common concerns and program developments.

15. Ask one or more teachers to help you establish a model lesson for teaching reading with social studies materials. Share this model with schools where different models are being developed.

16. Ask certain teachers to help you plan an orientation program for next year's new teachers.

17. Invite a researcher to discuss his or her findings with you and a group of interested teachers. Ask the researcher to stress implications for classroom practice.

18. Solicit teacher volunteers to help a reading researcher collect his or her data at your school.

19. Establish three-way conferences between yourself, the principal, and teachers to evaluate certain materials, discuss problem students, and discuss ways in which you might help the teachers identify and meet the needs of poor readers in their classes.

20. Ask a teacher to let you take her class for a week so you don't "lose your touch." Invite her to work with one or two problem students while you are teaching the class. Of course, you will need to know what he or she has been doing before you take over, and the teacher will need to know what you have been doing and your perceptions when you finish.

See response 6 for our scores.

Problem 7

When tackling problem 7, you may want to refer to chapter 10.

The following excerpt is from a principal's address to her staff delivered at the first meeting of the preschool orientation workshop.

Read the address and answer the four questions following it.

And now I would like to ask all of you to help me take a new approach to our in-service efforts to improve our reading program. Those of you who have been teachers at this school during my principalship know how committed I have been to the development of a strong reading program. You have enthused over or suffered through with me the presentations of experts whom we have employed to tell us how to teach our kids to be better readers. You know as I do that these presentations have ranged from informative and inspiring to dull and naive. The one thing they all had in common was the effect they had on changing our teaching behavior—practically none.

I think I know why our in-service programs through the years have been less than satisfactory in terms of our goals: We have followed the path of least difficulty. We have asked others to give us in an hour or two the insights that took them years of study and practice to acquire. In addition, we have expected them to be able to tell us in six easy steps what to do in a school they had to be given directions to find and with students they knew only as statistics or as test scores. I am convinced now that no one will make us reading experts in six easy lessons. We must become experts ourselves and we must realize that expertise is not achieved by spending several afternoons a year listening to different people tell us their biases on teaching reading. I think we are like many other staffs, who are expected to master the difficult, complicated process of teaching reading with a minimum of study and practice and a maximum of belief and hope that someone else could make it easy for us.

341

I am going to offer a number of recommendations that I hope you'll consider seriously.

1. I would like three classroom teachers to serve with me as a steering committee to guide our efforts in a continuing in-service program over the next several years.
2. I would like to use some of our staff meeting time and most of our in-service days to assess and discuss our efforts to improve students' reading skills and attitudes toward reading as we move along. We may invite specialists from outside our building to join us in our meetings for the purpose of discussing specific questions we feel we need outside help with. However, I think we should make it clear that we want outside resource people to discuss specific problems with us, not give us prepared presentations.
3. We will need to devise some kind of evaluation measures to let us know whether the new instructional practices and materials we employ are having a positive effect on our students' skills, attitudes, and habits.
4. I am enrolling in a graduate-level reading methods course. I urge all of you who can to join me in that class.
5. I am going to spend some money improving our faculty library, and I will ask each of you to spend one hour each week doing some professional reading in the area of reading.
6. I have received permission to use the funds allocated for new instructional materials for staff improvement purposes instead. I propose to use this money mostly for teachers aides and substitute teachers to provide us with more released time to study and discuss the strengths and weaknesses of our reading program. I'm tired of believing that there's an easy way to improve instructional programs. And I'm tired of being disappointed in the results of the in-service programs we've been having.

1. Would you describe this principal as realistic or unrealistic, honest or cynical?
2. Imagine that you are a teacher listening to this challenge. What questions might be raised in your mind? Would you feel inspired, angry, or indifferent?
3. If you were a university professor who did in-service work, how would you probably react to this principal's speech?
4. If you were a reading consultant in this principal's district, how would you react to his speech?

See response 7 for our answers to the four questions.

When tackling problem 8, you may want to refer to chapters 4, 5, and 9.

Respond to the following letter for help.

Dear Reading Consultant:

I've been a faithful reader of your column since my reading methods teacher in college called the attention of our class to it. For years I couldn't believe the messes some teachers get themselves into and certainly never thought I would some day be writing to you for help. But here I am, and I need help fast.

I'm about to begin my third year of teaching fourth grade. My first two years were great because I was in a modern school where the students were assigned to teachers according to the students' reading ability. I had the top group of fourth graders; those kids plowed through more materials than you can imagine. In fact, they finished the basal series through the sixth grade and absolutely devoured reading kits and workbooks. So I'm not an unsuccessful teacher.

Now here's my problem. I am moving and have accepted a job in a school district that is practically in the dark ages. In two months I will be faced with twenty-seven fourth graders who are not grouped in any special way for reading instruction. The principal told me to expect kids who are reading from the second grade level to the seventh grade level. When I asked her how I could teach reading to a class with a range of ability that wide, she smiled and said, "You're the teacher. I'm the principal." By the way, the principal also told me that I was expected to use a tri-basal approach with my class. I guess she thought I am older than I really am because I looked through my old class notes, and my methods teacher never even mentioned that. Evidently no one is even talking about tri-basal approaches anymore. I didn't embarrass her by letting her know I didn't know what she was talking about.

Well, Reading Consultant, you can see what I'm up against. Don't tell me to talk to the principal. I have, and she doesn't understand. Besides, how much can you tell your boss? Please answer soon as I can't sleep nights worrying about those poor kids next year.

Can't Sleep Nights

See response 8 for our response.

343

Problem 9

When tackling problem 9, you may want to refer to chapter 8.
Evaluate the following proposal.

A proposal for a reading-language arts learning center

CENTER GOALS

The goals of the reading-language arts learning center would
be:

1. To provide expert diagnosis and intensive remediation for
   students who have shown little or no reading improvement
   as a result of the work of the personnel and of the programs available to them in their regular schools.
2. To involve parents in the remediation process in a highly
   personal way.
3. To train classroom teachers and learning disabilities
   teachers assigned to regular school settings in a variety of
   diagnostic and remedial procedures.
4. To develop methods and materials for teaching students
   with severe reading disorders within a total language development curriculum.
5. To assist teachers and other personnel who work in the
   center on limited term bases to transmit their experiences
   and knowledge to their colleagues when they return to their
   regular schools.
6. To provide follow-up for enrolled students within regular
   school settings when they leave the center.

THE CURRICULUM

Although the center would exist primarily to remediate severe
reading disabilities, the instructional program would draw
heavily upon recommended activities for total language arts
development. Specifically the general approach to the remediation of reading disability would be through play reading,
dramatization, conversation, debating, creative writing, film
viewing, listening to music, and discussing art and other reading-related activities with a high potential for aesthetic appeal.
Specific reading skill instruction would be given within the

344

context of broadly conceived communications activities or projects. All instruction in the center would be highly individualized but would not exclude small-group activities. Frequent diagnostic evaluations would be an ongoing aspect of each student's program.

Considerable content from the social studies curriculum would be utilized so that students' development in that curriculum area would not be neglected because of their half-day enrollment in the center program. Students' schedules would be arranged so that they could receive their instruction in other curriculum areas in their regular schools and their reading-language arts and social studies instruction at the center.

THE STUDENTS

Thirty-two students would be enrolled in the center program on a half-day basis (9:00–11:30 or 1:00–3:30). Sixteen of the students would be drawn from grades 3 through 5 and sixteen from grades 6 through 8.

No student would be accepted into the center until a multidisciplinary diagnostic team had made the following judgments:

1. The student's reading achievement is clearly retarded in relation to his or her ability to learn skills and content in other curriculum areas.
2. The student's reading disability is so severe that he or she cannot extract ideas from print and respond to them intelligently.
3. The special personnel and programs available in the student's regular school have been tried for a reasonable period of time without appreciable improvement or indication of appreciable improvement to come.

Except in rare cases students would be expected to receive instruction in the center for one school year. At the conclusion of their one-year enrollments, each student's progress would be carefully evaluated using a review of the diagnostic data collected throughout the year and selected additional assessments. A decision would then be made for each student as to the advisability of his remaining in the center program or returning to his regular school full time. Suggestions for special programming within the regular school would be made at this time.

Two major criteria would be employed to determine a student's continuation or termination in the center program after each year of participation:

1. Whether the student had progressed sufficiently to return to his or her regular school curriculum without losing the gains made in the center.
2. Whether the student had improved sufficiently to conclude that the center's program was indeed more beneficial to his or her growth than regular school's program.

PERSONNEL

The teaching personnel would be recurited from among the ranks of classroom teachers in the elementary schools, classroom teachers in the middle schools, and teachers of children with learning disabilities in both elementary and middle schools.

The teachers would participate in a two-week workshop prior to their tenure as center teachers. In addition, they would attend a weekly seminar. The orientation workshop and the seminars would also be attended by the teachers who had worked in the center the previous half-year. The workshop and seminar meetings would be designed to help teachers improve their diagnostic and teaching skills and their ability to have a positive effect on the curriculums of their regular schools when they return.

The key staff members of the center would be two master teachers hired on a full-time basis. A major requirement for the master teachers would be successful experience in designing and implementing activities and materials for poor readers that incorporate all of the language arts methodologies. The master teachers would also need to possess teacher training skills and have a good sense of the aesthetic dimension of reading/language arts instruction.

An executive secretary would be hired on a full-time basis to handle budgeting matters, to schedule students, to perform necessary clerical tasks, and to remove the burden of typical administrative responsibilities from the master teachers.

STAFF ORGANIZATION

The teaching staff would work in two teams, each comprised of a master teacher and two other teachers. The assistance of specialized personnel from various sources would be obtained as the need for specialized services outside the expertise of the center staff was required.

One team would work with eight students from grades 3 through 5 in the morning and with another group of eight students in the afternoon. The other team would work with eight students from grades 6 through 8. Considerable changes in grouping arrangements to facilitate a varied instructional program would be an expected characteristic of the curriculum organization. The team working with students from the lower grades would be staffed by one of the master teachers, one classroom teacher, and one learning disabilities teacher. The team working with students from the upper grades would be staffed by one of the master teachers, a middle school classroom teacher, and a learning disabilities teacher.

PHYSICAL SETTING

The facility envisioned would require two regular-sized classrooms, two smaller conference-type rooms, and an office for administrative and supervisory personnel. One wing of a partly occupied elementary or middle school would be desirable. Easy access to an IMC would be essential.

The furniture should be movable chairs and tables. The facility would need to be well equipped with racks for book displays and cupboards to store special tests, instructional materials, and audiovisual equipment.

Since students from every school in the district would conceivably be enrolled from time to time, the school selected to house the facility should be centrally located. Parents would be required to provide transportation to and from the facility for their children. A location on a public bus route would be important.

EVALUATION OF THE CENTER PROGRAM

The evaluation of the center would rest most heavily upon the effect of its program upon students' reading improvement.

Students' attitudes, self-concepts, reading habits, and ability to express themselves orally and in writing would be assessed throughout their enrollment at the center. A bank of data would be collected for each student, and these data would be carefully examined to discover growth patterns, which would

347

be compared with those prior to the student's participation in the center program.

Evaluation data would also be collected from the parents of the enrolled students. Questionnaires would be constructed and administered to ascertain parents' evaluation of the center program and its effects upon their children and upon themselves.

Participating teachers would also be asked to evaluate the program in terms of its effect on them and their perceptions of the effects of the program on the children and their parents. Appropriate perception instruments would be constructed and utilized.

Finally, the classroom teachers in the students' regular schools would be surveyed to discover their perceptions of the program in terms of its effects upon the students who are presently or who have been in it and in terms of any effects it might have had or might be having on their own teaching.

See response 9 for our evaluation of the proposal.

Problem 10

When tackling problem 10, you may want to refer to chapter 7. Read this memo and answer the question following it.

MEMO: December 28

TO: All reading consultants and school principals

FROM: The office of the superintendent of schools

RE: Evaluation of student achievement in reading

I have become increasingly concerned about the lack of objective evidence that comes to my office regarding the effect of our instructional programs on students' achievement in reading at all academic levels. This is an age of accountability, and I must be accountable to the taxpayers for financial outlays for reading instruction.

Some of you have informed me of the questions of validity and reliability that surround standardized reading achievement tests. I can certainly understand your lack of faith in these evaluation instruments, and I am prepared in an academic sense to accept your reluctance to rely upon them. Nonetheless, the necessity to show results from our reading program remains.

Therefore, I am charging you with the responsibility of preparing a detailed plan for reading program evaluation that will permit us to find out if our reading program is doing its intended job. I remind you that our findings must be communicated to our lay citizenry if we are to gain their confidence and continued financial support. The plan you propose should also be useful to the classroom teachers in our district. They must know that they also are being held accountable.

I shall await your recommendations eagerly. Teaching students to read is the top priority in my administration. I am relying upon you to provide the evidence I need to gain the financial support necessary for that priority.

My best wishes for a happy and prosperous new year.

What plan would you propose in answer to the superintendent's memo?
See response 10 for our plan.

Problem 11

When tackling problem 11, you may want to refer to Chapter 9. Read the following speech, which was the opening talk in a workshop for elementary and secondary school principals at a state convention. Then respond to the questions following it. The speech was given by a university professor who did considerable work as a consultant with school districts throughout the state.

What administrators should know about their role in reading instruction

This is the first in a series of talks that have been prepared to help school administrators keep abreast of continuing changes in the teaching of reading and changes in reading curriculum development. Two beliefs prompted the offering of this workshop for school principals:

1. Administrators have a role in planning, implementing, and evaluating school reading programs.
2. Administrators at all academic levels want and need to be kept informed of the issues and trends in the teaching of reading.

The remainder of my talk this morning is divided into three parts. Part I is addressed to the role of administrators in reading curriculum development. Part II is addressed to the informational needs of administrators who play an active role in reading program development. And Part III is a list of questions

349

for administrators to ask of themselves at the end of every
month to gauge their involvement in the curriculum area of
reading on a month-by-month basis. The list of questions
in Part III will also serve to suggest various ways in which administrators can and should become involved in reading program development.

PART I: THE ROLE OF ADMINISTRATORS IN READING
CURRICULUM DEVELOPMENT

I was talking with a principal recently who told me that,
among other things, he was testifying in two school-related
lawsuits, defending some new instructional materials the
school had purchased to a community group that thought the
materials portrayed minority groups in an unfavorable light,
preparing a detailed report of the damage done to the outside
of the school building by vandals, discussing with representatives from the teachers' union the implications of certain ne-
gotiations that were made to settle the teachers' strike, trying to
help a substitute get organized with a class whose regular
teacher had emergency surgery, worrying about the lunchroom
where a fist fight had broken out and been broken up the previous day, preparing evaluation reports for two federally funded
programs, and getting ready to meet with the parents of a boy
who claimed that a teacher had slapped him and that he did
not call her a bleep-bleep-bleep.

Even with all the other matters that needed his attention
lying in waiting, this principal was talking to me, a reading
specialist, about his reading program. He obviously thought it
important that he do so. "Reading," he said "is a problem for
us and we need some help." Notice—WE need some help. In
this regard he was one of the teaching staff. He was concerned
and he wanted to be involved.

My work with his teachers will be more effective because he
took the time to speak with me. He will pave my way for meetings with teachers, he will participate in meetings I have with
his teachers, and he will evaluate the effects of the combined
efforts of his teachers, himself, and myself on students' reading
improvement. He is important to my work with his teachers and
to his teachers' work with their students.

For as long as I can remember, administrators have been
charged with the role of instructional leadership, not just in
reading but in all curriculum areas. Those of us who have written and spoken in this regard in behalf of reading curriculum

development have been especially adamant about the need for administrators to assume leadership positions. Apparently we have been more adamant than effective, because a survey of the literature shows that authors who have written on the subject are much more impressed with what administrators have not done than they are impressed with what they have done. I think we reading specialists must be praised for our zeal, but faulted for our lack of clarity about what administrators are wanted to do. As I reviewed the literature before writing this talk, I was struck with the unrealistic number and kinds of tasks that are sometimes explicitly and sometimes implicitly given to administrators by reading specialists, urging them to assume leadership positions. In effect, some authors imply that administrators should be reading specialists. That message has probably created more guilt feelings than positive action among conscientious administrators. Most principals *are not* reading specialists and *cannot* perform as reading specialists for three very good reasons:

1. They are required to take increasingly more academic work in school administration with fewer opportunities to take reading methods courses or courses in reading curriculum development.
2. The demands on administrators' time and energy for purely administrative rather than curriculum matters have been increasing at a rate that is considered alarming by many administrators.
3. Reading methodology and reading curriculum development have become increasingly sophisticated and specialized.

Obviously, administrators should not be expected to assume the role of reading specialist.

The question that arises, then, is what can and what should administrators do to plan, implement, and evaluate reading instruction? The answer as I see it, from my vantage point as a reading specialist who works closely with school administrators, lies in a four-step process:

1. Establishing a working relationship with a reading specialist. School administrators must learn what the family physician has learned—as a profession becomes increasingly specialized, generalists must refer to, and work with specialists. This does not mean turning the job over to specialists, but rather working together to achieve mutually desired goals. How to create access to a reading specialist

and establish good working relationships varies from
school to school. Some districts have specialists who
serve several schools, some schools have the luxury of
having a reading specialist all to themselves, and some
schools must look to their classroom teachers to find
someone or someones with special abilities, training, and
interest in reading. If a school has no specialist available,
the first order of an administrator's business is to find one
or to create one by giving special training and released
time to one or more members of the teaching staff. The
point to be made is that school administrators need reading specialists on their team just as surely as reading specialists need administrators on theirs.

2. Gaining staff acceptance for the reading specialist. There
are some aspects of administrative behaviors that remain a
mystery to me. I don't know what they do or how they do it,
but some administrators have a special talent for getting a
specialist and classroom teachers working together. I suspect it has a lot to do with the actual feelings the administrator has about using reading specialists and the kind of
relationship existing between the administrator and his or
her teachers. My sense is that administrators with talent for
orchestrating the work of teachers, reading specialists,
and themselves enjoy doing it. Their talent is probably one
part learned, one part personal charisma, and one part
dedication to reading improvement. Wherever the talent
comes from, administrators have to be born with it, learn it,
or stumble upon it to do the important and difficult job of
gaining teacher staff acceptance for reading specialists.

3. Providing resources for reading curriculum development.
One senior high school principal I worked with when I was
a public school reading consultant was always about three
years ahead of the principals in the other high schools in
the district when it came to providing resources for reading
curriculum development in his school. He had the first full-
time reading consultant in the district on his staff. He had
the first reading classes for college-bound students. He
had the first English teachers with master's degrees in
reading on his staff, and he had them teaching reading
classes as well as English classes. He declared the first
war on content area teachers who said they had no intention of incorporating the teaching of reading into their content area teaching. And he would have had me and the
other district reading consultants working in his building
forty hours a week if we hadn't been almost as shrewd as
he was. He knew that the squeaky wheel gets the grease,

and he squeaked to the right people—the superintendent of schools, the director of secondary education, school board members, community groups, parent groups, teachers' groups. He was shameless in his efforts to get resource people, paperbacks, developmental reading materials, in-service meetings, reading classes, and other goodies to improve the reading ability of the students in his school. And he got them, even though he bemoaned the impoverished resources available to his students, who in fact had more than the students in the other high schools combined. They had more because their principal got them more. I don't think they, or their teachers, ever realized how their principal was working in the background in their behalf.

Every school district has resources that administrators control or to which they have access. Administrators who have reading curriculum improvement as a goal will find ways to obtain these resources and to use them continually to improve the reading instruction students receive, even if using them for reading program development means postponing or passing up some curriculum developments or administrative programs that may be currently more fashionable, more visible, or more self-aggrandizing.

4. Evaluating reading program development. Perhaps the most difficult administrative responsibility in regard to reading curriculum development is evaluation. A satisfactory definition for reading is difficult to arrive at, instructional goals are hard to agree upon, and how to reach and measure the goals that are set are processes that are sometimes charged with fervor, sometimes heavy with apathy, and always surrounded by a variety of opinion resting precariously on a teacup full of solid research. Nonetheless, evaluation is the fourth step for administrators to climb or to trip upon. Other speakers at this workshop will also discuss the business of reading program evaluation. Suffice it for me to say that administrators must neither abdicate nor take complete responsibility for evaluation. They must be a part of the evaluation process, along with teachers, reading specialists, specialists in measurement, parents, students, and other interested and concerned people. Because of their central position in the school district and their administrative training, administrators are probably best able to (1) initiate reading program evaluation, (2) involve the specialists and members of the community who are necessary for a good and acceptable evaluation process, and (3) coordinate their efforts.

The four steps, then, that administrators must climb are: (1) establishing a working relationship with a reading specialist, (2) gaining staff acceptance for the reading specialist, (3) providing resources for reading curriculum development, and (4) evaluating reading program development.

And now to Part II of my message.

PART II: THE INFORMATION NEEDS OF ADMINISTRATORS

The intent of this workshop is to give administrators the information that the planners of the workshop and the individual speakers think they need. Therefore, listening to the speakers that follow me or studying the program will reveal the areas of information that at least some reading specialists think are the most important areas for administrators to be informed about. Administrators who listen to all the speakers will acquire, we hope, the background information and the inspiration necessary to tackle the job of reading curriculum development within their schools.

However, this workshop is not the only source of information available to administrators. Those of us who speak today will immodestly claim that it is the best source, but we will be quick to admit to the existence of other sources.

Most school districts employ one or more reading specialists or at least have access to a reading specialist who can keep administrators informed about the field of reading curriculum development. One or two hours a month could be regularly scheduled for administrators in groups of four or five to discuss informally their questions and concerns about reading instruction in their schools and in schools in other districts. A worthwhile adjunct to these monthly meetings would be the weekly mailing of an article from a professional journal, a newspaper article, or some other printed material about reading that administrators would find interesting and helpful to meet their informational needs. The reading specialist's job description could be written so that one responsibility would be to keep administrators informed about reading curriculum development, either through regularly scheduled conferences or through the mail.

Another source of information to keep administrators up to date about reading program development might be a nearby teacher-training institution. Many departments of education schedule reading classes to meet late afternoons, evenings, or Saturdays to take advantage of in-service teacher enrollments.

These classes are often relatively small and usually designed to allow considerable discussion and sharing of ideas and concerns. As a teacher of these courses I always welcome administrators who enroll generally more for their personal and professional interest than for the course credits. I also encourage administrator auditors. Most of my colleagues feel as I do because of the benefits to the other students in the classes and to ourselves, all of whom need to be reminded of, and kept up to date with the administrative aspects of public education. Administrators have much to contribute to as well as to take from university courses. As a postscript to this pitch to get administrators to enroll in university reading courses, I would like to mention a particular course, which is becoming a popular offering of many teacher-training institutions. The course is variously called "Supervising School Reading Programs," "School Reading Program Development," "Improving School Reading Programs," "Administering the School Reading Program," and other similar names. These courses are specifically designed to meet the needs of school administrators and should carefully be considered by administrators who want and/or need information about their several roles in reading curriculum development. Administrators who find it impossible or impractical to take such a course might find out what textbooks are being used in the course and read them. However, as the School Sisters of Notre Dame used to tell me repeatedly when I was in elementary and high school, "The road to hell is paved with good intentions." Enrolling in the course and paying the tuition will probably pay better dividends than buying a book and *intending* to read it.

PART III: QUESTIONS

So much for the second part of my talk. Now on to the third and final part—a list of questions for administrators to ask of themselves at the end of every month to gauge the level of their involvement in the curriculum area of reading on a month-by-month basis.

There are six questions in all. Each can be answered by a single "yes" or "no." I recommend that administrators have their secretaries prepare nine copies of the six questions and label each copy with a different month of the school year. I also recommend that the secretary be instructed to see that a copy of the six questions be placed on top of the pile of papers marked "MUST" on the morning of the last day of every month.

This will give administrators who are conscientious or just compulsive about getting good grades one more day to get more "yes" than "no" answers. At the end of the last day of every month (just as the secretary has finished counting the hot lunch money), the completed monthly check list should be returned to the secretary for another month. Now, every administrator knows that no secretary could resist peeking at his or her boss's report card, especially when the monthly hot lunch money is all counted. For obvious reasons, following the procedure I have just outlined will work.

Here are the six questions:

1. Have I done some professional reading in the area of reading curriculum this month?
2. Have I discussed some aspect of reading program improvement with a reading specialist this month?
3. Have I visited a classroom to observe a teacher helping students improve their reading this month?
4. Have I had a discussion with one or more classroom teachers this month about their successes and/or problems with their students and reading?
5. Have I asked for and studied some evidence of students' reading achievement this month? (Such evidence might be achievement test scores, taped oral readings, book reports, records of library book circulation, workbook pages, or taped discussions of textbook assignments in one or more content areas.)
6. Question six should be constructed by each administrator himself or herself. The question should relate to some individual project, program, or concern. This question may change from month to month or from year to year. The idea is to keep it focused on some current aspect of reading program improvement of concern or being emphasized in a school or district.

In summary, administrators can be powerful agents in reading curriculum development and improvement. They need information inputs on a regular and systematic basis. And they need to be active in reading program development and improvement on a regular and systematic basis. The remaining talks in this workshop will build upon this theme.

1. What effect would you expect this short speech to have upon the principals in the audience?

2. What do you find to be particularly praiseworthy about this speech?

3. For what, if anything, would you fault this speech?

See Response 11 for our answers to these three questions.

Response 1

The results of the teacher survey described in problem 1 are presented in Table 12.1. (See p. 358.)

Response 2

Our responses to the questions to the monologue in problem 2 follow.

1. We sympathize with the reading consultant who is about to come face to face with an angry young teacher who also needs some sympathy. In addition to being angry, the teacher also feels frustrated and betrayed. He wants to be a good teacher; and he can't, not until conditions change.

He is angry because the school has a reading consultant but no remedial reading teacher. His anger is understandable given his misperception of remedial reading. He thinks he has been betrayed by elementary teachers, the school principal, his former professors, a school board that hires a consultant when a remedial teacher is needed, and even his students, who don't remind him at all of himself when he was a student. He is frustrated because he does not know what to do next. His anger, his misperceptions, and his lack of understanding about how to deal with the situation he's in are all aspects of the problem with which the reading consultant will be faced.

2. Certainly the problem could have been avoided, at least to some extent. First of all, his history methods professors could have taught him about the differences in reading ability among high school students. They might also have taught him how to differentiate reading assignments and how to help students read the assigned material. He might have been encouraged or required to take a reading methods course as part of his pre-service training.

The principal might have explained when the teacher was hired that all the remedial teachers in the school district were assigned to the elementary grades, or that the reading consultant

Table 12.1 **Teacher Survey Results**

A: *Percentage of primary (P) and intermediate (I) teachers choosing each response category regarding the question: How well do you feel your pre-service education prepared you to teach reading in your first regular teaching assignment?*

Response	Level	Years of experience			
		1	**2–5**	**6–10**	**11+**
Very adequately	P	17.4(N = 28)	23.1(N = 52)	15.8(N = 19)	44.4(N = 27)
	I	0.0(N = 21)	10.0(N = 50)	7.7(N = 13)	10.0(N = 20)
Adequately	P	60.9	59.5	52.6	33.3
	I	47.1	28.0	38.5	25.0
Undecided	P	13.0	1.9	26.3	11.1
	I	9.5	16.0	7.7	25.0
Inadequately	P	8.7	13.5	5.3	11.1
	I	33.3	40.0	30.8	25.0
Very inadequately	P	0.0	1.9	0.0	0.0
	I	0.0	6.0	15.4	15.0

B: *Percentage of primary (P) and intermediate (I) teachers indicating need for information*

Response	Level	Years of Experience			
		1	**2–5**	**6–10**	**11+**
Grouping students	P	26.1	11.5	5.3	25.9
	I	23.9	16.0	38.5	0.0
Diagnosing individual instructional needs	P	78.3	55.8	47.4	48.1
	I	81.0	58.0	38.5	30.0
Using basal materials	P	34.8	3.8	5.3	3.7
	I	19.0	16.0	7.7	0.0
Using supplementary materials	P	60.9	44.2	52.6	18.5
	I	57.1	40.0	23.1	20.0
Different methods for teaching reading (ITA, programmed, etc.)	P	78.3	73.1	84.2	63.0
	I	95.2	74.0	84.6	85.0
Developing word attack skills	P	26.1	28.8	10.5	18.5
	I	47.6	44.0	15.4	20.0
Developing comprehension skills	P	39.1	32.7	15.8	22.2
	I	38.1	40.0	30.8	25.0
Providing for the disabled reader in the classroom	P	56.5	69.2	78.9	70.4
	I	66.7	54.0	69.2	70.0
Differentiating instruction for different ability groups	P	39.1	40.4	57.9	40.7
	I	57.1	36.0	38.5	35.0
Providing for the superior reader	P	56.5	32.7	42.1	22.2
	I	52.4	20.0	30.8	20.0

Table 12.1 **(cont.)**

B: *Percentage of primary (P) and intermediate (I) teachers indicating need for information*

Response	Level	Years of Experience			
		1	**2–5**	**6–10**	**11+**
Using the library or IMC properly	P	26.1	17.3	31.6	25.9
	I	9.5	8.0	30.8	25.0
Using writing, speaking, and listening	P	52.5	42.3	73.7	22.2
in the reading program	I	38.1	46.0	15.4	25.0

C: A desire for the kind of in-service help that meets the specific needs of individual teachers or of teachers of a particular grade was clear. Especially apparent was the desire of the first year teachers to have individual conferences with a reading specialist. Conversely, teachers with two or more years experience were considerably less interested in private conferences and more interested in noncredit classes for teachers of selected grade levels. University credit did not appeal as strongly to the older teachers as to the younger teachers. This finding suggests that public schools may be unwise to rely on university course offerings in reading to keep their experienced teachers updated. Noncredit classes offered within the school system may be well attended by the teachers who would not be attracted to university courses. Television programs, films, video tapes, and noncredit classes for elementary teachers who are not grouped according to special interests all had relatively little appeal. The teachers preferred personalized help with their instructional reading programs to general information.

Teachers in other school systems may, of course, have had quite different experiences from the group studied, and, therefore, might respond differently. Teachers for whom in-service programs are intended should be involved in the planning, and, whenever possible, exposed to a variety of approaches. (Smith, Otto, and Harty, 1970, pp. 446–447.)

was hired to help content area teachers deal with students with reading problems, or in some other way alerted the new teacher to which resources were available to him in that school.

The reading consultant could have had a meeting with all new teachers before school started to explain the reading program in the school and the teachers' and the consultant's respective roles in the program.

In short, some preparation for a typical problem might have prevented the problem from assuming tragic proportions and presenting seemingly unsurmountable obstacles to meeting his teaching objectives in the eyes of a new history teacher.

3. The reading consultant should probably not try to do much to help the teacher directly until he is in a better frame of mind. Certainly an emotional confrontation should be assiduously avoided. Probably the best approach would be to be sympathetic and make an appointment to meet with the teacher in his office or classroom within the next two or three days. The purpose of the meeting could be to plan for the consultant's visit to observe the class, examine some test scores, do some informal testing, examine the textbook, or in some other way identify the problem the teacher and the consultant will be dealing with together.

Response 3

Our responses to the four questions to the "Almost Finished
Short Play in One Scene" in problem 3 follow.

1. Although the play is intended to be humorous and might
be faulted for an exaggeration here and there, a thread of reality
runs through it. Most interviews contain a bit of sparring and
image setting, and most beginning teachers don't know all the
right answers. Most hiring officials know this to be more typical
than atypical because they've been beginners too.

2. Some lack of self-confidence is a healthy sign in beginning
teachers. How can anyone be sure of being a good teacher until
he or she has some actual teaching (not practice teaching) experience?

3. Although some persons might fault the candidate's teacher
training program for his feelings of insecurity, we would not
unless we had more damning evidence than is given in the play.
How could a methods professor be held responsible for telling a
student "exactly" how to teach an unknown class in an unknown
school? Some people might chastise the personnel director, but
we have interviewed enough candidates for teaching positions to
sympathize with the people on both sides of the table. Therefore,
we offer no chatisement at all.

4. Personnel Director:

Thinks: Thank heavens we have reading specialists to help this
man get started on the right foot.

Says: In this district we feel the job of learning how to teach
is never done. We have reading specialists available to
you who will give you the help you need to continue developing your knowledge about teaching reading and
your teaching skills. Come with me now. I'd like to introduce you to a principal who needs a teacher and
who has a reading resource teacher on her staff. We'd
like you to talk with the two of them before anyone
makes any commitments. They'll let me know how they
feel about having you join their staff after you've talked
with them, and I'll call you about their decision. I think
you have a good chance for the job.

Response 4

Our responses to the twenty phone calls described in problem 4
follow.

1. The question of the beginning first grade teacher who
wants to use language experience as a basic approach for her

class of low-ability first graders suggests conflicting answers. On the one hand, the language experience approach has many advantages for these children. The students quickly learn that reading is a communication process; what they read is closely tied to their oral language development and their experiential backgrounds; oral language and reading are developed simultaneously in a mutually reinforcing pattern.

On the other hand, this approach is difficult to implement with a whole class of low-ability first graders. The teachers we know who do it successfully had several years of experience with a basal program and sometimes help from a teacher's aide before they tried using language experience as the basic approach with a class similar to this one.

We would advise the teacher to use the adopted basal for a year or two to gain a better sense of the students' abilities and needs and to get a better understanding of the reading process and how to teach it. She could supplement the basal with language experience stories and thereby learn the intricacies of that approach in her first year or two of teaching. If an experienced aide and the close supervision of a reading specialist are available she might try the approach.

2. The parent who made this phone call needs a conference with her child's teacher, principal, or a reading specialist so that the language experience approach can be fully explained to her. She has some misunderstandings that need to be corrected. Parents' faith in the instructional programs their children are receiving is a factor in the learning process. A good explanation of the reason for the language experience approach and a description of it may allay this mother's fears. If an explanation does not suffice, she should be shown some tangible evidence of her son's progress in reading with an explanation of what constitutes reasonable progress in reading growth for children at his intellectual, emotional, and social levels of development.

3. This principal needs to catch up on his reading. We recommend that he read a chapter or two from textbooks that discuss the causes and correlates of reading retardation and the validity and reliability of standardized test scores for educationally disadvantaged students. Almost any remedial reading textbook will contain helpful material. We would send him the material to read through the school mail and suggest that he call again and arrange for an appointment after he's read it.

4. This parent should have a conference arranged, perhaps a three-way conference with the kindergarten teacher and a reading specialist. Most elementary reading methods textbooks contain a discussion of the individual nature of reading readiness and the advantages of initiating formal reading instruction only

when the child evidences the readiness to profit from it. The material in the textbook might be shown to the distressed parent and discussed with him. Most of the textbooks refer to research studies that can be used to convince the parent that what's good for one child may be detrimental to another in regard to the initiation of formal reading instruction in kindergarten.

5. Alas, we live in an imperfect world. If family physicians could treat all ailments, we would have no need for medical specialists. We wish the persuasive convention speaker had said, "If all classroom conditions could be made perfect, all children could be reading at the level to be expected of them given their development in other attributes that affect reading growth." But that wouldn't be so appealing to conventioneers. We recommend that the school board member read chapter 8 in this book and that the convention speaker be sent a letter explaining the damage his remark might have done to your program for disabled readers.

6. We recommend some guided visitation for the director of secondary education, plus an opportunity to talk about her concern with remedial reading teachers, preferably some who have taught both elementary and secondary students. The visits should be to both elementary and secondary remedial teachers at work. The director's attention should be directed to the potential for growth in reading skill development and in attitudes toward reading at both academic levels for the majority of the students in the program. It should also be directed to differences between students' motivation, absenteeism rates, and possibilities for coordinating remedial instruction with classroom instruction at both levels. The director might also be shown the materials and approaches available to poor readers at both levels so she can see that the remedial materials and approaches are more suitable for elementary than for secondary students with reading problems.

7. We would make every effort to supply the teacher requested, assuming that the teacher's work will be only with students from the district. The teacher's involvement will help to coordinate the philosophy and the procedures of the clinic program with the public school program. The clinic team will need to have an educator on it; and if the educator is also a member of the public school team, some serious theoretical and methodological conflicts might be avoided. The teacher should be a well-trained reading specialist with personal characteristics that allow him or her to stress and teach the educator's point of view to professionals who may view learning problems from a very different perspective and who may have some strong biases about diagnosing and treating reading disability. In other words, the teacher selected must not be cowed by medical specialists and their tests and jargon.

8. We would help the service club by making three suggestions: that the help in reading be given after breakfast, that the help be in the form of having club members who are good readers read to the assembled group and/or having a regular silent reading time for club members and children to read self-selected material together, and that the club officers work with a teacher or reading specialist in selecting materials for oral reading and/or arranging the silent reading sessions.

9. We do not support mandatory eye examinations for all children entering first grade as a major step in eliminating reading disability. Research has not supported the hypothesis that poor vision is a major or widespread cause of reading disability. The eye specialist's proposal is based on an unsupportable assumption and would drain limited financial resources away from programs and services likely to have a greater beneficial impact on reducing reading disability than vision examinations.

10. The alderperson who phoned is badly in need of some information about reading instruction. She probably wields a great deal of political power that could be used either to improve or to have a negative effect on reading instruction for poor readers. Therefore, it is imperative that she be brought up to date on reading theory and practice. We recommend arranging a conference with her to answer her questions and give her some facts about the place of phonics in reading instruction, the meaning of "grade level," and an understanding of the many factors besides phonics instruction that are important for reading achievement. We would also give her some material (selected chapters from textbooks and studies reported in professional journals) to read after the conference. A hoped for outcome of the contacts with the concerned alderperson would be an enlightened united effort to improve reading achievement in her ward.

11. The attitude expressed by the senior high school science teacher in her phone call is probably typical of that of senior high school teachers, who tend to reject the notion of individual differences in reading among students. We suspect that they feel reading is such a simple intellectual task that anyone who isn't mentally retarded can master it if he or she is properly taught—master it to the point of being able to comprehend sophisticated content, written in a difficult style, that is. This teacher and others with similar attitudes need to visit some elementary school classrooms and talk with some elementary school classroom teachers and remedial reading specialists. We would arrange for this teacher to spend a visitation day, an in-service day, or several preparation periods visiting elementary school classrooms and talking with some excellent elementary school teachers. We think familiarity might breed respect.

12. We think the major cause of reading disability in this country is lack of knowledge of the reading process and of precisely what to do with individuals who seem unable to master the process. If the answer to this student's question were known, educators and other professionals would be farther along in their quest to eliminate the problem. Instead, we would probably direct the caller to one or more remedial reading textbooks on the market, which posit that reading disability is probably caused by a number of interrelated factors, each of which exacerbates the other in a spiraling fashion.

13. Considerable controversy surrounds the condition called dyslexia. The term itself means different things to different people and is probably more misunderstood than understood. But to most people dyslexia is not untreatable. Therefore, the diagnosis made by the school psychologist and the prognosis and decisions resulting from it should be questioned.

Jimmy Brown may not be a good candidate for remedial instruction, but a better case needs to be built than the one expressed by the school psychologist. We recommend a staffing for Jimmy comprised of a remedial reading specialist, the school psychologist, Jimmy's teachers, his principal, his parents, and other professionals, if their advice is needed. After a complete diagnosis, including a history of Jimmy's instructional program, a decision can be made about remedial instruction for him.

14. Teachers have learned that using with all children an approach or materials that may be good for some is poor practice. Individual differences are as evident among poor readers as they are among students without reading problems. Without going into the controversy surrounding the effect of perceptual-motor training on reading development, we recommend that the school psychologist who phoned read a remedial reading textbook, watch some remedial reading teachers work with children and perhaps even try to teach a poor reader some word attack or comprehension skill. As is true of many people who comment upon remedial reading and make recommendations relative to that teaching specialty, the school psychologist needs to know more about the phenomenon for which he is urging reform.

15. Currently, modified alphabets for beginning reading instruction seem to be fading in importance. However, considering how the educational pendulum swings, we suspect they will return, disappear, and return again. There is no conclusive evidence to support the hypothesis that a regularized alphabet reduces reading problems. The i/t/a is well known to educators and has been used and tested widely enough to be generally recognized as a powerful tool if it were indeed more potent than other

approaches in reducing reading retardation at the national level.
We would tell the first grade teacher who phoned that the evidence to support the hypothesis that the teacher is more influential in reducing reading problems than the approach used is more convincing to us than vice versa. However, certain approaches in combination with skillful teaching may be more beneficial to certain students than others. We come again to the matter of individual needs, especially among poor readers.

16. Two problems may be involved in the failure of the four-year-old nursery school students to learn phonics: the teacher may be using an approach that is not well suited for them (such as deductive teaching of phonic generalizations) or the students may not have sufficient readiness for learning phonics. We would advise the nursery school teacher to administer a reading readiness test to her students. If their performance on the test indicates sufficient readiness to learn phonics, she might invite a reading specialist to examine the instructional materials she is using and to observe her teaching practices. We suspect that most of the nursery school students will profit more from readiness activities, developing sight vocabularies, and reading language experience stories than from structured phonics instruction.

17. Before the pediatrician's question can be answered, her definition of dyslexia must be ascertained. If the pediatrician wants to know the percentage of students reading below grade level, that information should be available from districtwide standardized test results. If the pediatrician wants to know the number of seriously disabled readers whose problem is suspected to be the result of minimal brain dysfunction, other sources of information will have to be consulted or collected.

We are aware of estimates that 10 to 20 percent of the school population suffers from a serious reading disability that results from a developmental lag in the central nervous system or from a central nervous system dysfunction that manifests itself in reading, spelling, and penmanship disorders. Our experience suggests that if such a condition exists, its incidence is much lower than 10 percent. We know of no school districts that have made systematic studies of the incidence of classic dyslexia (specific reading disability). Perhaps such studies are needed so that people who ask this kind of question can be given a response based upon systematic investigation rather than upon biased estimates.

18. The salesperson should send us the data upon which the claims for the new program are based and a sample set of the program materials. If data are not available, we would like a sample set of the program materials anyway.

365

19. The concept of a neurological lag as a factor in reading retardation implies a postponement of remedial instruction. Since
the concept is controversial, we think it advisable that remedial
reading teachers, who are trained and hired to work with perplexing problems, look elsewhere for explanations of instructional failure. The teacher who phoned needs another reading
specialist to help her assess the problem. Working together, they
may uncover some factor that suggests more positive action than
a neurological maturational lag suggests.

20. Reading improvement is more likely to have a positive effect on writing ability than the reverse. However, the English
teacher who phoned should be encouraged to do some classroom
research on the question. A simple experiment could be designed
that included a reading test given to a group of poor readers
before and after some intensive instruction in written composition. Teachers who speculate about ways to help poor readers
should be helped to test their theories unless their theories are il-
logical or seem likely to be harmful to students.

Response 5

Our counterarguments and concluding statement for problem 5
follow.

COUNTERARGUMENTS

1. Asking a teacher to provide a curriculum for a class that includes poor readers, average readers, and superior readers is
unrealistic. Individualization is easier, not harder, when the
range of abilities within a class is decreased. Poor readers are in
fact more alike than unlike in their skills needs; they need more
help with almost every skill.

2. Good teachers will form groups within the class of poor
readers. Poor readers vary in regard to the severity of their retardation. Assigning all poor readers to one class does not preclude
grouping within that class and movement from group to group.
Besides, skillful, sensitive teachers can help a child make the
transition to a different class and a different teacher without
undue upset. The opportunity to move upward may be a rewarding and motivating experience for a child.

3. The teacher can read to the children every day. Phonograph
records and audio tapes featuring good readers to follow along

with or listen to are easy to obtain, and the children will be able to hear their more able classmates reading in their other classes.

4. Heterogeneous grouping around interest themes is a good activity for the content areas. The purpose of a reading class is to teach children reading skills, not to entertain them.

5. Information about a child's reading can be easily communicated among teachers. If communication channels are poor in a particular school, then content area teachers can give the students in their classes to whom they do not teach reading an informal reading inventory periodically to stay abreast of their reading growth and needs.

CONCLUDING STATEMENT

The arguments for intraclass grouping seem stronger to us, although good counterarguments can be given. Improved assessment instruments and procedures, improved instructional materials, and improved teacher education programs (both pre-service and in-service) allow teachers to teach reading to students with a wide range of abilities in one class, thereby eliminating the dangers inherent in tracking students in the elementary grades.

Response 6

Our scores for suggestions for reading consultants in problem 6 follow in Table 12.2.

Response 7

Our responses to the five questions asked in problem 7 follow.

1. We think this principal is realistic and honest. We hope he or she also has the energy and commitment to carry through with this plan. Its success will depend upon the rapport and working relationship this principal has with the teaching staff. We're assuming this principal has the personal characteristics of a first-rate instructional leader.

2. The answer to this question depends much upon the relationship this principal has developed with his or her staff. If the principal had the respect of the staff, we think many teachers would be inspired. They might be a bit skeptical too, but the implementation would eliminate the skepticism.

Table 12.2 **Sources for reading consultants in terms of their
potential for helping teachers improve their
teaching.**

Suggestion no.	Score for elementary [a]	Score for secondary [a]
1	3	3
2	3	3
3	5	3
4	5	5
5	4	5
6	4	4
7	3	3
8	5	5
9	4	3
10	5	3
11	4	3
12	4	3
13	4	3
14	3	3
15	5	5
16	3	3
17	3	4
18	3	4
19	4	4
20	5	5

[a] The potential of each suggestion depends greatly upon individual
school conditions. All the suggestions warrant consideration.

3. We would be pleased. The principal has not eliminated
help from outside sources. However, resource people from outside the staff will be given direction for any help they are asked
to give. Resource people find it difficult to satisfy vague or broad
requests for assistance, such as, "Would you come out and tell us
how to improve comprehension?"

4. Hooray! Nothing is better for program improvement than a
principal and a staff actively engaged in self-evaluation and self-
improvement.

Response 8

Our letter to "Can't Sleep Nights" follows.

Dear Can't Sleep Nights:
    Relax, teacher. Your insomnia isn't going to help those "poor
kids." And since your first teaching job didn't prepare you very

well for your new position, neither will your two years' teaching experience. You're in a new ball game, Teach, so you'd better learn a few new rules:

1. Never go into a job with the kind of attitude reflected in your letter. You're making excuses for hitting into a double play, and you haven't come to bat yet. You've made some assumptions that are unwarranted: (a) you're a successful teacher (the proof of the pudding lies in teaching students who aren't in the top group how to read), (b) "plowing through material" leads to the development of reading maturity, (c) using a tri-basal approach with a heterogeneous ability group is a "dark ages" approach, and (d) your methods teacher or teachers had you copy into your class notes everything there is to know. Look upon your new job as a challenge with many opportunities for you and your students to grow, not as a penance levied by know-nothing administrators.

2. Find out if the classroom teachers in your new school have access to a reading consultant who can help you group your students and plan for the first two or three weeks of school. If no consultant is available, seek the advice of a teacher in your building. Be honest about your lack of training and experience for teaching a class with a wide range of abilities. If the first teacher you ask for help is no more help than your principal, try another teacher, and another if need be.

3. Dig out your old reading methods textbook. Read again the chapters on assessing students' needs, grouping students and individualizing reading instruction. You may even find some mention of the tri-basal approach, which means only that you group your students into three ability groups and use a different series with each group.

4. Most teachers have considerable autonomy in regard to how they teach. The school may purport to use a tri-basal approach, but you probably won't find two teachers teaching exactly alike. After you get to know your students, your fellow teachers, your reading consultant (if there is one available to you), and your principal better than you know them now, you'll probably learn that the system is not so rigid as it seems now and that your attempts to improve upon it will be welcomed.

Pleasant Dreams

Response 9

Our evaluation of the proposal for a reading-language arts learning center in problem 9 follows.

We think the proposal has a number of strengths, among them:

1. The students for whom the center is intended are clearly specified.
2. Students would receive half of their instructional program in their regular schools.
3. Parents are clearly acknowledged in the stated goals of the center.
4. Reading would be taught in a language arts context with concern for teaching students to value reading.
5. The center would bring classroom teachers and learning disabilities teachers together.
6. The center would provide in-service education for teachers, as well as remedial instruction for students.
7. The criteria for enrollment in the center and for cessation of enrollment seem sound and are clearly delineated.
8. The evaluation of each student's growth would be determined by a bank of data.
9. The executive secretary would permit the master teachers to devote all of their time to instructional matters.

Some potential problems are transportation to and from the center and the per pupil cost of instruction. If we were in a position to release funds for a program to assist seriously disabled readers, however, we would be inclined to fund the proposed center on a three-year experimental basis.

Response 10

Our plan in response to the superintendent's memo in problem 10 follows.

We are aware of the questionable validity and reliability of standardized reading achievement tests. However, we agree with the superintendent that scores on these tests are, for good or bad, very highly regarded and carefully scrutinized by parents and other community members interested in how tax dollars are spent for schools. Therefore, standardized reading achievement tests cannot be disregarded because of the criticism leveled against them by experts in the measurement of reading achievement, regardless of how justified that criticism is.

We suggest the following plan:

1. No formal reading achievement tests except on an individual student basis for specified reasons before the end of third grade.

2. Reports for all students of the results of informal testing by classroom teachers at the end of first grade and the end of second grade. The reports should include the following information about each student's reading with the materials being used for instructional purposes:

   a. The difficulty level (primer, first reader) of material that can be be read orally at the independent level (that is, no more than one uncorrected error per each hundred words).

   b. The characteristic oral reading errors in material slightly more difficult than material at the independent level (for example, omissions, substitutions, mispronunciations, lack of expression).

   c. The difficulty level of material that can be read silently at the independent level (student answers three or four comprehension questions correctly after reading a passage of approximately a hundred words with no prereading assistance).

   d. The difficulty level of material that the student can read and recall with good accuracy without any question prompts (unaided recall of a passage of approximately a hundred words).

3. Standardized reading achievement tests administered at the end of the third grade, at the end of the last grade in the student's elementary school experience, at the end of the last grade of the student's middle school experience, and at the beginning or middle of grade 12. (A test administered at the end of grade 12 might be a better reflection of "senioritis" than of reading ability.)

We would prefer that the standardized tests that are given all be from the same series of tests so that the philosophy of the authors and editors of the testing program is consistently reflected throughout the testing program.

We would also urge all teachers, reading specialists, and principals to collect, display, and discuss with interested parents tangible products that reflect students' reading growth (for example, tape-recorded play reading, book reports, illustrations of books, taped discussions of books featuring student readers, taped examples of good oral reading performances). Standardized reading achievement test scores tell only part of the story. Many times examples of students' performances with other kinds of reading ac-

tivities can be used to give parents a better picture of the effectiveness of the school's instructional reading programs.

Response 11

Our responses to the three questions at the end of Problem 11
follow. We have an advantage over our readers because we know
how the principals who heard the speech responded.

1. The principals were generally informed, inspired, and entertained. In a postworkshop evaluation, they gave this talk high
marks.

2. We find the direct approach, the general tone, the humor,
and the specificity of the message to be especially praiseworthy.

3. We find no fault. We think the speaker accepted a difficult
challenge and got the workshop off to a good start. How many
principals followed through on the suggestions and how successful they were is not known.

Smith, Richard J., Wayne Otto, and Kathleen Harty. "Elementary Teachers' Preferences for Preservice and Inservice Training in the Teaching of Reading." *The Journal of Educational Research* 63 (July–August 1970): 445–449.

Appendix

List of skills and objectives

This list of skills and objectives relates to the discussion in chapter 3. We have found variations of the list to be useful in our attempts to develop workable approaches to teaching the basic reading skills. The skills covered are basic to success in reading; thus the list (and variations of it) has proved useful for developmental programs at the elementary school level and for corrective/remedial programs at the secondary and adult levels. We offer the list as an example of what a reasonably definitive list might be like. Any list must, of course, be adapted for use in a given situation.

Teachers and administrators should find the list useful as a starting point for building a skill base for their local reading programs. Students of reading instruction will benefit from doing a careful critique of the list, considering such matters as the following:

1. Which of the skills/objectives—if any—appear to be essential to success in reading? Which are desirable but optional? Which appear to be superfluous or inappropriate for certain settings?
2. Given the skill list, are the objectives realistic? That is, are the outcomes observable and assessable; in effect, are the skills teachable insofar as demonstration of the outcome is possible?
3. What additional skills should be brought to the list to round out the important aspects of reading instruction or to meet specific needs?

Teachers can use the list just as it is to organize instructional materials, to devise record-keeping systems, and/or to build a systematic approach to skill assessment.

In short, the list may be perused as an example of a skill list that has had considerable input from practitioners, it can be critiqued as a starter list and adapted for local use, or it can be accepted and used as it is. Its potential uses are as extensive as the inclinations and the creativity of the users.

Characteristics of the list

The list has certain characteristics that reflect the opinions, beliefs, and concerns discussed in the first section of chapter 3.

1. "Reading" is rather broadly defined, with skills identified in six areas: word attack, study skills, comprehension, self-directed reading, interpretive reading, and creative reading.
2. Prescriptive objectives are stated for all of the skills in the word attack, study skills, and comprehension areas. The objectives for the self-directed reading, interpretive reading, and creative reading areas are merely descriptive.
3. The skills for each area are clustered at three to seven levels that correspond roughly to traditional grade levels, as shown in Table A.1. The clusters are tied to grade levels only because the grade-level referent has meaning for most teachers and in relation to many instructional materials and activities. Of course, the rate of any individual progress should be determined by performance, not grade in school.
4. Word attack objectives are limited to the first four levels only because we feel that those skills should be taught before the end of the primary experience.
5. The prescriptive objectives are stated at a mid-level of specificity.
6. The prescriptive objectives do not set a competence level of performance.

Table A.1 **Skills by area and by level**

Area	K	1	2	3	4	5	6
				Traditional grade level			
Word attack skills	A	B	C	D	–	–	–
Study skills	A	B	C	D	E	F	G
Comprehension skills	A	B	C	D	E	F	G
Self-directed reading		A–C			D–E		F–G
Interpretive reading		A–C			D–E		F–G
Creative reading		A–C			D–E		F–G

Word attack skills and objectives

LEVEL A. THE CHILD . . .

1. Listens for rhyming elements: words.
   Objective: Given familiar words pronounced by the teacher, the child indicates which of three word rhymes with a stimulus word or tells whether two words rhyme.
2. Listens for rhyming elements: phrases and verses.
   Objective: In real or nonsense verses read by the teacher, the child supplies the missing words in a couplet (for example, The little red hen/Lived in a ————) or identifies the rhyming words.
3. Notes likenesses and differences: pictures (shapes).
   Objective: The child identifies shapes that are the same or different in form and/or orientation.
4. Notes likenesses and differences: letters and shapes.
   Objective: The child selects the letter (upper or lower case) or number in a series that is identical to a key letter or number.
5. Notes likenesses and differences: words and phrases.
   Objective: The child selects the word or phrase in a series that is identical to a stimulus word or phrase (for example, *down:* wand, down, bone, find).
6. Listens for initial consonant sounds.
   Objective: Given familiar words pronounced by the teacher, the child indicates which of three words begins with the same consonant sound as the target word.

LEVEL B. THE CHILD . . .

1. Has a sight-word vocabulary.
   Objective: Given a maximum one-second exposure per word, the child recognizes selected words from a high-frequency word list.
2. Follows left-to-right sequence.
   Objective: The child reacts to number or letter stimuli in a left-to-right sequence.
3. Has phonic analysis skills: beginning consonant sounds.
   Objective: Given real or nonsense words supplied by the teacher, the child identifies the letter that stands for the initial sound and tells whether two words begin alike; or supplies another word that begins with the same sound.
4. Has phonic analysis skills: ending consonant sounds.
   Objective: Given real or nonsense words pronounced by the teacher, the child identifies the letter that stands for the ending sound and tells whether two words end alike; or supplies another word that ends with the same sound.

5. Has phonic analysis skills: beginning consonant blends.
   Objective: Given real or nonsense words that begin with the consonant blends *pl, gl, tr, fr, sl, br, dr, gr, pr, cr, fl, cl, bl,* the child identifies the two letters that stand for the initial blend in words pronounced by the teacher; or identifies words that begin with the same blend as a stimulus word pronounced by the teacher and pronounces words that begin with the blends listed above.
6. Has phonic analysis skills: rhyming elements.
   Objective: Given a word, the child selects a rhyming word based on structure (for example, *man, pan,* and *fan* are from the same word family), or supplies a real or nonsense word based on structure.
7. Has phonic analysis skills: short vowels.
   Objective: Given one-syllable words with a single short-vowel sound pronounced by the teacher (for example, man, duck, doll), the child identifies the letter that stands for the vowel sound or reproduces the vowel sound.
8. Has phonic analysis skills: simple consonant digraphs.
   Objective: Given real or nonsense words pronounced by the teacher, the child identifies the letters in the simple two-consonant combinations *ch, th, sh, wh* that result in a single new sound.
9. Has structural analysis skills: compound words.
   Objective: The child identifies compound words or specifies the elements of a compound word.
10. Has structural analysis skills: contractions.
    Objective: The child identifies simple contractions (for example, I'm, it's, can't) and uses them correctly in sentences.
11. Has structural analysis skills: base words and endings.
    Objective: The child identifies the root word in familiar inflected words (for example, *jump*ing, *catch*es, *run*s).
12. Has structural analysis skills: plurals.
    Objective: The child tells whether familiar words (noun plus *s* or *es*) are singular or plural.
13. Has structural analysis skills: possessive forms.
    Objective: The child identifies the possessive forms of nouns used in context.

LEVEL C. THE CHILD . . .

1. Has a sight vocabulary.
   Objective: Given a maximum one-second exposure per word, the child recognizes selected words from a high-frequency word list.

2. Has phonic analysis skills: consonants and their variant
   sounds.
   Objective: Given words containing variant sounds of *s, c,*
   and *g* (for example, *s*it-trees, *c*ake-*c*ity, *g*o-*g*iant), the child indicates whether the italicized letters in given pairs of words
   have the same sounds.

3. Has phonic analysis skills: beginning consonant blends.
   Objective: Given real or nonsense words beginning with the
   consonant blends *st, sk, sm, sp, sw, sn, sc,* the child identifies
   the two letters that stand for the initial blend in words pronounced by the teacher; or identifies words that begin with
   the same blend as a stimulus word pronounced by the
   teacher and pronounces words that begin with the blends
   listed above.

4. Has phonic analysis skills: long vowel sounds.
   Objective: The child identifies the letter that stands for the
   single vowel sound in real or nonsense words pronounced by
   the teacher (for example, *nose, bribe, cheese, seat, labe*) and indicates whether the sound is long or short; or pronounces
   real or nonsense words with a single vowel sound.

5. Has phonic analysis skills: vowel plus *r*.
   Objective: The child identifies the vowel that is with *r* in real
   or nonsense words pronounced by the teacher (for example,
   dearl, der, mur, form); or pronounces words with *r*-con-
   trolled vowels (for example, part, for, hurt, bird).

6. Has phonic analysis skills: *a* plus *l*.
   Objective: The child identifies the letters that stand for the *al*
   sound in real or nonsense words pronounced by the teacher
   or pronounces words in which there is an *al* combination (for
   example, salt, ball, yall).

7. Has phonic analysis skills: *a* plus *w*.
   Objective: The child identifies the letters that stand for the
   aw sound in real or nonsense words pronounced by the
   teacher or pronounces words in which there is an *aw* combination (for example, draw, saw, blaw).

8. Has phonic analysis skills: diphthongs.
   Objective: Given words containing *oi, oy, ou, ow, ew,* the
   child identifies the diphthong in nonsense words pronounced by the teacher or pronounces words containing the
   diphthongs.

9. Has phonic analysis skills: long and short *oo*.
   Objective: The child indicates whether the *oo* in words has
   the long (for example, choose) or the short (for example,
   book) sound or pronounces words in which there is an *oo*
   combination.

10. Has phonic analysis skills: short vowel generalization.
Objective: Given real or nonsense words in which there is a single vowel and a final consonant (for example, bag, his, cat, gum), the child tells whether the real words are pronounced according to the generalization or pronounces the words, giving the vowel its short sound.

11. Has phonic analysis skills: silent *e* generalization.
Objective: Given real or nonsense words that have two vowels, one of which is a final *e* separated from the first vowel by a consonant (for example, cake, tube, mape, jome), the child tells whether the real words are pronounced according to the generalization or attempts pronunciation by making the first vowel long and the final *e* silent.

12. Has phonic analysis skills: two-vowels-together generalization.
Objective: Given real or nonsense words that have two consecutive vowels, the child tells whether the real words are pronounced according to the generalization or attempts pronunciation by making the first vowel long and the second vowel silent.

13. Has phonic analysis skills: final vowel generalization.
Objective: Given real or nonsense words in which the only vowel is at the end (for example, go, she, thi), the child tells whether the words are pronounced according to the generalization or attempts pronunciation by making the first vowel long and the second vowel silent.

14. Has phonic analysis skills: common consonant digraphs.
Objective: Given real or nonsense words pronounced by the teacher, the child identifies the letters in the two-consonant combinations *ch, th, sh, wh, ph, nk, ng, gh, ck* that result in a single new sound.

15. Has structural analysis skills: base words with prefixes and suffixes.
Objective: The child selects base (root) words with or without affixes that are appropriate to the context.

16. Has structural analysis skills: more difficult plural forms.
Objective: The child tells whether more difficult plural forms (for example, mice, children, ladies) are singular or plural.

17. Distinguishes among homonyms.
Objective: Given a sentence context, the child chooses between homonyms (for example, Mother bought some *meet/meat* for dinner).

18. Distinguishes among synonyms and antonyms.
Objective: The child tells whether words in a pair have the same, opposite, or different meanings.

379

19. Applies independent and varied word attack skills.
    Objective: In both self-directed and teacher-directed reading, the child uses a variety of skills (for example, picture clues, context clues, structural analysis, sound/symbol analysis, comparison of new to known words) in attacking unknown words.

LEVEL D. THE CHILD . . .

1. Has a sight vocabulary.
   Objective: Given a maximum half-second exposure per word, the child recognizes selected words from a high-frequency word list.
2. Has phonic analysis skills: three-letter consonant blends.
   Objective: The child identifies the letters in the three-letter blends *scr, shr, spl, str, thr* in real or nonsense words pronounced by the teacher.
3. Has phonic analysis skills: silent letters.
   Objective: Given words containing silent letters (for example, knife, gnat, write), the child identifies the silent letters or pronounces words containing silent letters.
4. Has structural analysis skills: syllabication.
   Objective: The child divides words into single-vowel sound units by applying syllabication generalizations.
5. Has structural analysis skills: accent.
   Objective: The child indicates the accented part (syllable) in familiar words, primarily two-syllable ones.
6. Has phonic analysis skills: the *schwa*.
   Objective: Given words that he or she knows, the child identifies the syllable containing a *schwa* sound; given unfamiliar words, the child used the *schwa* sound when sounding.
7. Has structural analysis skills: possessive forms.
   Objective: The child identifies possessive nouns and pronouns used in context.

Study skills and objectives

The skills identified here fall mainly into three categories: map skills, graph and table skills, and reference skills.

LEVEL A. THE CHILD . . .

1. Describes position of objects.
   Objective: The child is able to describe or respond to descrip-

tions of the positions of objects in his or her environment in relation to himself or herself by using the following terms: up-down, on, between, near (beside), behind-in front of (front-back), below-above (over-under).

2. Describes relative size.

Objective: The child is able to use descriptive terms (for example, bigger-smaller, taller-shorter, lower-higher) to express comparisons of the size of objects in his environment.

3. Determines relative distance.

Objective: The child is able to use descriptive terms (for example, closer-farther, long way-short way) to express comparisons of distance in the environment.

4. Follows simple directions.

Objective: The child is able to perform the actions in simple one- and two-stage directions (for example, "Mark an X in the middle of your paper," "Please come and take one of these boxes of paper shapes to your work area").

5. Is able to remember details.

Objective: The child is able to remember sufficient details from an oral presentation (for example, a story or show-and-tell) to respond to questions (for example, four questions about specific facts based on a hundred-word presentation) and/or from an event he or she is describing to give an intelligible account of what happened.

6. Has attention and concentration span suitable for his or her ability.

Objective: The child is able to demonstrate active participation in classroom listening situations by attending an oral presentation and responding appropriately (for example, follows directions, reacts with relevant questions, and/or makes contributions).

7. Has beginning of independent work habits.

Objective: The child shows independence in assigned work by asking questions that are necessary for clarification of the task, not asking attention-seeking questions once the task is understood, keeping the necessary tools (for example, pencil, paper, crayons, scissors, etc.) at hand, accepting responsibility for completion of quality of work, and pacing himself or herself to complete a task acceptably in the allotted time.

8. Has basic book-handling skills.

Objective: The child demonstrates basic book skills by selecting books appropriate to his or her interests and ability level, handling books reasonably (for example, right-side-up, from front to back), and referring to books by their main character or subject (for example, "the book about the butterflies").

9. Is familiar with procedures within the library (book table,
book corner, etc.).
Objective: The child locates groups of books appropriate to
his needs and is able to check books in and out of the collection.

LEVEL B. THE CHILD . . .

1. Identifies representational relationships.
Objective: The child is able to place three-dimensional representations of objects to reflect their actual locations in the environment (for example, place blocks that represent houses on a large floor map, build models in a sand box).
2. Locates objects in relation to other objects.
Objective: The child is able to describe or respond to descriptions of the positions of objects and representations in the following terms: right-left, up-down, on, between near (beside), behind-in front of (back-front), below-above (over-under).
3. Locates points in relation to a simple picture grid.
Objective: Given axis and coordinate referents, the child is able to locate points and describe the location of points in relation to a simple picture grid.
4. Describes relative size.
Objective: The child is able to use descriptive terms (for example, bigger-smaller, taller-shorter, lower-higher) to express comparisons of size of representations of objects (for example, scale models, pictures).
5. Determines relative distance.
Objective: The child is able to use descriptive terms (for example, closer-farther, long way-short way) to express comparisons of distance in representations of objects (for example, sand box, pictures).
6. Interprets picture graphs.
Objective: Given a simple vertical picture graph in which each symbol represents a single object and there are no more than three to five columns of pictures, the child is able to determine the purpose of the graph, compare relative amounts, and extract information from the graph.
7. Interprets single-column tables.
Objective: Given a single-column table containing three to five rows, the child is able to determine the purpose of the table, locate a particular cell within the table, and use the table to compare relative amounts.

8. Follows oral directions given to a group.
   Objective: The child is able to follow two-stage oral directions when the directions are administered to a group (ten or more pupils), of which the child is a part.
9. Follows oral directions given individually.
   Objective: The child is able to perform the actions in two-stage directions that require some judgment when the directions are given directly to him or her.
10. Follows written directions.
    Objective: The child is able to follow a series of three to four brief written directions.
11. Begins locational skills (letters and digits).
    Objective: The child is able to indicate the correct symbol when letters and digits are presented orally and match capital and other allographs of one letter.
12. Expands book skills.
    Objective: The child demonstrates expanded book skills by continuing to select appropriate books, beginning to identify books by their titles, and using the table of contents in textbooks.
13. Expands use of the library.
    Objective: The child demonstrates expanded use of the library by using more materials, such as picture dictionaries, asking for help in finding books about a specific subject, continuing to observe local rules, and attempting to apply other skills (for example, locating a book in the card catalog by title).
14. Uses a picture dictionary for spelling new words.
    Objective: The child is sufficiently familiar with a picture dictionary to locate the spelling of words, which you pronounce orally.
15. Arranges pictures and words in sequence.
    Objective: The child can recreate the sequence of a story or event by arranging pictures or by arranging key words in order (for example, *The Three Bears:* "hot-bears walk-Goldilocks-breakfast-chairs-beds-bears come home").
16. Classifies ideas.
    Objective: Given five ideas or facts, the child is able to determine which are relevant to a given topic.

LEVEL C. THE CHILD . . .

1. Uses realistic picture symbols to interpret maps.
   Objective: The child is able to use realistic pictures to derive information from maps.

2. Uses semipictorial symbols to interpret maps.

 Objective: The child is able to use semipictorial symbols, which are explained in a key (legend), to derive information from maps.

3. Uses color key to interpret maps.

 Objective: The child is able to use distinct colors (for example, brown, red, yellow, blue), which are explained in a key, to derive qualitative information from different maps (for example, blue may denote water, grocery stores, or parks on different maps).

4. Locates points in relation to a simple grid.

 Objective: The child is able to locate points and describe the location of points in relation to a simple street grid.

5. Indicates cardinal directions on a globe.

 Objective: The child is able to indicate on a globe: north and south with reference to the North Pole, South Pole, and the equator and east and west with reference to north-south.

6. Interprets relative size.

 Objective: The child is able to interpret the relative size of areas in semipictorial maps (for example, lakes, parks, forests).

7. Expresses relative distance.

 Objective: The child is able to use familiar nonstandard units of measurement (for example, blocks, houses) to express distance and comparisons of distance on semipictorial maps.

8. Has picture graph skills.

 Objective: Give horizontal picture graph in which each symbol represents more than one unit (between two and ten), the child is able to determine the purpose, compare relative amounts, extract directly, and determine differences between numbers extracted.

9. Has bar graph skills.

 Objective: Given a vertical bar graph with one group of bars and a small interval on the coordinate (two to ten), the child is able to determine the purpose of the graph by examining its title and contents, compare relative amounts (for example, most-least, taller-shorter), and determine the exact amount represented by each.

10. Interprets multicolumn tables.

 Objective: Given a simple, multicolumn table with from two to four rows and columns, the child is able to determine the purpose, locate a cell, compare relative amounts in a single dimension, and determine relationships among cells.

11. Shows increasing independence in work.

 Objective: The child shows independence and acceptance of responsibility by asking the questions required to clarify a task, keeping the materials required to complete a task available and organized, showing an awareness of a standard or general quality in assigned work, and pacing himself or herself to complete assigned tasks in the time allotted.

12. Groups and orders words by initial letters.

    Objective: The child is able to group words by their initial letters, order words by their initial letter, and choose appropriate encyclopedia volumes by letter (for example, "Look in the *E* volume for information about elephants").

13. Expands book skills.

    Objective: The child demonstrates expanded book skills by identifying books by their titles, finding the title page in a book, associating authors with books, finding the author's name on the title page, locating the table of contents in a book, and locating the index in a book.

14. Expands use of library.

    Objective: The child is able to find easy books for independent reading, locate fiction books by the author's last name, locate nonfiction books, encyclopedias, and dictionaries, and ask for assistance in using the card catalog.

15. Begins to use reference materials.

    Objective: The child is able to select pictures appropriate to a given topic from a picture file, differentiate in his or her use of encyclopedias and dictionaries, use encyclopedias for browsing, and use some nonfiction materials as authoritative sources.

16. Reads to find answers; takes notes.

    Objective: The child is able to read for answers to direct questions and take simple notes to answer the questions at a later time (two to three days).

17. Keeps simple reading record.

    Objective: The child is able to list the titles of books consulted about a given topic.

18. Recognizes organization of ideas in sequential order.

    Objective: The child is able to recognize sequential relationships among two or three ideas.

19. Begins to make judgments and draw conclusions.

    Objective: Given facts, the child is able to respond correctly to questions requiring that he or she make judgments and draw conclusions on the basis of the facts presented.

LEVEL D. THE CHILD . . .

1. Uses a key containing nonpictorial symbols to interpret maps.

Objective: The child is able to use a key containing nonpictorial symbols (for example, lines, dots) to derive information from maps.

2. Uses a color key to interpret maps.

Objective: The child is able to use a color key (in which colors identify classes, and no more than three shades of any color identify subclasses) to derive information from maps (for example, the child reports that there are two areas of marshland—light blue—and one area of swamp—dark blue.

3. Locates points on a number-letter grid.

Objective: The child is able to locate points and describe the location of points on a number-letter grid.

4. Determines cardinal directions on globes, in the environment, and on maps.

Objective: The child is able to determine cardinal directions to describe relative location of two points on globes, in the environment, and on maps and relate the location of points in the environment (for example, the child matches objects pictured on a map with objects in the environment to determine direction).

5. Uses scale to determine whole units of distance.

Objective: The child is able to use a scale bar referent or verbal referent (for example, 1 inch = X standard units of measure) to compare and determine distances between points one or more referent units apart when one referent unit equals one standard unit of measure, and one referent unit apart when one referent unit equals more than one standard unit of measure.

6. Has picture graph skills.

Objective: Given a picture graph in which each symbol represents more than one unit (for example, two, ten, twenty), the child is able to determine the purpose, compare relative amounts, extract directly, determine differences between numbers extracted, and make a summary statement of the data presented (for example, from a graph showing the number of ships built in various countries, the child concludes which country is the major source of production).

7. Has bar graph skills.

Objective: Given a horizontal or vertical bar graph that has one group of bars and a small interval (for example, two, ten, twenty), the child is able to determine the purpose, compare relative amounts, extract directly, determine differences between numbers extracted, and make a summary statement.

8. Has circle graph skills.

Objective: Given a circle graph with from two to four divisions, the child is able to determine the purpose and compare relative amounts.

9. Interprets multicolumn tables.

   Objective: Given a multicolumn table with from five to eight rows and columns, familiar units for denominate numbers (explained in a key), and/or totals included for each column and row, the child is able to determine the purpose, locate a cell, compare relative amounts in a single dimension, determine relationships among cells, and make a summary statement.

10. Follows oral or written directions independently.

    Objective: The child is able to remember and follow a series of directions in sequence and generalize from directions for one task to a similar task.

11. Begins to do research assignments independently.

    Objective: The child shows independence or acceptance of responsibility by working independently on assigned projects and pacing himself or herself to complete long-term tasks in the time allotted.

12. Applies basic alphabetizing skills.

    Objective: The child is able to alphabetize words by first and second letters and locate words in dictionaries and encyclopedias.

13. Uses guide words in encyclopedias and dictionaries.

    Objective: The child is able to locate the appropriate alphabetical section of a reference book for a given topic or target word by attending to the alphabetic section of a reference book for a given topic or target word by attending to the alphabetic sequence of guide words.

14. Uses see references in encyclopedias.

    Objective: The child locates the topic referred in response to a see reference (for example, having located "Plains Indians. See Indian, American," the child locates the topic referred).

15. Uses table of contents.

    Objective: The child refers to the table of contents to determine if a book is relevant to his or her specific purpose (for example, interest, research topic) and/or locates a particular chapter or section in a book.

16. Uses glossary.

    Objective: The child locates and uses the glossary in a book, rather than a dictionary, to look up the meaning(s) of words as they are used in the context of the book (he or she finds new meanings for familiar words and unfamiliar words as they are used in a given context or subject area).

17. Begins to use indexes.

    Objective: Having identified a general topic, the child uses the indexes of books to locate information about the topic.

18. Uses study aids in textbooks.

    Objective: The child finds and uses such study aids as bold-face type, italics, and/or marginal notes in textbooks.

19. Expands use of library.

    Objective: The child is able to locate magazines and nonfiction books relevant to his or her interests and assigned work and continues to attempt higher-level skills. (for example, using the card catalog with the assistance of the librarian).

20. Begins to expand use of reference materials.

    Objective: The child will independently seek additional reference sources if the first source consulted does not give sufficient information, and/or pursue an interest aroused by initial stimulation (for example, having found a picture of an igloo in the dictionary, the child consults the encyclopedia to learn about the construction of igloos).

21. Begins to adjust reading rate to material.

    Objective: The child skims materials at a rapid rate when seeking to verify or locate specific information (for example, a date, a name).

22. Uses headings and subheadings.

    Objective: Having located a topic in a reference book, the child uses the format of the material to search efficiently for target information.

23. Recognizes that printed statements may be fact or opinion.

    Objective: The child is able to make a considered decision as to whether given statements represent fact or opinion.

24. Evaluates relevance of materials.

    Objective: Given an assigned list of topics, the child is able to choose from among available sources those that are likely to include relevant information on specific topics.

25. Checks accuracy of statements.

    Objective: The child is able to identify discrepancies between simple factual data from two sources (for example, the number of parks in a city).

LEVEL E. THE CHILD . . .

1. Uses point and line symbols to interpret maps.

    Objective: The child is able to use point and line symbols (for example, circle of different sizes, lines of different widths) to derive qualitative and quantitative information from maps (for example, the child identifies the largest city on a map as the one represented by the largest circle).

2. Applies rectangular grid to earth's sphere.

   Objective: The child is able to use lines of latitude as referents for describing general locations (for example, north of equator) and lines of longitude as referents for describing general locations (for example, west of prime meridian).

3. Determines intermediate directions on globes, in the environment, and on maps.

   Objective: The child is able to determine intermediate directions to describe relative location to two points on globes, in the environment, and on maps and to relate the location of points on globes and maps to the location of points in the environment (for example, the child matches objects pictured on a map with objects in his environment to determine direction).

4. Makes limited use of scale to determine distance.

   Objective: The child is able to use a scale bar referent or verbal referent (for example, 1 inch $= X$ standard units of measure) to compare and determine distances between points one or more referent units apart when one referent unit equals two or more standard units of measure (for example, when 1 inch $= 3$ miles, the child concludes that 3 inches $= 9$ miles).

5. Has picture graph skills.

   Objective: Given a picture graph in which each symbol represents more than one unit (for example, two, ten, twenty) and half-symbols are used, the child is able to determine the purpose, compare relative amounts, extract directly, extract by interpolating, determine differences between numbers extracted, make a summary statement, and make projections and relate information.

6. Has bar graph skills.

   Objective: Given a horizontal or vertical bar graph that has one group of bars and a small interval (for example, ten or twenty), the child is able to determine the purpose, compare relative amounts, extract directly, extract by interpolating, determine differences between numbers extracted, make a summary statement, and make projections and relate information.

7. Interprets multicolumn tables.

   Objective: Given a complex multicolumn table with denominate numbers (explained in a key or the title) and/or totals included for each column and row, the child is able to determine the purpose, locate a cell, compare relative amounts in

389

a single dimension, determine relationships among cells, make summary statements, and make projections and relate information.

8. Has independent classroom and research work habits.
   Objective: The child is able to focus all previously mastered study skills in independent study and/or research.
9. Utilizes alphabetical system.
   Objective: The child is able to alphabetize words.
10. Uses guide words and guide letters.
    Objective: Given the guide words and page numbers from three to six pages in a reference book, the child is able to specify the page on which specific words could be found, and/or given the guide letters and drawer numbers of a card catalog, the child is able to specify the drawer in which specific words, names, or topics can be found.
11. Uses alphabet skills related to card catalog.
    Objective: For locating information in the card catalog, the child uses guide cards in the drawers to locate his or her target word quickly and ignores initial articles.
12. Refines use of indexes.
    Objective: Having identified or been given a general topic, the child uses the indexes of books or the index volume of an encyclopedia to locate specific information about subtopics, (for example, Space, Space travel: development of flight plan, history of).
13. Uses dictionaries independently.
    Objective: The child uses dictionaries to check the spelling and/or meaning of words.
14. Consults encyclopedias and atlases.
    Objective: The child locates information on one topical heading in more than one encyclopedia by adapting his or her locational skills to the idiosyncrasies of each set (for example, some have individual volume indexes, some have no indexes, some have a multivolume index) and maps in atlases.
15. Uses magazines and newspapers.
    Objective: The child selects magazines and newspapers as sources of current, topical information.
16. Uses selected specialized reference books.
    Objective: The child selects *World Almanac* and/or *Information Please Almanac,* or *Junior Book of Authors,* or a dictionary, or an encyclopedia, or an atlas, or a nonfiction book, whichever is most appropriate to answer specific questions.
17. Adjusts reading rate to difficulty.
    Objective: The child adjusts his or her reading rate appropriately as reading materials become more or less difficult as

purposes change. For example, the child reads a given type
of material (such as science material) written at his or her independent reading level of difficulty at a more rapid rate
(greater number of words per minute) than similar material
written at his or her instructional level of reading difficulty.

18. Adjusts reading rate to purpose.
    Objective: The child skims materials at a rapid rate when
    seeking to verify or locate specific information; reads material
    at a slower (but still rapid) rate when seeking an overview or
    general idea about content; and scans material at a relatively
    slow rate when his or her purpose is to master, locate to ver-
    ify, or recall factual information.

19. Has beginning outlining skills.
    Objective: Given the major points in a formal outline, the
    child is able to select and fill in second-order points from
    well-organized paragraphs written at his or her instructional
    level of difficulty.

20. Makes simple bibliographies.
    Objective: The child lists books he or she has consulted by
    author and title.

21. Evaluates information in terms of his or her own experience
    and/or known facts.
    Objective: The child relates new information to his or her
    personal experiences and/or known facts and evaluates both
    new information and the past experiences and knowledge in
    terms of the relationship.

LEVEL F. THE CHILD . . .

1. Uses point, line, and area symbols.
   Objective: The child is able to use point, line, and area symbols to derive qualitative and quantitative information from
   maps.

2. Has location skills.
   Objective: The child is able to use lines of latitude and longi-
   tude to locate points on a map or globe (for example, New
   York City is 40° north latitude and 74° west longitude).

3. Identifies differences among maps drawn to different scales.
   Objective: The child is able to identify differences (amount of
   detail) among maps of the same area drawn to different scales
   (for example, 1 inch = 1,000 miles, 1 inch = 100 miles, and 1
   inch = 50 miles).

4. Makes use of scale to determine distance.

391

Objective: The child is able to use a scale bar referent or verbal referent (for example, 1 inch = X standard units of measure) to compare and determine distances between points that are combinations of fractional and whole referent units apart when one referent unit equals two or more standard units of measure.

5. Has bar graph skills.

Objective: Given a horizontal or vertical bar graph with two groups of bars, the child is able to determine the purpose, compare relative amounts, extract directly, extract by interpolating, determine differences between numbers extracted, make a summary statement, and make projections and relate information.

6. Has circle graph skills.

Objective: Given a circle graph with four or more divisions, the child is able to determine the purpose, compare relative amounts, extract directly, and make a summary statement.

7. Has line graph skills.

Objective: Given a single line, noncumulative line graph, the child is able to determine the purpose, compare relative amounts, extract directly, extract by interpolating, determine differences between numbers extracted, make a summary statement, and make projections and relate information.

8. Interprets schedules.

Objective: Given a simple schedule (such as a boat or bus schedule), the child is able to determine the purpose, locate a cell, compare relative amounts in a single dimension, determine relationship among cells, and make a summary statement.

9. Has independent classroom and research work habits.

Objective: The child is able to focus all previously mastered study skills in independent study and/or research.

10. Refines card catalog skills.

Objective: The child is able to locate target card quickly by applying these filing rules: names beginning with either Mac or Mc are filed together as if all were spelled m-a-c; an abbreviated word (for example, Mr.) if filed as if it were spelled out; and numbers are filed as if they were spelled out.

11. Refines cross-references skills.

Objective: The child applies the cross-references skill described at Level D, Objective 14, to all types of reference books.

12. Expands facility in using library.

Objective: The child is able to locate any book or material by its call number and/or many subject areas by using the ten major groupings of the Dewey decimal system (000, general works; 100, philosophy; 200, religion; 300, social science;

400, language; 500, pure science; 600, technology; 700, art; 800, literature; 900, history).

13. Uses dictionaries for pronunciation.

Objective: The child is able to use the diacritical markings in a dictionary to interpret the pronunciation of unfamiliar words (for example, Charybdis, escutcheon, imbroglio).

14. Adjusts reading rate to difficulty.

Objective: The child adjusts his or her reading rate appropriately as reading materials become more or less difficult as purposes change. For example, the child reads a given type of material (for example, science material) written at his or her independent reading level of difficulty at a more rapid rate (greater number of words per minute) than similar material written at his or her instructional level of reading difficulty.

15. Adjusts reading rate to purpose.

Objective: The child skims materials at a rapid rate when seeking to verify or locate specific information; reads material at a slower (but still rapid) rate when seeking an overview or general idea about content; and scans material at a relatively slow rate when his or her purpose is to master or locate to verify and recall factual information.

16. Makes notes of main ideas and supporting facts.

Objective: The child is able to identify main ideas and supporting facts in a selection and make notes in his or her own words.

17. Summarizes materials.

Objective: The child is able to write concise summaries (for example, identify major issues or main points of view expressed, of expository materials).

LEVEL G. THE CHILD . . .

1. Identifies likenesses and differences between two or more areas.

Objective: The child is able to make comparisons of geographic areas in terms of topographic, climatic, political, and demographic information provided on maps.

2. Synthesizes information about an area.

Objective: The child is able to use a variety of maps (for example, topographic, climatic, political, demographic) of an area to determine specific characteristics. For example, the child infers that since a particular area has an average rainfall, gently rolling hills, and moderate climate, the occupations of the inhabitants may be mostly related to farming.

393

3. Uses meridians and parallels to determine directions on any projection.

   Objective: The child is able to use meridians and parallels to determine directions on any projection. For example, on an elliptical projection with the prime meridian at the center, the child traces the meridian from a given point to the pole to show north or south.

4. Locates the same point or cell on various projections.

   Objective: The child is able to locate the same point or cell on various projections (for example, polar, Mercator).

5. Uses inset maps to determine relative size of areas.

   Objective: The child is able to determine the relative size of two or more areas drawn to different scales by comparing the inset maps, which are drawn to the same scale. For example, the child determines that even though his or her maps of Rhode Island and Texas are the same size, Texas is indeed larger, since the area outlined on the inset map (which is of the United States) is much larger than that area outlined for Rhode Island.

6. Has bar graph skills.

   Objective: Given a horizontal or vertical bar graph with three or four groups of bars, the child is able to determine the purpose, compare relative amounts, extract directly, extract by interpolating, determine differences between numbers extracted, make a summary statement, and make projections and relate information.

7. Has line graph skills.

   Objective: Given a single or multiline cumulative or non-cumulative line graph, the child is able to determine the purpose, compare relative amounts, extract directly, extract by interpolating, determine differences between numbers extracted, make a summary statement, and make projections and relate information.

8. Interprets schedules.

   Objective: Given any schedule, the child is able to determine the purpose, locate a cell, compare relationships among cells, and make a summary statement.

9. Has independent classroom and research work habits.

   Objective: The child is able to focus all skills developed to this point on one problem and apply all relevant skills in all subject matter areas.

10. Increases understanding of Dewey decimal system.

    Objective: The child is able to locate numbers for sections more specific than the ten major groupings as his or her interests become more specialized (391, costumes; 394, holidays; 520, astronomy; 540, chemistry; 597, fish; 796, sports;

92 or B, biography; 917, travel in North America [information about states]; 970, Indians; 973, American history).

11. Expands use of reference materials to current periodical indexes.

    Objective: The child uses the *Subject Index to Children's Magazines* for locating materials in children's magazines and the *Abridged Reader's Guide* for locating material in general adult magazines.

12. Adjusts reading rate to difficulty.

    Objective: The child adjusts his or her reading rate appropriately as reading materials become more or less difficult as purposes change. For example, the child reads a given type of material (for example, science material) written at his or her independent reading level of difficulty at a more rapid rate (greater number of words per minute) than similar material written at his or her instructional level of reading difficulty.

13. Adjusts reading rate to purpose.

    Objective: The child skims materials at a rapid rate when seeking to verify or locate specific information; reads material at a slower (but still rapid) rate when seeking an overview or general idea regarding content; and scans material at a relatively slow rate when his or her purpose is to master or locate to verify and recall factual information.

14. Gains skill in note taking.

    Objective: The child is able to take notes from varied sources in a form that is useful to him or her and permits him or her to retrieve needed information.

15. Makes formal outlines.

    Objective: Given selections at his or her instructional level of difficulty, the child is able to select and order main points in a formal outline.

Comprehension skills and objectives

The skills identified here fall into four categories: word meanings skills—word parts and context clues; sentence meaning—details and paraphrase; passage meaning—central thought (main idea) and relationships/conclusions; and sequence.

LEVEL A. THE CHILD . . .

1. Derives meaning from passages.
   a. Identifies a topic: pictures.

395

Objective: Given three pictures, the child identifies the
picture that best illustrates the topic of an orally presented
passage with an organizer (topic sentence) and only relevant details (details that support or describe the general
topic).

b. Identifies descriptive relationships.

Objective: Given three pictures, the child identifies a picture that demonstrates synthesis of information given in
an orally presented statement of a descriptive relationship.

2. Determines sequence: first or last event.

Objective: The child identifies the pictured event that occurs
first or last in an orally presented selection.

LEVEL B. THE CHILD . . .

1. Derives meaning from sentences: notes detail.

Objective: Given a short written-oral selection of simple sentences, the child selects details: verbs, modifiers, direct objects, and objects of positional prepositions.

2. Derives meaning from passages.

a. Identifies a topic: explicit organizer.

Objective: The child identifies the topic of an orally presented passage with an organizer and only relevant details.

b. Identifies comparison/contrast relationships.

Objective: Given three pictures, the child identifies the
picture that demonstrates synthesis of information given
in an orally presented statement of a comparison/contrast
relationship.

3. Determines sequence.

a. Identifies event before.

Objective: Given an orally presented sentence containing
a "before" clause, the child determines the order of two
events.

b. Identifies event after.

Objective: Given an orally presented sentence containing
an "after" clause, the child determines the order of two
events.

LEVEL C. THE CHILD . . .

1. Derives meaning from sentences.

a. Notes detail.

Objective: Given a short written selection of simple positive and negative sentences, the child selects details: pronouns, indirect objects, objects of infinitives, and objects of directional prepositions.

b. Paraphrases negative and positive sentences.

Objective: The child is able to restate simple negative sentences in the negative and in the positive, plus simple positive sentences in the negative and in the positive by rearranging the order of words in the sentence and/or substituting for one or more words.

2. Derives meaning from passages.

a. Identifies a topic: implicit.

Objective: The child identifies the topic of a passage without an explicit organizer and only details relevant to the implicit topic.

b. Identifies cause-effect relationships.

Objective: Given a passage, the child determines whether a stated cause-effect relationship is correct on the basis of the cause-effect relationship given in the passage.

3. Determines sequence: calendar markers.

Objective: The child determines the order of two events in a sentence when the sequence is indicated by calendar markers (for example, today, yesterday, tomorrow, morning, afternoon, noon, night, names of days).

LEVEL D. THE CHILD . . .

1. Determines word meaning.

a. Identifies word parts: prefixes

Objective: The child recognizes that a prefix is a meaning-bearing unit that can modify the meaning of a word in one of the following ways: to signify range (for example, *ab-, ad-, en-, ex-, sub-, super-, inter-*); to indicate time (for example, *pre-, post-, re-*); to signify approval or support (for example, *com-, pro-,*); to signify opposition (for example, *de-, dis-, un-, anti-, mis-, non-, in-*); to signify number (for example, *bi-, tri-, di-, semi-*).

b. Identifies explicit context clues.

Objective: The child uses explicit context clues (for example, synonym, definition, equivalent phrase, summary) to determine the meaning of an unfamiliar word in context.

2. Derives meaning from sentences.

a. Notes detail in sentences with subordinate clause.

397

Objective: The child attends to detail in sentences that are
written in the active or passive voice and contain tem-
poral and/or abstract prepositional phrases and either a
terminal clause or an embedded part.

b. Paraphrases active and passive sentences.

Objective: The child is able to restate sentences with no
more than one subordinate clause in the passive voice and
in the active voice by rearranging the order of words in
the sentence and/or substituting for one or more words.

3. Derives meaning from passages.

a. Classifies details as relevant or irrelevant.

Objective: The child determines whether details are relevant or irrelevant (not supporting or describing the general topic) to the topic of a passage with an organizer and
both relevant and irrelevant details.

b. Identifies conclusions: explicit relationships.

Objective: The child identifies a conclusion based on relationships explicitly stated in a passage.

4. Determines sequence: event before or after.

Objective: Given a sentence in which the sequence is indicated by either "before" or "after," the child determines the
order of two events.

LEVEL E. THE CHILD . . .

1. Determines word meaning.

a. Identifies word parts: suffixes.

Objective: The child recognizes that a suffix is a meaning
bearing unit that can modify a base word and with that
modification identify the grammatical function of that
base word as noun (for example, -ance, -ation, -ism, -ure,
-ity, -ment, -hood, -ness, -ty, -ess, -ist, -er, -or, -let); adjec-
tive or adverb (for example, -less, -able, -ous, -ful, -ant,
-ish, -al, -ly, -est); or verb (for example, -en).

b. Identifies explicit context clues: application.

Objective: The child determines the meaning of an unfamiliar word in a context that contains explicit clues (for
example, synonym, definition, equivalent phrase, summary) and then applies that meaning in a second context
where the same unfamiliar word appears but no explicit
clues are present.

2. Derives meaning from sentences.

a. Notes detail in sentences with more than one subordinate
clause.

Objective: The child attends to detail in sentences containing no more than two subordinate clauses.
b. Paraphrases complex sentences.
Objective: The child restates sentences containing no more than two subordinate clauses by rearranging and/or substituting for more than a short phrase.
3. Derives meaning from passages.
a. Identifies main idea statements.
Objective: The child identifies a stated main idea for a passage that has an organizer and both relevant and irrelevant details.
b. Identifies conclusions: implicit relationships.
Objective: The child identifies an appropriate conclusion based on relationships that are implicit but not stated in a passage.
4. Determines sequence: explicit cues.
Objective: The child determines the order of events in a selection when that order is indicated by common, specific sequential markers (for example, next, then, later, soon, finally, until, while, when, as soon as, during, meanwhile).

LEVEL F. THE CHILD . . .

1. Determines word meaning.
a. Identifies word parts: combining forms.
Objective: The child recognizes that combining forms (for example, bio, geo, graph, logy, meter, phone, photo, tele, zoo, homo, pseudo, auto, hydro, micro, aero, demo, psycho, astro, gram, magni, petro) are meaning-bearing units that join together to constitute new English words.
b. Identifies implicit context clues: application.
Objective: The child determines the meaning of an unfamiliar word in a context containing implicit clues (for example, cause-effect, contrast, example, modifying phrase) and then applies that meaning in a second context where the same unfamiliar word appears but no explicit clues are present.
2. Derives meaning from sentences: paraphrases complex sentences with two or more prepositional phrases.
Objective: The child paraphrases complex sentences containing two or more prepositional phrases by rearranging words and substituting for more than a short phrase.
3. Derives meaning from passages.
a. Identifies main idea statement.

399

Objective: The child identifies a given main idea statement of a passage that has no organizer and has both relevant and irrelevant details.

b. Recognizes supported and unsupported conclusions.

Objective: The child determines whether given conclusions are supported by the information given in a passage that embodies one or more explicit or implicit relationships.

4. Determines sequence: implicit cues.

Objective: The child determines the location of a specific event within the framework of a series of events when that location is indicated by implicit sequential cues.

LEVEL G. THE CHILD . . .

1. Determines word meaning.
   a. Identifies word parts: word roots.

   Objective: The child recognizes that some unfamiliar words may consist of prefixes or suffixes combined with word roots (for example, fac, sta, pos, fer, mit (mis), tend, spect, ten, part, cat(t), duc(t), pli, that have their origin in a language other than English.

   b. Identifies context clues: obscure meanings.

   Objective: The child uses explicit and implicit context clues to determine an obscure meaning of a familiar word in context.

2. Derives meaning from sentences: paraphrases more than one sentence.

   Objective: The child paraphrases one long sentence into two or more sentences, or paraphrases several sentences by rearranging words and substituting for more than a short phrase.

3. Derives meaning from passages.
   a. Generates a main idea statement.

   Objective: The child generates a main idea statement for a passage that may or may not have an organizer and has both relevant and irrelevant details.

   b. Modifies conclusions.

   Objective: The child forms a tentative conclusion on the basis of limited information and then modifies that conclusion as additional facts or evidence are given in passages that embody one or more explicit or implicit relationships.

4. Determines sequence: Explicit and implicit cues.

Objective: The child determines the location of a specific event within the framework of a series of events when that location is indicated by explicit or implicit sequential cues.

Self-directed reading

LEVELS A–C. THE CHILD . . .

1. With teacher guidance selects books appropriate to his or her independent reading level and begins to develop automaticity in word and phrase recognition.
2. Uses basic book skills (for example, locating the title, author, title page, table of events, and index) to determine whether a book contains needed information.
3. Responds to brief oral and written directions.
4. Exhibits self-direction by asking appropriate questions about an assigned task for purposes of clarification and by attending to an assigned task.
5. Locates and uses basic areas of the library appropriate to his or her needs and interests.

LEVELS D–E. THE CHILD . . .

1. Selects books appropriate to his or her independent reading ability and develops automaticity in word recognition.
2. Practices scanning to find a specific fact and skimming to determine the general theme.
3. Responds to written directions that have been explained by the teacher.
4. Paces himself or herself with minimal teacher supervision to complete a task within an allotted time.
5. Locates and uses basic references according to his or her needs and interests.

LEVELS F–G. THE CHILD . . .

1. Selects books appropriate to his or her independent reading ability and refines automaticity.
2. Adjusts rate in view of purpose for reading.
3. Responds independently to written directions contained within an assignment.

401

4. Exhibits self-direction by finding answers to questions independently and by pacing himself or herself independently to complete a task within an allotted time.
5. Independently uses library facilities appropriate to his or her purpose.

Interpretive reading

LEVELS A–C. THE CHILD . . .

1. Considers writer's purpose.
2. Notes reality or fantasy.
3. Notes character traits and motives.
4. Notes emotional reactions.
5. Notes sensory imagery.
6. Predicts outcomes.

LEVELS D–E. THE CHILD . . .

1. Identifies writer's purpose and attitude.
2. Identifies fact or fiction.
3. Identifies character traits and changes.
4. Notes characters' emotional reactions.
5. Notes figurative language, metaphors, and similies.
6. Predicts outcomes.

LEVELS F–G. THE CHILD . . .

1. Considers writer's opinion.
2. Identifies elements of fact in fiction.
3. Identifies and compares character traits, attitudes, changes, and motives.
4. Identifies with characters' emotional reactions.
5. Notes use of connotative and denotive words.
6. Predicts outcomes.

Creative reading

LEVELS A–C. THE CHILD . . .

1. Dramatizes characters, emotions, and movements from literature.

2. Gives oral and musical interpretations of literature.
3. Tells stories based on characters or themes in literature.
4. Writes (or dictates) stories based on characters or themes in literature.
5. Creates a visual representation of a scene, object, character, or idea from literature.

LEVELS D–E. THE CHILD . . .

1. Dramatizes themes from literature in relation to own experiences or contemporary situations.
2. Presents oral and musical interpretations of literature read and related literature.
3. Creates original stories about personal experiences or contemporary situations based on literature.
4. Writes stories or plays that relate some aspect of literature to personal experiences or contemporary situations.
5. Creates visual representations that apply certain themes from literature to own experiences or contemporary situations.

LEVELS F–G. THE CHILD . . .

1. Uses drama to transform the content of literature to different modes, moods, or points of view.
2. Alters mode, mood, or point of view of literature through oral and musical interpretations.
3. Creates stories by transforming the mode, mood, or point of view of literature read.
4. Rewrites a piece of literature with mode, mood, or point of view transformed.
5. Creates a visual representation of some aspect of literature read that transforms it into a different mode, mood, or point of view.

Index

BCDEFGHIJ—H—79